THE INVISIBLE RESOURCE:
USE AND REGULATION OF THE RADIO SPECTRUM

HARVEY J. LEVIN

THE INVISIBLE RESOURCE

Use and Regulation of the Radio Spectrum

published for Resources for the Future, Inc.
by The Johns Hopkins Press, Baltimore and London

Resources for the Future is a nonprofit corporation for research and education in the development, conservation, and use of natural resources and the improvement of the quality of the environment. It was established in 1952 with the cooperation of the Ford Foundation. Part of the work of Resources for the Future is carried out by its resident staff; part is supported by grants to universities and other nonprofit organizations. Unless otherwise stated, interpretations and conclusions in RFF publications are those of the authors; the organization takes responsibility for the selection of significant subjects for study, the competence of the researchers, and their freedom of inquiry.

This book is one of RFF's appraisal studies, which are directed by Hans H. Landsberg. Harvey J. Levin is Augustus B. Weller Professor of Economics at Hofstra University, Hempstead, N.Y., and Senior Research Associate at the Center for Policy Research. His research was supported by an RFF grant to Hofstra University. The manuscript was edited by Roma K. McNickle. The charts were drawn by Frank and Clare Ford. The index was prepared by Eloise T. Lee.

RFF editors: Henry Jarrett, Vera W. Dodds, Nora E. Roots, Tadd Fisher.

The Johns Hopkins Press, Baltimore, Maryland 21218
The Johns Hopkins Press Ltd., London

Library of Congress Catalog Card Number 71–148951

International Standard Book Number 0–8018–1316–6

CONTENTS

Part Four: Allocation, Regulation, Prices, and Service

TABLES

FOREWORD

In this book Harvey Levin has attempted to describe and analyze the economic characteristics of the radio spectrum—that portion of electromagnetic waves used to transmit information through the air. In addition, he identifies the participants in this industry and their roles, analyzes the economic efficiency with which the radio spectrum is utilized, and suggests some alternatives for management.

When it was suggested to RFF's Board of Directors, in the spring of 1964, that it approve a grant in support of research for the work that has now resulted in this book, one of the directors suggested that, while the matter was really quite "far out," it was proper for a nonprofit research organization to make "venture capital" available for such a purpose.

In the intervening six years, the problem of how best to utilize and manage the radio spectrum has worked itself from the domain of a few technical experts into a prominent position on the nation's agenda. The timeliness of the book is thus well established.

In supporting Levin's research, RFF did, strictly speaking, enlarge its definition of natural resources to embrace air as a medium of communication. But the extension was anything but arbitrary. Like land or water, the radio spectrum has at any given time a fixed capacity, and use of it by one limits the use of it by others. Likewise, technology can expand the spectrum's capacity, either extensively by rendering useful those portions that formerly were barren, or intensively by utilizing traditional space more effectively. Congestion, here called interference, results when the spectrum's capacity is overtaxed, just as pollution arises on a crowded highway or in a body of water that receives effluents.

However, the radio spectrum differs from most other resources in that no private rights are acquired in it; its use is determined wholly by government regulation; and transfers between specific uses are not permitted. By and large, absence of cost as a factor in acquiring the right to use the spectrum robs the user of incentives to economize the spectrum or even to calculate the value of spectrum use to him or to the next-best user.

Because the radio spectrum offers an instantaneous and direct way of communicating across space, its significance in this age of rapidly mounting information congestion has greatly increased. So have the problems that burgeoning demand causes: to the transmitter and recipient, private or public, to the regulator, to the policymaker, to the equipment manufacturer, to the information media, singly and as a category, and, last but not least, to those who are concerned with the content of the information rather than the technology by which it is transmitted.

Levin's contribution to the debate is a dispassionate, detailed explanation of the workings of the communications system to the extent that it uses the radio spectrum; in addition, it is a guided tour through feasible institutions and mechanisms other than the regulatory machinery in use today. To our knowledge, this is the first attempt by an economist to look comprehensively and in depth at the technical as well as the socio-political aspects of this "invisible resource."

JOSEPH L. FISHER
30 September 1970   *President, Resources for the Future*

PREFACE AND ACKNOWLEDGMENTS

The principal economic value of the radio spectrum lies in its capacity to carry information. But physical and technical capabilities alone cannot guarantee effective utilization of the radio spectrum resource. This also requires favorable economic conditions and affirmative administrative action.

Thus radio spectrum management clearly has an economic dimension as well as problems for the engineer, the scientist, the technologist, and the lawyer. Yet engineers and technologists normally prevail in the basic allocational field, and the lawyer–public administrator has long dominated the licensing and regulation of public and private users of spectrum. Neither group, apparently, has been aware of the help it might get from the economist.

This study seeks to help rectify some of the present imbalance in an undertaking that requires the cooperation of specialists in all these fields. The growing demands today for radio frequencies and their short supply in critical regions leave the government administrator harassed and beleaguered. They also dramatize the timeliness of a serious exploratory economic study which one would hope could never really be "too late" or, for that matter, "too early."

The book describes and evaluates the goals, policies, and performance of the American system of interacting spectrum users, managers, and developers in the light of conceivable modifications. Within the legal, technical, and economic constraints that govern the present system, special attention will be paid to the government's allocational, promotional, and regulatory responsibilities. For spectrum management must be evaluated from the viewpoint of at least three areas of concern: efficient allocation, level of development, and specific regulatory policy. I shall in fact examine alternatives in management, levels of spectrum development, and allocation-regulation-prices-and-service as they impinge on these areas. Part One lays out the broad economic and regulatory framework; the rest of the study will (a) consider the economic and administrative implications of organizing and managing the spectrum resource without markets; (b) examine the ways by which price incentives could be better injected into current management and regulatory practice; and (c) identify the areas where market forces would not *ipso facto* further national policy goals.

My focus will in any case be on aspects of the interplay between the technical-engineering base, the economic-political structure, and the legal-administrative framework. This may appear excessive, but the problem required no less. By its very nature, the use and regulation of the radio spectrum demands perusal of the widest range of issues. To keep the study manageable, some of them had to be omitted or reviewed cursorily. For example, I could no more than touch on the international aspects, crucial though they obviously are in any review of spectrum management generally or of space communication in particular. I also had to stop short of all but the barest mention of new technologies in the broadcast field and certainly of the thorny problems posed by wired city television. Even so, the study extends far beyond the normal scope of spectrum management viewed narrowly as an allocational-engineering problem.

More than seven years have now elapsed since the inquiry was first conceived. During this period, a field where only the hardiest of my colleagues had dared to tread a decade ago has now shown signs of coming of age. The going is tough, but consider the indicators.

To survey the terrain in broad terms, Resources for the Future and the Brookings Institution held the first national conference on the use and regulation of the radio spectrum in 1967 at Airlie House in Warrenton, Virginia. Since then several million dollars have been spent on studies with important economic dimensions by the Rostow Task Force on Communications Policy, by the Federal Communications Commission's Research and Policy Studies Program, by the Executive Office of Telecommunications Management, and, starting a year or two earlier, by the Department of Commerce. The Council of Economic Advisers in its latest Annual Report to the President has for the first time explicitly recognized the problems of radio spectrum scarcity, problems which surely played their part in the recent White House decision to create a new cabinet-level Office of Telecommunications Policy. Finally, the FCC's traditional preoccupation with broadcast regulation alone has been broadened to include a spate of new activity on the spectrum generally, and in particular its usage by the terrestrial common carriers, the mobile radio services, and the users of satellite technology.

At each point, economic factors have been given greater attention not only by the lawyer-administrator but also by the physical scientist, technologist, and engineer. Even the flow of journal literature has started to reflect the broadening. The law journals, traditionally the major outlet for economic-regulatory research on broadcasting, have begun to look at the radio spectrum more generally. The pathbreaking economic analysis of spectrum allocation by a few stalwarts a decade ago is being followed by at least a modest flow of related papers in major economic and scholarly reviews. Finally, the range of approaches to spectrum economics and the problems of spectrum management have shown healthy diversity during this formative stage in an area of inquiry which virtually demands cooperative endeavor among many different specialists.

In a field as primitive as this one was when I began in 1964, one vital source of information had to be the expertise and files of many scholars and practitioners in communications, technology, economics, and law. These were located principally at university and other research centers; in the broadcast, communications carrier, and equipment manufacturing industries; at the Federal Communications Commission, the Executive Office of Telecommunications Management, and the Department of Commerce (Boulder Labs). Because so many insights and materials in the book emerged from personal contacts with such individuals, a rather detailed set of acknowledgments is in order. Without the cooperation and sometimes exceptional assistance of the persons and organizations cited below, the investigation could not have been conducted the way it was. However, neither my findings of fact, conclusions, or recommendations are necessarily shared by any of them, and I assume full responsibility for the final statement.

At the outset, Mark S. Massel, then at Brookings, gave invaluable advice on general scope and overriding business, economic, and legal interrelations. For many subsequent exchanges on legal-regulatory aspects, I am also much indebted to William Kenneth Jones of Columbia Law School whose related work was most helpful at a formative stage. I must further acknowledge perceptive detailed comments on the economics and technology by Leland L. Johnson of the President's Task Force on Communications Policy. While the Task Force cooperated fully on matters of mutual interest, my research and analysis were completed without prior knowledge of any Task Force staff paper or final report. The study is indebted, finally, to Ronald H. Coase and William H. Meckling, whose pioneering studies provided a crucial starting point for several sections which admittedly moved in other directions.

On specific portions, special thanks are due to Merton J. Peck for persuasive advice on the thrust of Parts One, Two, and Three (Professor Peck had just served as a member of the Communications Task Force); to Alfred E. Kahn for comments on Chapters VI and X; to Joel B. Dirlam, Kenneth Jones, and Herman Schwartz for careful readings of Chapters X, XI, and XII. I also want to acknowledge critical responses and suggestions from Sidney S. Alexander, Paul W. MacAvoy, Almarin Phillips, Peter O. Steiner, and Oliver E. Williamson, and several valuable sessions at the outset with William S. Vickrey on key analytical concepts.

In government, major thanks are due William E. Plummer for his painstaking review of technical details in an interim draft, and for frequent talks with him, Paul Miles, Harold Johnson, Wilfrid Dean, and Ralph Clark, all of the Office of Telecommunications Management. At the Federal Communications Commission, Saul M. Myers and Curtis B. Plummer gave assistance on difficult frequency allocation problems, while Asher Ende and Bernard Strassburg helped me to unravel some of the intricacies of satellite and common carrier organization and control. Major acknowledgments are due also to Commissioners Nicholas Johnson and Kenneth A. Cox and their staffs for exceptional assistance in data collection where the pickings were often slim, and for many thoughtful reflections on political, economic, and technical-legal interrelations. At the Department of Commerce and the Institute of Telecommunication Sciences (Boulder), I learned much from Kenneth A. Norton, Richard A. Kirby, Robert S. Kirby, and Louis A. Rose; from early exchanges with C. Gordon Little; and, toward the end, from sessions with Walter Hinchman whose work helped clarify Chapter IV. Acknowledgments are due also to Carl Loeber of the State Department's Telecommunications Division, and for the cooperation of frequency management officials in many federal government agencies. At Stanford Research Institute, Ray Vincent, Donald R. MacQuivey, and George Hagn gave valuable help, as did John Hult at The Rand Corporation.

Among persons in industry, I am much indebted to Richard P. Gifford of the General Electric Communications Products Division, then Chairman of the Joint Technical Advisory Committee; to William J. Weisz of Motorola, key man on the Electronic Industries Association Land Mobile Frequency Card Study which was used extensively in Chapter VIII; to Edward H. Weppler, George V. Cook, and their associates at American Telephone and Telegraph Company; to Louis B. Early and Emric Podraccky at ComSat; to James Hillier of RCA Laboratories; to James P. Veatch, Wayne Mason, Raymond Simonds, and Leonard Tufts of RCA Communications; to Leroy Spangenberg of

World Communications, International Telephone and Telegraph Corp.; to David Blank and James D. Parker of Columbia Broadcasting System, Inc.; and to Victor G. Reis of the Communications Committee, National Association of Manufacturers. I must also acknowledge the cooperation of the Electronic Industries Association, National Association of Broadcasters, National Association of Educational Broadcasters, and National Cable Television Association.

Major parts of the analysis benefited greatly from invited participation in a number of communications conferences—not only the Airlie House Conference on the Radio Spectrum but conferences on rate base regulation and innovation in the telecommunications industry at the Brookings Institution (1968–69); on public utility economics at the University of Chicago (1965) and at Michigan State University (1969); on global satellite television at The George Washington University (1965); and on spectrum economics and technology at conference sessions of the Institute of Electrical and Electronics Engineers in Philadelphia (1968) and Boulder (1969).

During the long research period, some of the issues were advisedly examined in separate journal articles. Parts One and Two utilized much of an Airlie House Conference paper, "The Radio Spectrum Resource," which appeared in the *Journal of Law and Economics* in October 1968. Those chapters were also developed from parts of three theoretical, policy-oriented papers: "Spectrum Allocation without Markets," *American Economic Review*, May 1970; "New Technology and the Old Regulation in Radio Spectrum Management," *American Economic Review*, May 1966; and "There Is Always a Substitute for Spectrum," *Telecommunication Journal*, January 1969. Much of Part Two was actually revamped in line with an advisory briefing I gave the Telecommunications Committee of the National Academy of Engineering and members of the Office of Telecommunications Management in August 1968. Chapter XI drew extensively on my testimony for the Justice Department on satellite organizational structure (FCC Docket No. 16828—the proposed ABC–ITT merger); Chapters X and XI both benefited from consultative work I did for the Ford Foundation's satellite television project in 1966–67. Finally, Chapter XIII drew in part on research published separately in the *Journal of Political Economy* in April 1964 and in *Columbia Law Review* in May 1970.

Initiated under a grant from Resources for the Future in 1964–65, the full study was subsequently completed with some additional RFF help and, throughout the period, support from the Augustus B. Weller Chair in Economics at Hofstra University. At RFF, the project was aided substantially by Hans H. Landsberg to whom I am personally very much indebted. I am grateful also to John V. Krutilla for insights on important analytical points; to Francis T. Christy, Jr., and Allen V. Kneese for helpful suggestions; and to Roma K. McNickle for a most painstaking and imaginative job of editing. At Brookings, my principal debts are to William M. Capron (now at Harvard) and to Joseph A. Pechman, Director of Economic Studies. At Hofstra, I must thank Dean Joseph G. Astman and Jacob Weissman for the continued and vital support of the Weller Chair, and, for comments on specific points, Howard Kitt, Marshall Kolin, and Dean Harold L. Wattel of the School of Business. Unless otherwise indicated, the basic statistical work was prepared at my specification by the Hofstra Computer Center, under the supervision of its Director, Nathan Goldfarb, and his staff.

The final word of gratitude, however, must go to my wife Rhoda and my son Adam, who endured so much, so long.

Garden City, New York   HARVEY J. LEVIN
September, 1970

THE INVISIBLE RESOURCE:
USE AND REGULATION OF THE RADIO SPECTRUM

INTRODUCTION

The communication frequencies that constitute the radio spectrum are a natural resource essential to living in the modern world. Without radio and radar, travel by land, sea, and air would be much slower and less safe. The construction, mining, manufacturing, and distribution industries use spectrum in the processing and delivery of materials. Public safety and national security depend heavily on radio and other uses of spectrum. Whatever the payoff of the space program, it would have been impossible without the most sophisticated use of spectrum. Television and radio broadcasts are as much a part of modern life as the air man breathes.

Yet the spectrum is by no means unlimited in supply relative to the growing claims of its users. Though a resource of great economic and social value, market considerations still play almost no part in its allocation. No price is paid for spectrum even though huge private and public investments are based upon its use.

Anyone in the United States who wishes access to spectrum must obtain permission from the Federal Communications Commission or, in the case of a federal agency, from the Director of Telecommunications Management acting for the President.[1] Those authorized to use it pay nothing, and they cannot sell or share any portion of what they have been allocated. Thus they lack incentives to economize use, to withhold use today if the value would be greater tomorrow, or to transfer rights to others who value them more highly. Moreover, large portions of spectrum are allocated to groups of users in various "services"—radio,

---

[1] Effective April 20, 1970, the DTM's functions were transferred to the Director of a newly created Office of Telecommunications Policy, successor of the Executive Office of Telecommunications Management. *Federal Register*, April 22, 1970, Title 3. Reorganization Plan No. 1 of 1970.

1

television, land mobile, local government, for example—across the board and across the country, with no chance for transfer between services.

Some consequences of this highly centralized and inflexible non-price system have been aptly described by the President's Task Force on Communications Policy which reported late in 1968:

> Police and other public safety radio services in major metropolitan areas may be unable to obtain vital spectrum resources, while those resources allocated to other user categories go unused in the same area (e.g., frequencies reserved for forestry services were only recently made available to the New York City Police Department). The business community and the general public throughout the nation may be denied access to otherwise unused spectrum bands simply because these bands are used for other services in a few metropolitan centers (e.g., land mobile services are unable to use spectrum allocated to television in areas where the allocations are unusable for TV). One class of users may be forced to adopt costly equipment modifications to meet growing demand, while another class, favored with an abundance of similar spectrum resources, may use them wastefully (e.g., private land mobile users have undertaken three major equipment revisions since 1950 to conserve spectrum, while certain other mobile services continue to use wider bandwidths than required by existing technology). New spectrum dependent services, irrespective of potential social or economic benefit, may be denied allocations or forced to adopt uneconomic design and operating practices to protect established services, without even the option to indemnify existing users against harmful interference (e.g., satellite services are forced to locate earth terminals in remote areas and to adopt sub-optimum system trade-offs and operating constraints to ensure absolute interference protection for microwave relay systems).[2]

This state of affairs, where some industries and services have been allocated much more spectrum than they have used and others are unable to obtain allocations that will permit them to use radio at all, has been termed "the silent crisis" by another advisory group.[3]

[2] President's Task Force on Communications Policy, *Final Report* (U.S. Government Printing Office, 1968), Ch. VIII, pp. 16–18.

[3] Telecommunication Science Panel, Commerce Technical Advisory Board, *Electromagnetic Spectrum Utilization: The Silent Crisis* (U.S. Government Printing Office, 1966). Other publications describing the incidence and magnitude of present or projected spectrum scarcities include: *The Radio Frequency Spectrum: U.S. Use and Management*, App. B to Staff Paper No. 7, President's Task Force on Communications Policy (U.S. Department of Commerce: Clearinghouse for Federal Scientific and Technical Information, June 1969); and Advisory Committee for the Land Mobile Radio Services, Federal Communications Commission, *Final Report* (U.S. Government Printing Office, 1967).

In terms of economics, a newcomer is kept from sharing, borrowing, or preempting spectrum directly from incumbents even though (a) such options would be less costly to him than developing a new system higher up, or turning to some costly substitute; (b) he would therefore be willing to reimburse incumbents to accommodate him; and (c) the social priorities to further which the government managers stockpile spectrum are either vaguely conceived or could be equally well implemented otherwise. By the same token, incumbents are permitted to retain unused or underused spectrum notwithstanding the outputs which the community thereby forgoes, the extra costs imposed on excluded next-best users, and the highly valued uses to which it could be put. Finally, the relatively deprived users are virtually forced to innovate spectrum-economizing, spectrum-developing technology regardless of its true economic or social merit, whereas those favored with abundant allocations lack any incentive to innovate at all.

How has this silent crisis come about, and what can be done to resolve it? Such scarcities, irrationalities, and economic inefficiencies in the use of a "critical natural resource," as President Kennedy called it,[4] cannot be properly understood or remedied without careful examination of the American spectrum system which includes the federal managers, the public and private users and hardware manufacturers, and the developers. The latter are often federal too, in funding if not in operation.

ALLOCATION OF SPECTRUM AMONG THE NATIONS

Essential to understanding of the spectrum system is some knowledge of the evolution of allocation and the necessity for it. The radio spectrum is international in character. Very early in the development of radio communication it became apparent that some agreement would have to be reached between nations as to the spectral location of different uses and users. A message beamed at a receiver in another nation could not be received at all if transmitter and receiver were located in widely separated regions of the spectrum. The unconfinability of radio emissions which readily crossed national boundaries was all too apparent to the earliest users of the lowest spectral regions; viz., the so-called High Frequencies (below 30 megacycles). There, even strictly domestic communications could interfere with emissions from other sources thousands of miles away. The International Telecommunications Union, to which 135 nations are now parties, has served as the organizing

[4] Executive Order 10995, February 16, 1962.

mechanism through which "bands," or groups of radio frequencies, are assigned to particular types of radio services.

One basic presumption throughout this book is that there nonetheless exists an area of national discretion where nations can explore ways to improve their own spectrum systems without being vetoed at the international level. This presumption seems sound enough in an era of line-of-sight technology. The viability of strictly national experiments in spectrum management derives from the greater predictability and directionality of the newer technologies, compared to older propagation modes lower in the spectrum. Yet the scope of national discretion must not be exaggerated. International coordination is obviously crucial in the case of communication near a neighbor's border and throughout the international mobile, fixed, and space services. But the real dilemma is posed by the unpredictable transformation of what is a strictly domestic service today into an international one tomorrow. Space satellites and radio astronomy illustrate the kind of new international services which may have wide ramifications for strictly national uses of spectrum too. Additional constraints devolve from the economic advantages to all nations in the buying and selling of standardized equipment and especially to those involved in global movement of security forces. More work is needed to determine the precise weight to assign these general international constraints in formulating management policies at the national level.

However much such factors may act to impede the establishment of a full-fledged domestic market, it seems safe to assume they need not block something less extreme. Nevertheless, assignment of specific frequencies (channels) to each user within as well as between nations, is necessitated by the fact that the radio resource is subject to pollution by interference when two signals are being transmitted on the same channel at the same time and place. How widely spaced assignments must be depends on the use which is being made.

FCC ALLOCATIONS: RADIO AND TELEVISION

Since 1927, first the Federal Radio Commission and then the Federal Communications Commission have allocated spectrum for all users in the United States except federal agencies. In 1928, the FRC enunciated a set of allocation principles which subsequently guided its successor, the FCC, in a major communications task of the 1930s and early 1940s—the assignment of frequencies to AM (standard) radio stations on a case-by-case basis.

In discharging this responsibility, the FCC sought to put into effect social priorities which were later codified in its TV Allocation Plan of 1952 and in 1963 in a permanent FM Allocation Plan. In all three allocations, the Commission sought to diffuse the benefits of spectrum utilization widely, and to ensure diversified programs of high quality. As stated in the TV Plan, the allocational criteria were fivefold:

Priority No. 1: To provide at least one television service to all parts of the United States.

Priority No. 2: To provide each community with at least one television broadcast station.

Priority No. 3: To provide a choice of at least two television services to all parts of the United States.

Priority No. 4: To provide each community with at least two television broadcast stations.

Priority No. 5: To assign to various communities any channels which remain unassigned under the foregoing priorities, according to community size, geographical location, and the number of TV services available to such communities from TV stations located in other communities.

Although not included in this list, a sixth criterion also figured in allocating TV and FM radio, but not the AM broadcast spectrum. This pertained to the reservation of special channels for noncommercial educational use. Program choice was to be widened and benefits diffused not just by structural diversity but by institutional diversity as well.

The advent of TV and FM radio right after World War II posed far-reaching economic and physical problems. Unlike AM radio, FM and TV operate on a line-of-sight basis, so that signals do not go over the horizon and may be obstructed by large buildings or high elevators. FM radio and the voice component of TV (which is FM) require wider frequency bandwidths than AM radio, since they operate on the frequency modulation principle. An AM station requires only 10 Kc/s-wide channels compared to 20 Kc/s for FM channels, and 600 Kc/s for television. Therefore, a single megacycle of bandwidth, in a given geographic area, can accommodate far more AM than FM radio or TV stations.

Today about 3,000 commercial FM assignments are potentially available on 80 channels carved out of the 20 Mc/s of FM spectrum. Likewise only some 1,200 commercial TV assignments can be made on the 82 channels that FCC has laid out in 492 Mc/s of TV broadcast spectrum. In contrast, almost 4,300 commercial AM stations already operate within the 1.07 Mc/s allocated to standard broadcasting, and some 15,000 to 20,000 could technically be accommodated there if one assumed low-power local operations only. The per market maxima which the FCC imposes on broadcast stations, finally, range about 10 to 15 in TV and 15 to 18 in FM in contrast with the AM band where, without any comparable Allocation Plan, social-technical factors have long set per market limits of some 30 to 34 outlets.

Economic factors are better able than social-technical maxima to explain the effective degree of spectrum utilization within and between the three broadcast services. In 1968, a per market average of only 16.2 AM and 4.2 TV stations was actually authorized in the 50 leading markets, less than one-half the technical maxima therein. Even more dramatic is the contrast between VHF and UHF television—a per market average of 3.1 VHF stations as compared with 1.0 UHF in the top 50 markets; and 2.6 VHF as against 0.9 UHF in the top 100 markets. In the 71 leading markets with independent commercial FM stations, finally, the average number authorized per market was only 3.4, a scant one-third of the technical maximum.

The economic, technical, and regulatory factors which underlie this pattern can best be described as follows. In television, the national AM radio networks were prepared to rush into the new field in 1945 just as soon as wartime materials limitations had eased. They naturally preferred to acquire TV affiliates and stations of their own through their then existing radio interests. The FCC also preferred TV applicants with past broadcast experience, which at the outset necessarily meant AM radio experience.

In its first postwar VHF-only plan, set up in 1945, the Commission had assigned some 400 outlets entirely to 140 major market centers; early-comers quickly preempted 100 of these choice VHF assignments. Perceiving that both the number and distribution of TV assignments would soon create critical problems, the FCC forbade establishment of any TV station between 1948 and 1952. This "TV freeze" ended in 1952 when the Commission announced a new Television Allocation Plan in its so-called Sixth Report and Order. Working with 70 UHF and 12 VHF channels, the new Allocation Table provided over 2,000 assignments in almost 1,300 communities across the nation with 242 reserved explicitly for educators. Subsequent rule changes have left somewhat fewer assignments today—about 1,850 in 850 communities—but of these over one-third are earmarked for educational purposes. Minimal co-channel spacing for TV remains 170 miles in the Northeast, 220 miles in the Gulf region (owing to ionospheric interference), and 190 miles elsewhere.

The technical development of FM radio was somewhat different. Before the wartime "freeze" on all new station construction, few assignments had been made under the Commission's first FM Plan introduced in 1940. Further disruption and delays resulted when, for technical reasons, the FCC in 1945 shifted FM higher up in the spectrum. The temporary partial Allocation Table adopted at that time remained in force until 1958, when a more comprehensive table for all 80 commercial FM channels was proposed. Adopted in 1963, that table simply extended the principles underlying the earlier ones. Some 2,830 outlets (now over 3,000) were assigned to 1,858 communities across the nation, according to the same priorities codified in the TV Allocation Plan a decade before. However, applications to operate on those 20 FM channels reserved exclusively for noncommercial educational use were (and still are) handled on a case-by-case basis.

The economic factors which have deterred FM's growth are similar to those still operating in UHF television. In both cases, few home sets were at the outset equipped to receive the new FM or UHF signals. Even today, AM–FM receivers or FM-only sets are but a fraction of total radio receivers; and UHF set penetration is still far smaller than VHF penetration. Advertisers will be reluctant to buy time on stations with such limited markets, and this further acts to compound the broadcaster's difficulties in gaining access to popular network or syndicated programming. As a consequence, the set owners' incentives to convert to all-channel receivers will be reduced still further.

In 1962, a requirement that all TV sets be built as all-channel receivers helped but actually came too late to arrest the demise of many UHF pioneers in the early 1950s, a pattern closely reminiscent of a slightly earlier but equally spectacular decline in FM grants. (Not until 1961 did the number of FM authorizations recover and surpass the level actually reached in 1948). Even now, with theoretical access to over twice as many allocated channels as VHF broadcasters have, UHF licensees operate only one-fourth of all TV stations on the air. Likewise FM radio, despite its quickening pace, still lags financially well behind AM broadcasting. Of 2,100 commercial FM stations on the air today only 300 operate independently of an AM station, in contrast with almost 4,300 AM stations of all types.

The Microwave and Space Satellite Allocations

Following World War II, yet another allocation crisis arose when microwave developed as a relay device and spectrum had to be earmarked for the common carriers (1945), and then for the private or independent specialized point-to-point systems (1959). The question was whether the latters' higher spectrum costs were more than compensated for by the competitive rate adjustments which private system entry was expected to induce from common carrier incumbents; or whether the latters' loss of business from the big specialized users would force the carriers to shift more of their common costs from those users onto the small general user; or whether the carriers would do so all the more because spectrum costs were excluded from their cost of service for rate determination purposes.

Related questions are already being posed by the allocation of spectrum for space satellites in the international market. They may soon be posed again even more vividly with the opening up of space satellite spectrum for domestic purposes, in competition with terrestrial microwave and cable systems.

The Land Mobile Allocation

Meanwhile, land mobile and other special radio services have had little relief from the narrowness of their spectrum allocations, though they have developed remarkably efficient transmitters and receivers. They have repeatedly asked to be allowed to use spectrum allocated to TV but still unused. In reply, the TV industry cites Congressional and FCC commitments to a fully activated UHF band as a structural guarantee of wider program choice. The unique public value of broadcast spectrum for news, public affairs, culture, and education has been increasingly cited by those who support an allocational status quo, whereas the land mobile interests, to justify a change, emphasize their own important contributions to economic productivity, public safety, and public convenience.

In the present contest, one frequently hears arguments and counterarguments reminiscent of those exchanged almost twenty years ago between commercial and noncommercial broadcasters over access to the then newly allocated TV spectrum. At that time, commercial TV licensees rejected the educator's urgent plea for extra time to activate his assignments. Instead they offered the FCC a speedier development of allocated spectrum and at far lower costs in periods of protracted nonuse by noncommercial broadcasters than under the ETV reservation. Today, ironically, the commercial broadcaster confronts a very similar claim by the land mobile interests; namely, that land mobile's speedier activation of the long underutilized UHF (or even FM) spectrum would generate net economic outputs otherwise forgone through nonuse. In both episodes one critical task is to devise reliable measures of the net social benefits (and net social opportunity costs) of any management policy to stockpile spectrum for favored classes of users over long time periods.

REGULATION, LICENSING

In addition to its allocation function, FCC regulates the domestic and international common carriers in the communications field, all of which use spectrum. The Communications Act, which is the organic law for the FCC, specifically states that broadcasting is not a public utility. Yet to some extent the licensing of TV and radio also performs an important regulatory function, one with considerable effect on economic viability and programming. And it is important also to recognize the close linkage between allocation and regulation. Sound allocational practice virtually requires knowledge of the end effects of allocation decisions in terms of their stated objectives and of regulatory norms more generally.

THE GOVERNMENT AS PROMOTER

The Federal Communications Commission and the Director of Telecommunications Management have had little to do directly with those federal programs that most promote the nation's electronic communication capabilities. The major advances there are associated with two wars and the government's space-defense programs. The Navy's electronics research contributions have been crucial from the outset, though more recently the Defense Department (DOD) and National Aeronautics and Space Administration (NASA) have also played growing roles.

The booster-launching-satellite technology which currently promises to revolutionize the communications industry is merely the most recent and spectacular in a long series of technical advances extending the intensive and extensive margins of spectrum. The government's role is well illustrated by the Navy's in-house development of radar during the 1930s and early 1940s; the new war-stimulated development of microwave; and the dramatic advances which culminated in communications satellites.

The problem for spectrum management is twofold: first, to accommodate this flood of new communications technologies, inadvertent byproducts of huge military and space programs, which often pose serious problems of congestion and interference; and second, wherever appropriate, to induce all spectrum users to adapt and install spectrum-economizing hardware at no less than the rate they would be motivated to do so if spectrum were sold, like timber and land, in a full-fledged market.

WOULD A MARKET HELP?

It is obvious from this glimpse that management centralized in the federal government unifies the spectrum system as the market does in other spheres. It determines where, how, and by whom the resource shall be used, though not at what price. In so doing, it takes into account the engineering facts of life and the social priorities laid down by Congress. But it pays scant, if any, heed to the economic consequences of its acts except in the regulatory field.

Many of today's problems in management of the spectrum resource arise not only because the managers rather than the market have to integrate the components of the spectrum system, but also because they are compelled to override such market values as could in fact be available to them. On both counts, the immediate question becomes how to articulate economic factors more effectively in allocational-management decisions. Some academic economists argue that a market should be established in this field, as in forests, land, and other resources. These proposals have brought little positive response from the FCC or DTM— quite the opposite, in fact.

A REGULATED MARKET-TYPE SYSTEM WITH PRICES

It is my thesis in this book that, while a full-fledged market would have theoretical advantages, we will get much farther with a regulated market-type system with prices. My conclusion is that now is the time to pay far more attention to the mechanics of promising middle-range options which lie between the polar extremes of a complete market and the present framework. In this, my position jibes with that of the President's Task Force on Communications Policy which, in rejecting a full-fledged market at this time, endorsed a more "eclectic approach."

The fact is that the long use of a regulated nonprice spectrum system in this country has built into government agencies opposition to almost any attempt to utilize economic incentives more directly. As a result, the possibility of valuable progress short of a full-fledged market has too long been ignored. Aside from their crucial non-economic objections to any complete spectrum market, many government officials simply believe it cannot work.

It may be that we shall always want to preserve unified management and to allocate spectrum in line with social priorities. Many of the same basic economic problems could well remain whatever the precise legislative-administrative relation of the FCC and the OTM. But the managers ought to be able to state what a decision costs in opportunities for other uses forgone. Only with such knowledge can intelligent decisions be made.

Various methods of identifying opportunity costs are known to economists. Short of a full-fledged market in spectrum, other devices can allow prices to be set. Among them are rentals and auctions. The nature of the resource and the wide variety of uses also seem to argue for secondary rights. Wide use of certain administrative devices, such as frequency clearance, would also help.

But it should be noted that there are areas where even effective reliance on market forces will not necessarily suffice to further national policy goals. Anyone familiar with the task of spectrum management is well aware that market-type efficiency considerations are not enough. Maintenance of safety, internal and external security, cultural and educational values, and wide dissemination of information are also important.

In regard to overall organizational structure, finally, the greatest ingenuity of administrative lawyers and public administrators is needed to insure continued civilian ascendancy over the major military users of spectrum and to reconcile due process safeguards with the secrecy that still shrouds the federal government sector. However, substantive work is equally crucial today, and here economics has much to offer in what must necessarily be a joint effort at reform. Because the nation badly needs new tools and new principles for a more efficient spectrum system, economists should be encouraged to make their own overdue contributions even as the lawyer-public administrator wrestles with the problems of overall organization and procedure.

PLAN OF THE BOOK

The book is divided into four sections. Part One will describe the American spectrum system with special emphasis on economic and physical characteristics, international aspects, and the interacting role of users, managers and developers of spectrum—all from the viewpoint of prevailing national goals. The chapters in Parts Two, Three, and Four will then examine, respectively, the current principles and practice of spectrum allocation, the government's promotional responsibilities, and the interrelated tasks of competition and regulation. Throughout, the focus is on the implications of organized markets and their absence for the several areas in question.

The absence of market prices for spectrum is the source of many (though not all) of the nation's management problems. For that reason Part Two examines, as a crucial starting point in the quest for new management criteria and tools, a range of techniques through which the behavior of spectrum users can be made economically more rational. Notwithstanding the spectrum's peculiarities as a natural resource and the special obstacles to a full-fledged market, there is no question that regulated market-type constraints can be introduced to good effect.

Market-type incentives take us farthest in the allocational arena. However, there is need to inject them also into the government's promotional role. In Part Three we therefore try to draw a line between what the government must do because there are no prices and what it must do anyway. For whether we continue to tolerate the pattern of technological change associated in part with the current simultaneous spectrum congestion and underutilization, or institute instead a relative price structure closer to what would emerge in a full-fledged spectrum market, special criteria will be needed to help us determine the most suitable form and magnitude for the federal contribution to telecommunications R&D. Of necessity, only a small start has been possible in this book.

Finally, the government's regulatory function would clearly remain even if certain major regulated industries were to acquire their spectrum in an organized market. Yet without a spectrum market, the urgency of effective regulation is even greater. Even the institution of middle-range options like rental charges, shadow prices, and intraband auctions or of such strictly administrative techniques as frequency clearance and secondary rights would still leave a suitable role for competition and regulation in the broadcast and common carrier fields. Part Four therefore reviews basic aspects of several regulatory policies in the context of spectrum scarcity.

PART ONE

THE SPECTRUM SYSTEM

CHAPTER I

ECONOMIC AND PHYSICAL CHARACTER OF THE RADIO SPECTRUM

Electromagnetic radiation has been defined as "a form of oscillating electrical and magnetic energy capable of traversing space without benefit of physical interconnections."[1] The rate of oscillation, expressed in cycles per second, is its frequency. Of the whole range of frequencies which together constitute the electromagnetic spectrum, only that portion from about 10,000 cycles to 3,000 billion cycles is classified as the radio spectrum. Of this range, only up to 40 billion cycles is officially allocated for radio usage today (Table 1).

The principal economic value of the spectrum resource lies in its use for conveying information of widely varying sorts at varying speeds over varying distances. The multi-billion dollar television industry is of course built on the use of spectrum. So are the land mobile services which direct taxicabs and the delivery of everything from diapers to concrete mix. Spectrum was used dramatically in putting men on the moon.

Like other natural resources, spectrum is developed in relation to supply and demand. On the supply side, it has intensive and extensive margins. On the intensive margin, technical advances have improved the use of spectrum along its dimensions of time, space, and frequency. At the extensive margin, technology is now making it possible to use spectrum at higher and higher frequencies. Demand for spectrum reflects mainly growth in levels of population and per capita income and changes in taste.

Again as with other natural resources, favorable economic conditions are a prerequisite for effective utilization of the spectrum. Unlike

---

[1] President's Task Force on Communications Policy, *Final Report* (U.S. Government Printing Office, 1968), Ch. VIII, p. 2.

others, however, access to and development of the spectrum resource require affirmative action by the federal government.

As a resource that is often (if not always) interchangeable between alternative uses and users, spectrum poses all the familiar problems of economic choice. But, though subject to significant economic constraints, spectrum is allocated without a price system.

Radio spectrum is today not only a resource but a scarce resource in specific spectral regions, services, and geographic areas, even though only a minute fraction of the known radio spectrum is in use. Scarcity reflects in part the fact that spectrum, though it is not depleted by use like some other resources, is subject to degradation and pollution which stem from congestion and intolerable interference. Pollution in this context refers to the decreasing utility of the spectrum for radio communication due largely to its growing use for noncommunication purposes.

In the light of growing scarcity and congestion, as noted in the Introduction, and the grave policy problems thus posed, the present chapter examines four basic issues:

1. The physical possibility of interference as a basic precondition of spectrum scarcity.

2. The role of technological change and substitution as accommodating responses on the supply side.

3. The "inherent" economic and legal characteristics of spectrum which now generate scarcity through congestion and pollution.

4. Those additional characteristics which further dramatize the need to articulate economic factors more effectively into spectrum management decisions.

PHYSICAL CHARACTER OF THE SPECTRUM

For present purposes, the term "spectrum" will refer to an arbitrarily defined range of radio waves utilized in communication, with the "dimensions" of frequency, time, and physical space.[2] As noted, it has

---

[2] It is standard engineering practice to identify these three dimensions as "occupied" by radio waves in all radio communications. See two studies by the Joint Technical Advisory Committee, *Radio Spectrum Conservation* (McGraw-Hill, 1952), pp. 181–82, and *Radio Spectrum Utilization* (New York: Institute of Electrical and Electronics Engineers, 1965), p. 5.

However, since the "spatial" dimension is itself three-dimensional, including height as well as area, Norton identifies five dimensions of spectrum. See K. Norton, *The Five-Dimensional Electromagnetic Spectrum Resource* (Boulder, Colo.: Environmental Science Services Administration, Institute for Telecommunication Sciences, rev. Dec. 12, 1967, unofficial multilith), pp. xv, II–1 to II–6, and Appendix I, 4 to 7.

Hinchman identifies eight dimensions of "electrospace": three-dimensional

intensive and extensive margins, and these respond to research and development (R&D), technical innovation, and a variety of economic and administrative or regulatory constraints.

The mere fact that spectrum is physically available does not *ipso facto* mean that it is technically usable, and technical usability does not necessarily imply economic usability. Nor need economic usability mean administratively sanctioned usability. As technology advances, however, more of the spectrum's resource base is transformed into technically usable "spectral resources"; and as cost constraints ease, "spectral resources" become economically usable as "spectral reserves."[3] Effective utilization in that case requires only affirmative administrative sanction.

Although the radio spectrum has a number of noncommunication uses—radio determination (as in radar), medical diathermy, and radio astronomy among them—its use in communications is of paramount importance in the economy and the primary focus of this study. Uses of the spectrum for communications include: defense- and space-related activity; radio–TV broadcasting; police, fire, and other local government services; the communications common carriers; business and industrial radio; air, marine, and land transportation; space, atmospheric, and geophysical research; amateur and citizens radio.

Effective spectrum utilization is delimited by electrical interference on one hand and by the propagation characteristics of different frequencies on the other. Where two or more users radiate signals on the same frequencies, at the same time, and in the same geographic area, the resultant interference may make one or all signals unintelligible. For a long time, a primary role of technological advance has been to facilitate a growing volume of transmissions without inacceptable interference.

In addition, the physical properties of particular frequencies may make them more or less suitable for some purposes than others.[4] Radio waves at the lower frequencies are best suited to long-distance communication, either because they bounce off the ionosphere, as in Band 7, or propagate along the ground or water and thus follow the earth's curva-

---

physical space, frequency, time, and the polarization, intensity, and directivity of radiated signals. See W. Hinchman, "Use and Management of the Electrospace: A New Concept of Radio Resources" in *Conference Record*, IEEE International Conference, Boulder, Colo., June 9–11, 1969, Sess. 13, pp. 1–5.

For convenience, we retain the simpler three-dimensional concept of spectrum space in this book.

[3] See threefold distinction in S. Schurr et al., *Energy in the American Economy, 1850–1975* (Johns Hopkins Press for Resources for the Future, 1960), pp. 296–300.

[4] See Joint Technical Advisory Committee, *Radio Spectrum Conservation*, Ch. 2, and *Radio Spectrum Utilization*, pp. 95–208.

ture, as in Bands 4–5.[5] At higher frequencies, the radio waves transmit on a line-of-sight basis or scatter somewhat over the horizon (Bands 8–9), but these frequencies are far less subject to severe fading than some of those lower down (Bands 6–7). The highest frequencies (Band 11) are subject to excessive attenuation or absorption by the atmosphere.

Physical Dimensions of the Resource Base

The term "bandwidth" refers to the number of consecutive frequencies needed to transmit designated bits of information. The radio spectrum refers to all frequencies ranging from 10,000 cycles per second to 3,000,000,000,000 cycles per second, a range usually described in terms of 10 kilocycles (Kc/s) to 3,000 gigacycles (Gc/s). Of these 3,000 Gc/s, only 40 Gc/s (1.3 percent) are now allocated by the International Telecommunications Union (ITU), and even this small percentage is by no means fully occupied. Above this point—i.e., from 40 to 300 Gc/s—only 10 percent is even spasmodically used, and this for experimental purposes.[6]

Nonetheless, the perennial concern with spectrum scarcity is understandable because technical and physical restraints rule out more extensive use at present. It should be noted, however, that physical-technical "saturation" has frequently been alleged in the past, only to be eased by subsequent technical advances, so that the economics of telecommunications research and development activities may be the ultimate determinant of spectrum utilization.

As spectral dimensions, time and space are most readily illustrated by reference to the time period and three-dimensional physical space within which radio signals are transmitted by users of any frequency. Signals transmitted on a given frequency over a designated area (including height) can be said to occupy all three dimensions of the spectrum utilized—time, space, and frequency. The degree to which the volume of physical space the signals pass through is in fact occupied depends on radiated power intensity. Extreme power intensity will so saturate the volume of physical space as to preclude any other signal from being received intelligibly within it.[7]

---

[5] These bands, determined by the International Telecommunications Union, are identified in Table 1.

[6] Although there is considerable use of the infrared, visible light, ultraviolet, and X-ray spectrum, we have not yet learned enough, or developed the equipment, to justify international allocations above 40 Gc/s. Meanwhile, work is under way to develop national allocations up to 1,000 Gc/s to guide research and development.

[7] See R. Gifford, "Maximizing Our Radio Resource," an address before the Electromagnetic Compatibility Group of the Institute of Electrical and Electronics Engineers, Washington, D.C., May 12, 1966, p. 6.

This conception can be clarified further as follows. Two spectrum users may utilize the identical frequencies and transmit at the same moment if they are far enough apart in terms of three-dimensional physical space. If they occupy the same frequency at the same time, they will occupy different spectrum in the spatial sense. If they operate at the same place, on the same frequency, and with the same intensity, but at different moments in time, they can be said to occupy different spectrum in the temporal sense. Effective communication is also possible when users operate at the same time, place, and intensity but use different (and nonadjacent) frequencies.[8]

How close to each other different users may come in regard to any or all of the three dimensions of spectrum before the resulting interference becomes intolerable depends on (a) the character of the information being transmitted; (b) the technical parameters; and (c) the state of the engineering arts. Historically, technical advances have facilitated closer and closer spacing in all three dimensions without destroying effective communication and at the same time extended the range of usable frequencies and the areas over which they are usable. However, though technical criteria alone may help determine acceptable levels of interference, optimality is clearly an economic concept.

For example, technical advances may help reduce some given level of interference, but their economic viability will depend on the opportunity costs of the necessary investment in R&D. The most one can say is that spectrum scarcity and congestion will at some point make economical that R&D needed to reduce spectrum requirements that has hitherto been considered too costly.

The Extensive Margin

Extensive spectrum development refers to the ability to manufacture hardware that can communicate information at higher and higher (and "newer") frequencies, notwithstanding severe physical constraints. Sometimes extensive development is facilitated by the advent of some new communications capability, as when technology developed during World War II later enabled us to open up spectrum above 100–200 Mc/s. Extensive development may also come through a related non-

---

[8] Hinchman focuses explicitly on the additional possibilities offered by varying the polarization, intensity, and directivity of radio waves. His more refined conception is basically consistent with the analysis here. See W. Hinchman, "The Electromagnetic Spectrum: What It Is and How It Is Used," App. A to Staff Paper No. 7, President's Task Force on Communications Policy (U.S. Department of Commerce, Clearinghouse for Federal Scientific and Technical Information, June 1969).

communications breakthrough, as in the case of booster-launching-tracking facilities for communications satellites which utilize hitherto unusable dimensions of spectrum for great distances.

Steady progress in developing the extensive margin is clearly reflected in the range of technically usable frequencies allocated at successive international conferences, up to 1 Mc/s in 1912, 23 Mc/s in 1927, 200 Mc/s in 1938, 10,500 Mc/s in 1947, and 40,000 Mc/s in 1959. The pattern of spectrum development is revealed further by the relatively large additions made at the two postwar conferences in 1927 and 1947. Finally, the historical pattern is suggested by the fact that the "older," earlier-developed regions are by and large those most intensively utilized today.

Table 1 provides a relevant backdrop of general information. Listed are the major spectral regions in descending order of frequency, together with some typical uses of the itemized bands. Starting with the highest radio frequencies, a region neither allocated nor used even experimentally,[9] we pass down through successively lower, older, and in general, more intensively utilized bands. Thus the uppermost Band 11, the Extremely High Frequencies, while officially allocated by the International Telecommunications Union up to 40 Gc/s and mainly devoted to radar and radio navigation, accommodates radio astronomy at 88–90 Gc/s and experiments even higher. Moving down, we pass through Band 10 (SHF), with its microwave and satellite relay systems; Band 9 (UHF), with TV broadcast, land mobile, tropospheric scatter, radar, and additional microwave relay systems; Band 8 (VHF), with its comparable versions of most of the above, plus FM broadcasting; Band 7 (HF), with its medium- and long-range point-point systems and international HF broadcasting; and Band 6 (MF), with its standard (AM) broadcast service and maritime/coastal radio services. Still lower are the oldest regions: Band 5 (LF), with its long- and medium-range point-point communications; and Band 4 (VLF), with its still longer-range capabilities. A detailed picture of the present distribution of all communications and noncommunications uses of the radio and optical light spectrum, appears in Figure 1, which is enclosed in the pocket at the end of the book.

Location of the several services in different spectral regions reflects physical suitability, of course, but also the state of the engineering arts at the time of the successive allocations. For example, the designation

---

[9] Still higher, there is the optical spectrum with still other uses, which lies beyond the scope of a study of the radio spectrum extending only to 3,000 Gc/s. However, there are uses of the infrared, visible light, and ultraviolet portion of the optical spectrum which could substitute for certain uses of radio frequencies.

TABLE 1. TYPICAL USES OF SPECTRUM, BY MAJOR ITU BAND

Frequencies	Band number	Band	Typical uses
300–3,000 Gc/s			Unallocated radio spectrum
30–300 Gc/s[a]	11	Extremely High Frequencies (EHF)	Microwave relay; space research; radar; radionavigation; amateur, experimental; radio astronomy
3–30 Gc/s	10	Super High Frequencies (SHF)	Microwave relay; deep space, space research, telemetry, communications satellites; radar; aeronautical radionavigation; meterological aids; amateur, citizens; radio astronomy
300–3,000 Mc/s	9	Ultra High Frequencies (UHF)	Short-range communications; microwave relay; over-horizon "scatter" communication. UHF television, instructional TV; land mobile; weather satellites, meteorological aids; space tracking and telemetry; radar; worldwide aeronautical radionavigation; amateur, citizens; radio astronomy
30–300 Mc/s	8	Very High Frequencies (VHF)	Short-range line-of-sight communication; over-horizon "scatter" communication. VHF television, FM broadcasting; space tracking and telemetry, satellites; aeronautical distress; worldwide radionavigation; land mobile; amateur; radio astronomy
3–30 Mc/s	7	High Frequencies (HF)	Medium- and long-range communication. International broadcasting; international point-point; air-ground; ship-shore; space research; amateur, citizens, radio astronomy
300–3,000 Kc/s	6	Medium Frequencies (MF)	Medium- and short-range communication. AM broadcasting; aeronautical mobile, radionavigation, marine radiophone, Loran; international distress, disaster; amateur
30–300 Kc/s	5	Low Frequencies (LF)	Long- and medium-range point-point communications; radionavigation aids; aeronautical mobile
10–30 Kc/s	4	Very Low Frequencies (VLF)	Very long-range point-point communications (over 1,000 nautical miles)

Source: Joint Technical Advisory Committee. See Appendix A. For abbreviations see Glossary.

[a] Allocations by the International Telecommunications Union extend to 40 Gc/s only, but the spectrum above that point is available for experimental uses.

of 550–1,600 Kc/s (in Band 6) for standard broadcasting was understandable in the 1920s, given technical know-how and prior allocations at the time. But short-range local broadcasting is far better suited to the FM frequencies in Band 8, whereas the long-range clear channel broadcast service could have capitalized on the propagation characteristics of spectrum below 550 Kc/s. There are indeed many examples of the second-best, pragmatic character of service allocations today. However, there is little question that physical-natural constraints will *ipso facto* rule out practical utilization of certain bands for certain purposes.[10]

Extensive development may result from R&D activity and innovation sponsored by either private or public agencies, but many of its most crucial advances have been governmentally sponsored. The governmental contributions have frequently been inadvertent, coming as an unexpected byproduct of large R&D, systems development, or other "crash" programs geared to quite different goals. This was obviously true of radar (at most a locational and surveillance device) and in the more recent case of satellites, which are heavily indebted to the whole space and defense program.

The Intensive Margin

Technical advances have also facilitated the intensive development of spectrum by operating on each of its three dimensions. Many of these advances are the result of private R&D (with or without federal financial assistance) by hardware manufacturers, communications carriers, and electronics laboratories.

Advances in the more intensive use of the spatial dimension have come through improved transmitters and directional antennas, which has facilitated closer and closer geographical spacing of users, even in the broadcast field, standard (AM) radio being the outstanding example. But the most dramatic development has been the close directional beaming made possible by line-of-sight microwave radiation, at first terrestrially and then in conjunction with space satellites. A comparable advance has come about through improved filters and receivers which facilitate better communication at lower power and thereby reduce the need for wide geographic spacing.

The most dramatic recent extension of the intensive margin of the frequency dimension has occurred in the land mobile service. During the past 15 years, in the face of recurrent spectrum congestion, land mobile channels have been "split" several times, first in the so-called Low Band (25–50 Mc/s), then in the High Band (150–174 Mc/s), and most recently in the Ultra High Band (450–470 Mc/s). Each time, the bandwidth required for two-way mobile radio was cut in half through technical improvements incorporated in higher-cost equipment. In the High Band alone, technical advances facilitated a decline in needed channel spacing from 240 Kc/s in 1940 to 15 Kc/s in 1966. Proposals

[10] Joint Technical Advisory Committee, *Radio Spectrum Conservation*, Chs. 3–4.

for further potential reductions to as little as 7½ Kc/s are sometimes heard. During the same period, equipment was developed to operate in the Ultra High Band, though at a substantially higher initial cost. Extension of the intensive margin through channel-splitting was therefore closely intertwined with extension of the extensive margin. On both counts this provided temporary relief to the divergence between the demand and supply of mobile radio spectrum.

Further exploitation of the frequency dimension has occurred through techniques to transmit a given kind and amount of information in a single, rather than a double, sideband. Effectively halving the necessary bandwidth in some services, this too is a major step in extending the intensive margin. Specifically, needed bandwidth depends on the kind of information transmitted—telegraphic, voice, or picture. As the information becomes more complex and sophisticated, more data must be carried by the radio signal: hence, the wider the sidebands and the greater the spectrum bandwidth required. The conversion to single sideband simply means that the same (or more) information can theoretically be transmitted in less space within the same time period.

Important here also are technical improvements that increase the frequency stability of transmitters and receivers and thus eliminate undesirable excursions from the assigned frequency which necessitate wider bandwidths than where the emissions are steadier and more predictable. As the state of the arts advances, it becomes possible to build at the same (or lower) costs equipment with greater stability that is less likely to emit wasteful side emissions.

We have not yet advanced so far in exploiting the time dimension. But as the spatial and frequency dimensions become more fully occupied and as moving upward to higher frequencies becomes more difficult, we may extend the temporal dimension too. For example, it is technically possible to pool several voice channels and use the pauses in the messages being transmitted, thereby raising the aggregate capacity of these channels by 30 per cent or 40 per cent with the use of so-called TASI equipment. Comparable equipment is available in microwave radio, too, though not yet economical to use. Installation at some future date could facilitate a more refined intensive use of the time dimension of spectrum. So-called time-division multiplex is not yet economical, let alone conducive to spectrum economy, but it could eventually facilitate more intensive use of the time dimension by enabling us to transmit as many as ten simultaneous conversations on the same frequency.

Mere availability of equipment able to transmit more information with less spectrum does not of itself produce the ability to use spectrum more efficiently. This also depends on the cost of the hardware and its degree of effective utilization. Where spectrum economy is achieved through higher-cost hardware associated with higher-capacity but under-utilized radio systems, such economy is clearly not economically effi-cient. On the contrary, economic efficiency would presumably require that more (not less) spectrum be used to reduce the hardware invest-ment per communications channel generated.

Substitutes for Spectrum

In the clamor to limit spectrum access to users who have "no alter-native," it is sometimes forgotten that, strictly speaking, there are *always* substitutes for spectrum.[11] Substitutes for radio include open wire, sunken or hardened coaxial cable, and submarine cable. Although the communications common carriers also use microwave radio today, their traditional hallmark has long been that of a wireline service. It has even been proposed on past occasions to exclude them from radio en-tirely. Transportation is still another substitute for radio.

Moreover, if mobile radio systems may reduce the need for vehicles, drivers, and fuel in a fleet of taxis or trucks, it must also be true that these displaced factor inputs may in turn replace radio. Likewise, just as radio may reduce the manufacturer's need for personnel and storage space, so increasing the latter may enable him to dispense with radio. Even in the broadcast field, wire systems financed by subscriber arrange-ments are coming to look like viable economic alternatives to the advertiser-supported air network service.

The main problem in finding substitutes for radio is less technical than economic. If one is willing to pay the price there *are* substitutes. The trouble comes mainly from the fact that the added costs of alterna-tive uses of spectrum are rarely quantified or weighed in any allocation decision.

Perhaps the most dramatic example of uses for radio for which there appear to be no meaningful substitutes are those involving the safety of moving vehicles, their passengers, and freight. But even in the case of aeronautical, marine, or police radio, or military use, the basis for any judgment about radio's "unique" role is less technical or even economic than social and political. It obviously reflects the high value

---

[11] To the spectrum manager-cum-radio engineer who asks how to communi-cate with aeronautical, marine, or space vehicles without radio frequencies, the simple answer is that even he can vary systems design at the margin to economize spectrum, albeit short of eliminating radio entirely. See H. Levin, "There Is Always a Substitute for Spectrum," *Telecommunication Journal* (January 1969), pp. 33–35.

we place on safety. Yet even safety is clearly no absolute value in transportation, fire prevention, crime control, and so on. It is all a matter of degree. The value of additional safety must be weighed off against the outputs forgone by additional investment in it. The question becomes one of how much spectrum to divert to safety from other uses and at what price in forgone outputs.

The most one can say, then, is that there are ranges of substitutes for radio, of varying adequacy and for varying purposes. Yet the spectrum user is not now free to determine how to balance between these substitutes and the real thing; nor does he normally confront the appropriate price incentives in striking his balance.

Regarding the direction of substitution, it is not true that radio always has, or necessarily must, displace the older communications modes, or that it is inherently superior for all purposes to what came earlier. Appearing after the early wire lines—of course, after transportation—radio has in some sense acted to displace these modes for certain purposes. But it is more likely that radio will supplement them, or cater to new needs which its availability has helped create, rather than supplant them.

Just as VLF and HF radio systems challenged the first primitive ocean cables, so the newer high-capacity submarine cables have threatened to displace these less reliable, lower-capacity radio services. And even before high-capacity satellite relays arise to challenge the need for new submarine cable, plans have been announced for a superior broadband transistorized cable with several times the capacity of any now in use. Just as microwave links are helping to promote cheaper transcontinental telephone service, so we have come to rely on a hardened coaxial cable as terrestrial back-up for national security purposes. Just when intercontinental satellite TV has become a reality, AT&T's new 720-circuit cable and projections of even greater channel capacity may offer still another competitive option. Indeed in the foreseeable future flying TV tapes of certain kinds to and from Europe by jet transport could be at least as practical as satellite and high-capacity channels, if not more so.

What this suggests is that outright replacement of wire modes by radio, or vice versa, rarely occurs. Rather, the several modes supplement each other, the older ones being retained within limits as a hedge against natural or man-made uncertainties. The reliability of communications in services where even momentary outages can have drastic effects is increasingly cited to defend the retention of seemingly obsolete modes in the face of newer developments. It is sometimes hard to evaluate these claims or to determine whether the price we pay in excess capacity and duplication is really offset by the facilitation of commensurate security and reliability or merely operates to maintain the current value of the preponderant investments in older communications equipment.

The most spectacular potential substitutes for radio communication are the laser, a device which employs guided light waves, and the circular waveguide tube, a two-inch diameter conduit down which radio signals are sent. Insofar as the laser uses light waves and the waveguide tube uses cable technology, they can both presumably be classified as substitutes for radio spectrum. Neither radiates radio waves or poses any new threat of interference for existing radio signals. Yet both promise to add immensely to new communication capability. Indeed the problem today, according to Bell Laboratories, is that the waveguide's capabilities still so far exceed those needed on any known or foreseeable communications link anywhere in the world as to make it uneconomic. As with the satellite relay, economic and not technical factors constitute the major stumbling block.

ECONOMIC CHARACTERISTICS OF THE SPECTRUM

Thus we come to the more strictly economic characteristics of the spectrum; its stock and flow attributes and unique freedom from depletion; its character as a common property or shared resource subject to special international constraints; its interchangeability as between different uses; and its overriding value for public information, education, and security. Two major issues will be scrutinized: first, the spectrum's inherent tendency, under present institutional arrangements, toward scarcity through congestion and pollution; second, those basic features which further underscore the relevance of opportunity costs and the need to articulate economic factors better in major allocational decisions.

Stock and Flow Attributes

"Stock" resources, such as minerals or fossil fuels can be regarded as inventories or stocks that await further processing.[12] The stocks are finite, irreplaceable, and require further "winning, processing, transportation." Although ultimately depletable, the stocks are normally expansible within limits through exploitation, at a price in added investment

---

[12] For a standard characterization of stock and flow attributes, see A. Scott, *Natural Resources: The Economics of Conservation* (University of Toronto Press, 1955), Ch. 1. See also the critique by J. Bain, "Resource Policies in Relation to Economic Growth," in J. Spengler, ed., *Natural Resources and Economic Growth* (Washington: Resources for the Future, 1961), pp. 246–76.

and higher costs per units of output. These rising costs are due to: the declining quality of reserves exploited; their diminishing accessibility; and in certain cases, the bidding up of costs due to external diseconomies where competing administrative units manage the same resource pool.

On the other hand, "flow" resources, such as arable land, fisheries, or water flow, are at least potentially restorable, replaceable, and reproducible. Like stock resources, they are also expansible at a price in new investment and higher costs. The basic difference is simply that in stock resources less use today leaves more for use tomorrow, whereas in flow resources a reduced use rate today only leaves more for someone else to use today.

Although stock resources are exhaustible, optimal use is by no means zero use. The best economic use is simply one that equates the net revenue which users could derive by producing and selling outputs today with what they could earn if they waited. In flow resources, too, the user-owner will maximize the current value of his property. But here he must select both an optimal time rate of use and a rate of investment in maintenance and renewal that just forestalls physical conditions which would make it uneconomic to reverse depletion, i.e., an investment whose current value at the margin just equals the current value of the revenues otherwise forgone through irreversible depletion.

On the face of it, the spectrum can be said to possess both stock and flow attributes. On one hand, the frequent magnitude and specialized character of needed hardware investment and the length of its amortization period clearly imply that the more spectrum that is occupied or used today, the less there remains to occupy or use tomorrow. Such indeed is a major reason for the longstanding practice of spectrum stockpiling as an instrument of spectrum management. On this count therefore spectrum is a stock resource, indeed one whose physical magnitude is known with a higher degree of certainty than in the case of many others. However, like other resources, whether stock or flow, the spectrum's usable portions depend on technology, economics, and regulatory administration. Thus the distinctions between a "resource base" set by natural-physical limitations; potential "resources" set by conjectural levels of technology and cost conditions; and (effective) "reserves" determined by current economic-technologic factors, also apply here.[13]

In addition to the constraints set by sheer physical scarcity, technology, and economics, there is an oft-decisive set of regulatory-administrative constraints. For example, the UHF spectrum is not only phys-

[13] See fn. 3 above.

ically available and technically usable for broadcast television but also administratively available. However, it is still largely unusable for TV on economic grounds. Yet it is both technically and economically usable by nonbroadcast private, public, or common carrier users or indeed by the military. To explain the longstanding nonuse of the UHF notwithstanding the variety of outputs forgone and the substantial costs imposed on next-best users forced to inferior alternatives, we must turn to administrative intervention rationalized as an attempt to implement a number of broadcast regulatory priorities.

Notwithstanding the mere 1.3 per cent (40 Gc/s) of the known spectrum currently allocated by the ITU, the bulk of which has actually become usable only since World War II, users and managers have long confronted recurrent congestion and spectrum scarcity in the face of technical, economic, and administrative constraints. Congestion and scarcity are indeed in part symptomatic of the absence of a system of frequency markets and prices to distribute radiation rights efficiently.[14] Without such markets and prices, both spectrum managers and users have accommodated to scarcity through a system of central allocation. They have also accommodated by deliberate efforts to develop the intensive and extensive margins of spectrum as well as its substitutes. Nevertheless, the pattern and intensity of these developmental or substitutional efforts need not coincide with those that would prevail under a market-type system of resource allocation.

Insofar as it is free from depletion upon use, the spectrum has characteristics of a sustained-yield (flow) resource of a unique sort, perhaps most similar to solar or water power. There is no need for investment in spectrum to restore or renew it, as in the case of fisheries, arable land, or forests, where to maintain a sustained yield requires not only that equipment remain intact but also that the resource itself be renewed upon use. In the spectrum, if equipment is maintained intact, then the same flow of information is possible indefinitely, with no depletion of the resource itself.

Like water resources or air, however, the spectrum too is subject to degradation through pollution or congestion. Pollution may be due partly to noncommunications uses of radio like arc welders and medical or industrial diathermy or to noise levels generated by communications

---

[14] There is, of course, an economically optimal level of interference (congestion). A free spectrum market may therefore facilitate more (not less) interference while enhancing the economic value of the spectrum resource. Nevertheless, market-clearing prices for spectrum would still induce some users to reduce their usage and otherwise act to eliminate longstanding divergences between supply and demand.

use. Or it may be due to the absence of markets and of market-clearing prices and in particular to a variety of externalities incorporated inadequately into the user's cost parameters. (See Chapter IV.)

Unlike other flow resources, to be sure, the spectrum returns at once to its original virginal state just as soon as the congestants or pollutants are removed. However, once large hardware investments are made, the sources of spectrum pollution or congestion may not be easy to eliminate on short notice; enforcement costs may be substantial. Hence the difference in restoration costs as between spectrum, water, and air resources should not be exaggerated.

Common Property Attributes

As presently constituted, the spectrum has many attributes of a common property (shared use) resource.[15] Users of such resources will normally lack incentives to refrain from use rates which raise costs against themselves and others. That is, unless assured that all others will refrain from using up the resource before they do, the initial users have no reason to postpone or reduce their own use. In this case, there is bound to be excessive use of labor, capital, and raw materials. It is no surprise therefore that the tendency towards depletion, congestion, and economic inefficiency will result in attempts to appropriate rights unilaterally (as by extension of offshore fishing rights) or by joint cooperative arrangements among the users (as in unified ownership of oil pools and international agreements on migratory fisheries). Even more frequently, there will be a call for public control of output and/or entry.[16]

In the spectrum field, there has indeed emerged an international clearinghouse of information on frequency use, and also a practice of mutual forbearance on the part of different nations in their recognition of a principle of priority of registration or priority of use. In some domestic cases, local industry advisory committees play a less effective

---

[15] Common property resources are characterized in A. Scott, *Natural Resources*, Chs. 5, 11; F. Christy and A. Scott, *The Common Wealth in Ocean Fisheries* (Johns Hopkins Press for Resources for the Future, 1966), Ch. 2; and in H. Jarrett, ed., *Environmental Quality in a Growing Economy* (Johns Hopkins Press for Resources for the Future, 1966), pp. 47–65. Theoretical aspects are best set forth in H. Gordon, "The Economic Theory of a Common Property Resource," *Journal of Political Economy* (April 1954), pp. 116–24.

[16] In fisheries there have been numerous regulations short of entry control, but entry control is also essential to prevent overuse and may be instituted by a tax on catch or on fishermen or by restrictive licensing. See especially A. Scott, "Economics of Regulating Fisheries" in *Economic Effects of Fishery Regulation* (Rome: U.N. Food and Agriculture Organization, 1962), pp. 27–58.

role in controlling access. In still other cases, entry has been formally restricted by the Federal Communications Commission (FCC).

The fact is that no spectrum user will reduce his power or service range to keep from entering another's frequency space or invest in costly spectrum-economizing R&D unless assured that he will benefit personally thereby and not merely help a rival. In the absence of clearly defined property rights in spectrum (including the right to exclude unwanted signals),[17] the only ways to prevent congestion are intra-industry or international agreements among all users and public regulation of entry, power, time on air, and similar factors.

By way of illustrating the problems posed by the common property attributes of the spectrum we may turn briefly to the situation in domestic land mobile and the international High Frequency Band.

Land Mobile Radio.   One major constraint in the land mobile service is that the suitable frequencies are largely limited to the region below 890 Mc/s, over half of which on the nongovernment side (i.e., frequencies not allocated to the federal government) is currently allocated to FM and TV broadcasting. The growing congestion since World War II has resulted in successive innovations to reduce mobile radio channel spacing. Indeed this innovative response to congestion has actually been the major focus of attention in most discussions to date.[18] High federal officials recognize what the industry is quick to identify as its sustained contributions in developing spectrum-economizing hardware. However, the economic factors which gave rise to the congestion in the first place have been notably neglected. The tendency is to view the phenomenon in largely technical-physical or in administrative terms.

Entry into many land mobile services has long been virtually unlimited for eligible operators. In such cases as business radio or land transport radio, the operators are permitted to enter with full knowledge that they may well interfere with others on various frequencies. Before issuing new licenses, however, the FCC will normally require certification of any applicant's proposed frequencies by one of the industry's voluntary advisory committees or user associations.[19] In actual practice, these user associations coordinate frequency requirements in virtually all the mobile radio services; they also resolve interference complaints.[20]

----

[17] The reasons for, and economic consequences of, their absence are discussed in Ch. IV below.

[18] Systematic analysis of this response appears in Ch. VIII below.

[19] *FCC Rules and Regulations*, para. 93.9.

[20] Joint Technical Advisory Committee, *Spectrum Engineering: The Key to Progress* (New York: Institute of Electrical and Electronic Engineers, 1968), Supp. 2, pp. 24–29, 39.

Through such arrangements the Commission has tried (albeit unsuccessfully) to keep interference to a minimum.

Because radio's productivity in any case depends on the speed and reliability of communication, there is a real question as to whether some firms would have entered at all could they have predicted the growing delays that would plague them. In one sense this is a case of external diseconomies pure and simple, where private and social costs diverge. The last entrant is simply unable to predict the degree to which his entry will increase waiting time and decrease reliability for all. Or, more precisely, his prediction of future economic yield due to radio is falsified by the cost-increasing, value-reducing effects of his own entry, as well as later entries.

Some of this divergence of private and social cost may of course be due to deficient market knowledge. In the case of small, impoverished users, more complete and accurate market information could facilitate more economically rational investment decisions. But it is sometimes implied that there is an irreducible core of ignorance here which even a perfect market would not eliminate.

Because no one can be sure that his withdrawal will not simply confer a competitive advantage on a rival by facilitating his more efficient use of radio, the argument goes, it is hard on sheer competitive grounds for anyone to withdraw. The upshot has in any case been a dramatic excess of demand over supply of spectrum, lengthy delays in placing calls, an excess of capital and labor in the land mobile band, and persistent underutilization of radio equipment beyond that which flows from the intermittent nature of the mobile radio services.

However imperfect the economic logic of this explanation of congestion,[21] it unquestionably underlies a number of recent proposals to "correct" the situation. These proposals include: restrictive entry limitations; access to unused frequencies now assigned to others in FM and television; permission to share presently occupied television channels in the VHF band; authorization of one-way tone coding, a service that requires little spectrum but hopefully satisfies the needs of some present users of two-way voice service. Also suggested has been greater reliance on unitary management of land mobile frequencies, to be ac-

----

[21] A distinction must actually be drawn between the facts that (a) firms do not take into account the effects of their acts on others (external economies) and (b) they are ignorant of how far others will subsequently enter the market. Ignorance of future entry could exist even where the market is working perfectly in other respects, and economics therefore normally ignores it. Moreover, optimal degrees of congestion need not require tighter administrative controls on entry if externalities are internalized through spatial or temporal modifications of radiation rights.

complished by permitting individual users to pool their frequencies or otherwise to coordinate usage through the existing industry advisory committees, even if this requires an informal antitrust exemption, or by authorizing a more extensive common carrier service to handle these needs centrally. These methods, of course, are not mutually exclusive.

Without pressing the analogy too far, several of the proposals (for example, those for unitary management) are very much the kind instituted in managing other common property resources. In land mobile radio, entry control and/or redefinition of radiation rights seems essential at some point, however much temporary relief is possible through other alternatives.

International High Frequency Band. The solution that appears to have emerged in the international High Frequency Band makes an interesting contrast. HF radio has long been the work horse of international broadcasting, radiotelephone, and radiotelegraph. Notwithstanding viable substitutes like submarine cable and now satellites, the HF band is still retained as a back-up in last resort by the carriers and the military. Here too, congestion has produced two sets of remedies. First, ITU authorities have encouraged more intensive use of the spectrum through moving to single sideband modulation, greater use of substitutes through cable, landlines, and satellites, and relocation of incumbent services where possible and appropriate through shifting land mobile to the UHF band.[22] Second, there has been a spontaneous informal process of pragmatic accommodation centering around the clearinghouse of international frequency assignments recorded at the ITU's International Frequency Registration Board (IFRB) in Geneva. It is this second arrangement that mainly concerns us here.

All nations are free to claim rights to use spectrum at will and have their claims recorded at the IFRB, provided only that they do not conflict with the prior right of others. Since squatters' rights have more legal standing in the case of international frequency management than they do domestically, most sovereign nations tend to claim far more space than immediately needed out of fear that none will be available when they do need it and/or a national pride that sees in advanced communications systems a sign of having arrived. Hence all available HF space has long been nominally claimed by someone.

Nonetheless, congestion and full occupancy on paper have not prevented potential users without satisfactory assignments from "borrowing" the space staked out by others which is not being used. Priorities are

[22] International Telecommunications Union, *Final Report of the Panel of Experts* (Geneva: The Union, 1963), Ch. 2.

in fact respected here more out of mutual forbearance and fear of retaliation than out of a desire to forestall international adjudication. Within these constraints and the principle of priority by notification or registration, unused spectrum is "borrowed" on a pragmatic trial-and-error basis, with few head-on collisions and still fewer cases requiring international adjudication.

New users hunt out unused HF space, irrespective of the legal claims thereon, and use it on a pragmatic basis. All nations have thereby come to use more space than they otherwise would, on a secondary or temporary basis. Yet international adjudication is rarely resorted to in order to determine who has prior rights or to dislodge the borrower with secondary rights. Rigorous enforcement of formal priorities, it is widely agreed, would have reduced the use of these frequencies. Even attempts to define priority according to first use, or longest continuous use, rather than first registration have apparently provided no better answer than this pragmatic accommodation of interests. It must be said, of course, that the provision of accurate up-to-date information on actual frequency usage by the IFRB could facilitate more efficient utilization.

In short, the system of legalized squatters' rights which ITU members have accepted out of mutual fear has established a kind of property right system through frequency listings at the IFRB, one that is ultimately defensible before the World Court. So long as users do not interfere with any other registrant's higher priority, they may ostensibly seek out and use idle spectrum on a pragmatic ad hoc basis. The results are: a flood of claims to establish squatters' rights throughout the spectrum, irrespective of the immediate prospects of use; a pragmatic acquiesence of incumbent nations in the borrowing of idle space by latecomers or nonpriority users; and a consequent increase in radio-frequency utilization, reduced congestion, and reduction in excess radio plant capacity.

From the viewpoint of spectrum management, perhaps the most relevant points may be summed up as follows. The several national managers and users have spontaneously coordinated their claims and counterclaims to spectrum within the context of primary and secondary rights on file at the IFRB, using it as an international clearinghouse for information on recorded rights and assignments, and now gradually for more complete and up-to-date usage information. They have felt less compelled to use their spectrum prematurely than they would have without such chances to borrow idle space later on an ad hoc basis or without the priorities on file at the IFRB; and licensees have poured less capital and labor into the HF band and congested it less.

Without outright entry control and pre-engineered allocations or a system of private or national radiation rights,[23] no long-run solution to the congestion problem seems likely, notwithstanding the ITU's deliberate encouragement to extend the intensive margin, to move to other spectral regions, and to substitute wire or cable. The pragmatic process described here may have operated as a partial, but only a partial, remedy.

In addition to the economic factors conducive to recurrent congestion in the radio spectrum, three other characteristics underscore the need to articulate the economic dimensions of allocational decisions more explicitly. The overriding public value of spectrum makes economic analysis more essential, for no rational rating or reevaluation of social priorities in spectrum utilization is possible without careful reference to opportunity costs. By the same token, opportunity costs are significant only where spectrum is technically interchangeable among alternative users and uses. As a practical matter, finally, the possibility of articulating economic factors in national management decisions will depend at least partly on the kind of international constraints to which the spectrum must be subject.

Overriding Public Value of Spectrum

Few natural resources have been as frequently or exclusively viewed from a strictly social vantage point as has the spectrum. Public waterways and national forests have recreational uses; public lands, educational uses; strategic materials, military value. But in each case there are strictly economic or business uses, too, and even strictly noncommercial utilization may be constrained by the managers' knowledge of market price in the resource's best-alternative private use. Market value may well figure in decisions on whether to divert such resources to public purposes.

With spectrum, however, there is no organized market. The market for tangible radio assets does not appear to perform any truly comparable function or provide the spectrum manager with an appropriate yardstick. The absence of a market tends to exacerbate the users' and managers' sense of "spectrum scarcity." Hence the managers' strong

---

[23] Had two-sided radiation rights been initially defined as coterminous with national boundaries and nations been permitted to buy and sell them freely, centralized ITU controls might be far less urgent today. See W. Meckling, "History of International Allocation and Assignment," paper presented at the Conference on Economics of Regulated Public Utilities, University of Chicago, June 20–25, 1965. A move in this direction would now pose serious practical and political problems, though possibly none greater than would a move toward a fully engineered spectrum.

compulsion to husband the resource and parcel it out only after the most careful evaluation, in social terms at least.

Why the spectrum managers have, almost from the outset, minimized or neglected the economic aspects of their allocational decisions, notwithstanding their undeniable performance of an obvious and crucial economic function, is another matter. It may reflect in part those elaborate Congressional directives which underline the public character of spectrum and in part also a longstanding recognition of the resource's "unique" potential for social, political, cultural and military purposes, for internal and national security, for public information and education, for exploration and experimentation, and for recreation and entertainment.

However, another important reason for the managers' apparent neglect of opportunity costs is their understandable desire to maximize administrative discretion in furthering social priorities. Yet the nation's commitment to such priorities cannot be presumed out of hand without a prior articulation of all the alternatives forgone in any allocational decision. The extra costs imposed on next-best users must clearly be taken into account. To recognize these economic consequences is not necessarily to deny that they may be worth incurring. But to ignore them is to perpetrate a subterfuge by deciding without full knowledge and divulgence of all the facts.

In using land for educational purposes, water for recreation, fisheries or forests for sport, we are increasingly called upon first to consider economic value in best-alternative use. To know the price we must pay in forgone benefits may presumably help us decide whether some particular social need is best met in this way or through some other means. The public's demand for recreation or education may be hard to estimate, but tentative estimates along with other relevant data will surely help us avoid the anomaly of using highly valuable resources to meet public needs of relatively little importance. So too with the radio spectrum, too long and incorrectly viewed as a free good, at least by favored classes of users.

The relevance of opportunity costs, however, clearly depends on the technical interchangeability of spectrum among alternative users and uses. If A, but only A, can use a given frequency, the problem of economic choice does not arise.

Technical Interchangeability

The spectrum is a resource with a potentially high degree of interchangeability among alternative users. Technical properties are in fact

less important as constraints here than are the costs of developing
unused spectrum higher up, conversion costs for existing equipment, and
international factors like the economic advantages of hardware standardization. Thus while certain services, such as radio astronomy, simply
cannot be accommodated elsewhere in the spectrum, most services could
in fact be relocated, the frequencies in many spectral regions having at
least a limited number of different possible uses. Hence, if the present
user were displaced, someone else could enter; and unused frequencies
now assigned to one service could in all likelihood be used by another
if the managers permitted. In some cases a mere swap of spectrum by
different incumbents could enhance the technical and economic efficiency of both.

Even a limited technical interchangeability of spectrum among users
underlines the importance of opportunity cost calculations for efficient
spectrum management. The opportunity costs of spectrum utilization in
some regions presumably approach zero, as in much of the abundant
microwave band or in the presently unusable regions above 30 Gc/s.
But in other regions the costs may be extremely high. This would
apparently be the case in television where land mobile users might well
pay large sums for access to unused UHF (or occupied VHF) spectrum, or where broadcasters have sometimes sought out military spectrum. In addition, the low opportunity costs of point-point microwave
occupancy outside the urban areas doubtless reflect the capability there
for narrow directional beaming, whereas the high opportunity costs of
broadcast or land mobile occupancy reflect their omnidirectional beaming and the resulting need for more spectrum that is interference-free.

In this regard, technical interchangeability not only permits choices
among alternative users but makes such choices a necessary condition
for a socially and economically desirable use of the spectrum. Such an
objective requires, of course, recognition of the costs imposed on potential claimants who are forced into more costly or lower-quality alternatives by being excluded from their preferred place in the spectrum.

Nonuse of spectrum is wasteful, on the other hand, only if some
excluded potential user actually exists and would enter; and this also
depends in the first instance on technical interchangeability. Furthermore the justifiability of continued exclusion depends in part on the
availability of equally suitable alternative spectral assignments for users
with current access to unwanted spectrum.

International Constraints

Will the international character of spectrum as a shared resource
permit the careful weighing of opportunity costs at the national level?

Or will the constraints on national discretion make this unlikely? Although the full discussion of this issue is reserved for Chapter IV, some general comments are in order here on the nature of international constraints.

Insofar as all radio communication "uses" the national airspace, the spectrum may superficially appear to be a national resource subject to national sovereignty.[24] Yet one clearly cannot communicate by radio with another country without its cooperation as to frequency, time, power, and place of communication. In some cases one cannot even use radio within one's own boundaries without the forbearance of other nations. These and other limits on national discretion could be said to make the spectrum an international resource comparable in theory to airspace over the high seas, to international waterways, or even to migratory fisheries.

The question is how much discretion any nation has in utilizing various frequencies as it sees fit without reference to the needs or actions of others. Unlimited national discretion obviously implies exclusive national jurisdiction not only over rights to emit signals therein but also to exclude the emissions of others.[25] To the extent that such national discretion exists, the spectrum may indeed be characterized as "belonging" to the nation in question, but where national discretion is narrowly circumscribed by the machinery and requirements of international coordination, the spectrum would more nearly assume the character of a shared international resource. Between these two polar extremes there could conceivably be a different practical status for different spectral regions, depending on their physical characteristics and the state of the engineering arts.

Stated otherwise, radio communication transmitted and received wholly within the United States and posing no interference to any other country occupies spectrum for all practical purposes "belonging" to us under present international arrangements. But we are free also to use

[24] Today nations exercise sovereignty over the airspace above their territory at least up to the height at which aircraft can operate. (Convention of International Civil Aviation, 61 Stat. 1180, Pt. I, Ch. I, arts. 1–3.) The status of contiguous space beyond this designated national airspace remains ambiguous. One common view is that nations should rightly be permitted to claim rights as high into stratosphere, ionosphere, and exosphere (beyond the region usable by aircraft) as the most advanced technology will facilitate, but never in any case into "outer space" beyond the region of the earth's attraction. See papers in Senate Committee on Space, 87th Cong., 1st Sess., *Legal Problems of Space Exploration*, 1961, especially J. Cooper (pp. 66–73); J. Hogan (pp. 129–40); and W. Heinrich (pp. 271, 284–305, 316–19).

[25] Meckling states that nations have exchanged unlimited discretion to emit signals on all frequencies for right to emit on some frequencies without interference, giving up "some *em*ission jurisdiction in exchange for jurisdiction over *ad*mission." ("History of International Allocation and Assignment," p. 24.)

frequencies beyond our boundaries or within them when potential conflicts with foreign countries are precluded or resolved through priorities
recorded in the Master Frequency Register of the IFRB in Geneva. Such
international recognition of priority rights based on first assignment,
first use, or longest continuous use, can be construed as establishing a
kind of national property right system in spectrum even where national
discretion is not unlimited initially because emissions are likely to cross
national boundaries.[26]

The possibility of injecting economic factors into national management decisions will obviously be greater, the greater the range of national
discretion. Where such discretion is circumscribed by the plans, policies,
and goals of foreign partners, the possibilities will diminish, as in the
case of international broadcast, fixed, mobile, and space services. Communication in the border areas of different nations also requires coordination and agreements. For example, discretion of the United States
and Canada—and the United States and Mexico—is reciprocally circumscribed by each other's needs and requirements within some specified distance of the border. For certain European countries problems of
border area coordination loom particularly large, and even in countries
as big as the United States the propagation characteristics of some frequencies require agreements with neighbors far from the border areas.

Within these designated border strips, however, and aside from such
problems as the nighttime skywave interference caused by high-powered
standard broadcast stations hundreds of miles beyond their official service range, a large geographic area can be carved out where communication appears to be strictly national, as in the VHF and UHF bands and
the microwave region generally. This area is presumably the best suited
for new attempts to inject economic incentives into spectrum allocation.
Yet even here the spectrum's strictly national usage may still be constrained by the factors named above and also by the economic and
security advantages of internationally standardized equipment, and by
the mutual advantages to all nations in using the same frequencies to do
the same things domestically, notwithstanding the technical interchangeability of spectrum among alternative uses. Thus more work is clearly
needed to determine just how far opportunity costs can at best be
articulated in seeking a more rational approach. (See Chapter IV.)

There is of course no question about the economic benefits of

[26] See F. Nicotera, "The Structure of the ITU," *Telecommunication Journal*
(June 1964), pp. 160–62; P. Miles, "International Radiofrequency Management,"
Telecommunication Journal (October 1954), pp. 170–73; and Note, "The Master
Radio Frequency Record," *Telecommunication Journal* (December 1955), pp.
216–21.

international standardization of hardware. The equipment-producing nations enjoy greater economies of scale; the nonproducing buyer nations benefit from the greater number of options they can choose among on the supply side. On the other hand, the "common use of common frequencies" has emerged historically for administrative convenience in the accommodation of new services. Most nations normally find it advantageous to coordinate even strictly national frequency usage through the ITU. To that extent, even the most characteristically national usage can be said to be broadly subject to important international constraints.

For example, in the case of space communication, the question was whether to place it in a band then occupied by U.S. radar and by the Soviet Union's terrestrial microwave or in another band occupied by their radar and our microwave. Both nations had placed these two domestic services in different bands during the wartime hiatus in the rule of common usage, between the ITU Conferences of 1939 and 1947. Space communication could be kept compatible with domestic microwave at a small cost, but not easily with radar. Hence, depending on where space communication was lodged, substantial displacement or conversion costs would have been placed on the U.S., or the U.S.S.R. In the face of cold-war sensitivities, not even a generous amortization period for microwave or radar hardware would have provided a really satisfactory answer. The compromise struck was for each side to stay clear of its own radar bands, while allowing enough overlap in the frequencies selected for space communications so that future U.S. and U.S.S.R. systems could communicate with each other.

The rule of common usage would have prevented this problem from arising and acted to distribute the displacement or conversion costs more equitably on the parties involved, without having to determine first whose incompatible usage had priority over whose. What is less clear is how far the above constraints might preclude the injection of economic incentives. The answer probably lies in large part on the mechanism used for the purpose. In Chapter IV I conclude that, while these two pervasive international constraints may intensify the considerable difficulties in establishing any strictly domestic system of freely transferable rights, they by no means rule out a new approach short of that, an approach based on shadow prices, rental charges, and auctions.

CHAPTER II

MAJOR COMPONENTS
OF THE SPECTRUM SYSTEM

Although students of telecommunications economics normally examine nonatmospheric (wire) as well as radio communication, it is
still useful to think loosely of a "spectrum industry," or at least a "spectrum system,"[1] made up of users, their end customers and hardware
suppliers, the underlying R&D facilities, and the national spectrum
managers. The fact that spectrum has a number of viable substitutes of
varying degrees of closeness does not preclude analysis of how the
communication capability it facilitates is produced, distributed, used, and
developed.

Spectrum users compete for access to limited frequencies within the
same service and between different services. They compete also within
(and between) the federal and the nongovernment sectors. This compe-
tion is largely backwards, to the spectral reserves. But some users, like
those in business and manufacturers radio, may also compete forward
for the business of the same end customers. These are the users most
likely to treat spectrum like any other factor input, to be combined in
ways that minimize their total costs. Here the main problem is that the
cost of the spectral inputs is normally, if incorrectly, equated with the
cost of communications hardware alone. Most other users, like those in
public safety and local or federal government radio, are not directly
constrained in their use of spectrum by pressures in any "markets" for
their end products or services. There, administrative rules of thumb
assume even greater importance for efficient utilization of the spectrum.

---

[1] In formulating and developing this construct, I am indebted to J. Bain, R.
Caves, and J. Margolis for insights derived from their book, *Northern California's
Water Industry* (The Johns Hopkins Press for Resources for the Future, 1966).

Some user groups, such as the common carriers and federal agencies, actively choose between new investment in spectrum-using and non-atmospheric communications modes. Others are less likely to do so—aeronautical, marine, and land mobile for obvious reasons and broadcasters for more complex ones. But it is well to bear in mind that in principle at least, there is always a substitute for spectrum.

The hardware suppliers of any and all spectrum users, and the performers of underlying telecommunications R&D on which they draw, constitute the developers of spectrum par excellence. User and hardware laboratory entities can be said to play this developmental role jointly. In a resource field where recurrent congestion and pollution are as much a result of the limited proportion of the total resource that is effectively usable as of the intensity of demand for particular frequencies, the historical extension of intensive and extensive spectral margins has played a role of exceptional importance.

Nonetheless, national spectrum management is still very much a problem in allocation without markets. In the absence of spectrum markets, the competing and interacting users necessarily vie for access rights under a set of administrative-regulatory constraints imposed by federal managers. It seems valid and useful to presume that any and all classes of spectrum users, both within the federal and nongovernment sectors, act as if they seek to maximize an internal preference function. This would range from the corporate preferences of the business-industrial user, where profit-maximization or "satisficing" is the normal assumption, to a more complex preference function in the case of public safety, local government, or educational users. It is true, however, that even the private commercial users operate to maximize preferences which are shaped partly at least by the administrative-legislative-judicial doctrine which enmeshes American spectrum management today.

Under these administrative constraints, the interaction of rival users within discrete services (and between them) produces a distribution of frequencies between uses different from what would emerge if there were a market. Moreover, because different users within the same services or in different services cannot at present compete for spectrum in any organized market, there is no readily available market valuation of frequencies in alternative uses. Nor is there any market-type constraint to guarantee that spectral inputs will be combined optimally with other factor inputs by any or all users to maximize their contributions to the Gross National Product. Neither is it clear therefore that the economic efficiency impaired by particular allocational policies is offset by furtherance of the regulatory-legislative priorities presumably incorporated in the managers' preference function.

Spectrum Users

American spectrum users can be classified as fixed, mobile, broadcast, and space, and further distinctions can be made between domestic and international, as well as between government and nongovernment users. In addition, one must distinguish between communications and noncommunications uses of spectrum, the latter including industrial, medical, and scientific uses.

The major nongovernment users are the broadcasters, common carriers, users of safety and special radio services, and the amateurs. The government users are broadly grouped as: military agencies plus the Department of Transportation which together hold almost 80 per cent of government frequency assignments; and agencies ranging from old-line departments such as Agriculture, Interior, Commerce, and Justice, to the newer ones such as the Atomic Energy Commission, the National Aeronautics and Space Administration, and the U.S. Information Agency. (All state and local government users are grouped along with the "nongovernment" services; the "government" sector includes federal government users only.) On the government side, all other uses of spectrum are overshadowed by the requirements of national security (see Table 2).

Different classes of users compete for spectrum within each service and between different services. This is true whether the competing users are located wholly on the government or nongovernment side or distributed between the two. Thus in the nongovernment sector, broadcasters compete for spectrum among themselves and also vie with public and private nonbroadcast users, common carriers, and even with the federal government. Most other nongovernment users compete in the same fashion, and so do federal agencies.

The main difference is that broadcasters and the common carriers are also subject to competition in markets for their end products. A second difference between the several users lies in (a) the cost and availability of the next-best alternatives to which an excluded party must turn if deprived of spectrum; (b) the relative portion of the user's total investment accounted for by radio equipment; and (c) the differing regulatory constraints imposed.

In the absence of any market for spectrum, the nation has relied on a system of central allocation by managers at the federal level. These managers seek not only to distribute spectrum in an orderly, efficient way among competing users and services and between the government and nongovernment sectors but also in ways that further social-alloca-

TABLE 2. ESTIMATED U.S. INVESTMENT IN ELECTROMAGNETIC TELECOMMUNICATIONS
SYSTEMS, EQUIPMENT, AND R&D FACILITIES, 1963

	Depreciated value
	(*millions*)
U.S. Government:	
Department of Defense and other national security agencies	$ 9,000
Federal Aviation Agency	635
National Aeronautics and Space Administration	250
Treasury (Coast Guard)	450
Commerce (Maritime Administration, Weather Bureau, National Bureau of Standards, etc.)	70
U.S. Information Agency	90
Others, including Atomic Energy Commission, Agriculture, Interior, Justice, Tennessee Valley Authority, Veterans Administration, St. Lawrence Seaway, etc.	75
Manufacturing, net fixed assets	1,000
Non-U.S. Government communications services, facilities, and equipment:	
Broadcasting, television	370
Broadcasting, radio	260
Common carrier	1,700
Safety and special services, including state and local government	1,500
Research and development, equipment and facilities not reported elsewhere:	
Government, industry, and educational and other nonprofit institutions	350
Repair and installation services, and test and measuring equipment and facilities	300
Wholesale and retail trade	450
Consumer electromagnetic telecommunication equipment:	
Television receivers	5,500
Radio receivers	4,000
Total	$26,000

Source: H. Booker and C. Little, "Atmospheric Research and Electromagnetic Telecommunication—Part I," *IEEE Spectrum* (August 1965), p. 45.

tional priorities related to wide diffusion of benefits and the growth of communications capability.

The Federal Communications Commission is authorized to classify all nongovernment radio services, allocate frequencies, and license individual users. As noted, "nongovernment services" include services of all public agencies except those of the federal government. The FCC does have jurisdiction over spectrum use by state and local governmental entities.

The management of federal use of spectrum rests with the President and his duly appointed representatives. The President has delegated these responsibilities to the Director of the Office of Emergency Planning and, in turn, to an assistant director now known as the Director of Telecommunications Management (DTM). This arrangement has been in effect only since 1962. The federal government, which has used radio for many decades, began in 1922 to coordinate its needs for spectrum through an Interdepartment Radio Advisory Committee. IRAC, initially created to assist the President in executing his responsibilities under the Radio Act of 1912, still plays an important role in spectrum management.

Of crucial import in the spectrum system today is the need to coordinate government and nongovernment demands, much dissatisfaction having arisen over the effective use and nonuse of military and broadcast spectrum. Another problem relates to the urgent need to identify and quantify the costs imposed on next-best users by allocational decisions, incumbents usually being favored over newcomers notwithstanding the injuries imposed by exclusion. These exclusionary costs set the maximum price any excluded claimant would pay for spectrum at the margin and are thus related to (though not identical with) "shadow prices" for spectrum—that is, those prices that would emerge under competitive bidding if a market did in fact exist.

A third problem arises from the very fact of central allocation, which necessarily intervenes with market processes and thus confers advantages on some at the expense of others. To justify continuance of the status quo, the spectrum managers have virtually been thrust into formulating techniques and criteria to provide the wide diffusion of benefits to which the law directs them.

Nongovernment Users

Nongovernment users can be classified as included in the broadcast service, the common carrier service, or the safety and special radio services.

The principal classes of *broadcast service* are television, standard (AM) and FM radio, international (shortwave) broadcasting, facsimile, and a number of auxiliary services such as studio-transmitter links to relay programs from studio to transmitter, pickup equipment, and experimental stations. Broadcasting is basically characterized by omnidirectional transmissions throughout a wide area to individual receivers. The broadcast use is distinguished also by relatively expensive and high-powered transmitters and relatively simple, inexpensive, widely distributed receivers.

The wide distribution of sets is crucial because, if receivers could be readily changed or improved without hardship, the broadcast industry and the FCC might both be more willing to institute improved technical standards more quickly. If the receivers were better, the transmitters might use less bandwidth and power and, on those counts at least, require far less spectrum. In addition, TV receivers would be less susceptible to interference from adjacent channel operations.

Paramount in the broadcast service is the cheap and wide dissemination of entertainment, information, cultural, and educational matter to large numbers of persons. Such "service to large numbers" is frequently cited to justify the industry's large share of choice VHF and UHF spectrum. The question is whether the discharge of public service responsibilities truly compensates for industry access rights, especially in view of their rising marginal value to next-best users.[2]

The *communications common carriers* provide a mechanism to transmit private messages by telephone and telegraph, combined voice-record service, two-way teletype, or high-speed data processing. Originally wire services, the common carriers today also use radio links as an integral part of their overland and overseas service. AT&T, for example, employs open wire, terrestrial VHF cable, coaxial and noncoaxial cable, and several types of submarine cables. It also uses terrestrial microwave at home and HF radio circuits and tropospheric scatter overseas, and participates in ComSat's global satellite operations.

The relative shares of common carrier domestic investment have gradually shifted from cable to microwave radio, whereas submarine cable still dominates most transoceanic links (see Table 3). Even radio-oriented carriers like RCA Communications have turned increasingly to cable as more reliable than the older HF radio, and a new high-capacity transistorized cable is being developed by AT&T. At the same time, the advent of satellite relays has rejuvenated the use of spectrum in the international services. Beyond this, the carriers have long provided microwave relays for TV at home and for the marine and aeronautical-navigational services.

Like broadcasters, the carriers have enjoyed large exclusive spectrum allocations because of their essential service to "large numbers of people" who have no other recourse. The question is whether the FCC's rate and service policies have in fact successfully guaranteed such benefit-diffusion in view of the apparently rising marginal value of some common carrier spectrum to next-best users.[3]

The *safety and special radio services* include nonbroadcast private and public users (see Table 4). Among the nonbroadcast private users are the citizens service, which permits the use of radio for business or

---

[2] The rising marginal value of broadcast spectrum to the land mobile services is amply attested by its continuing attempts to borrow or preempt UHF channels (at one time FM channels too) or to secure sharing rights in the VHF band. Each option has been sought in the face of growing congestion, waiting time, and equipment costs in the move up to the UHF band at 450–470 Mc/s. See H. Levin, "New Technology and the Old Regulation in Radio Spectrum Management," *American Economic Review, Papers and Proceedings* (May 1966), pp. 344–45, Table 1.

[3] See generally Chapter VI below.

TABLE 3. BELL SYSTEM LONG-LINE CIRCUIT MILES, 1954 AND 1963 (PERCENTAGE DISTRIBUTION)

(per cent of total)

Type of facility	Open wire		Voice frequency cable		Noncoaxial cable carrier		Coaxial cable		Microwave radio	
	1954	1963	1954	1963	1954	1963	1954	1963	1954	1963
Message telephone	5.0	0.5	8.0	1.0	27.0	3.5	39.0	36.0	21.0	59.0
Private-line telephone	8.0	1.0	26.0	2.0	31.0	14.0	23.0	33.0	12.0	50.0
Voice frequency carrier telegraph	8.0	1.0	15.0	9.0	53.0	42.0	24.0	26.0		22.0
All other circuits	23.0	5.0	44.0	10.0	19.0	20.0	11.0	25.0	3.0	40.0
Total circuits	7.0	0.5	10.0	1.5	27.0	8.0	36.0	33.0	20.0	57.0

Source: FCC Docket No. 14650, AT&T Exhibit No. 70, Attachments 10–14 (1964). Percentage distribution from graphs in AT&T Exhibit.

Note: Mileage excludes video channels and overseas circuits.

personal activities (walkie-talkies); the amateur service which offers recreation and also permits experimental and exploratory radio techniques; the land transportation service, used by trucks, taxis, buses, and railroads; industrial radio, used by petroleum pipelines, lumber and power companies, manufacturers, public utilities, news radio services, and motion picture units on location. Nonbroadcast public includes: aeronautical and marine radio, and service for police, fire, local government, highway maintenance, special emergency, forest conservation, and state guard. The number and percentage of stations and transmitters licensed to users in the categories of safety and special services appear in Table 4. The nonbroadcast public service operates to safeguard public safety and security on land, in the air, and at sea, whereas nonbroadcast private service makes possible lower manufacturing costs and safer, speedier transportation, and more efficient homes and business services.

Federal Government Users

The uses of spectrum by federal government agencies cover the gamut of the duties and responsibilities of all user agencies. The Defense Department is the largest user in frequency terms; the Federal Aviation Administration (in the Department of Transportation) comes next, with its requirements for air traffic control and navigational aids.

Beyond radio's crucial national security functions—command and control, detection, surveillance, and radiolocation—other governmental bodies are primarily concerned with safety and security on the ground, in the air, and at sea. Moreover, radio figures as an instrument for furthering federal responsibilities in situations where other communication services are inadequate or unavailable. Thus Interior uses it for fire protection, stream gauging, and field investigations; Treasury for law enforcement; the Coast Guard for radionavigation and safety services; Commerce for weather prediction, coast and geodetic surveys, and refined precision instrumentation; Agriculture for the management of national forest preserves; NASA for space communication tracking and launching; USIA, for Voice of America broadcasting; Justice for law enforcement; the Post Office for the airmail service; the General Services Administration for government car pools and guard vehicles; and the State Department for diplomatic communication.

There has been surprising stability in the shares of spectrum allocated to government and nongovernment use notwithstanding the great wartime and postwar breakthroughs which opened up the spectrum from a ceiling of 200 Mc/s in 1939 to 10,500 Mc/s in 1947 and 40,000 Mc/s in 1959. In laying out plans for new spectrum allocations in 1945,

TABLE 4. SAFETY AND SPECIAL RADIO SERVICES: NUMBER OF AUTHORIZED STATIONS AND TRANSMITTERS, JUNE 30, 1968

	Stations		Transmitters	
Type of service	Number	Per cent of total[a]	Number	Per cent of total[a]
Aircraft group	114,897	6.68	183,835	2.88
Aeronautical and fixed group	5,740	0.33	9,184	0.14
Aviation auxiliary group	763	0.04	3,968	0.06
Aviation radionavigation land	1,049	0.06	1,364	0.02
Civil air patrol	18,350	1.06	27,525	0.43
Total, aviation	140,799	8.17	225,876	3.54
Ship group	160,590	9.32	192,708	3.02
Coastal group	1,305	0.08	2,088	0.03
Marine auxiliary group	124	*	124	*
Marine radar land	67	*	107	*
Alaskan group	1,914	0.11	4,211	0.07
Total, marine services	164,000	9.51	199,238	3.12
Police	20,394	1.18	263,083	4.12
Fire	11,787	0.68	152,052	2.38
Local government	10,867	0.63	118,450	1.85
Highway maintenance	6,986	0.41	69,161	1.08
Forestry conservation	5,317	0.31	50,512	0.79
Special emergency	7,793	0.45	30,782	0.48
State guard	16	*	416	*
Total, public safety services	63,160	3.67	684,456	10.71
Special industrial	37,885	2.20	394,005	6.17
Business	109,855	6.38	834,898	13.07
Power	17,367	1.01	204,931	3.21
Petroleum	11,341	0.66	100,935	1.58
Manufacturers	2,621	0.15	63,690	1.00
Forest products	3,473	0.20	34,730	0.54
Industrial radiolocation	642	0.04	1,669	0.03
Motion picture	66	*	1,188	0.02
Relay press	305	0.02	4,240	0.07
Telephone maintenance	1,491	0.09	48,458	0.76
Total, industrial services	185,046	10.74	1,688,744	26.43
Railroad	7,347	0.43	227,243	3.56
Taxicab	5,208	0.30	176,030	2.76
Automobile emergency	2,323	0.13	23,578	0.37
Interurban passenger (Motor Carrier)	125	*	1,225	0.02
Interurban property (Motor Carrier)	3,054	0.18	55,277	0.87
Urban passenger (Motor Carrier)	172	0.01	1,858	0.03
Urban property (Motor Carrier)	1,787	0.10	37,170	0.58
Total, land transportation	20,016	1.16	522,381	8.18
Citizens, Class A	6,578	0.38	25,984	0.41
Citizens, Class B, C, D	860,974	49.97	2,755,117	43.12
Total, citizens services	867,552	50.35	2,781,101	43.53
Amateur	269,591	15.65	261,503	4.09
Radio amateur civil emergency	12,727	0.74	25,454	0.40
Disaster	207	0.01	207	*
Total, amateur and disaster	282,525	16.40	287,164	4.49
Total, safety and special services	1,723,098	100.00	6,388,960	100.00

Source: Federal Communications Commission.

* Less than 0.01 per cent.

[a] Due to rounding, the sum of individual percentages may not equal percentage subtotals.

the U.S. spectrum managers used a 50–50 rule of thumb—hardly a proxy for a market verdict. Some 50 per cent of the choice 25–5,000 Mc/s region went to nongovernment usage, some 30 per cent was shared between government and nongovernment, and the remainder was for exclusive government use.

As between the several government users, it is clear in Table 5 that the three military services account for some 54 per cent of all government assignments today and, together with the Department of Transportation, for nearly 74 per cent of the assignments.[4] However, it must be remembered that requirements of the different agencies vary so much that interservice comparisons are not too meaningful. Still more indicative of the relative size of the spectrum-using activity of different government agencies are data in Table 2 above, which shows estimated investments in electromagnetic telecommunication in 1963.

Radio's contributions to national security have constituted an overriding priority from the very outset, first in regard to the Navy's needs for ship-shore or ship-ship communication and then for Army and Air Force requirements. The growing dependence of modern weapons systems and general security arrangements on radio communication have brought renewed attention to the military's large spectrum use.

For several reasons it is hard to know whether the government's use of the spectrum is fully justifiable. The whole government sector, especially the military assignments, is shrouded in secrecy. It is hard to challenge military expertise whenever security priorities are invoked. Information is lacking on actual frequency usage even for intramural purposes. And finally there is a great uncertainty regarding future military requirements and the need for supplementary or alternative assignments "to provide against the loss of service in emergencies, excessive traffic loads, and harmful interference."[5]

In addition, temporal sharing is impossible in those military services which require round-the-clock use (e.g., beacons and radars) or in the case of actual military operations. Even where temporal sharing is physically or technically feasible, there may be administrative delays in coordination, whereas geographic sharing may pose other interference problems in different spectral regions.[6]

The Joint Technical Advisory Committee—the best-known group of independent experts on spectrum utilization—recently summed up

---

[4] Owing to sharing of frequencies, the military plus DOT actually occupy 95 per cent of government spectrum.

[5] See U.S. Navy, *Frequency Management Handbook*, August 1965, para. 211.

[6] Ibid., paras. 222–23.

TABLE 5. GOVERNMENT AGENCY FREQUENCY ASSIGNMENTS, JULY 1969

Agency	Assignments		
	Number	Per cent of total	Number of frequencies[a]
Air Force	26,192	21.0	4,709
Transportation (Federal Aviation Administration and U.S. Coast Guard)	24,586	19.7	2,219
Navy	22,301	17.9	3,792
Army	19,104	15.3	3,365
Interior	7,675	6.2	974
Justice	6,810	5.5	394
Agriculture	6,610	5.3	277
Commerce	3,018	2.4	505
Atomic Energy Commission	2,612	2.1	825
Treasury	1,053	0.9	166
U.S. Information Agency	1,012	0.8	363
National Aeronautics and Space Administration	987	0.8	373
Federal Communications Commission	742	0.6	23
Tennessee Valley Authority	546	0.4	123
Health, Education, and Welfare	236	0.2	74
Veterans Administration	193	0.2	49
Post Office	122	0.1	34
National Science Foundation	89	0.1	48
General Services Administration	65	0.1	21
State Department	56	*	47
Federal Reserve System	30	*	9
International Boundary and Water Commission	21	*	10
Smithsonian Institution	10	*	9
Office of Economic Opportunity	7	*	1
Housing and Urban Development	1	*	1
Library of Congress	1	*	1
U.S. Capitol Police	2	*	2
Total	124,627	100.0	18,414
Military services	67,597	54.2	55.9
Military services plus Transportation	92,183	73.9	76.5

Source: Office of Telecommunications Management.

* Less than 0.1 per cent.

[a] Indicates total number of frequencies whether or not shared by more than one agency. The actual number of government frequencies is 12,200.

the crucial differences between military and nonmilitary communications-electronics needs, as follows:

The first and perhaps the most significant [difference] is the military need for an instantaneous and secure reaction capability. In an age of missilry and nuclear weapons, this need has come increasingly in the fore. It is imperative that a Commander-in-Chief have the capability to command and control the military forces at his disposition with great rapidity. Command and control must be exercised during normal as well as during emergency conditions. Constant readiness also must be maintained for wartime capability. Other important factors are the need for security and flexibility. A military establishment does not have complete freedom with regard to the development of operational requirements and the methods for satisfying such needs . . . Military requirements dictate the need for complete versatility in the use of communications-electronics anywhere in the world . . . Another factor not encountered in nonmilitary applications is the susceptibility of some weapons systems to electromagnetic radiation. Restrictions and precautions must be observed to ensure that spurious activation of ordnance devices does not occur.[7]

THE FUNCTIONS OF NATIONAL SPECTRUM MANAGEMENT

The nation's spectrum managers are, as noted, the Federal Communications Commission, with jurisdiction over all nongovernment spectrum, and the Director of Telecommunications Management, assisted by the IRAC, with control over the government spectrum. Both managers attempt to allocate frequencies in an orderly fashion among competing claimants and on a basis other than first come, first served. However, de facto squatters' rights generally operate to the contrary.

In addition to policing interference, the FCC has long sought to diffuse the benefits of spectrum use widely through a variety of licensing-allocation-rate controls and service standards imposed on the regulated communications industries. The DTM appears likely to focus increasingly on predicting, promoting, and integrating into telecommunications structure a variety of new technologies and capabilities.

Less familiar, but of growing importance, are the programs, plans, and telecommunications policies of the Commerce Department, in particular the activities of its Institute for Telecommunication Sciences, formerly the Central Radio Propagation Laboratories of the National Bureau of Standards. Long active in basic telecommunications R&D through its Boulder Laboratories, the Commerce Department has revealed new interest in systematizing the national program in atmospheric sciences in ways that enhance the economic value of spectrum utilization.

The Federal Communications Commission

Today no user other than a federal agency can occupy spectrum without the FCC's permission. Specifically, the Commission is authorized to regulate the radio communication activities of all state and local

---

[7] Joint Technical Advisory Committee, *Radio Spectrum Utilization* (New York: Institute of Electrical and Electronics Engineers, 1965), pp. 246–47. The committee is the joint undertaking of the Institute and the Electronics Industries Association.

governments, as well as those of private and nonprofit broadcasters, communications common carriers, business, industry, transportation, and other safety and special radio users.

In managing use of the spectrum, the FCC is explicitly empowered and directed by the organic Communications Act of 1934 to:

1. Provide to all the people of the United States a rapid, efficient nation-wide and worldwide wire and radio communication service with adequate facilities at reasonable charges, for the purpose of the national defense, for the purpose of promoting safety of life and property through the use of wire and radio . . . and for the purpose of securing . . . a more centralized authority to this end (sec. 1).
2. Classify all radio stations, prescribe the nature of their service, assign bands of frequencies to different classes of stations, and individual stations to particular frequencies, control their power, time of operation, and location; set technical standards, and otherwise prevent interference between standards (sec. 303-a through 303-f).
3. Study new uses for radio, provide for experimental uses of frequencies, and generally encourage the larger and more effective use of radio in the public interest (sec. 303-g).
4. Make such distribution of licenses, frequencies, hours of operation, and of power among the several states and communities as to provide a fair, efficient, and equitable distribution of radio service to each of the same (sec. 307-b).

FCC regulates the common carriers as public utilities and hence in a quite different fashion from the broadcast and private nonbroadcast services. The Commission must approve all common carrier rates, rate schedules, and routes (sec. 201-a), determine their reasonableness (secs. 201-b, 205-a), prohibit discriminatory or unreasonable charges (sec. 202-a), and periodically appraise the value of all common carrier assets towards that end (sec. 213-a). The Commission must also approve all carriers' plans to build additional transmission facilities (sec. 214-a), or to merge or consolidate their aggregate properties (sec. 222). The broadcast service, on the other hand, is not a common carrier. In the absence of rate controls, the Commission regulates it through an ingenious mixture of entry controls, service standards, and procompetitive policies—i.e., those favoring competition.

The basis for the Commission's dual functions (procompetitive and regulatory) is set forth broadly in the Communications Act. A procompetitive function is implicit first, in the declaration that broadcasting is not a public utility (sec. 3-h). Had Congress intended to confer a protective function on the FCC, it would not have gone to such pains to emphasize the limited character of the license rights (secs. 308-a,

309-d(1), 301), or to require broadcasters explicitly to waive all "continuing rights" based on prior usage (sec. 304).

Insofar as possible, competition, rather than direct regulation, is expected to determine the level of broadcast time rates and profits. Explicit designation of the Commission's procompetitive function appears in: sec. 313, which applies the antitrust laws to broadcasting; sec. 314, which forbids broadcasters from entering telephone, telegraph, or cable if this lessens competition substantially; sec. 311, which specifically instructs the Commission to refuse licenses or renewals to applicants who have attempted to monopolize trade in broadcasting or set manufacturing; and sec. 308-b, which pertains to the Commission's screening of an applicant's legal qualifications whereinunder past or current violators of the antitrust laws have been denied licenses. Equally relevant are the powerful procompetitive pronouncements in two decisions of the U.S. Supreme Court—*Federal Communications Commission* v. *Sanders Bros. Radio Station*, 309 U.S. 470 (1940), and *National Broadcasting Co.* v. *United States*, 319 U.S. 190 (1943). The full legal basis for the procompetitive function is detailed in the Commission's *Report on Chain Broadcasting* (1941) and the more recent *Report on Network Broadcasting* (1958).

On the other hand, the Commission's regulatory function was sketched in broad outline only. Section 301 lays the basis by establishing the spectrum's public character (as well as the limited license term) and thus providing an appropriate context for flexible regulation. In regard to *how* market forces would be modified, the provisions of sec. 303 have already been noted. However, broadcast regulation is grounded in the first instance in sec. 307-a, which subjects all entry to the Commission's licensing power and prescribes that licenses shall be granted only in the "public interest." The public interest standard reappears also in sec. 308-a (licensing, renewals, modifications) and sec. 310-b (transfers). It does not, then, suffice that an individual has capital which he is willing to risk. He must also be found legally, technically, and financially qualified.

By way of further guidance, sec. 307-b provides for a "fair, efficient, and equitable distribution of radio service" among the several states and communities. Here the initial presumption appears to have been that unregulated market forces would otherwise result in excessive concentration of facilities in the big urban markets in the East at the expense of rural markets. Section 315 prescribes that if a broadcaster grants time, free or paid, to any political candidate, it must provide comparable time to all legally qualified candidates, though it need not provide free time to any. Section 316 originally proscribed lotteries and the awarding of prizes by chance. Section 317 requires that all sponsors of broadcast programs be identified. Section 326 proscribes obscenity and profanity in program fare, and also proscribes any government censorship.

In short, public ownership of the spectrum resource and the limited character of the license privilege provide the basis for broadcast regulation, whereas the public interest standard states its general goal. Moreover, in promoting the public interest, the Commission is empowered to alter industry structure, conduct, and performance, subject to a proscription against censorship and to the requirements of due process.

The principal criticisms of the FCC's licensing-allocation practice are fourfold. First, the Commission is said too often to acquiesce de facto to first come, first served, and to be hostile to reallocations once heavy hardware investments are made. As a consequence, new services may be shunted off into spectral regions inappropriate for them (even when this inappropriateness is clearly known) and, when the technology improves, retrospective changes are hard to introduce.

Second, even new entrants are unable to buy rights to enter into the bands they prefer. Nor, in the case of competing applicants, will coherent administrative criteria necessarily govern the grant. In a market allocation the radiation rights would tend to go to those best able to use them economically. Deliberate modification of this tendency to further regulatory goals is one thing. But there is no systematic attempt today to weigh off the impairment of economic efficiency against any compensatory service provided. It is therefore impossible to say whether spectrum allocation is optimal with regard to any set of regulatory norms, let alone strictly economic norms. One cannot, of course, be certain that cost-benefit quantification will necessarily facilitate reallocations more consistent with such norms. But it is clearly a step in the right direction.

A third criticism relates to the inadvertent creation of franchise value. Related to this is the imposition of substantial costs on next-best users of allocated spectrum. On both counts, the allocator's integrating function becomes indistinguishable from its disruption of market norms.

While licensing and allocation provide a technical base for broadcast operations, they create differential economic values by limiting the entry of users in the same service. On the other hand, the exclusion of next-best users in other services from the allocated space necessarily imposes extra costs when the excluded claimant must turn elsewhere or do without radio completely. In either case, allocation alters the distribution of spectrum which would result in an organized market. The differential economic rents and extra costs that emerge actually represent a second basis for benefit-diffusion in the spectrum field, with special reference to broadcasting and communications satellites. (See Chapter VI.)

Office of Telecommunications Management and Interdepartment Radio Advisory Committee

Criticisms of FCC practice also figure in any appraisal of the widely cited shortcomings of the management of the federal government's spectrum. At the suggestion of Secretary of Commerce Herbert Hoover, the IRAC was organized in 1922 by the several interested Executive Departments to assist the President in telecommunications affairs. IRAC's role as Presidential adviser was reaffirmed in 1927 and again in 1934. It has continued to function since that time in matters pertaining to frequency allocations to the Executive Departments, with special reference to interference, safety, and security. Since 1962, IRAC has functioned as special advisory arm to the DTM. It has always included the main federal agencies that use radio, and today it has fourteen members including a representative of the FCC.

Among the allocational criteria cited by different governmental claimants within the IRAC forum over the years have been specific legislative directives, international commitments or treaty obligations, national defense requirements, internal security, protection of national resources, essential mobile communications, communications affecting safety of life or property, research and experimental services, and unavailability or inadequacy of other means of communication. Hence the several criteria that figure in IRAC actions are not unlike those invoked in the FCC's more formal licensing-allocation proceedings.

Although officially serving since 1962 only as an "advisory" arm of the DTM, IRAC still plays an important role in the actual determinations.[8] Hence its operations warrant further scrutiny here on their merits, and as a springboard from which to consider the DTM. We shall therefore examine first a few earlier criticisms of IRAC[9] and then consider

[8] See President's Task Force on Communications Policy, *Final Report* (U.S. Government Printing Office, 1968) (publication cited hereinafter as *Task Force Report*), Ch. VIII, p. 23 and Ch. IX, p. 10.

[9] See S. Metzger and B. Burrus, "Radiofrequency Allocations in the Public Interest: Federal Government and Civilian Use," *Duquesne University Law Review* (1965–66), pp. 1–96; V. Rosenblum, "Low Visibility Decision-Making by Administrative Agencies: The Problem of Radio Spectrum Allocation," *Administrative Law Review* (Fall 1965), pp. 19–54. For an earlier evaluation of similar criticisms, see R. Coase, "The Interdepartment Radio Advisory Committee," *Journal of Law and Economics* (October 1962), pp. 17–47. A frank statement in IRAC's report for January 1–June 30, 1966 (Attachment #1) acknowledges that some criticisms are valid.

several bits of evidence on how far and in what ways, if at all, creation of the DTM may now alter the situation.

IRAC can be described as an interagency committee of users constrained by a de facto rule of unanimity, where no one can or will make the "hard" decisions. Heavily dependent on internal bargaining and negotiation among its members, IRAC lacks the formal statutory directives and procedures which govern the FCC, where *all* licensing-allocation decisions are made on an open record, with safeguards against *ex parte* influence. In contrast with the Commission's more formal and detailed public scrutiny of civilian requests for spectrum, there is far less rigor on the federal government side, where grants have sometimes been made on the bare assertion of need and decisions are less readily subject to systematic Congressional scrutiny, let alone judicial review.

In further contrast with FCC's continuing supervisory power over civilian users, IRAC has never had formal control over federal government use, hoarding, or nonuse of frequencies. Excessive stockpiling of government spectrum is further attributed to the fact that federal users regard themselves as contestants who, with no independent body to choose among them and with no ready access to any frequency market, must necessarily stockpile heavily against future contingencies. And in contrast with an FCC assignment practice characterized by public decision-making with ample notice, open hearings, confrontation, cross-examination, right of counsel, decision on the record, and impartial tribunals, IRAC holds no open hearings, publishes no rules or opinions, and permits no public or industry participation.

The upshot has hitherto been said to be a built-in bias against nongovernment users on two main counts: first, the relative ease with which government users can secure spectrum assignments, in the absence of formal screening; and second, FCC's general willingness to accede to IRAC requests for frequencies otherwise available for civilian use, especially in view of the potential difficulty of challenging military expertise in national security determinations. In the absence of procedures for comparative evaluation of government and nongovernment requests, in short, government requests are said to prevail, wholly without regard to lack of rigorous screening in IRAC and lack of evidence that asserted federal interests necessarily represent the public interest.

Although IRAC has not formally operated with any rule of voting unanimity since 1953, there is little evidence as to just how far creation of the OTM (in 1962) will be able to correct the above-cited deficiencies. It is difficult to know whether the special problems posed by a bifurcated spectrum authority for government and nongovernment users could in any case be resolved short of creating a unified entity. There is, however, little question that the OTM was established in part to rectify many of these criticisms and that it has in fact made efforts towards that end.

In regard to the rigor with which federal agencies' requests for spectrum are scrutinized, the Director of Telecommunications Management personally reviews major requests, problems, and issues at special hearings. He has also assigned IRAC a new mission and status and had it report directly to him, thus assuming additional responsibilities for decisions on allocation, usage, and stockpiling which IRAC has traditionally lacked authority to implement.[10] To forestall large hardware investments from tying his hands or otherwise influencing allocation decisions, the DTM has urged all government agencies to require prior frequency clearance before approving development or procurement expenditures and to upgrade the administrative echelon of frequency management activities.[11] To forestall anticipated conflicts between old and new services, he contracts for projections of spectrum demand and supply for particular uses.[12]

In regard to the dangers of unsupervised government stockpiling, the DTM has sought to institute an ongoing inventory and annual review of usage with automatic data processing, to eliminate large numbers of unused assignments, and to initiate long-range studies of spectrum utilization.[13] To reduce the need for military allocations, he has tightened up on emission standards generally, with special reference to the radar bands. To safeguard civilian interests vs. military spectrum demands, finally, the DTM now conducts hearings jointly with the FCC chairman.[14]

Nonetheless, it seems doubtful that DTM's procedures will ever be fully comparable to FCC's. Hearings are closed to the public, reported in no open record, and apparently provide no formal basis for subsequent decisions. Because the procedures are highly secret, it is hard to

[10] Office of Telecommunications Management, *Manual of Regulations and Procedures for Radio Frequency Management* (August 2, 1965), para. 1.6.2; *Notice to . . . Federal Users of Telecommunications on Interdepartment Radio Advisory Committee* (December 10, 1964, rev. August 21, 1967); and *A Report on Frequency Management within the Executive Branch of the Government* (October 1966), pp. 16–17.

[11] Office of Telecommunications Management, *Report on Frequency Management* (October 1966), p. 16; *A Review of DTM Activities in Radio Spectrum Management* (March 8, 1967), pp. 4, 17. (OTM publications referred to hereinafter by title only.)

[12] *Report on Frequency Management* (October 1966), p. 17; *Review of DTM Activities* (March 8, 1967), pp. 17–18.

[13] *Manual of Regulations and Procedures*, para. 2.2.6; *Review of DTM Activities* (March 8, 1967), pp. 10–11, 35; *Report on Frequency Management* (October 1966), Appendix 5.

[14] *Review of DTM Activities* (March 8, 1967), pp. 3, 16, 34–38.

determine their substantive impact or the effects of efforts to institute improvements in frequency management practice through persuasion and negotiation.[15] Yet it hardly seems fair to compare the "ideal" of FCC practice with the "real world facts" of IRAC and FCC/DTM coordination. The deficiencies of FCC practice are well-known. Moreover, even if both entities were fully comparable or were themselves subject to review (or replaced outright) by some higher spectrum authority, the basic allocational problem would still remain.

Squatters' rights continue to plague the DTM as much as the FCC. The principle of noninterference with incumbents, whereby newcomers are saddled with extra entry costs, operates under both authorities. The problem on both sides is to identify next-best users, to measure the costs of exclusion and the benefits forgone through nonuse, and at the least to inject such information into the bargaining-negotiation process wherein rival spectrum claimants must now vie.

In regard to stockpiling and nonuse, broadcast allocations surely represent as serious a problem for FCC as military stockpiling does for the DTM. Spectrum managers on both sides appear to ignore opportunity costs, the better to retain maximum discretion in prosecuting their preferred priorities and to keep intact their "vision" of an integrated allocation plan. In both cases, opportunity costs must be more dramatically articulated and a careful line drawn between rational stockpiling for defensible needs and irrational hoarding for strategic purposes in the absence of price constraints, adequate records, and public scrutiny.

Even if, for argument's sake, the theory of FCC "subservience" to the federal government side were accepted as valid, the answer might lie not so much in formalizing a procedure for comparative evaluation (in view of the latter's striking failures elsewhere) as in developing a bargaining-negotiation process which operates with a fuller divulgence of factual data on costs and benefits, or in instituting rental charges and auction-type schemes within *both* sectors. (See Chapter V.)[16] There is in any case some question as to how "subservient" the Commission has really been.

There have been a few dramatic cases and even some litigation (the Bendix case). But the statistics on government and nongovernment spec-

[15] See *Telecommunications Reports* (January 18, 1965), pp. 8–11; *Industrial Communications* (January 15, 1965), pp. 2–4.

[16] There may even be merit in a total restructuring of spectrum management by consolidating the jurisdiction of DTM and FCC in a single new spectrum authority. See *Task Force Report*, Ch. VIII, pp. 50–62, 65; Ch. IX, pp. 30–33. However, many of the same problems will presumably remain unless major steps are simultaneously taken to upgrade economic factors in allocational decisions.

trum shares show no drastic changes. Some potential new civilian uses may have been disadvantaged by the government's failure to release unused spectrum, although here too intersector spectrum sharing has steadily increased.[17] Short of outright market bidding and subjecting government spectrum usage to formal budgetary review, it is hard to predict which way the frequencies would have moved, had fuller play in fact been given to market factors.

In theory at least, DTM seems potentially better able than FCC to dislodge incumbents for cause just because he need not contend with formal property rights under the Administrative Procedures Act. Moreover, insofar as the biggest user of all—the military—often has the necessary leverage to reclaim spectrum quickly for cause, one could argue that it is the most likely candidate on either side to be required to lend or share unused frequencies, wherever technically feasible and consistent with national security.

Creation of the Office of Telecommunications Management has in any case been no mere response to criticisms of IRAC. It was an attempt also to strengthen the government's promotional role. The strictly allocational function continues, but these additional responsibilities have been emphasized.[18] Indeed the new attention to growth and security brings us to a final word on the Department of Commerce which, under the Johnson Administration, had begun to reassert its traditional activity in basic fact-gathering and telecommunications R&D, bolstered by creation of a new center for extensive spectrum studies. Under this concept, FCC and OTM would largely work within current or emerging technological parameters, whereas Commerce would alter these parameters and constraints in ways that change the data with which spectrum management traditionally operates.

Department of Commerce, Institute for Telecommunication Sciences

The federal government's largest in-house effort in basic telecommunications R&D has long been housed in the Commerce Department's

[17] Note should also be taken of the DTM's action on June 3, 1968 to return 26 Mc/s in the 890–942 Mc/s band to the FCC for nongovernment use. This was facilitated by DTM review procedures, the recently revised operational requirements of certain military agencies, and the FCC's proposed rule-making in Dockets No. 18261 and 18262, July 26, 1968.

[18] See Executive Order No. 10995, February 16, 1962, secs. 2, 3, 6; Executive Order No. 11191, January 4, 1965, sec. 2; and "Establishment of the National Communications System," President's Memorandum, August 21, 1963. The DTM's positive promotional responsibilities are explicitly recognized also in *Manual of Regulations and Procedures* (rev. September 1968), paras. 2.1–2.3. See also Office of Telecommunications Management, *Five Year Spectrum Development Program*, July 1967.

Boulder (Colorado) Laboratories, now called the Institute for Tele-communication Sciences. Paramount in the ITS mission has been the identification of deficiencies in our basic knowledge of electromagnetic propagation, prediction, and control. Through ITS and more generally, Commerce seeks not only to provide a more adequate data base on which allocation decisions can be made but also to identify the tele-communications areas most in need of additional R&D.

In short, there appears to be new interest in having the federal government play a more active role in telecommunications R&D, virtually irrespective of the current rate and pattern of spectrum development and of substitutions between atmospheric and non-atmospheric transmission and whatever the byproducts of security- or space-related government programs. This would not only mean R&D support but also facilitate greater overall efficiency of total communications capabilities on the basis of economic contributions to the GNP. As such, the new conception[19] can be viewed as ancillary to the FCC/OTM management function, not as replacing it.

It seems unlikely, however, that the sole or even the major federal R&D activity will be housed at ITS or elsewhere in Commerce. The Department of Defense and NASA budgets will doubtless continue to provide the principal annual contributions. In fiscal 1967, the "electronics content" of the DOD budget was estimated at $8 billion, some $5.6 billion of which was spectrum-associated. This compares with an ITS budget of only some $13 million for the same period. But at this moment the expected future magnitude of the ITS operation is less important than the precise character of its basic R&D and systems design activity.

Following an interdepartmental study of the current and future national program for atmospheric sciences in 1964, ITS received a new mission. No longer limited to R&D in the lower spectral regions, it was authorized to support work in the higher ranges as well. ITS has even proposed to go beyond its traditional work in the diagnosis and prediction of propagation conditions to the study of their control, at least in ionospheric communication.

Although the ITS mission is now under review it has thus far been twofold. First, in support of the $20 billion annual national expenditure on electromagnetic telecommunication, to conduct "research and serv-

[19] Telecommunication Science Panel, Commerce Technical Advisory Board, *Electromagnetic Spectrum Utilization—The Silent Crisis* (U.S. Government Printing Office, 1966), pp. 39–42. For an independent account of what such a program might be, see K. Norton, *The Five-Dimensional Electromagnetic Resource* (Boulder, Colo.: Environmental Science Services Administration Institute for Telecommunication Sciences, rev. December 12, 1967, unofficial multilith), Part I and related appendices.

ices on how radio, infrared and optical waves [travel] from a transmitter to a receiver." This has required propagation analysis and research to determine how the atmosphere and earth's surface may affect electromagnetic waves in all spectral regions. Second, to conduct an ongoing space weather service for purposes of improved space environment forecasting, and to test the reliability of ionospheric communications. Toward these ends, ITS has served as a primary federal facility for basic telecommunications R&D; acted as a central repository for related information, reports, and data; furnished advice and consultative service to industry, government, and other entities; performed scientific liaison with other countries; and prepared and published predictions of propagation conditions and disturbances.[20]

THE SPECTRUM "DEVELOPERS"

No overview of the major components of the spectrum system could omit the third component, the spectrum "developers." The present examination will be brief, since the developers are reviewed in detail in Part Three below.

Although the FCC is legally authorized to promote the "larger and more effective use of the radio spectrum" and the DTM to promote the development of a global satellite relay and a national communications system, strictly speaking neither entity can really be called a "developer" of spectrum. For neither body now conducts the R&D or makes the hardware to generate new communications capabilities that extend the margins of spectrum space. Their main objective is to insure that technical standards are raised in response to rising levels of technology, the tacit point being that, with no clear price incentive to economize spectrum, the national manager must try to provide an equivalent by his periodic review of technical standards and imposition of new ones.

The major organizational innovation here may now occur in the Commerce Department's in-house program in telecommunications R&D on such basic determinants as atmospheric noise, propagation characteristics, and transmission technology. Nevertheless, neither FCC, ODTM, nor even Commerce at present conducts (or finances) the bulk of this country's spectrum-developing R&D. Federal support of telecommunications R&D in private labs is extensive and funded largely by the DOD, NASA, and Transportation. The magnitude of such R&D is actu-

[20] Institute of Telecommunication Sciences, *Resources and Management Information* (February 1967), pp. 1–4. Several changes recently initiated by the Nixon Administration may alter the picture.

ally far beyond the research capabilities of any but the largest hardware suppliers and common carriers—and also beyond NASA's current in-house function or its advisory role on satellite systems and advanced technical research. (See Chapter IX.)

In regard to private companies, the communications and electronics companies and their related laboratories have performed most of the actual work, largely as contractors of the government agencies, but they have also worked in company-supported projects. Among the sixty-odd hardware manufacturers are many independent companies (Motorola, Bendix, Lenkhurt, Hughes, General Electric, etc.), but other hardware entities are associated with the carriers and with major laboratory facilities (GT&E, RCA, ITT, and the Bell–Western Electric–AT&T complex). In one case, RCA–NBC, the ties even extend further into investments in TV broadcasting. Nonetheless, aside from the carriers it is the exception, rather than the rule, for spectrum users to integrate vertically into hardware-laboratory facilities.

The significance of vertical integration for spectrum development is therefore not entirely clear. On one hand, GT&E and ATT–Bell–Western Electric have contributed significantly to technical advances in the common carrier bands; but so have Motorola and General Electric in safety and special radio services and Lockheed and Hughes in space satellites. In broadcasting, on the other hand, the different relative dynamism of TV and AM signal standards and the existence of few vertically integrated broadcast entities suggest that other factors are undoubtedly at play. (See Chapter VIII.)

In any event, much of the space- and defense-related telecommunications R&D today takes place in the communications equipment and electronic components industry. There the federal government finances about twice as much of such R&D as the companies do. Indeed the DOD alone accounts for some four-fifths of the R&D expenditures on atmospheric noise. Thus whatever the actual impact of vertical integration on telecommunications R&D (and hence spectrum development),[21] the government's promotional role appears to be determinative. This subject will be discussed further in Chapter IX.

[21] The innovative impact of vertical integration is still uncertain. See *Task Force Report*, Ch. VI, pp. 37–42.

CHAPTER III

THE GOALS OF NATIONAL SPECTRUM MANAGEMENT

The primary aim of central frequency management has been variously described as "maximizing the use of the spectrum," "minimizing interference in its use," or "maximizing the flow of information through a channel per unit of time." Efficient or optimal usage as narrowly defined has been said also to require that no service be accommodated which could in fact use a wire substitute.[1]

Yet clearly, "maximum use" or "full occupancy" as such may run directly counter to the minimization of interference, which is best achieved, technically, through no use at all. Likewise, greater occupancy may be facilitated by uneconomic R&D which extends the intensive and extensive margins of spectrum to the point where the resulting economic and social gains fall short of the R&D costs. Maximizing the flow of information per channel per unit of time offers little guidance without explicit reference to costs, since this flow can always presumably be increased at some price. Finally, the rule that access to spectrum be foreclosed wherever a wire mode is conceivable confuses technical-physical possibilities with economically viable substitutes. It would clearly preclude uses for spectrum which more than pay their way in terms of the outputs and cost-savings.

The ideal, of course, is some norm of optimal interference, information flows per dollar cost, and frequency sharing per dollar of R&D investment cost. Even short of the ideal, no meaningful criterion for frequency management is possible without some grasp of the economic magnitudes involved.

Looking at the goals of spectrum management more broadly con-

---

[1] See critical review in Telecommunication Science Panel, Commerce Technical Advisory Board, *Electromagnetic Spectrum Utilization: The Silent Crisis* (U.S. Government Printing Office, 1966), p. 36.

65

strued, we confront similar problems once again. There have been recurrent references not only to "full occupancy" (and use) but also to "efficient use" in narrow technical terms, "sustained development," "wide diffusion of benefits," and the closely related "equal nondiscriminatory access." Yet from a strictly economic viewpoint public officials should really be concerned with estimating optimal degrees of occupancy and use, optimal rates of development, and an optimal diffusion of benefits.

At the least, the value of the final outputs of spectrum utilization must just cover the added costs of generating them. Additional occupancy (or use) will be warranted economically if, but only if, the extra outputs are worth more than they cost. In regard to development, too, additional telecommunications R&D is justifiable only if the dollar benefits that result from the extra capabilities created exceed the dollar cost of the investments required. A "wide diffusion of benefits" refers, first, to the cost-price-product adjustments which would have emerged in a competitive spectrum system, notwithstanding the actual monopolistic character of many user entities; and, second, to the additional benefits which would flow from internal or external subsidization of unprofitable service by users of spectrum where private and social benefits diverge. On both counts, too, equal nondiscriminatory access becomes a vehicle for wide diffusion as well as a goal in its own right.

How does this conception compare with the proposal that spectrum should be distributed so that the resultant use pattern maximizes its contributions to the GNP?[2] To those who view management primarily as an allocational problem, there is much appeal in the criterion of GNP-maximization. Such a criterion is advocated as more precise and operational than the broad concept of "public interest, convenience, and necessity"—and more likely also to produce a predictable pattern of behavior on the part of spectrum managers. The user would therefore be in a better position to know what he can expect, the managers' discretion would be narrowed accordingly, and the chances for favoritism or arbitrary action reduced. It is suggested that the criterion of GNP-maximization will tend to optimize the rate of technological innovation in telecommunications and the permissible degree of interference, and to reduce hidden government subsidies to grantees as well as the real resource cost of licensing and allocation.

These asserted advantages of the GNP criterion are broadly valid

[2] A less ambiguous formulation would be to distribute spectrum so as to maximize its economic efficiency in use. This may, but need not, coincide with maximizing its contributions to the GNP. However, the discussion that follows applies equally well to the efficiency criterion too.

but they fail to qualify it as a really adequate single desideratum. While maximum contribution of spectrum to the GNP is a useful point of departure, in itself it is by no means determinative in every case, and must not be the sole consideration. What we really want in national spectrum management is not to maximize the user's contributions to GNP so much as to equate the marginal social benefit of each spectrum policy, in terms of specific regulatory priorities furthered, with its marginal social cost in terms of forgone GNP. That is, we want added safety and security, wider diffusion of service, wider viewer choice in broadcasting, and similar desiderata, but we want them with the smallest possible decrements of potential GNP due to economic misuse of the radio spectrum.

This formulation is analogous to that underlying the use of cost-effectiveness analysis in evaluating alternative military weapons systems.[3] Despite the impossibility of putting dollar values on additional defense capability, economic analysis can help us choose between projects "likely to have the same effect on defense capability" and also between the alternative ways to increase those capabilities.[4] Comparative cost analysis is of paramount importance here.

The goals of security and safety do not of course have any nice, discrete level of attainment; we can surely attain some levels with no loss of GNP due to economic misuse of spectrum, as well as higher levels with such loss. Nevertheless, not all social benefits are taken into account through conventional measures of GNP. Therefore the policies to maximize the user's contribution to GNP may not always jibe with policies to safeguard some desired level of safety or security. Up to some point, GNP may be higher with policies that permit accident rates, interference levels, and degrees of urban concentration of facilities and service greater than those which would be politically or socially tolerable. Likewise, the nation may be willing to pay some price in forgone GNP to raise safety standards, widen the distribution of facilities, and reduce the level of permissible interference.

This is not to say that no standards of safety, signal clarity, or geographic dispersion which public officials choose to implement can ever be truly rational (or defensible) without explicit consideration of opportunity costs, nor that the estimation of such costs is any simple matter.

---

[3] See F. Scherer, "Government Research and Development Programs" in R. Dorfman, ed., *Measuring Benefits of Government Investments* (Brookings, 1965), pp. 12–34, and discussion on pp. 58–70.

[4] See R. Nelson, "The Allocation of Research and Development Resources" in R. Tybout, ed., *Economics of Research and Development* (Ohio State University Press, 1965), pp. 294–95.

Perhaps the most we can hope is to inject enough factual knowledge about costs into the decisional arena as to produce tighter ceilings on the standards than spectrum management appears to permit (or is intent on sustaining). Here the balance struck would not be one that necessarily maximizes each user's contribution to GNP so much as one which minimizes the GNP sacrificed for specific priorities furthered.

Admittedly any such rough balancing will in some ways be less appealing than the precision of a GNP criterion. Yet we must not exaggerate the ease of applying the latter in practice. Furthermore, to dismiss "public interest" standards as nonoperational is to confuse a broad legal mandate with the far more detailed and explicit regulatory priorities that could be formulated to concretize it. The really relevant question in spectrum management is this: By what dollar cost will some prevailing (or marginally adjusted) level of safety, security, educational service, or signal clarity be reduced or raised by relying on telecommunications systems that use a little more or a little less spectrum?

For spectrum management, in short, the practical question is: What happens at the margin and, specifically, what balance is struck between contributions to GNP and other regulatory priorities? In the absence of any coherent management preference function, the dollar trade-offs between GNP and other priorities will necessarily remain imprecise. Yet devising a greater role for market criteria and market incentives does not and need not mean that all administrative criteria must be jettisoned. The task is to limit administrative discretion, not eliminate it, spurring public administrators to justify more rigorously and persuasively any deliberate decision to override market considerations. Systematic analysis of trade-offs would give us a badly needed constraint on administrative discretion without entirely eliminating it. Lacking the necessary measures and incentives, spectrum managers may well be unaware of decisions that could seriously (and needlessly) impair economic efficiency.

In sum, the task of management today is twofold: first, to integrate the spectrum system as a series of markets and prices would do if one in fact existed; and second, to tolerate or justify any impairment of economic efficiency or divergence from optimal utilization only where the economic costs in question fall short of the social benefits that result, at least in terms of explicit regulatory priorities furthered. With this in mind, the present chapter will undertake to indicate briefly how the price mechanism could integrate the present components of the spectrum system; consider in passing how each of the several tacit goals of spectrum management and the goal of market efficiency may diverge;

and identify the areas where past experience suggests the community would want to alter market performance in spectrum in order to safeguard explicit social priorities.

The Price System as an Integrating Mechanism

In the absence of any system of markets and prices, national spectrum management clearly has one major unavoidable task—to integrate the supply of and demand for spectrum. The formal economic problem is to allocate scarce resources with alternative uses to maximize graded ends. Optimal resource allocation requires that all productive factors be so distributed as to equate their marginal value productivity in terms of any and all competing ends. Moreover, unless the supply of a resource is so limited that users are willing to forgo other goods and services to acquire additional units, it can command no price. On this account, resource scarcity and economic choice are closely intertwined.

Central allocators and competitive markets are in any case alternative mechanisms for obtaining optimal allocation, as defined. In theory at least, the central allocators can attempt to simulate market-type solutions in maximizing economic efficiency by utilizing the proper decision rules.

Under either framework, economic efficiency requires that all resources (including spectrum) be so allocated among competing claimants that no new assignment can increase their aggregate economic value. Reassignments must continue until each unit of each resource (including spectrum) is assigned to its highest-valued use. Short of that, some reallocation from lower- to higher-value uses and users will act to raise total economic value. However, the existence of so-called uncompensated costs and benefits means that private decisions on resource use alone will not suffice to maximize aggregate value. Where private costs fall short of the social costs of spectrum utilization, in the absence of public intervention "too much" spectrum will be used from the economist's viewpoint. Where private benefits fall short of social benefits, "too little" will be used. In both cases, public action of some sort (taxes, bounties, legal constraints) is needed to assure optimal utilization and maximum economic value.

With such qualifications in mind, "efficient" or "optimal" resource allocation can be described as one where the dollar value of any small unit of any resource is the same for all uses and users. It is an allocation also where no further substitution of other resources (say, of wire for spectrum) will increase the user's output value more than it raises his input costs.[5] This standard of economic efficiency helps articulate the constraints that market organization could provide if allowed to do so. It identifies one of the prime tasks of spectrum management—to integrate the several components of the "spectrum system" and safeguard the efficiency with which radio communication is used as one productive resource among many.

The efficiency criterion also provides an economic yardstick against which furtherance of the managers' various social priorities can be measured. Any regulatory decision that disrupts the balances cited above must be carefully justified by its compensatory enhancement of some explicit noneconomic standard. The failure to do so, by neglect of market-price standards or an inability to account for them without a formal market, may seriously impair the overall performance of spectrum management along lines described below.

Economic Efficiency Aspects of Spectrum Management Goals

There are several trade-offs between economic efficiency and the several stated goals of spectrum management. "Full occupancy" may no longer be the truly overriding goal of spectrum management, but it is still an engineering ideal.[6] Whether it would ever be economical to occupy all known spectrum, or even all that is technically usable, is quite another question. The *degree* of occupancy is the important thing for economics. This depends, in turn, on the relative cost and value of spectrum compared to conceivable substitutes, and the total demand for communications facilities. No matter how cheap spectrum might become and how expensive its substitutes, full occupancy might require a higher level of aggregate demand for communications capabilities than that which now exists.

Stated otherwise, it may simply not be economically worthwhile for private or government users to occupy all technically usable spectrum. The degree of occupancy that actually results from free market pricing will tend to coincide with what is economically worth using in meeting the several users' competing needs. Falsification of the price of spec-

---

[5] Users may of course be government agencies, nonprofit entities, or private commercial firms. Resource allocation to maximize user preferences is no different here than where the users are all commercial. For an attempt to evaluate the efficiency of water allocation as between public and private users, see J. Bain, R. Caves, and J. Margolis, *Northern California's Water Industry* (The Johns Hopkins Press for Resources for the Future, 1966), pp. 8–17, 273–85, 597–623.

[6] For a standard definition and discussion of technical impediments to achieving full occupancy, see Joint Technical Advisory Committee, *Radio Spectrum Conservation* (McGraw-Hill, 1952), pp. 181–85.

trum—say, by giving it away—would raise this degree of occupancy but in an economically wasteful way. The fuller occupancy might be warranted on overriding noneconomic grounds, but this is never self-evident. It must be carefully demonstrated, with administrators bearing a heavy burden of proof.

Any concept of economic spectrum utilization requires that spectrum remain unused when some other resource can do the same job more effectively, per dollar of expenditure. And the cost of using spectrum must not only include the cost of the needed equipment and personnel but also the benefits forgone by excluding some other potential user. Thus, additional occupancy is economic if, but only if, the incremental benefits generated exceed the incremental costs, including the benefits forgone by excluding the next-best user.

In the absence of any alternative user to bear the costs of exclusion, the question is simply whether radio equipment and personnel cost more or less to do a given task than transportation, land lines, submarine cable, mail, or some other substitute. But where some alternative user may in fact be excluded, the difference between the net benefits that his service would have produced and those which the present incumbent will produce must be included as part of the "cost" of using the radio spectrum. This is what economists call its "opportunity costs."

In "frequency development" we come to less familiar ground. Little is known about the empirical relation between relative factor prices and the inducements to develop any resource at its intensive and extensive margins. Nonetheless, one can argue a priori that, whenever the demand for a resource exceeds its supply at the going price, not only do the prices rise until demand equals supply but the divergence itself unleashes the forces of technological change. Thus inflated demand prices for a resource can be expected to provide incentives for suppliers to produce more, bringing forth even what has hitherto been uneconomic to sell. Suppliers will do so in part by more fully utilizing or over-utilizing present capacities to produce the resource. More important, they will try to institute new techniques to develop the resource's useful outputs intensively (e.g., more thermal power from a barrel of crude oil), as well as to develop its extensive margins (deeper oil wells, drilling on the outer continental shelf). High supply prices, on the other hand, will tend to divert users to cheaper substitutes, including some which had hitherto been not quite economic to use. There would even be an inducement to discover new substitutes or to use old ones more intensively or extensively.

In short, other things being equal, one would expect some rate of intensive and extensive development of the spectrum to flow from the incentives generated by a freely working spectrum market. But just as it is conceivable that spectrum management may want to raise the degree of occupancy above that level determined by economic factors, economically wasteful though this may be, so it may stimulate or condone a rate of frequency development above or below that which would result from the ordinary price incentives that reflect relative spectrum scarcity. And this too could be considered economically wasteful. However, the factors that govern spectrum resource development are far more complex than these alone, and special attention should therefore be paid (as in Chapter IX) to the peculiar risks, large capital requirements, and long planning periods for spectrum development and to the tendency for private and social net benefits to diverge. On each count there may be familiar reasons to ignore any strict market calculus.

The goals of "equal access" and "wide diffusion" are intimately associated with the distribution of spectrum in organized markets. For competitive conditions in such markets imply that all users can enter readily as buyers, as potential developers (or hardware suppliers), or as owners of the spectrum resource. By definition, that is, there must be no artificial restraints on access to spectrum, with regard either to direct occupancy by potential users or to unencumbered access by all to the facilities of other users.

Likewise, a wide diffusion of benefits would normally be furthered by competitive pricing of spectrum insofar as this implies prices no greater than opportunity costs, though presumably greater than zero costs. Nevertheless, where private and social benefits diverge, the spectrum manager may conceivably seek to enable users to buy spectrum who cannot afford to, or to make those who would not normally choose to buy it (even if they could) more likely to do so. In such cases, pricing to diffuse benefits would diverge from competitive pricing. But if the ultimate economic benefits which result from below-cost pricing are sufficiently large, it may still be economically justifiable.

It is in any case useful to distinguish between economic and uneconomic but politically or socially desirable access and diffusion. The norms themselves present basic ideals whose attainment may be constrained by economic realities.

In short, the total performance of spectrum management today really cannot be determined without reference to an optimal allocation of frequencies as between competing users. When available spectrum is distributed so as to equate its value for all users and uses, there will then follow not only an economically efficient allocation but also some economic degree of occupancy, access, and diffusion, and some corresponding rate of frequency development.

If the pattern of allocation, occupancy, access, diffusion, and development dictated by economic factors is deliberately altered, this should be done on one ground only: because costs and benefits external to the market have not been taken fully into account by the users of spectrum. Where these external costs and benefits are quantifiable in dollar terms, the needed adjustments will be readily apparent, though not always easy to effectuate. But where benefits are vague and defy any measurement as precise as costs, the manager must bear a special burden of proof in overriding a strict market calculus, or even a corrected one. And he must do so only in the light of all the data on costs.

At best, we are left with a range of administrative discretion, intuition, and judgment greater than that where GNP-maximization is the sole criterion, but far smaller than that which characterizes the present centralized nonprice system.

The Tacit Goals of Spectrum Management

In light of this somewhat theoretical discussion we may now examine each goal again a little more closely and consider what the public officials themselves seem to have in mind.

Full Occupancy

The OTM is directed to promote the full and efficient use of the spectrum resource;[7] the FCC to promote "the wider and more effective use of the radio spectrum." Once the moment has passed, the economic or social benefits forgone by having left the spectrum unused in all its dimensions simply cannot be recaptured. These losses due to nonuse being irrevocable, the managers' concern with at least "fuller" occupancy seems superficially understandable and the waste of nonuse is surely viewed as no negligible matter today.[8]

In all fairness, however, the managers do appear increasingly aware that full occupancy is not the only goal, or the most important one, or that it is necessarily consistent at all times with all other goals. The "unrecoverable" output lost through nonuse may not in fact have been economic to recover. Or less than full occupancy may be the temporary price of swift technological breakthroughs (opening up new spectral regions) which would never have occurred unless the systems developer-

[7] Executive Order No. 10995, February 15, 1963, sec. 6.
[8] Joint Technical Advisory Committee, *Radio Spectrum Utilization* (New York: Institute of Electrical and Electronics Engineers, 1965), pp. 4–5.

sponsor had expected some period of grace to capitalize on his new capability. The spectrum also has a crucial supportive role in furthering national goals outside of communications.[9] Of all this the managers seem fully cognizant.[10]

It is less clear whether the managers always take adequate steps to ensure that nonuse or underuse is fully compensated for by the further-ance of other specific social priorities,[11] or to determine whether dis-placement costs or other costs to accommodate new uses in the future (in the event of "fuller" occupancy during the interim), will necessarily exceed the losses that would arise from interim nonuse to avoid said costs. For this reason alone the managers sometimes seem too ready to hold spectrum idle even when secondary interim grantees would come forth to utilize it.

Finally, because the radio spectrum is a natural resource, to occupy any portion of it "fully" may be uneconomic simply because some sub-stitute (say, wire communication) makes the latter more suitable and efficient, or because technical know-how is not yet adequate. As with other natural resources, only when technology improves may it be pos-sible to occupy greater expanses of spectrum more intensively and at lower costs. On all these counts, even the goal of "fuller occupancy" is no longer viewed simplistically.[12] And yet spectrum managers clearly lack authority and/or investigative facilities to weigh the costs and suitability of wire (or other) substitutes before allocating frequencies or authorizing their use. Managers may therefore often appear more com-mitted to promoting spectrum usage as such than they really are, or would be in full light of all the facts.

Efficient Usage

In economic terms, optimal spectrum utilization occurs when the value of any unit of spectrum is equal in all conceivable uses. At this point the value of the frequencies in their best-alternative use is no greater than in the currently effective use.

As presently conceived, however, the managers' goal of "efficient

---

[9] Office of Telecommunications Management, *A Report on Frequency Manage-ment within the Executive Branch of the Government*, October 1966, p. 26, para. e, and Appendix 5. (Publication referred to hereinafter by title only.)

[10] Ibid., p. 24, para. c, items 1–4.

[11] Spectrum allocation to radio astronomy illustrates well both (a) the man-ager's willingness to forgo full occupancy for important social-scientific purposes (radio astronomy is a passive service and does not radiate); and (b) his neglect of opportunity costs in reaching this decision.

[12] *Report on Frequency Management*, pp. 12, 20–21, paras. f–n.

use" is far less demanding. They are normally confronted by a limited number of contests where a few contestants vie for the same frequencies within the same service, or in different services, and where a choice must therefore be made. In choosing, economic factors are usually weighed impressionistically, if at all. Economic considerations will at most figure as one element among many and, even when quantified, will rarely be determinative. In short, efficient spectrum usage will normally be defined pragmatically by a manager within a far narrower range of users and uses than that which concerns the economist in analyzing "allocative efficiency."

Among other things, the manager seeks to assure that the wrong users do not use the wrong spectrum at the wrong time. "Wrongness" relates to users who (a) do not need all their bandwidth for the intelligence they transmit; or (b) really require for reliable service more spectrum than is now assigned; or (c) could generate greater benefits from the occupancy of spectrum with different propagation character-istics (and other users from theirs).[13]

Hence the incidence of use and nonuse is not the only relevant criterion. There is also concern about efficient use in these rather special senses. The first precondition for it is approached when, assuming different users could trade their assignments, they would have no further private financial incentive to do so either because of the magnitude of the conversion costs or even if conversion costs were zero (via ade-quate amortization periods, reimbursement, etc.). A second precondi-tion is approached when there is no potential benefit in frequency trad-ing by which the community in economic, social, or technical terms can justify regulatory action to bring it about, granting that present users may themselves lack the private financial motivation to do so.

Some users occupy the wrong slots from the engineer's viewpoint; trade-offs might enhance signal quality or reliability and, conceivably, net economic or social benefits. One well-known case is the present assignment of distress signals at 500 Kc/s and other ship-shore service at 300–500 Kc/s. Distress, it is widely agreed, could be handled more effectively from a technical viewpoint higher in the spectrum (perhaps up around 2,000 Kc/s), whereas the spectrum from 535 Kc/s down to 500 Kc/s, or even to 200 Kc/s, could be better devoted to long-distance standard broadcasting.[14] A second case would be the hypothetical move-

<hr/>

[13] See Joint Technical Advisory Committee, *Radio Spectrum Conservation*, Ch. 3; and *Radio Spectrum Utilization*, p. 5, item 5. See also *Report on Frequency Management*, pp. 6–7, Appendix 5.

[14] Joint Technical Advisory Committee, *Radio Spectrum Conservation*, pp. 156–57, 195–97; *Radio Spectrum Utilization*, pp. 218–19.

ment of all local standard broadcast licensees from the AM to the FM band, AM frequencies being far better suited for long distance than for local transmission.[15]

The question is how such technically suboptimal frequency assignments arose in the first place, and why exchanges have not occurred since. In this regard, the historical development of different services has created a major problem: state-of-the-arts constraints limit the range of options open to different services at the time they are first initiated. What may be the "best" frequency assignment at one time is simply not the "best" later, in view of new scientific-engineering knowledge or changing economic conditions.

In addition, there is the practice of allocating spectrum according to a single uniform national plan, wherein particular frequency bands are earmarked for particular classes of users and services. This may have been administratively convenient at the outset, but it is at best inflexible and unsuited to present needs. Today frequent variations in local demand among users and services create serious problems of over- or under-utilization of spectrum.

Nevertheless, de facto property rights have generally gone to the earlier, older services. A principle of first-come first-served has long prevailed in the international field; and, as a practical matter, the radio user gains a legal equity or continuing right in his frequency space at home too. With no right to sell the spectrum he may vacate, an incumbent will simply lack financial incentives to permit latecomers to share his frequencies. Nor will he be willing to incur the higher hardware costs associated with any movement upwards, even though latecomers might be more than willing to reimburse him. Whether it pays the community to bring about these reallocations is quite beside the point for any individual user.

But why has the government itself not acted to reallocate in such cases more frequently? Here we can fruitfully turn to another episode. The military VHF spectrum is well-suited to television and in 1959 could theoretically have accommodated that burgeoning service, had the military been willing (and able) to accept in return the broadcasters' UHF spectrum as a place to develop an alternative set of military systems.[16]

The FCC had proposed to exchange at least some of the UHF channels assigned to broadcast television (518–890 Mc/s) for as much

---

[15] Joint Technical Advisory Committee, *Radio Spectrum Utilization*, p. 233; *Radio Spectrum Conservation*, p. 197.

[16] House Commerce Committee, 86th Cong., 1st sess., *Hearings on Spectrum Allocation*, 1959, pp. 193–94, 232–37.

as practicable of the military VHF (225–400 Mc/s).[17] Such an exchange was advocated as a more expeditious way to implement the Commission's TV Allocation Plan than continued assignment of the UHF with steps to activate them; reduced geographic spacing of VHF stations; and the promotion of CATV systems as a microwave-interconnected wire alternative. In reply, the military and OTM rejected the Commission's proposal because of (a) an estimated $5 billion cost to develop new military systems elsewhere; (b) interim loss of U.S. and Allied defense capability until the move was completed; (c) uncertainty as to whether future military capabilities would be fully comparable to those lost.[18]

The main point is that there was simply no administrative mechanism whereby the potential extra net economic benefits enjoyed by turning the military VHF over to the TV industry (net of a half billion dollars in TV conversion costs) could be compared to the cost of developing new military systems in the vacated UHF band.[19] Obviously, no government department (let alone one with the military's leverage in spectrum matters) would willingly agree to move elsewhere at considerable cost to do the same thing no better, and indeed at some risk of possible deterioration.

Because the defense-producing value of DOD dollars would at best be no greater after such a switch, it is understandable that the DOD should be reluctant to move even if its conversion-reallocation-systems development costs were fully reimbursed by the TV industry or by the community generally. On the other hand, industry was never asked whether the military VHF was worth to it a sum greater than the necessary cost of moving the military elsewhere without the loss of interim or long-range capabilities and converting TV transmitters and the public's receivers to the new VHF allocations.[20]

Even granting the strategic importance of the military's "final" word as to what constitutes "comparable defense capability elsewhere" and the difficulty of making accurate cost-benefit estimates, there is no ques-

---

[17] For a brief outline of the two FCC plans for an exchange, see Office of Civil and Defense Mobilization, "Position With Respect to TV Allocation Proposals," August 8, 1960, pp. 2–5. (The OCDM, in existence in 1958–62, was the organizational antecedent of the present Office of Telecommunications Management.)

[18] Ibid., pp. 5–13.

[19] See commentary in R. Coase, "The Interdepartment Radio Advisory Committee," *Journal of Law and Economics* (October 1962), pp. 42–45.

[20] In all fairness, TV was at no time precluded from making an economic case, but no appeal was filed after the OCDM's decision was made public. Sometimes overlooked may be the fact that existing VHF TV licensees wanted no more VHF competition and that the public itself was not pressing for more channels.

tion but that a quantification and injection of cost data into the decisional arena would have made for a more rational and orderly resolution of the issue.

Sustained Development

As noted in Chapter II, the Communications Act instructs the FCC to "promote the wider and more effective use of the radio spectrum." Executive Order No. 10995 instructs the OTM to encourage telecommunications R&D generally, and in particular the development of satellite technology, to facilitate the full, efficient use of the spectrum resource.[21] Such promotional responsibilities relate to the sustained development of the intensive and extensive margins of spectrum for any or all users. Users and managers may thereby accommodate better to spectrum scarcity and congestion.

We return to these matters in Part Two, with special reference to the federal government's role in telecommunications R&D. Suffice it to note here simply that public officials must reconcile "sustained development" with the other goals of national spectrum management. Experimentation requires the reservation of frequency assignments to test new techniques which could conceivably extend the margins of spectrum and does so even though the temporary stockpiling will interfere with full occupancy. The policy of equal access by all spectrum developers to the communications hardware market may militate strongly in favor of a separation of the operating common carriers from hardware/ research entities, whereas some observers see vertical integration as more conducive to innovative advance in telecommunications.

Equal Access and Wide Diffusion

"Equal access" means unrestricted opportunities by all potential radio users to combine spectrum freely with other factors in their production functions. This they may do either by building and operating their own private communications systems or by buying service from the carriers.

On the other hand, the policy of "wide diffusion" is endorsed by sec. 1 of the Communications Act, wherein the FCC is instructed to bring to all people at home and abroad the most economical wire and radio communication service at the lowest rates. A comparable provi-

[21] See fn. 18 in Ch. II above and associated textual discussion. See also *Report on Frequency Management*, pp. 21–23, 26, para. d.

sion, regarding the lower rates which potential satellite economies may facilitate in international and ultimately domestic communication appears in sec. 201(c) of the Communications Satellite Act.[22]

Wide diffusion also includes sharing in the fruits of government-supported R&D in such fields as radar, satellites, and atmospheric noise. And, finally, it refers to the imposition of varied service standards and, in particular, to the requirement that common carriers, ComSat, and radio-TV broadcasters shall serve uneconomic markets at home and abroad. Related to this criterion is the priority in allocation proceedings normally given users who serve "large numbers of people" with cultural, educational, or informational material (broadcasters), useful private information (common carriers), or in ways that safeguard life and property (police, fire, aeronautical-marine mobile, the military).

Stated otherwise, once spectrum is allocated under a variety of market and administrative criteria, the government proceeds to impose rate controls on the common carriers and conduct standards (via entry controls) on virtually all grantees (business, government, common carrier, broadcast). But competition is also maintained within and between many classes of spectrum users, backward to the spectrum reserves and to other factor inputs and forward in the contest for customers and revenues. Pursuant to this, the government purports to maintain equal nondiscriminatory access by the suppliers of factors to all broadcast, common carrier, or satellite facilities. This may conceivably require antitrust scrutiny by the Justice Department, as in the case of TV network program procurement and access to prime-time markets by independent program suppliers and nonnetwork advertisers, or the case of vertically integrated hardware/common carrier entities in their competition with independent equipment producers. Or it may simply mean the safeguarding of equal access by the FCC in regulatory decisions under the Communications Act or the Communications Satellite Act.

The upshot is twofold. First, there is an attempt, once the spectrum is allocated, to maximize and diffuse the benefits of its use as widely as if it were traded in an organized market and its user groups were themselves competitively structured. Second is an attempt to diffuse benefits even further when private and social benefits diverge and, as a consequence, the spectrum user's service must be subsidized internally or externally. On both counts, the tacit goal of spectrum management can really be said to coincide with the criterion of economic efficiency though, in the second case, not with market efficiency.

---

[22] See also sec. 201(c)(1) regarding competitive hardware procurement.

INTERRELATIONS OF THE GOALS

Having examined the management goals separately, we must now take note of their interrelations. Realism in mounting any serious program to improve the performance of American spectrum management requires continued awareness of these interrelations. They are in any case readily illustrated by a brief reference to the FCC's TV Allocation Plan of 1952.

The Plan allocated roughly half of the nongovernment spectrum below 890 Mc/s to broadcast television, with specific assignments on a community basis geared to bring at least one service to all areas, at least one station to most communities, and then as many additional services and stations to as many areas and communities as consistent with economic and technical constraints. A number of channels were reserved also for noncommercial educational use. Actually, it is virtually impossible to discuss the Plan meaningfully without going beyond the mere distribution of radiation rights to consider the industry structure which the Plan is intended to nurture and the structural constraints and incentives it provides for widening and diversifying program choice.

Intimately related to the Allocation Plan is the Commission's licensing power, which governs the distribution of particular rights to particular users within the broad framework which the Plan lays down. As noted, these licensing policies are geared largely to govern licensee conduct. Hence, without question, the composite licensing-allocation function not only distributes rights and integrates the several components of this broadcast system but also seeks to diversify and enrich the end product—i.e., to diffuse the benefits of communications technology through all relevant markets in social and economic terms.

Less familiar, perhaps, are the Plan's indirect effects on the level of spectrum development. However, the constraints imposed by niggardly allocations and the blunting of incentives where allocations are lush clearly affect the users' desire to extend the margins of usable spectrum. More familiar is the allocators' need to accommodate to the flood of new technologies, whether by finding the spectrum without which they cannot be instituted at all or by allowing the technologies to facilitate the release of spectrum by incumbent services. On both counts it is perfectly clear that allocation bears crucially on the level of spectrum development.

What this means is simply that one major managerial tool—the Allocation Table—cuts across three areas of major concern to spectrum management today: efficient spectrum allocation, the level of spectrum development, and specific regulatory criteria. Therefore its impact must be scrutinized from each of these viewpoints. Such standards of appraisal are relevant also to evaluating other major policies and tools of spectrum management, reviewed presently—the principle of temporary interim use of idle spectrum by the users and suppliers of communications facilities, rate base regulation, the conduct standards imposed by common carrier and broadcast licensing policies, and others. The following chapters examine the relative merits of alternatives to the present centralized nonprice system of spectrum allocation. Subsequently we shall consider the level of spectrum development and then certain management norms as standards for evaluating the impact of different regulatory policies and techniques.

PART TWO

ALTERNATIVES IN SPECTRUM
ALLOCATION AND MANAGEMENT

CHAPTER IV

FREELY TRANSFERABLE RIGHTS

Few would deny that the present centralized nonprice spectrum system is economically inefficient or that it fails to further many overriding national priorities. Without markets and prices for radio frequencies, it is impossible to tell whether spectrum has been allocated optimally among alternative users and uses, whether users have struck correct balances in their mix of radio and nonradio substitutes, whether they have sufficiently developed spectrum at its intensive or extensive margins. Yet when a scarce resource is given away, as spectrum is, there is a strong presumption, supported by numerous examples, that the wrong people often use the wrong frequencies at the wrong time; and that they innovate spectrum-economizing (or spectrum-developing) equipment in the wrong places for the wrong reasons.

What should we do about it? The public administrator traditionally looks to new administrative concepts and tools, normally devoid of substantial economic content. On the other side, university economists are too often associated exclusively with a single remedy: a full-fledged spectrum market wherein spectrum would move virtually automatically from lower- to higher-valued uses and users, and its imputed economic value as a factor input in the production function of any and all public and private users would be maximized.

This latter proposal has considerable merit in theory and also has value as a point of departure for empirical work. But in their almost exclusive concern with it, economists have needlessly polarized the issues. In the process we may have overlooked certain important middle-range options between a complete market, which many high officials believe simply cannot work, and the current framework, which they admit is unsatisfactory in some respects.

My contention here is that we must now pay far more attention to

85

the mechanics of several modified market-type arrangements, shown in Table 6, which meet those critical noneconomic objections which the government still has to almost any market system. These modified options (auctions, user charges, and shadow prices), being far more "salable" than a complete market in practical political and strategic terms, need bear only a modest burden of economic proof. For that reason they offer the best hope of moving us off dead center at this time.

TABLE 6. ALTERNATIVES TO THE CURRENT SYSTEM OF SPECTRUM ALLOCATION

A. Freely Transferable Rights
   1. Rights created in the courts under tort law, through inclusion and exclusion, with spectrum bought and sold outright like land.
   2. Federal designation of rights, leaving them freely transferable after their subsequent sale outright.
   3. Federal designation of rights, periodic competitive leasing for limited periods, with lessees substantially free to transfer at will.

B. Auctions of Federally Designated Radiation Rights
   1. Interband contests to determine reallocation as between different services, in addition to intraband contests limited to like users within the same service.
   2. Interband contests to ration grants among like users, within different services competing for the same spectrum, with managers free to utilize the resultant values in further reallocation of spectrum between the two services.
   3. Intraband contests within a single service to ration rights there, with results used to set user charges elsewhere too.

C. Charges to Users
   1. Charges applied on three-dimensional spectrum occupied by a user, as measured by some index of physical use.
   2. Per unit rates might be (a) derived from intraband auction values or estimated shadow prices; or might be (b) set at some arbitrary flat dollar rate.

D. Shadow Prices
   Prices derived from maximum sums that current spectrum users and systems designers would be willing to pay rather than do without some small amount of spectrum.

E. New Administrative Techniques
   1. Greater role for frequency clearance, with government users required to secure prior authorization (from the Director of Telecommunications Management) before disbursing funds to develop or build any communications system.
   2. Secondary rights—i.e., rights to share or borrow frequencies contingent upon noninterference with rights of the primary user.
   3. Heavier burden of proof on spectrum managers when they deliberately override economic considerations.

Note: Alternatives are here ranked inversely to their nearness to the current non-price management framework.

THE REQUIREMENTS OF REMEDIAL REFORM

Before examining the key obstacles to institutional change, it will be helpful to describe the full range of issues in question from a different vantage point—that is, in terms of five principal requirements of any viable alternative to current allocational practice.

First of all, any serious proposal for remedial reform must be sufficiently close to the current institutional-regulatory framework to be relevant on practical and political grounds. For beyond some point, any radical restructuring is bound to provoke concerted opposition from virtually all the parties at interest. Industry and regulatory officials alike will be understandably reluctant to trade an ongoing certainty, however imperfect, for the paper promises of a hypothetical ideal which, however persuasive in theory, are still only paper promises. The complete market would virtually replace the public administrator's allocational function and render obsolete the buttressing skills and know-how of the frequency management establishment. The modified middle-range options would limit but not eliminate administrative discretion. Without replacing the central allocator outright, these options would force him to justify far more rigorously and systematically any deliberate decision to override market indicators. Working within the existing matrix of social-administrative criteria developed over past decades, the public administrator would simply be given a new economic tool to inject price incentives more effectively into allocational decisions.

A second requirement for any viable reform is that it speak directly to the problems posed by the public official's commitment to regulatory priorities of a noneconomic sort, such as the commitment to avoid pricing the small unit out of the market, that has long been a rallying point for those who oppose a complete spectrum market. The specter of economic concentration and opinion manipulation at home and of anti-American sentiments abroad are often cited in opposition. Yet in a competitive market, spectrum (like other resources) will go not to the wealthiest users but to those relatively best able to use it. Large and small users alike will theoretically get the amounts they can most efficiently utilize, the question being only whether the public administrator is committed to a diffusion of access rights consistent with economic efficiency. Where the designated distribution diverges from an economically efficient one, there is no question that those sensitive to the plight of small units, or small nations, will prefer modified middle-range options to any complete market. Surely the explicit safeguards of a zoned auction system, or a set of user charges introduced under current FCC rules on multiple ownership of TV stations, will be more tolerable to those suspicious of markets in any form than the mere knowledge that antitrust law can be invoked after the fact to alter any market-determined distribution of access rights.

A third and closely related requirement is to devise options directly responsive to the problems posed by the large benefit externalities now associated with public spectrum usage by federal, state, and local gov-

ernment services, education, public safety, information, and even commercial TV under present arrangements. Part of this problem is probably
spurious. If public users cannot command adequate fiscal resources to
retain their currently allocated spectrum, let alone acquire more, it may
rightly be questioned whether they should have it in the first place.

True, there are well-known imperfections in the appropriations
process as an adequate indicator of community preferences. The public
sector may be relatively deprived both because consumers need not pay
directly for all the benefits they derive from many collective services and
because they actually want less of what economists call merit goods
than is "good for them" and for society. Nevertheless, this does not stop
us from forcing public and private users of common resources to compete elsewhere in the economy. Nor is it self-evident that spectrum
should be treated differently.

In opposing a full-fledged market, however, the public administrator
may still have an arguable point of a more practical sort. If public spectrum users are suddenly dropped into a complete spectrum market, there
could well be drastic short-term transitional adjustments. To say that
their failure to command sufficient fiscal resources means that the community rates public use of spectrum lower than private, hardly speaks
to the lethal opposition which the most influential public lobbies could
and would make against almost any move towards a system that
threatened to dislodge them. By working within the existing allocational
framework, on the other hand, the middle-range options would force
public users to economize on spectrum and to consider its economic
value in determining their mix of communications hardware investment.
But the explicit safeguards of a regulated market-type system would
substantially reduce short-term reallocational pressures. The chances of
instituting price incentives in some form would therefore be commensurately greater.

A fourth requirement relates to the phasing in of a remedial option.
The more gradual this process, the less disruptive the economic impact,
and the less likely that concerted opposition will arise. A full-fledged
market may be more difficult to phase in than is sometimes believed. To
institute such a market, to be sure, one need only vest rights in the current rightholders, who will indeed become aware of the market only
when they subsequently decide to sell their rights voluntarily. Nevertheless, even these incumbents will be subject to full-scale market pricing
as soon as they seek to acquire additional spectrum. Therefore they, no
less than the newcomer, will presumably fight bitterly to keep from paying for access rights hitherto awarded gratis. In addition, the inequity

of grandfathering the current incumbents may in its own right exacerbate still more the political opposition to change.

In contrast, the middle-range options can be phased in gradually over long time periods, with far less impact on incumbents or newcomers alike and with far more explicit safeguards of their interests. Thus those who had entered in reliance on free spectrum grants could eventually be made subject to market incentives without excessive economic injury or the gross inequities of vesting their rights outright.

A fifth requirement relates to the strictly economic merit of a remedy and, in particular, the burden of proof it must bear. On this count, an option which rates decisively higher on the several practical political-strategic counts just described, need not bear so heavy a burden of economic proof as one which rates low. Here the full-fledged market unquestionably operates under a serious political handicap, and its mere improvement of present economic performance will therefore not suffice. The complete market must be shown to be *decisively* superior, if one is to assume its political liabilities. That is, one must first be sure that a full-fledged market is not only better than the present system but better than other more "salable" options as well.

This burden of economic proof cannot be discharged on a priori grounds with abstract deductive theorizing alone. Careful empirical study of a sort not yet made is absolutely essential. This work can and should be done. But meanwhile, the more modest economic promise of middle-range options must command unstinting short-term effort as the most likely way to improve the present system.

ECONOMIC OBSTACLES TO A FULL-FLEDGED MARKET FOR SPECTRUM

Any bona fide market for frequencies must include the owners' rights to deliver such signals, to exclude others who would cause harmful interference, to use the frequencies for any and all purposes, and to transfer or sell them at will.[1] That is, there must be *emission* rights to

---

[1] The classic delineation of a system of freely transferable rights appears in R. Coase, W. Meckling, and J. Minasian, "Problems in Radio Frequency Allocation," unpublished study for The Rand Corporation, Santa Monica, Calif., Ch. 4. My discussion throughout has benefited from early access to this thought-provoking document. Valuable recent amplifications and modifications, published after most of my research was completed, appear in A. De Vany, R. Eckert, C. Meyers, D. O'Hara, and R. Scott, "A Property System for Market Allocation of the Electromagnetic Spectrum," *Stanford Law Review* (June 1969), pp. 1499–1561. See also L. Rose, "Marketable Spectrum Rights," *Conference Record*, 1969 IEEE International Conference, Boulder, Colo., June 9–11, 1969, sess. 13, pp. 7–12.

radiate energy on specified bandwidth, at a specified time, within a designated area, at some maximum permissible power level; *admission* rights that exclude others from radiating energy greater than some predetermined level on a frequency, at a time, and in an area to which one's rights pertain; *freedom to use* the above rights for any purpose and to *combine* inputs in so doing; and *freedom to transfer* one's rights to others at will.[2] Properly conceived, these rights should operate to safeguard the users' ability to transmit signals of acceptable clarity and also to insure that spectrum is used in its highest-valued use.

In the present regulated nonprice spectrum system, centralized spectrum management provides only an imperfect equivalent of what a decentralized system of freely transferable property rights would ideally facilitate. Today, the managers define emission rights by specifying transmission inputs in some detail, and admission rights are normally protected by limiting the number and radiation patterns of transmitters permitted to operate in any area.

Most proposals for a complete spectrum market would require rights to be specified as signal outputs bounded in time, frequency, and three-dimensional space.[3] Radio users would then be permitted to combine transmission inputs—transmitter power and location, antenna heights, directivity and polarization, signal intensity and modulation—provided that these inputs were kept consistent with maximum authorized signal strength at the perimeter of their area and also with some maximum allowable percentage of spurious emissions on adjacent or harmonic channels therein.[4]

Leaving users free to combine factors this way, on a cost and revenue basis, makes it possible to maximize the net economic value of authorized levels of signal output. At the margin, value to any user must equal value of the rights in their best alternative use; if not, it would pay him to continue trading until this is so and thus until net economic product is maximized.[5]

What then are the principal economic impediments to creating such a system of freely transferable rights? Its practicality cannot be judged without empirical answers to the following questions, among others. Do the magnitude and complexity of interference now associated with spectrum utilization make the cost of internalizing its external effects so

[2] Coase et al., "Problems in Radio Frequency Allocation," p. 101.

[3] See ibid., pp. 102–8; W. Meckling, "Management of the Frequency Spectrum," *Washington University Law Quarterly* (Spring 1968), pp. 26–34; De Vany et al., "Property System for Allocation of the Spectrum," pp. 1512–29; and Rose, "Marketable Spectrum Rights."

[4] Coase et al., "Problems in Radio Frequency Allocation," pp. 99–100.

[5] Ibid., pp. 102–4.

high as to eliminate any net economic gain derived from moving spectrum from lower- to higher-valued uses? Does the dynamic interactive physical character of radiation create such uncertainties and ambiguities in rights definition as to require centralized specification of inputs for any system of clear, reconstitutable, and transferable rights? If so, at what point does any necessary degree of input specification make prohibitively costly the free transferability of rights across any and all service lines in all spectral regions? At what point, that is, will the minimal degree of input specification needed for "sufficient" clarity and certainty in rights definition so increase the number of parties to representative market transactions as to render transfer costs uneconomic to incur?

Cost Externalities, Uncertainties, and Transferability of Rights

Several important externalities now impede the efficient definition, enforcement, and reconstitution of rights in spectrum, and hence the creation of a viable market via private contract and common law. These external effects of individual uses of spectrum, reflective of their strong interactions, mean that fungible, discrete, quantifiable, and certain rights cannot be readily defined, transferred, subdivided, or combined. These interactions also make it at best complex and costly to protect rights, to resolve conflicts between the rightholders, and hence for a full-fledged market to work efficiently.

Three representative cost externalities may be briefly identified, leaving until later any scrutiny of externalities on the benefit side. One problem relates to variability in signal outputs due to natural phenomena beyond the user's control which produce extensive and unpredictable patterns of interference. Here the best examples are the nighttime skywave of the AM broadcast band and the outages and aberrations of HF radio transmission during the periodic sunspot cycle.[6] In either case, radio signals may extend over very long distances and interfere with the authorized emissions of many other transmitters.

A closely related externality arises from the general unconfinability of radiation irrespective of spectral region or transmission mode. Here rights to radiate on designated frequencies in designated areas often have unpredictable or unauthorized effects on other frequencies in other areas. This is the problem of spurious emissions generally and of harmonic and adjacent channel interference in particular.

---

[6] See generally Joint Technical Advisory Committee, *Radio Spectrum Utilization* (New York: Institute of Electrical and Electronics Engineers, 1964), pp. 112–42; *Radio Spectrum Conservation* (McGraw-Hill, 1952), pp. 33–36, 53–55, 65–91, 156–57, 159–63.

A third externality relates to intermodulation effects where several different services operate simultaneously on different frequencies but in the same limited physical area, such as a mountain top, urban roof, or a naval vessel. Unlike the first two externalities, neither C nor B alone would harm A; but, in C's presence, B does harm A through no fault of his own, while C harms neither. A further complication follows from the fact that B's interference with A's reception (in C's presence) may be due more to the low quality of A's receiver than to the power of B's transmitter.[7] With neither C nor B liable for these effects on A, there is an uncompensated external cost which may result in "excessive" inter- ference. That is, the degree of intermodulation interference will be non- optimal unless the cost externalities can be internalized through proper designation of spatial and temporal radiation rights.

Each of these major cost externalities could make the definition of rights far less clear and certain than otherwise and, on that score at least, impair the efficiency of any market for spectrum. But one uncer- tainty often cited by opponents of a market system is really irrelevant. It is best summed up in the question: How can even the government define and guarantee radiation rights whose reliability lies beyond its control and is subject, say, to the actions of nations who are not even members of the ITU? This issue can be dismissed by noting that one well-known earmark of the business system is its ability to cope with normal risks of the trade. The spectrum field is no exception, and there seems no reason why private spectrum users should be spared having to bear all the customary risks borne by business entities elsewhere. Even the problem posed by unpredictable actions of non-ITU members seems no more onerous than the risks of expropriation that some American companies have long had to face in making investments abroad.

Those special characteristics of the spectrum which explain the prevalence of these complex external effects and interactions have been variously described. Reference has been made in Chapter I to the spec- trum's multiple dimensions, its nondepletability upon use, its capacity for simultaneous use and reuse in given geographic areas and, above all, to the fact that electromagnetic energy can be spatially confined only in a very probabilistic sense.[8] To such characteristics have been further

---

[7] A thorough explanation of the technical aspects appears in Joint Technical Advisory Committee, *Spectrum Engineering: The Key to Progress* (New York: Institute of Electrical and Electronics Engineers, 1968), Supp. 6. See also De Vany et al., "Property System for Allocation of the Spectrum," pp. 1520–22.

[8] See President's Task Force on Communications Policy, *Final Report* (U.S. Government Printing Office, 1968), Ch. VIII, pp. 31–33 (referred to hereinafter as *Task Force Report*). See also Ch. I above.

attributed[9] the technical impossibility of creating absolute (or even conditional) emission rights under which rightholder A could locate his transmitter freely within a designated area or freely select his power, intensity, polarization, or directivity, without potentially preventing other rightholders from doing likewise on the same frequency in an adjacent area. Nor could rightholder A protect his receivers from harmful interference caused by others without keeping their transmitters several times as far from his boundary as his own transmitter is.

On both counts, it has at least been argued that the creation of exclusive, flexible, and freely transferable emission rights for any user A and their protection against co-channel interference from adjacent areas will require the nonuse of some (conceivably large) area beyond the perimeter of A's authorized service range. Likewise, access to some range of frequencies including but not limited to those A uses, must also be foreclosed to others. Otherwise, A's rights cannot be protected against interference by users who operate in the same area on different but adjacent or harmonic frequencies, or whose transmitters intermodulate with his.

Space limitations preclude any detailed recapitulation of the technical analysis on which these propositions rest, or any evaluation of the important ongoing effort to define a viable system of marketable rights nonetheless.[10] For present purposes we shall simply accept as fact the postulated direct relation between (a) the degree to which output rights can be defined on a certain, flexible, exclusive, and transferable basis and (b) the magnitude of unusable areas and frequency ranges that result. This direct relation, due in large part to spillover effects and dynamic interactions, must be further distinguished from but related to the problem of input specification. Here the question is whether the degree to which inputs must be specified to insure relative clarity, certainty, and exclusivity in rights definition—and on that score to facilitate exchange—will for any other reason impede the ready transfer, subdivision, and reconstitution of the rights. If so, generally defined, freely transferable output rights would require considerable nonuse of the spatial and frequency dimensions of spectrum, and thereby might impose sizable economic losses. But the specification of inputs which

---

[9] See W. Hinchman, "The Electromagnetic Spectrum: What It Is and How It Is Used," Appendix 8 to Staff Paper No. 7, President's Task Force on Communications Policy (U.S. Department of Commerce, Clearinghouse for Federal Scientific and Technical Information, June 1969). The following paragraphs draw heavily on Hinchman's ideas, especially pp. 32–60.

[10] See especially De Vany et al., "Property System for Allocation of the Spectrum," pp. 1512–52. See also Rose, "Marketable Spectrum Rights."

could reduce this nonuse would itself prevent spectrum from going to those economically best able to use it.

The choice would then be between two imperfect alternatives. One common-sense criterion would be to strike a balance whereby the spectrum's output value relative to its enforcement and exchange costs is maximized. However, in seeking out arrangements towards this end a number of economic and noneconomic problems must be met.[11]

The principal problem in grounding a market system on rights defined as signal outputs derives from the external effects and interactions just described. These externalities introduce considerable uncertainty as to precisely how much of what dimension of any user's radiation rights he can expect to utilize successfully. It is easy enough to define the output rights. But the degree to which they will be meaningful and productive depends on the way all other users in the same or neighboring areas use the same or related frequencies.

Following Hinchman, the technical argument can be illustrated further as follows.[12] Let rightholder A transmit in an assigned area adjacent to eight other areas in each of which another rightholder also operates. Let each rightholder operate freely within his assigned area, on the same frequency, at a level of power sufficient for acceptable service at his outlying perimeter. It can be shown that, if no one else were operating, rightholder A alone could operate freely within his perimeter, deciding at will on transmitter location, directivity, and intensity. However, his ability to do so would become increasingly constrained as each of the other users utilized his comparable rights. So that, unless rightholder A knew beforehand the precise inputs of the others, he could not predict how much or how little of his area rights he could in fact use without harmful interference.

The same holds true for A's ability to use his assigned frequency rights. Suppose, for instance, that each of the eight other rightholders operates on other frequencies, but fully within A's authorized perimeter. Spillover effects would this time occur in the frequency (not the spatial) dimension. With no one else on the air, A would of course have full, unimpaired use of his assigned frequency. But suppose the other users operate on adjacent or harmonic frequencies, or with transmitters which

[11] My approach contrasts with that of De Vany et al., notwithstanding these externalities, who attempt to define spectrum rights so as to facilitate a distribution of frequencies which would "increase the value of the spectrum resource relative to exchange and enforcement costs." "Property System for Allocation of the Spectrum," pp. 1512–52.

[12] See Hinchman, "The Electromagnetic Spectrum," pp. 52–60.

intermodulate with A's or with his receivers. In that case, as each user commenced to utilize his authorized frequency, rightholder A's ability to use his frequency would be increasingly limited. Once again, without knowledge of the other users' precise inputs (in power, location, directivity, etc.), A cannot predict the degree to which his rights are in fact substantive.

There are at least two ways to reduce A's uncertainties about his rights and hence to facilitate their greater divisibility, transferability, and reconstitutability. Either all inputs of all users can be specified (as at present), or the users can be permitted to negotiate with each other concerning who will use which frequencies, with and without which transmission inputs. The price paid for certainty, clarity, and exclusivity of rights and for low-cost protection from harmful interference will presumably be that of reduced flexibility, transferability, divisibility, and reconstitutability. But in either case the key question is whether aggregate net spectrum value will increase in the process, and this is by no means self-evident.

Careful prior analysis is needed as to: how uncertain the rights can become before rendering market transactions impractical; how far the inputs must be specified to reduce this uncertainty; and how costly and impractical such input specification would itself render market transactions. What one presumably wants is enough input specification to eliminate the extreme uncertainties and make the rights readily marketable on that score without at the same time raising enforcement and exchange costs substantially relative to spectrum value on other counts. Far more work is needed on this crucial issue, largely ignored in the recent discussions. Short of this, it seems highly premature to focus exclusively on freely transferable rights. Less extreme market-type arrangements may offer less ideal but perhaps more manageable ways to inject economic factors into the present centralized nonprice spectrum system. At this stage of theoretical and empirical work, the latter also deserve scrutiny on their merits.

Any system of transferable rights constrained significantly by input specification raises the likelihood that the number of rightholders who must negotiate even the simplest transfer, subdivision, or combination of rights will be very large indeed. Take the situation confronting the Midwest Program for Airborne Television Instruction in 1964 when it applied for six unused UHF channels to broadcast instructional programs to some 1,200 schools in a six-state area, using airborne transmitters. Among other things, MPATI had to demonstrate that it would not interfere with the conventional ground-based TV stations then

projected for the area in question.[13] But suppose that the TV grantees
had already been selected, though without yet starting to build their
stations. And suppose also that MPATI had somehow to induce those
with whom it might potentially conflict to make necessary adjustments
in their transmission inputs. In a market for input rights under these
postulated constraints, MPATI would have had to negotiate with 45
commercial licensees and one ETV grantee in 38 areas to modify their
transmitter locations, frequencies, directivity, polarization, and the like.

Now if one further postulates that, once the parties had struck their
bargain, the FCC could approve all the needed adjustments forthwith,
then the negotiations, complex and cumbersome at best, would have
stopped there. But under a fuller market-type version, suppose MPATI
also had to induce each of the 46 "adjusting" rightholders to sell some
of its input rights and acquire those of still other grantees who are at
the time postulated to enjoy the preferred locations, frequencies, power,
etc. The transaction would now have become so unwieldy and costly as
to make it almost inconceivable. Its unmanageability on any market
basis derives simply from the unique value of input rights to the individual rightholders.

In short, the cost externalities described earlier raise some question
as to whether single-valued radiation rights can readily be defined,
measured, and enforced. Without these prior conditions, such rights
cannot be bought, sold, or reconstituted efficiently in a bona fide market.
Yet property rights will emerge to internalize external costs and benefits only where the cost of internalization falls short of the gains that
result. Where interactions of the rightholders immediately involved affect
many others besides, or are in turn affected by them, this will simply
not be the case. Enforcement and transfer costs will be too high where
the number of transacting parties is very large and the withdrawal of
any single participant can prevent a satisfactory agreement.[14] Private
negotiations to reconstitute and police the rights will normally be deemed
inappropriate,[15] even in the absence of a more efficient government

[13] See "Comments by the Midwest Program for Airborne Television Instruction" in FCC Docket No. 15201 and 14229, April 3, 1964, Exhibit No. 1 (prepared by Steiner and Barnett), pp. 57–154. The episode is discussed further in Ch.
VII.

[14] R. Coase, "The Problem of Social Cost," *Journal of Law and Economics*
(October 1960), pp. 15–18; H. Demsetz, "Toward a Theory of Property Rights,"
American Economic Review, Papers and Proceedings (May 1967), pp. 347–50.

[15] See Demsetz, "Toward a Theory of Property Rights," pp. 348–49, 357; and
Coase, "The Federal Communications Commission," *Journal of Law and Economics* (October 1959), pp. 29–30.

mechanism to do so, in which case efficiency requires that the externalities be ignored.[16]

In any event, it is widely agreed that individual negotiation and enforcement are impractical in the case of man-made noise, such as that due to medical, industrial, or scientific radiation, to auto ignition switches, or to street cars. Here the number of independent sources of radiation is very large, their detection costs high, and the number of people transmitting and receiving the noise excessive. Special administrative regulation is therefore needed to set standards in regard to receiver quality, hardware design, transmitter shielding, and wiring.[17] Would individual negotiation and enforcement be very much more manageable in regard to major communications or locational uses of the spectrum? The answer cannot be stated in black and white.

Radiation Rights and Changing Technology

There have of course been important technical advances in many spectral regions over the years. What is unwieldy and prohibitive at one state of the arts may not be so at another, and the cost of internalizing the externalities would respond accordingly. So the really relevant question is not whether we could have created a viable system of property rights in spectrum with the empirical knowledge we had forty years ago, but whether we could now do so if we had it to do all over again. That is, do advances in technology permit the needed definition and enforcement of rights more readily today than in 1927?

Even assuming that property rights had initially been created by a federal commission rather than by the courts under tort law, considerable knowledge of radio propagation characteristics would have been needed. The uncertainties that confronted spectrum users in the major reaches of the then available spectrum are well-known. But our growing technical knowledge has presumably operated to lower the cost of internalizing the externalities since then.

These costs have probably declined somewhat, for example, in response to major technical advances in directing and confining AM broadcast transmissions and in predicting the propagation conditions of

---

[16] See Coase, "The Problem of Social Cost," pp. 15–18, 26–28, 41–44; and Demsetz, "Exchange and Enforcement of Property Rights," *Journal of Law and Economics* (October 1964), p. 12.

[17] Coase et al., "Problems in Radio Frequency Allocation," pp. 128–33. See generally Joint Technical Advisory Committee, *Spectrum Engineering: The Key to Progress*, Supp. 9, pp. 2–6, 19–25.

HF radio.[18] Even more dramatic improvements are implicit in the advent of line-of-sight technology as such. In the VHF, UHF, and microwave regions generally, our ability to predict the precise three-dimensional space any spectrum user will occupy, and to define radiation rights accordingly, is doubtless superior to comparable predictions in the older, lower spectral regions. This probably deserves all the fanfare it has recently received, for there is no question that propagation vagaries have significantly colored our whole attitude towards the spectrum and its management.[19]

On the other hand, we must not exaggerate the significance of technological advance. Both HF and AM broadcast transmission continue to pose serious interference problems.

The Unwieldy AM Broadcast and HF Radio Bands

To cope with AM broadcast skywave, detailed regional agreements must still be negotiated periodically with Canada, Mexico, Central America, and Caribbean countries. Even within the United States, difficult AM radio interference patterns show up in complex hearings where numerous parties from far-apart communities may protest some particular licensee's application for greater signal power or a longer broadcast day. The detail in which the FCC must now specify transmission hardware requirements, in order to reconcile acceptable signal standards with new AM station entry, further underlines the kind of agreements that would otherwise be needed between the individual users affected.

In the HF band, global interference patterns still require complex negotiations. These vagaries of ionospheric propagation remain the classic example of radio emissions that affect a multitude of parties over far-flung areas. The complicated multilateral negotiations needed to maintain a viable system in HF are nowhere better illustrated than in the voluminous HF Broadcast Schedule wherein all 134 ITU members now coordinate daily broadcasts by some 500 HF stations in 74 geo-

[18] See U.S. Department of Commerce, *Ionospheric Radio Propagation* (U.S. Government Printing Office, 1965), Chs. 6–7; D. Patterson, *A Survey of Techniques for Improving Utilization of the Radio Frequency Spectrum*, NBS Report No. 7630 (U.S. Department of Commerce, National Bureau of Standards, 1962), pp. 41–51; and Joint Technical Advisory Committee, *Radio Spectrum Utilization*, pp. 142–58.

[19] On the administrative and engineering constraints imposed to cope with natural variability, see S. Myers, *Technical Aspects or Consideration of Frequency Assignment*, FCC Report No. F-6601 (Federal Communications Commission, 1965), pp. 9–13, 23–27.

graphic broadcast regions, 24 hours a day, over some 300 to 350 separate HF radio frequencies.[20]

Line-of-Sight Technology: The Hazards of Overgeneralization

Even with line-of-sight radiation, special interference problems may render the definition, enforcement, and transfer of rights difficult and costly. Rights can be far more precisely delineated for terrestrial users in the microwave region than much lower down in the spectrum. Microwave radiations, characterized by narrow directional beaming, directly affect very few parties beyond the immediate vicinity of their transmitters or relay towers. Even satellite earth stations can be shielded in ways that, thus far, minimize their effects on the terrestrial systems.

Without the proper (and possibly costly) hardware adjustments, however, a TV broadcast satellite could conceivably interfere with numerous aeronautical, marine, or land mobile systems and particularly with conventional broadcast and microwave transmissions. It could do so on the same, adjacent, or harmonic channels over one-third of the earth's surface.[21] Individual negotiation of the necessary transmission standards would obviously be impossible.

The line-of-sight land mobile services pose still other problems. Aside from such freak occurrences in the Low Band, as when local BBC broadcasts have sometimes interfered with the U.S. police or highway maintenance services, mobile radio users may interfere with TV stations. Specifically, TV reception may suffer where low-quality TV receivers are tuned to a TV station on a channel adjacent to one which the mobile system utilizes in a given city, or to a second station located in another city and using the same channel.[22] In addition, erratic interference within and between services due to a long-distance "skip" phenomenon still plagues all mobile radio below 50 Mc/s during the high period of the eleven-year solar cycle.

Radar offers a still better example of the dangers of overgeneralizing

[20] See International Frequency Registration Board, *Tentative Frequency Broadcast Schedule* (Geneva: The Board, 1967).

[21] See generally R. Haviland, "Space Telecasting for World Education," XVI IAF Congress, Athens, September 13–18, 1965, mimeo., pp. 8–14; "Selected Studies of Space Broadcasting," *Telecommunication Journal* (February 1965), pp. 77–85.

[22] Strictly speaking, the complaints about co-channel interference with outside TV stations have no "standing" with the FCC, but the issue may become muddied where viewers reside in a fringe area between the two broadcast facilities. See Federal Communications Commission, *Report of Land Mobile Frequency Relief Committee*, January 19, 1968, p. 5.

about the new line-of-sight technology. Spurious emissions on adjacent and harmonic channels are much harder to contain in the radar bands than elsewhere in the microwave region or in the FM and TV broadcast bands. The number of parties affected by radar is excessive in part because of its high radiating power and "dirty" splattering emissions, and interference is all the more extensive because the several radar bands are not harmonically related.

In short, radar interference problems are far more complex than those of any radio communication service in the VHF, UHF, or micro-wave regions. Indeed, unless properly engineered, a radar facility over-looking a sizable city could potentially interfere with all radio services operating there across the whole spectrum. The individual transactions needed to negotiate an optimal level of interference would be far too numerous, cumbersome, and costly to handle on any market basis. It is inconceivable that the owners of all transmitters and receivers affected could deal directly with the radar facility, in or out of the courts, to secure the installation of necessary filters or other hardware components.

As with medical, scientific, and industrial radiation, then, an admin-istrative designation of transmission standards and design objectives for radar is essential. So too is the concentration of all transmitters in a few wide exclusive bands. It must also be noted that radar operates in a full 39 per cent of all spectrum between 30 and 1,000 Mc/s (16 per cent on an exclusive basis), compared to only 11 per cent allocated to broad-casting, and 2 per cent to land mobile. Even the prime radar bands account for one-half of the region between 1,000 and 10,000 Mc/s, roughly the same fraction which broadcasting occupies below 890 Mc/s. This is no negligible handicap to the efficiency of a complete market system.

In the absence of property rights and a market system, to be sure, the proper objective in all such cases should still be to strike a judicious balance between the cost of shielding, hardware adjustments and filters on one hand, and the economic value of the alternative uses of spectrum thereby protected on the other. But this merely underscores the need to consider the economic factor in *some* fashion, as by user charges, auc-tions, and shadow prices.

Uncertainties of Intermodulation and the Principle of Unitary Management

In the case of intermodulation on a mountain top or urban building roof, it is at least conceivable that the rights could be defined, liability for damages assessed, and individual negotiations conducted to untangle the situation. But the practicality of such individual negotiation is another matter.

Examples of intermodulation are scattered throughout the spectrum, wherever antennas are clustered within narrow physical constraints. The question is whether this represents the kind of externality that precludes any market-type solution of the interference problem. Discussion here will be limited to the phenomenon as it appears on a crowded mountain top. Let us assume that:

A gets a right to transmit and moves to the mountain top. *B* then follows suit, without interfering with *A*. Then *C* arrives. Though he does not interfere with *A* or *B* directly, *B* now, through no fault of his own, starts to interfere with *A*. Several questions arise. Shall *B* be compelled to install equipment to protect *A*? If so, who shall bear the cost? Can *A*'s radiation rights be defined before *B* and *C* arrive on the scene so as to take such eventualities into account in order that *A* can judge the value of his rights accurately enough to bid for them rationally in the first place?

There is in principle nothing insuperable about handling this phenomenon in a market system, provided that the transaction does not become unduly cumbersome. Like the simpler case of interference which *A* suffers when *B* or *C* operates on an adjacent or harmonic channel (or the simplest case of interference on the same channel), once the rights of the three parties are designated and liability for damages assigned, individual negotiation should theoretically be possible.

Without intermodulation, the normal practice is that newcomer *C* must bear the full cost of correcting any interference he causes *B* or *A* on the same, an adjacent, or a harmonic channel. And this is true even though these costs might be far lower had *B* and *A* designed their equipment in the first place to minimize the opportunity costs of their occupancy, as represented by latecomer *C*'s difficulties in entering. But here, government and nongovernment users, a mobile system, a TV broadcaster, and a microwave station may all operate in a narrow physical space. Intermodulation is intense, and the old rule of noninterference by latecomers breaks down.

To strike individual bargains over who should pay whom how much to do what is obviously much more difficult where latecomer *C* no longer has any direct effect on *A* or *B*, and where *B*'s effect on *A* is in an important sense due to *C*'s presence rather than to *B*'s transmitter. The problem becomes even more complex where *B*'s interference with *A* (as induced by *C*) is due not to deficiencies in *B*'s transmitter so much as in *A*'s receivers. Because *A*'s receivers, perfectly adequate before *C*'s arrival, are no longer adequate, *C* now makes *B* interfere with

A. And just to add one final complication, suppose *A* is a TV station whose receivers are sets watched in 25,000 homes in the valley below, and not a base station transmitting to a handful of mobile units.

One way out might be to lease or sell outright the whole mountain top to a single licensee, leaving him free to sublet physical sites and frequencies to different users. The licensee would presumably pre-engineer the whole system (receivers and transmitters), spacing and charging each user so as to maximize total rental income.[23] But the question is whether unitary management would emerge efficiently, if at all, through individual negotiation alone, via an interfirm agreement, merger, or otherwise, or whether any such solution would initially require explicit federal designation of spatial and temporal tenure arrangements, with subsequent lease/sale to the highest bidder.

Another approach might be for the government to award special leases with contingency provisions requiring that, if *x* or *y* should occur, then the lessees must install this or that filter, trap, or other equipment to correct the transmitter or receiver intermodulation. Once again, would something comparable to such a pre-engineered system in fact emerge spontaneously, and at no higher cost, from the free trading of radiation rights?[24]

In short, cost externalities will pose a potent economic obstacle to the emergence of any efficient market system through private contract and common law. And this is true notwithstanding the technical advances just described.

Benefit externalities pose still another impediment to market efficiency, although it is easier to handle through appropriate regulation. The broadcaster's access to virtually all resource inputs, including spectrum, will now be nonoptimal simply because advertiser-supported broadcast television cannot collect payments from all who view its programs. The institution of pay-TV would presumably eliminate many such externalities.[25] Under the present system of broadcaster-subsidized blue-ribbon programming, moreover, external public service grants-in-aid might help handle still others. Meanwhile the obstacle posed for an efficient spectrum market seems quite clear. This is true also of scien-

[23] See generally Joint Technical Advisory Committee, *Spectrum Engineering: The Key to Progress*, Supp. 6.

[24] For a definition of spectrum rights and a formulation of general rules assessing liability that purport to optimize the degree of permissible intermodulation interference, see De Vany et al., "Property System for Allocation of the Spectrum," pp. 1512–18, 1520–22.

[25] See J. Minasian, "Television Pricing and the Theory of Public Goods," *Journal of Law and Economics* (October 1964), pp. 77–80; and P. Samuelson, "Public Goods and Subscription Television," *Journal of Law and Economics* (October 1964), pp. 81–83.

tific, educational, and governmental spectrum users, which are equally unable to collect direct payments for all the services they render.

The analysis of economic obstacles to a full-fledged market does not imply that valuable work cannot now be undertaken to define spectrum use rights, specify reciprocal rights and obligations for rightholders, assign liability for infringements, and generally formulate statutory rules to eliminate such difficulties. As one approach among several, freely transferable rights may well merit more scrutiny than many government officials apparently believe. But the problems just described, together with the noneconomic objections reviewed later in this chapter, make it quite clear that we must continue to explore other options as well.

This necessity is further underscored by the major simplifying assumptions which even the most painstaking of recent efforts to construct a property system for market allocation has had to make. For these assumptions appear to raise questions about the scheme's general relevance to the spectrum. For example, property rights are deliberately defined only for the 50–1,000 Mc/s region, a band free of those intractable interference problems which now plague radiation in the HF radio and AM broadcast services where international considerations also complicate matters.[26] However, the 50–1,000 Mc/s region accounted for only one-half the estimated value output associated with spectrum usage in 1962. Indeed on a per megacycle basis this actually worked out at a slightly lower rate than the output associated with the band below 30 Mc/s (see Table 5). Nor is it clear precisely how, if at all, the property rights analysis could be applied to the federal government users which now occupy exclusively over one-fourth of the region under scrutiny and share another 8 per cent with nongovernment users.

Furthermore, the proposed rights are explicitly defined for transmitter (and not receiver) owners.[27] Yet in a very real sense, broadcast transmitters and receivers both share the TV spectrum. Unlike the situation in other services, moreover, separate parties own the two components. Spectrum economy for TV transmitters is therefore possible only if the set owners are willing to buy higher-priced sets where expensive nonspectrum inputs are substituted for free spectrum. But will they be so motivated unless they too can sell the spectrum which their more costly narrow-band sets would release to the same next-best users who then seek the transmitter owners' spectrum? That is, how much higher a price must (say) land mobile users pay a television licensee to cut

[26] See De Vany et al., "Property System for Allocation of the Spectrum," p. 1502.

[27] Ibid., p. 1518.

his transmitter bandwidth in half where the set owners' sole incentive to cooperate is to continue to receive a particular station's programs at all, or at least as clearly as at present?

Incentives for the set owners to accommodate to the proposed transaction will clearly be far greater where they too hold rights to spectrum, that is, reception rights. But in that case, may not the transactions needed to negotiate optimal levels of interference become as multipartied as those which already plague transmitter owners in the AM broadcast, HF radio, and radar bands? May not individual negotiation then become too costly and unwieldy to make such transactions attractive? These considerations are too important to be excluded from painstaking review in any scheme of property rights deliberately limited to the TV broadcast and mobile radio bands.[28]

NONECONOMIC OBSTACLES TO A FULL-FLEDGED SPECTRUM MARKET

The major opposition to a full-fledged spectrum market, and even to market-type systems, arises from several subjective judgments of the frequency management establishment. For the most part, these judgments are grounded on untested assumptions regarding the consistency of such markets with prevailing regulatory doctrine. Indeed, noneconomic considerations may be so persuasive today just because policymakers incorrectly equate market incentives with a full-fledged market and fail to distinguish the latter from management systems that utilize shadow prices, user charges, or stratified auctions.[29] Some of the government's objections to markets or market-type systems, which have been mentioned briefly, may now be examined in greater detail.

The U.S. Image Abroad

One major obstacle to serious consideration of the merits of any international spectrum market has been the government's fear that it would price out the less affluent newcomer nations. Government officials believe that the U.S. image abroad is already damaged by neo-Marxist

---

[28] One further indication of the difficulty of limiting the definition of rights to transmitter owners appears in the radio astronomy service. Radio astronomy has no emission rights at all, but its reception rights are all-important and must be rigorously protected.

[29] Although too often blurred in the literature, these important distinctions were clarified and made explicit in W. Jones, "Use and Regulation of the Radio Spectrum: Report on a Conference," *Washington University Law Quarterly* (Spring 1968), pp. 85–105.

stereotypes about monopoly capitalism and economic imperialism and that the serious exploration of any scheme to sell rights to the highest bidder among nations could only exacerbate foreign sensitivities.[30]

They have apparently discounted the possibility that a redefinition of rights coterminous with national boundaries could enable the poorer nations to share in spectrum value by leasing theirs to others, without using it directly at all. Such a leasing system could hardly be interpreted as U.S. aggrandizement. If phased in gradually over time, this arrangement would raise far fewer questions of equity or political acceptability than any scheme to vest ownership (without compensation to the government) in those who currently use it.

Perhaps the exploration of any such international system has seemed too risky in view of the questions it raises about the defensibility, equity, and efficiency of present allocations, wherein the U.S. figures as the major user of spectrum. For it is hard to accept at face value the apparent belief of high U.S. policy-makers that the mere exploration of any lease or sale system would be greeted abroad with great suspicion.[31] As the major user of spectrum beyond its borders, this nation may appear to have most to lose from any such change. But even future U.S. access to new spectral regions (as for satellites) could be impaired by claim-staking developing nations with no other recourse. A U.N.-supervised international spectrum-leasing system geared to sustained U.N. funding has been proposed as one way to phase in market-type incentives internationally without compromising U.S. interests. Since the United States is already the chief financial supporter of the United Nations, it is urged that, on balance, the United States need pay no more under such a scheme than it now pays.[32]

---

[30] See K. Norton, Annex of Letter from K. A. Norton to Arthur J. Goldberg, Aug. 14, 1965, analyzing letter from James D. O'Connell, Director of Telecommunications Management, to Norton, July 10, 1964 (Boulder, Colo.: Environmental Science Services Administration, Institute for Telecommunication Sciences, 1964, unofficial multilith).

[31] One recent outstanding exception that suggests that the climate may eventually change appears in Task Force Report, Ch. VIII, pp. 28–38, 63–64. See also the searching prior outside study, commissioned by the Task Force, of the economics of spectrum management, "Electromagnetic Spectrum Management: Alternatives and Experiments," App. G to Staff Paper No. 7 of President's Task Force on Communications Policy (U.S. Department of Commerce, Clearinghouse for Federal Scientific and Technical Information, June 1969), elaborated in De Vany et al., "Property System for Allocation of the Spectrum."

[32] See K. Norton, *The Five-Dimensional Electromagnetic Spectrum Resource* (Boulder, Colo.: Environmental Science Services Administration, Institute for Telecommunication Sciences, rev. December 1967, unofficial multilith), App. 10, pp. 1–4, Annex to Letter to Dean Rusk, July 6, 1965; Letter to Sen. Warren G. Magnuson, June 26, 1964; and Letter to A. M. Andrus, May 14, 1963.

There are, on the other hand, obvious difficulties in converting at this late date to any system of "contiguous jurisdiction." At present, nations secure rights to use spectrum on a first-come-first-served basis by notifying the ITU. But under a system of "contiguous jurisdiction," each nation would hold exclusive emission and admission rights for all the spectrum coterminous with its national boundaries[33] and buy or sell use rights accordingly. Any such move today would raise serious practical and political problems—all the difficulties of dislodging well-entrenched incumbents or charging them for occupancy they have hitherto enjoyed gratis. Rights could not be readily vested in the present technically advanced occupants unless they were willing to pay compensation, presumably to the less-developed countries. It is therefore easy to see why the former should hesitate to move in this direction, but less clear why the developing nations are equally reticent.

Meckling outlines the path of contiguous jurisdiction that the international community might have taken but did not:

1. Contiguous jurisdiction would have resolved the question of who (what nations) would capture the value of the newly discovered resources with far less dissension than we have experienced. Since each nation would have had admission and emission control coterminous with its geographic boundaries, each would have enjoyed some part of their value, and there would have been no occasion for the objection levelled at the priority system that the share of value a nation has received is a function of the rate at which it developed the use of radio. Even the incentive to claim-staking that characterized the priority system would have been eliminated.

2. The evolution of clearly defined rights would have been fostered—rights for which the nations of the world would gradually have developed more and more respect. By covering the admission as well as the emission side the specification of rights would have been made symmetrically complete.

3. The suggestion that nations *pay* for using other nations' "airwaves," implied the development of a truly international market for frequencies, a market that would have enabled use of individual frequencies to adjust to where their value was greatest. . . . In brief, nations could have been induced to auction off some of their frequencies to the highest bidder even though the . . . . bidder might be in some other

[33] The dual character of radiation rights and their bearing on national jurisdiction over spectrum, are expounded at length in W. Meckling, "History of International Allocation and Assignment," a paper presented at the Conference on Economics of Regulated Public Utilities held at the University of Chicago, June 20–25, 1965. Meckling draws a useful distinction between rights of "emission" and "admission."

country. It is important in this context to distinguish between exchanges or sales of (government) dominion over a frequency and exchanges of the right to use a frequency. What is important from an efficiency point of view is only that potential users have the opportunity to acquire rights to use frequencies by bidding for them. It is much more difficult to induce a nation to give up sovereignty over spectrum than to induce it to permit an outside party (as the highest bidder) to use that spectrum, subject to whatever laws and conditions the sovereign nation chooses to impose.[34]

The path we did take was that of noncontiguous jurisdiction with access to spectrum on a claim-staking basis and the ITU as a central clearinghouse. This has been fraught with many problems. As Meckling notes, to capture the value of their own spectrum today nations are often forced to use it prematurely and in less efficient ways than other potential users could. In the absence of rights to exclude others and hence to charge them for access rights, the developing nations simply lack any incentive to allow in the more efficient users with the more advanced capabilities. Even assuming that the development of common hardware standards for the international fixed, mobile, and space services might in principle have emerged under a system of contiguous jurisdiction and freely transferable rights,[35] it is still doubtful whether at this late date the tide can be turned and a movement initiated in that direction.

Nevertheless, it is one thing to dismiss an international spectrum market because it requires the definition of contiguous rights and a costly adjustment by incumbents who have the political power to thwart it. To go further and rationalize it by citing fears that the U.S. image must thereby suffer reveals either a lack of candor, a misreading of economic incentives, or both. This misreading becomes even more patent in the outright rejection of a more modest spectrum-leasing system which clearly could be phased in gradually and better reconciled with the requirements of national sovereignty.[36]

In the long run, no incumbent nation can benefit from an international allocation system which places a heavy premium on all countries'

[34] Ibid., pp. 31–32.

[35] Meckling contends that equipment costs, sharing possibilities, and the premium placed on reliability and convenience would have induced all nations to "use uniform frequencies around the world for mobile services" (pp. 42–43). "[E]quipment cost considerations would call for using a limited number of frequencies in communicating with a given mobile unit, while time-sharing suggests standardizing frequencies so that different mobile units can use the same bands" (p. 43).

[36] On the advantage of permitting nations to sell use rights in spectrum instead of outright dominion over it, see ibid., p. 32.

staking excessive claims on all newly available frequencies, whatever the economic merits. As a practical matter, to be sure, claim-staking by one country need not keep another from using the same frequency, provided that the IFRB foresees no interference or that none actually materializes because the original registrant does not use the frequency. Even so, the latecomer may have to accept a secondary status, contingent on the firstcomer's subsequent usage. Hence, unless we are willing to condone the developing nations' practice of buying telecommunications systems far in advance of their effective needs through aid from the U.N., the U.S., or the U.S.S.R., we have no choice but to open up other options that would enable them to benefit from "their" spectrum without actually using it.

The bearing of these international considerations on a domestic market for spectrum is far less clear. The phasing in of a domestic market is presumably less of a problem just because the current rights can be more readily vested in the rightholders than is true where the incumbents are advanced nations. There may of course be good reason to oppose a free spectrum market, in favor, say, of an auction scheme under zonal constraints. But to oppose a domestic market simply because a bona fide international market poses special problems reveals an erroneous view of the necessary relationship between domestic and international mechanisms in this field.

International Constraints on a Domestic Market

There are, however, a number of more substantive international constraints on the creation of a domestic market. Even when radiation can be confined to U.S. territorial limits (as in large portions of the VHF, UHF, and microwave bands), the character of the international fixed, mobile, broadcast, and space services virtually requires the close cooperation and coordination of many foreign partners.[37] Furthermore, other seemingly domestic services may require comparable foreign cooperation and coordination, either because the service, though confinable, operates within several hundred miles of our territorial borders, as in the case of land mobile, FM, or TV broadcasting, or because, though far from our borders, the service is technically hard to confine, as in AM broadcasting and HF fixed service.[38]

Line-of-sight transmission technology appears to facilitate substan-

[37] S. Myers, *Technical Aspects or Considerations of Frequency Assignment*, p. 2.
[38] Ibid., p. 6.

tial national discretion in spectrum utilization today in the case of domestic point-point services in the VHF, UHF, or microwave regions and in portions of the domestic land mobile or TV broadcast services. However, as previously noted, basic constraints are imposed by the economic and security advantages of international hardware standardization and by the rule of "common use of common frequencies."

Perhaps the only really substantive international constraint is subsumed under this last factor. As noted in Chapter I, frequencies allocated to a strictly domestic service, and thereby ostensibly suitable for a market, may subsequently be needed for a new international service. To accommodate the new space satellite and radio astronomy services, ITU members have had to clear certain domestic bands and/or make subsequent costly internal adjustments in the hardware of a number of other prior spectrum users. Such accommodation was doubtless rendered more difficult and costly just because the several nations had failed to synchronize their spectral location of various domestic services during the wartime hiatus of ITU meetings.

The transferability of spectrum among alternative domestic services would clearly be constrained by such factors—all the more in the absence of an international market for spectrum or of domestic markets within foreign countries. Whether a domestic U.S. market is nonetheless conceivable really depends on the frequency with which such far-reaching technical changes are likely to occur and the adequacy of eminent domain in handling them. Such a market would in any case best be limited to services that use the line-of-sight technology, subject to border-area and regional coordination.

Social Values in a Domestic Spectrum Market

A full-fledged domestic market is generally opposed as likely to prevent wide diffusion of rights among all potential users and adequate accommodation of public, educational, charitable, and scientific users, both of which are major social norms.[39] The fear of "spectrum concentration" is really nothing new in frequency management circles. Numerous FCC policies have long sought to forestall concentrated control of broadcast facilities, tantamount to control of the spectrum itself. A deep concern over "monopolizing the airwaves" harks back to the very

---

[39] See colloquy cited in Jones, "Use and Regulation of the Radio Spectrum," p. 92. See also Meckling, "Management of the Frequency Spectrum," pp. 32–33; House Committee on Appropriations, 87th Cong., 1st sess., Hearings on Independent Offices Appropriation for 1962, 1961, Pt. 1, pp. 633–34; and Hearings on S. 2926, Senate Commerce Committee, 83rd Cong., 2d sess., 1954, p. 20.

outset of broadcast regulation[40] and may indeed help explain: (a) the early and continued attempts to limit signal power of the big clear channel licensees; (b) the rigorous limits imposed on multiple station ownership generally and on dual station ownership within the same market; and (c) the consequent rise of the national networks and of a network-affiliate relation subject to FCC review, hopefully, as a way to reconcile the economies of large-scale programming with the diffusion of economic and political power.

Our experience in broadcasting actually suggests that safeguards can prevent undesirable changes in industry structure even in a market system.[41] The absence of a market for spectrum has not prevented the wealthier interests from increasingly acquiring broadcast facilities. In a market system, spectrum would go, not to those best able to buy it but to those most willing to do so; i.e., for whom it had greatest relative value, or who could use it most efficiently.[42] The antitrust laws and procompetitive element in the public interest standard both provide at least potential safeguards against tendencies towards excessive concentration and monopoly control.

These are matters to which we return in the following chapter. It will serve here to note only the deep-seated conviction among broadcast regulators that any market for spectrum would seriously exacerbate the monopoly problem; and that, once the broadcasters had bought their spectrum outright, the basis for many diffusionist licensing policies would be badly undermined. Valid or not, therefore, these regulatory fears still constitute a serious impediment to change.

In regard to public users, on the other hand, it is indeed true that, once rights are bought and sold in a market, the political feasibility of stockpiling spectrum for high-priority services will become more difficult. For public accountability and budgetary review regarding governmental usage would become more rigorous when all allocational decisions must be made in full light of the market value of spectrum. As a consequence, the allocators' discretion would presumably decline, as would the public users' discretion to combine spectrum with other inputs at will. Small

[40] See H. Warner, *Radio and Television Law* (Washington: Bender, 1948), p. 546. Most Congressional concern in the 1920s was over monopolization of the radio equipment and receiver industry. See House Committee on Merchant Marine and Fisheries, 68th Cong., 1st sess., Hearings on HR 7357, 1924, pp. 40, 71, 95, 131, 203; *Congressional Record*, LXIV (1924), pp. 2336–42, 2781–84. But note also concern shown in these hearings over monopolization of program distribution, pp. 10 ff., also at 40–51, 80–98, 157, 207.

[41] See, e.g., H. Levin, "Regulatory Efficiency, Reform and FCC," *Georgetown Law Journal* (Fall 1961), pp. 29–31.

[42] See Coase, "The Federal Communications Commission," pp. 19–21.

wonder then that spectrum managers and the big government users often appear opposed to almost any move toward a market system.

How defensible are these fears? To say that public users cannot collect payment for all the benefits they generate is true, but quite beside the point. This is true of virtually any public goods; it explains why the government normally tax-finances their production and distribution. In other words, the inability of public users to retain their radio frequencies in a spectrum market would merely signify their failure to substantiate a claim on public fiscal resources against the counterclaims of rival services. For such reasons public officials often view free access to the public spectrum as a convenient safeguard of vital public services.

The economic and fiscal objections to this tacit circumvention of the budgetary process are well known. But they have not prevailed in other fields and therefore provide little hope that this misconception will not continue to underscore the regulator's suspicions about markets and market-type modifications of the present system.

The alleged subversion of broadcast program balance and diversity in any spectrum market raises still other issues. The presumption here is twofold: first, that there are significant noneconomic standards by which the broadcast service can be properly evaluated; and second, that an economically efficient allocation of spectrum does not necessarily mean that all relevant dimensions of industry performance will be optimized.

The most explicit statement[43] of these fears can be pieced together from the arguments cited in opposition to the distribution of broadcast licenses by auction, namely that:

1. Large wealthy buyers of TV stations who have ready access to an imperfect capital market and whose strategy requires entry into choice urban centers notwithstanding a severe scarcity of licenses, will have greater incentives and resources than other companies to absorb any public license charge and to bid up station sales prices accordingly.

2. The result will be greater concentration of broadcast facilities in fewer hands, greater geographic concentration, a bidding up of capital charges (depending on the degree to which buyers absorb the initial license charge), new pressures to spread the higher capital charges over increased time sales, and a cutback in public service programming and in general program balance and diversity toward that end.

3. The danger of program deterioration is further aggravated by the elusive character of the Commission's service standards, for, against the

[43] The statement is spelled out more fully in H. Levin, "Federal Control of Entry in the Broadcast Industry," *Journal of Law and Economics* (October 1962), pp. 57–58.

present improbability of being forced to live up to his promised program standards should higher capital charges make this impossible, a licensee must weigh the certainty of losing all rights if he fails to bid enough.

If their logic is valid, the opponents of spectrum markets may have stumbled on an extremely sensitive point and one with great political significance. The frequent trading of broadcast stations over time *has* bid up sale prices with those same adverse effects on ownership and area concentration predicted to result from the buying and selling of new licenses or renewal rights. (See Chapter XIII and Appendix C.) Forward shifting of license charges could well have similar consequences. Even the FCC's fears that auctions will so bid up sales prices and capital charges as to result in program deterioration and narrowing of program choice are not entirely unreasonable. They are based on two assumptions accepted by many students of this industry: (1) that the public service responsibilities which broadcast licensing now imposes on broadcasters deter them from seeking maximum profits, and (2) that the increment to capital charges caused by inflated sales prices may act to reduce both a station buyer's capacity and his incentives to maintain public service and program balance.

One possible answer to these "dangers" is simply that they already exist under the present centralized nonprice system. There is little reason to expect competitive bidding for federally defined rights to raise station prices and capital charges still more, above the point to which the trading of stations has already brought them.[44] But once again, past experience makes one wonder whether economic logic will finally prevail or whether regulatory concern over the impact of any organized spectrum market on broadcast program balance and diversity will remain a continuing obstacle to innovative steps in that direction.

The Narrowing of Administrative Discretion

There is of course no question that, wherever allocators encounter adjudicable property rights, administrative discretion in furthering any number of regulatory priorities will be narrowed. Taking these priorities as a sine qua non of public policy, it is at least understandable that spectrum markets should for so long have been viewed with a jaundiced eye.

For this very reason, indeed, the Communications Act initially directed that the United States should retain sole possession of the radio spectrum and that licensed private users must explicitly waive rights of

---

[44] See analysis of this point, ibid., pp. 59–64.

continuing access on the basis of prior use. Those who would bring "order out of chaos" in the late 1920s rightly believed that property rights in spectrum would seriously impair the administrative flexibility needed to dislodge incumbents and otherwise keep industry structure consistent with emerging social priorities in the wake of then unpredictable technological change.[45]

Any serious move to create bona fide property rights today would be viewed with similar alarm. Yet the spectrum managers' concern about administrative rigidities reflects their long experience with the present centralized system wherein de facto private property rights *have* made allocational decisions more difficult.[46] Here the question is twofold. Do property rights themselves so much as the absence of a free market system make for these rigidities, since the only way one can now be entirely sure of access rights precisely when one wants them is to stockpile spectrum for long periods? And are the favored regulatory priorities threatened by free trading in spectrum rights in fact worth safeguarding through central allocation, cumbersome and inefficient as the present system appears to be?

Similar frictions and constraints apparently plague the central allocation of rights among government users too, even without private property rights. It can be argued further that those priorities subverted by a market-type system which are not attainable anyway without a degree of economic inefficiency that we are unwilling to incur ought not to be pursued. At least, one can question the candor of trying to implement *any* set of regulatory priorities without considering their full costs.

Finally, the fact that de facto property rights in spectrum may impair the working of a centralized system through stockpiling and protracted litigation by no means implies that they must also impair a market-type system *once it is operating*. This depends on how the rights are defined and how well the market works. The problem meanwhile is that allocators do not anticipate the institution of anything so extreme as a bona fide market, whereas they do rightly see even limited property rights as obstacles to their unencumbered discretion under the present system. Thus here too the frequency management establishment can be expected

---

[45] The optimal length of the license term was directly an issue here. See Hearings on HR 7357, pp. 15 ff., 27, 206–7. See also letter from Secretary Hoover to Representative White dated December 5, 1924 in *Congressional Record*, LXVIII (1927), pp. 2572–73. See finally Federal Radio Commission, *First Annual Report* (U.S. Government Printing Office, 1927), p. 1.

[46] Alleged property rights in spectrum figure (unsuccessfully) in early FCC attempts to reduce the number of radio stations on the air. See citations in H. Levin, *Broadcast Regulation and Joint Ownership of Media* (New York University Press, 1960), Ch. 7, fn. 36.

to oppose almost any attempt to introduce legal property rights unless perhaps they can somehow be shown to leave basic administrative discretion intact.

The Problem of Vested Rights

Still another reason for the regulators' resistance to a market system is the fear of triggering thoroughgoing opposition by users who had hitherto obtained their spectrum for nothing and would therefore fight bitterly against charges of any sort. These fears are understandable and surely must not be minimized as critical impediments to any move to a full-fledged spectrum market. But neither must they be permitted to obfuscate the varying ease with which different modified market-type systems could in fact be instituted, or the possibility of "phasing in" any system gradually, to minimize the initial disruption. It is also important to distinguish between the practical enormity of any total overhaul of the present system and the special opposition grounded in the incumbent rightholders' vested interests.

Even the most ardent critics of the current framework concede its probable irreversibility. Coase observes: "[T]he belief that broadcasting . . . is unique and requires regulation of a kind which would be unthinkable in the other media . . . is now [so] firmly held *as perhaps to be beyond the reach of critical examination.*"[47] The same has been said about radiation rights more generally, at home and internationally. It may also be true, as Coase writes, that:

> The history of regulation . . . in broadcasting . . . demonstrates the crucial importance of events in the early days of a new development in determining long-run governmental policy. It also suggests that lawyers and economists should not be so overwhelmed by the emergence of new technologies as to change the existing legal and economic system without first making quite sure that this is required.[48]

So far as radiation rights go, however, the cat is clearly well out of the bag. The question is: Where do we go from here, and how?

Short of the most extreme abuse, the momentum of an ongoing system goes far to explain the regulators' widespread reluctance to consider any market system seriously. Numerous skills would be made obsolete, deeply ingrained habits of thought scotched, and the certainty derived from having immediate access for priority uses lost. Whenever

[47] Coase, "The Federal Communications Commission," p. 40. Italics added.
[48] Ibid.

an ongoing system, however imperfect, is compared to any hypothetical alternative, however persuasive, the existing system has all the advantages of actuality. Given the far-reaching institutional changes required, this is especially true of spectrum. It is true all the more because modified market-type remedies, though far from ideal, can still be instituted to improve the situation.[49]

On the other hand, what of the regulators' reluctance to precipitate the protracted opposition in judicial, political, and regulatory channels almost certain to meet any attempt to charge spectrum users for rights hitherto given away? Here, as elsewhere, a review of alternatives is in order.

Our objective in this chapter has not in any case been to anticipate all conceivable ways that the many critical noneconomic objections to freely transferable rights might be met. But even its staunchest advocates will concede that concerted political opposition will very likely preclude the creation of a full-fledged market in the foreseeable future. Therefore, we shall now consider in greater detail those modified market-type or administrative options which represent the real contributions of the market model to spectrum management.

---

[49] The fact that markets are not a novel mechanism to distribute resources by no means minimizes the magnitude of the legal-institutional changes required to introduce them into the current centralized nonprice spectrum system. But see discussion, ibid., pp. 17–18.

CHAPTER V

TOWARD A REGULATED MARKET-TYPE SYSTEM WITH PRICES

The analysis in Chapter IV has held that there is much to commend something less radical than a full-fledged market for spectrum. Properly conceived, a number of middle-range options could help us overcome the major obstacles to such a system—high enforcement and transfer costs—in a fashion that would also sidestep important sources of political opposition.

Ranked inversely to their nearness to the current nonprice management framework, the major options and sub-options were listed in Table 6. From an economic point of view, there seems little question that, if we had it all to do over again, a system of freely transferable rights that worked would be by far the best. However, such a system seems farthest from current real-world practicalities and the option least likely to gain national acceptance. Nor does the version discussed most widely of late, which is based on interband auctions, transferable rights, and their eventual sale outright (options A–2, 3), appear viable in any case.

On the other hand, progress has been made in giving greater weight to economic considerations through administrative techniques like frequency clearance and secondary rights (option E). More work can and should be done on this approach, and valuable advances can probably be made. But if we are serious about articulating economic factors into spectrum management today we cannot stop with this administrative attempt to find "equivalents" for the pricing system. Just as we are nowhere near ready for a full-fledged market for spectrum, so we are already well beyond the point where we can stop with a purely administrative approach.

As noted above, we really need a more eclectic strategy that is sufficiently close to the current framework to be relevant, contains enough economic merit to make it attractive on that score as an important step forward, and is amenable to being phased in gradually so as to reduce the likelihood of lethal opposition by those with "line authority." And because today's managers and users of spectrum will understandably feel that an ongoing reality, however imperfect, is decidedly preferable to the paper promises of any hypothetical ideal, the allocational innovator must bear a heavy burden of proof.

The approach that best meets these requirements would be a sequential strategy grounded in options D, C, and B–2 of Table 6: shadow prices, user charges, and intraband auction values.[1]

MARKET SIMULATION AND SHADOW PRICES

The term "shadow prices" as used here means the maximum sums that users of spectrum would be willing to pay rather than do without some marginal amount of bandwidth. These are at best only very tentative and imperfect approximations of the true shadow prices, whether the "commercial" prices which would result from unregulated (perfect) competition or the "ideal" prices that would measure marginal social opportunity cost for all users, public and private.[2] A distinguishing characteristic of shadow prices is their estimation of the value of spectrum without any actual buying, selling, or leasing of frequencies. Once shadow prices are calculated, the spectrum manager has three options: to allocate spectrum accordingly; to override the "economic verdict" for cause; or to translate the shadow price into a set of charges on occupied bandwidth.

Under the third option, a tax on user A equal to the extra costs incurred without some marginal unit of spectrum would reduce A's use to a degree depending on his elasticity of derived demand for spectrum.[3] If A were a big commercial user, the "commercial" shadow price for

---

[1] The President's Task Force on Communications Policy emphasized user charges. See its *Final Report* (U.S. Government Printing Office, 1968), Ch. VIII, pp. 34–37. It also made (pp. 37–38) proposals to "permit greater transferability of licenses among legitimate spectrum users within broad service classifications." (Publication cited below as Task Force Report.) Shadow pricing is explicitly endorsed by the National Academy of Engineering in *Report on Selected Topics in Telecommunications: Final Report to Department of Housing and Urban Development*, November 1968, p. 54. The kind of auction scheme outlined below, however, appears in neither document and differs substantially from the one described in "Electromagnetic Spectrum Management: Alternatives and Experiments," App. G to Staff Paper No. 7 of President's Task Force on Communications Policy (U.S. Department of Commerce, Clearinghouse for Federal Scientific and Technical Information, June 1969).

[2] J. Bain, R. Caves, and J. Margolis, *Northern California's Water Industry* (The Johns Hopkins Press for Resources for the Future, 1966), pp. 240–42.

[3] Ibid., pp. 252–53.

spectrum would fall accordingly. By the same token, the prevailing shadow price at the outset (as inferred empirically from the shadow demand price for spectrum) could give a rough feel of the spectrum value in question. This could further help set a proper unit rental charge to apply against the total volume of occupied spectrum. Rental rates could also be set on an arbitrary flat basis or according to auction values derived in selected services.

Even assuming a systematic governmental estimation effort, little more than the crudest shadow prices are likely to be available for a long time. Furthermore, shadow price values will presumably reflect economic values in the current rather than the potential uses of spectrum. Yet, in view of the necessarily arbitrary element in allocational decisions today, even crude measurements are better than none. Finally, it should be possible to look to the actual trade-offs implicit in the existing stock of communications hardware for some tentative feel of the actual values involved. This would obviate any excessive dependence on the costs the hardware designer says he would incur without x units of spectrum.

Basically, what we want to know is how net value output (net of exclusionary cost) will vary as additional bandwidth is allocated to A and B, or reallocated as between A and B. Therefore, even crude estimates of the value of spectrum to alternative users must consider: (a) the extra value of output generated in either service after an allocation of additional bandwidth; (b) the extra costs incurred by either service; and (c) the amount of extra bandwidth allocated.

Strictly speaking, the relative value of some small unit of bandwidth to alternative services can be estimated only if we take into account all three factors. For in many real-world cases the contending services require different amounts of extra bandwidth, and hence the extra net value output cannot be directly compared. Where the probable value output and exclusionary costs both remain constant, however, the service that uses less bandwidth should clearly be favored on economic grounds. Where the services use comparable bandwidth, the one that generates greater net output (over and above the extra costs due to exclusion) should be favored.

Finally, if the net economic value output is constant or even favors A over B, the spectrum managers may still conceivably favor B over A when the regulatory priority associated with B's output (safety, security, or education) is demonstrably higher than A's (industrial usage). But even here, applicants' claims about "merit" uses will obviously be subjected to much closer scrutiny under an allocation system that uses shadow prices.

For illustrative purposes let us now consider two hypothetical examples. In Case I, we postulate competing claims on a band of micro-wave frequencies by a space satellite and a terrestrial microwave system; in Case II, rival claims by land mobile and TV broadcast systems on a designated portion of the VHF spectrum. In both cases we want to estimate the maximum price the rival claimants can be presumed to be willing to pay rather than do without the frequencies in question. This will in turn be derived from the hypothetical trade-offs between band-width and other factor inputs in generating varying numbers of com-munications circuits, with varying degrees of reliability. In Case I, the two services are assumed to have comparable priority ratings; in Case II this issue is left open.

Space Satellites and Terrestrial Microwave

In this example we shall assume that the two systems seek the same frequencies, that this spectrum is added to prior allocations to each service and is in that sense a marginal increment; and that both services are essentially domestic. This latter assumption permits us to abstract from major international complications. Further to simplify the analysis we also postulate a microwave band sufficiently utilized, and earth sta-tions sufficiently numerous, to make sharing uneconomic if not technically impossible. We postulate, finally, that both services seek more spectrum to generate 4,000-mile voice circuits at lower costs than hitherto, with some acceptable degree of reliability.

The "no sharing" assumption may strike some readers as unrealistic, and it does clearly abstract from the many interesting possibilities which spectrum sharing in this field offers today. Others may consider the as-sumption a valid projection of long-term trends wherein satellites are already predicted as eventually requiring exclusive allocations of their own. We do not wish to prejudge these issues or to minimize the im-portant economic and technical trade-offs which could help us *now* to accommodate space satellites and terrestrial relays within the same microwave bands.

Trade-offs hypothesized in Table 7 could indeed be modified to reflect some of these considerations. However, we deliberately exclude them from what follows in the interest of analytical simplicity and clar-ity. This seems appropriate in the present instance where we want to formulate a fairly elementary exposition of relative shadow price calcu-lations for hypothetical allocational purposes only.

Holding constant the state of the arts and industry structure, crude estimates of shadow demand prices will now be very tentatively under-taken as follows. First, for satellites we may analyze the trade-offs be-

Table 7. Hypothetical Dollar Trade-Offs between Satellite Bandwitdh, Power, Antenna Diameter, and Type of Modulation, in Generating Varying Numbers of 4,000-Mile Voice Circuits

Option	Satellite type	Modulation	Cost of satellite with launch ($ million)	Antenna diameter	Cost of antenna ($ million)	Cost of earth station[a] ($ million)	Degrees kelvin	Power (watts)	Bandwidth (Mc/s)	Number of voice circuits
S-1	II	A	6.5	85'	1.7	5.0	50	20	100	240
S-2	III	A	7.5	85'	1.7	5.0	50	240	500	1,200
S-3	IIIa	B	7.5	85'	1.7	5.25[b]	50	240	1,000	2,400
S-4	III	A	7.5	210'	10.4[c]	13.7	50	240	100	1,200
S-5	III	A	7.5	125'	3.7[c]	7.0	50	240	500	2,400

Total system costs

Option	2-sats, 2-stations		1-sat, 2-stations	
	Total ($ million)	$ per 4,000-mile circuit	Total ($ million)	$ per 4,000-mile circuit
S-1	23.0	95,830	16.5	68,750
S-2	25.0	20,833	17.5	14,583
S-3	25.5	10,625	18.0	7,500
S-4	42.4	35,333	34.9	29,083
S-5	29.0	12,083	21.5	8,958

Source: Derived largely from unofficial estimates of ComSat staff members (see text footnote 4).
[a] Cost of station = cost of antenna plus fixed cost of $3.3 million.
[b] Arbitrary sum of $250,000 to develop new improved modulation.
[c] Minimum antenna costs (without R&D cost).

121

tween power, antenna diameter, modulation, and frequency bandwidth in generating varying numbers of voice circuits. Other things being equal, the extra costs associated with some specified bandwidth reduction would represent the maximum sum the space satellite service would be willing to pay for that amount of bandwidth.

Second, because virtually all the long-haul microwave systems operate with 500 Mc/s bandwidth, we must devise some other way to examine the implications of bandwidth variations. Here we will analyze the trade-offs between building reliability against rain outages and fading through the use of extra protection frequencies (frequency diversity) and through antennas, transmitters, towers, and buildings (space diversity). The value of spectrum to any microwave system will be inferred from the net cost-savings in using the protection bandwidth for reliability over the costs of achieving comparable reliability through space diversity and using the released protection bandwidth for extra circuits instead.

Third, we would want to compare the cost of generating 4,000-mile voice circuits by both systems (terrestrial and satellite) within the same amount of bandwidth. The relative economic value of the designated spectrum to the two services can then be crudely estimated under the hypothetical postulated conditions.

In Table 7 are tabulated hypothetical data for several satellite options, designed to point up a number of conceivable trade-offs between bandwidth, power, antenna diameter, reliability, and modulation.[4] The basic technical trade-offs are then summarized in dollar terms by making a few heroic assumptions, and the dollar trade-offs appear in columns 12–15.

The most dramatic dollar savings per circuit occur in the move from a Type II to a more advanced Type III satellite. Here in the shift from satellite option #1 (S–1) to option #2 (S–2), a fivefold increase in bandwidth utilized (associated with the new technology) results in an 80 per cent reduction in per circuit costs.

A further doubling of bandwidth in the move from S–2 to S–3, with

---

[4] In drawing up this illustrative table I was greatly aided by the expertise of several ComSat staff members, although I assume personal responsibility for its use here. For a valuable source of background material on trade-offs between bandwidth and other inputs, see Communications Satellite Corporation, "Satellite Broadcasting, A Preliminary Report on Technical and Economic Aspects," rev. B, July 1969, unpublished, especially Appendices I–III; "Economic Comparisons of Alternative Domestic Satellite TV Systems—A Technical Memorandum," No. SAD-9-66, December 5, 1966, unpublished; and, most recently, National Academy of Sciences, *Useful Applications of Earth-Oriented Satellites—Broadcasting* (Panel No. 10), 1969, especially sections 2, 3, 5, and Appendix D.

antenna diameter and power constant, facilitates a further halving of per circuit costs, this time by means of a relatively modest technical improvement in type of modulation. In view of the technical changes associated with S–2, and to a lesser extent with S–3, one would thus far be reluctant to speak of trade-offs between spectrum and nonspectrum inputs as such. But such trade-offs do become clear in comparing S–3 with S–5. There, holding technology and power relatively constant, a halving of bandwidth from 1,000 Mc/s to 500 Mc/s is associated with a rise in per circuit costs of 14 to 19 per cent. Likewise, in moving from S–2 to S–4, bandwidth reduction of 80 per cent is associated with a rise in per circuit costs of 70 to 100 per cent. In both cases there is a clear trade-off between spectrum bandwidth and antenna diameter, all other factors remaining virtually constant.

Still another way to look at the trade-offs is to note the relation between rising bandwidth utilization and falling per circuit costs, moving from S–4, to S–5, to S–3; or, if the growth in demand for circuits were slower in the early years, in the move from S–4, to S–2, to S–3.

Such trade-offs facilitate no more than the crudest estimate of the maximum value of spectrum to the designer of space satellite hardware. But, more fully and systematically developed, they should help us construct a demand schedule for space satellite spectrum under the postulated conditions, as derived from the estimated savings in per circuit costs.

A comparable demand schedule could presumably be derived also from the cost-savings in allocating extra bandwidth to the terrestrial microwave systems, and here too the question is what happens at the margin. It must also be borne in mind once again that (a) shadow demand prices, let alone true shadow prices, are extremely hard to calculate in any but the crudest form; and (b) the postulated trade-offs would generate these crude estimates only with regard to existing technology and hardware, not with reference to other potential uses for the spectrum in question.[5] It must also be noted that (c) the postulated area of spectral overlap for a domestic satellite system is far greater, the consequent chances for systematic sharing far smaller, and the need for a hard choice far greater, than present factual realities indicate to be the case.

In Table 8 the estimated costs per 4,000-mile voice circuit for two types of long-haul microwave systems are tabulated. Estimates are also

---

[5] There is, however, some minor attempt to consider technological options in the satellite case in the distinction between Type II and Type III satellites and Types A and B modulation.

TABLE 8. HYPOTHETICAL COMPARATIVE COST DATA FOR TWO MICROWAVE RELAY SYSTEMS, EACH BUILDING RELIABILITY BY FREQUENCY OR SPACE DIVERSITY TECHNIQUES

Number of 2-way working channels	Number of 2-way protection channels	Bandwidth (Mc/s)	Total route costs for all channels	Number of voice circuits for all working channels	Costs per 4,000-mile voice circuit	Costs per 4,000-mile voice circuit per megacycle bandwidth
			M-1 System			
Frequency diversity						
(a) 10	2	500	$ 86,620,000	6,000	$14,436	$28.87
Space diversity						
(b) 10		500	120,257,000	6,000	20,042	40.08
(c) 12		500	130,670,000	7,200	18,148	39.29
			M-2 System			
Frequency diversity						
(a) 6	2	500	$131,940,000	10,800	$12,216	$24.43
Space diversity						
(b) 6		500	187,696,000	10,800	17,379	34.75
(c) 8		500	218,972,000	14,400	15,206	30.41

Source: Derived mainly from data provided by AT&T (see text, fn. 6–9).

included for building reliability into such systems by means of so-called frequency diversity and space diversity techniques.[6] The per circuit cost estimates permit a very tentative comparison with per circuit cost estimates for the satellite options. But because the two long-haul microwave systems both operate with 500 Mc/s bandwidth there is no easy way to make bandwidth trade-offs comparable to those in Table 7. Hence we have had instead to examine such trade-offs in the context of building system reliability.

In this latter regard, microwave system reliability can be defined in terms of outages due to rain, atmospheric fading, bursts of excessive noise, or other sudden departures from specified transmission standards.[7] To safeguard the desired level of reliability, frequency diversity employs one extra protection channel for varying numbers of working channels, depending on the type of system in question. The ratio is generally one protection channel for every five working channels for long-haul systems at 4 Gc/s or 6 Gc/s and a ratio of one to one for short-haul systems at 6 Gc/s or 11 Gc/s.[8] Space diversity is a more costly way to build system reliability, but it requires no extra spectrum space. It hedges against outages by using almost double the receiving and transmitting hardware, more switching equipment, higher antenna towers, greater power, and more floorspace. Thus space diversity uses 20 to 100 per cent less spectrum than frequency diversity but costs 25 to 33 per cent more.[9]

Before interpreting Table 8, let us make explicit the protection costs we have assumed in constructing it. These include under microwave

[6] The data tabulated here and examined below have benefited from AT&T expertise and, in particular, from "Response of AT&T to the FCC in Docket No. 15130: Reliability and Related Design Parameters of Microwave Radio Relay Communications Systems and Resultant Impact Upon Spectrum Utilization," especially pp. 21–35, on economic considerations of diversity systems. See also, AT&T "Notes on Economies of Scale," in FCC Docket No. 14650, Exhibit No. 64, items #7, #8, July 1964. Of value, finally, is the historical review of TD-2 and related systems in A. Dickieson, "The TD-32 Story," *Bell Laboratories Record* (October, November, and December 1967), pp. 283–89, 325–31, and 357–63. The conversion of data into "costs per 4,000-mile voice circuit" and the hypothetical comparisons of postulated microwave and satellite dollar trade-offs are of course my own.

[7] See "Response of AT&T in FCC Docket No. 15130," pp. 1–5.

[8] On the long-haul routes, the extra channels facilitate emergency restoral of service and routine maintenance without interim loss of protection. But on short-haul routes, even the one-for-one protection ratio may not suffice due to rain outages at 11 Gc/s. To cope with these dangers and to salvage its systems on these frequencies, Bell has instituted crossband diversity for short-haul systems in the 6 Gc/s and 11 Gc/s bands. Ibid., pp. 6–7.

[9] On the character of frequency diversity and space diversity techniques see ibid., pp. 6–9. Still other techniques to improve reliability can be derived from increased transmitter power and larger antennas, but here too the cost would be prohibitive.

system M–1, $10 million for frequency diversity and $44 million for space diversity; and under system M–2, $20 million and $76 million, respectively. On these assumptions, protection costs for M–1 run 11.5 per cent of total route costs for frequency diversity, but some 36.6 per cent for a comparable space diversity system. For system M–2, the respective costs range from 15.2 per cent for frequency diversity, to 40.5 per cent for space diversity. In each case, then, without extra bandwidth the desired level of reliability would require outlays between 2½ and 3 times greater relative to total route costs than would be the case with the extra spectrum. Even considering the extra circuits each system could generate by using its protection bandwidth for working circuits (the space diversity approach), these rough proportions still hold.

Derivable also from the data in Table 8 is the greater relative value of the spectrum in building reliability for either system (M–1 or M–2) than in generating extra circuits where extra antennas, towers, and transmitters would provide comparable reliability for all circuits. Looking at columns 1–3, 500 Mc/s of bandwidth can accommodate 12 two-way working channels for M–1, and 8 for M–2. Therefore, the bandwidth for 2 two-way protection channels must be roughly 83 Mc/s, and 125 Mc/s, respectively. The net value of this protection bandwidth can be inferred next from the *difference* between data on line (a) and line (c) in column 6. In system M–1, that is, 83 Mc/s of protection bandwidth are worth no less than the $3,712 in extra costs per 4,000-mile voice circuit which one incurs by using this bandwidth to generate new circuits instead, building reliability through space diversity. In system M–2, by the same token, the net value of the 125 Mc/s protection bandwidth would be the $2,990 in extra costs incurred per 4,000-mile voice circuit.

Taking the above figures one step further, finally, the extra bandwidth used for protection must be worth almost twice as much in cost-savings per voice circuit per Mc/s for system M–1 ($45) as for system M–2 ($24). From the viewpoint of spectrum utilization only, system M–1 thus appears to be the more economic of the two terrestrial systems.

At this point we must make an interservice comparison of these illustrative data in both tables. Let us therefore look at systems which use 500 Mc/s bandwidth only, and at those satellite systems (in Table 7, col. 13) with reliability comparable to that of the microwave options. It is clear that the lowest cost per terrestrial voice circuit ($12,216 in system M–2) contrasts favorably with satellite options S–2 and S–4, and approximates S–5. Also, microwave system M–1's lowest per circuit cost ($14,436) compares favorably with S–2 and S–4, but not with S–5. The same is true of the higher-cost terrestrial options (which use space diversity) with one exception: microwave option M–1(b) approximates the costs of S–2. The decisive advantages of satellites actually appear in S–3, with 1,000 Mc/s bandwidth, where the per circuit costs clearly outclass those of all six postulated microwave options,[10] none of which utilizes the larger bandwidth.

In sum, in allocating an extra 500 Mc/s to facilitate the lowest possible per circuit cost in the two services, assuming demand to be no constraint,[11] the grant would presumptively go to satellite option S–5, though with microwave option M–2(a) a very close second. Following that, the choices would be: third, M–1(a); fourth, M–2(c); fifth, M–2(b); sixth, M–1(c); and seventh, M–1(b), with S–2 a very close eighth.

Clearly, satellite option S–5 requires special R&D to develop a new 125-foot antenna and new modulation capabilities. If spectrum were no constraint, a 1,000 Mc/s allocation (for S–3) would reduce per circuit satellite costs still further with far less additional R&D. A 1,000 Mc/s grant to microwave in the present model, on the other hand, would presumably facilitate the construction of two long-haul M–2(a) systems, at double the total cost of one, with per circuit costs remaining constant.[12]

What the spectrum managers should attempt to do is to allocate spectrum to the service for which it has the highest net value at the margin, and this yardstick might actually yield a somewhat different result. Using our earlier figures of $24 and $45 per voice circuit per megacycle as an index of value of the released protection bandwidth in microwave systems M–2 and M–1, respectively, we may now calculate the trade-offs between extra satellite bandwidth and other components in moving from S–4 to S–5 to S–3, or from S–4 to S–2 to S–3.

In each case the declining per circuit costs are associated with rising bandwidth allocations. Placing these cost changes on a per mega-

---

[10] Needless to say, if one were willing to drop the requirement of launching a second satellite for insurance against satellite failure, the satellite options would all look somewhat better. But even then, only S–3 and S–5 would clearly outclass the lowest-cost terrestrial microwave options.

[11] Microwave system M–1 offers circuit capacity some 2½ to 5 times greater than most satellite options; the other terrestrial system provides circuit capacity some 4 to 10 times greater. For the comparative cost estimates to be meaningful, one must clearly presume sufficient projected total demand to warrant installation of such systems. What the tables compare, in short, are per circuit costs under fully utilized capacity with all scale economies realized.

[12] Our sole interest here is in how per circuit costs of different communications modes vary with variations in available spectrum. Deliberately excluded for analytical convenience is the possibility of increasing microwave system capabilities without more spectrum. This can be done through improved techniques and minor modifications. See FCC Annual Report for 1968, p. 58.

cycle basis and combining the figures with those derived earlier for microwave, the following pattern emerges:

1. Had satellites been forced to work within only 100 Mc/s bandwidth, then clearly any move from S–4 to S–5 would yield $50 to $58 cost-savings at the margin, in excess of those enjoyed in either microwave system. On the other hand, a move from S–4 to S–2 would yield savings of $36, in excess of those in M–2 but not in M–1. A move from S–1, with its less advanced technology, to S–2 or S–5 would also outclass both microwave systems, and do so by the greatest margin of any option.

2. Had satellites in fact been operating with 500 Mc/s bandwidth and could they now secure an additional 500 Mc/s, the move from S–5 to S–3 would yield few additional cost-savings ($3 per megacycle), nowhere comparable to those in M–1 or M–2. Even the move from S–2 to S–3 would yield smaller per circuit cost-savings ($14 to $20) than in either M–1 or M–2.

Although the cited values are only crude approximations of what a final megacycle of bandwidth is worth to the two services, they do suggest the relative value, per megacycle, of a full 500 Mc/s band to either. Viewing the whole band as a marginal increment to prior allocations as postulated at the outset, the presumptive allocational choice as between satellites and terrestrial microwave would depend on which configuration we had in mind.

Land Mobile and TV Broadcasting

Case II pertains to the relative value of a final channel of bandwidth to mobile radio users and TV broadcasters as inferred from illustrative data on the extra costs either would incur in being deprived of it.[13] For analytical purposes only,[14] we shall follow Casselberry and

[13] The data appear in Federal Communications Commission, *Report of the Advisory Committee for the Land Mobile Radio Services* (U.S. Government Printing Office, 1967), pp. 393–423. Publication cited hereinafter as LMAC Report. The cited chapter was prepared mainly by R. Casselberry. However, the basic conceptualization owes a heavy debt to R. Gifford, so that we cite the work here as jointly written.

[14] The most detailed critique of this important pioneering study appears in Letter from Lester W. Lindow to FCC Chairman Rosel H. Hyde, dated Jan. 30, 1968, with Attached Comments on LMAC Report on Behalf of Maximum Service Telecasters Inc. See also Letter from NAB President Vincent T. Wasilewski to Rosel H. Hyde, Jan. 19, 1968, plus Comments on LMAC Report on Behalf of the National Association of Broadcasters (reprinted in *Industrial Communications*, Jan. 26, 1968, pp. 2–7). See, finally, Casselberry's general response and rebuttal to NAB comments, reprinted in *Industrial Communications*, Feb. 9, 1968, pp. 15–22.

Gifford in estimating the relative value of bandwidth to the two services by considering first, the cost of spectrum usage (i.e., cost of ownership); and second, the cost of replacing spectrum with other factor inputs.

Once again, we are interested mainly in cost-savings at the margin, in response to a shift of some small amount of bandwidth from one service to the other. In the absence of marginal values, however, we must start our discussion by looking at the data on total costs for the whole service.

Cost of Spectrum Usage. Table 9 summarizes Casselberry's cost-of-ownership estimates for land mobile, television, and radio on a per megacycle basis. Costs in each case include estimates of operating costs, maintenance, and amortization of all physical plant. Land mobile plant includes all base stations, mobile units and antennas for public safety, industrial, and transportation services. In radio and television, plant includes not only physical station plant but also the public's investment in and maintenance of broadcast receivers.

The authors cite comparative costs to contrast the relative value output of the respective land mobile and broadcast spectrum. The frequencies, in other words, are assumed to facilitate the cited investment and operating expenditures. And insofar as such frequencies are technically interchangeable between the two services, the question is whether some diversion of bandwidth from television to land mobile would be likely to raise the spectrum's aggregate net benefits.

Aside from the uncertainty about marginal values, however, "costs of ownership" as thus defined refer to a heterogeneous group of end products and intermediate products (station plant) and therefore contain a good deal of double counting. Consumer expenditures on TV sets represent some minimum value to the audience of the radio-TV service,

TABLE 9. ESTIMATED COMPARATIVE COSTS OF OWNERSHIP FOR SELECTED RADIO SERVICES

Service	Costs of ownership[a] ($ million)	Allocated bandwidth (Mc/s)	Costs of ownership per megacycle bandwidth ($ million)
(1) Broadcast TV	4,236 (4,630)	492	8.6 (9.4)
VHF only	4,186 (4,575)	72	58.0 (63.5)
(2) FM and AM radio	1,222 (1,351)	21	58.2 (64.3)
(3) Land mobile[b]	1,606 (1,606)	43	37.3 (37.3)

Sources: Federal Communications Commission, *Report of the Advisory Committee for the Land Mobile Radio Services* (U.S. Government Printing Office, 1967), Vol. 2, Pt. 2, pp. 415–19. Parenthetical figures represent adjustments made by R. L. Casselberry in *Industrial Communications*, February 9, 1968, pp. 15–22, pending further review.

[a] Includes annual amortization, maintenance, and operating costs.

[b] Includes public safety, industrial, and transport services.

lacking any direct demand-price for programming and advertising. More-over, the costs of running a broadcast station are costs of an intermediate product of sorts bought by the advertiser, to reach the consumer, so that consumer outlays on sets, while a minimum value, subsume at least part of the investment in stations and the expenditures on advertising.

One can equally well call land mobile equipment an intermediate factor whose value is ultimately reflected in the mobile radio users' revenues. In that sense one would really want to compare broadcast revenues with revenues due to land mobile equipment. But while we can readily compare AM, FM, and TV revenues on a per megacycle basis, there is no easy measure of revenue due to mobile radio equipment as such. For present purposes, what one really wants to know is how these ownership costs vary at the margin when some small amount of spectrum is added or taken away, and this is clearly not apparent in Table 9.

In estimating the value of bandwidth to alternative users from their respective expenditures in using it, Casselberry and Gifford explicitly assume that the spectrum must be worth at least these "costs of owner-ship" and possibly more.[15] But this is wrong, for the same reason that it would be wrong to estimate the value of oil from a summing up of the operating costs, maintenance, and amortization of all oil users. Auto-mobiles do use oil, of course, and cannot operate without it. But neither can they operate without many other cooperating factor inputs. To attribute their total economic value to any one of these "essential" factor inputs is fallacious simply because the same reasoning applies to any other input, and because the net result would be massive double-counting in the calculation of GNP.

Even on the basis of "per megacycle of bandwidth occupied," esti-mated costs of ownership have serious limitations as any indicator of relative economic value. Like comparable measures of capital stock per unit of bandwidth, to be sure, the cost of ownership values provide a guidepost for managers ever sensitive to allocational changes that could disrupt the value of existing plant. However, there are ambiguities. If high costs of ownership per unit of bandwidth are associated with greater economic productivity and extra spectrum is allocated accord-ingly, the larger, older, stable industries would be favored over small but growing new ones. The favored service might for a time fall behind in

[15] See LMAC Report, Vol. 2, pp. 394–98; R. Casselberry and R. Gifford, "Mobile Spectrum Farming," G.E. Communications Products Division (1964), pp. 2–3 and Appendix; R. Casselberry and R. Buesing, "A Look into the Future of Land Mobile Communications," G.E. Communications Products Division, pp. 4–5.

investment per unit of bandwidth occupied but would normally exploit its new allocation with a still larger plant and thus strengthen subsequent claims on still more spectrum. In addition, when two services located in substantially different spectral regions compete for some other common unit of bandwidth, the one housed higher up would tend on that score alone to show a higher per unit investment record, irrespective of whether it had utilized its then-allocated frequencies more intensively.

Costs and Cost-Savings at the Margin.   At best, all that Table 9 really tells us is something about the total spectrum assigned to the three services in question. For allocational decisions the more relevant comparisons must be made at the margin, and here a rather different set of questions must be asked. Are the extra costs incurred by using a final few megacycles of bandwidth in service *A* or *B* greater or less than the average costs incurred for all previous bandwidth? What cost-savings would either service enjoy through reallocation of a minimal unit of bandwidth from one to the other? This brings us to consideration of hardware costs under varying spectral constraints and, in particular, the cost of replacing spectrum outright.

The value of spectrum at the margin can best be derived from estimated cost-savings due to radio or from the extra costs a present user would incur were he forced to his next-best alternative. It will be convenient to review the issues here; first by comparing the marginal and average costs of spectrum utilization in the several broadcast and land mobile bands today; and then by considering, in each case, the extra costs of using a "next-best" nonspectrum alternative.

Under the postulated constraints, our analysis will make explicit the economic conditions under which cross-band reallocations would theoretically be in order. Given the data in question, however, all one can actually say is that it would be less costly for the whole television service to shift to its next-best nonspectrum alternative, than for land mobile to shift to its next-best alternative. This is of course quite different from concluding that the reallocation of the marginal channel from television to land mobile would increase the net economic benefits of both.

Average and Marginal Costs of Spectrum Utilization.   In land mobile it is well-known that the choicest band (150 Mc/s) is the most crowded and that room is more readily available in the more recently developed Ultra High Band (at 450 Mc/s). However, hardware at 450 Mc/s costs more than comparable hardware lower in the spectrum, even taking into account the longer response time in the more congested lower bands. It is also well known that there are virtually no legal limits on eligible entrants in many mobile radio bands today.

The upshot is that new entrants have two alternatives. They can lengthen the response time for all in the lower and more congested bands, thus reducing the value productivity of radio equipment there. Or they can incur higher hardware costs in the more arduous, newer spectral regions at 450 Mc/s or higher. In our illustration, therefore, the marginal cost of spectrum utilization for land mobile will presumably exceed its average cost.

This is also true for the saturated VHF and AM bands, though for different reasons. However, it is clearly not necessarily true for the underused UHF and FM bands. In AM broadcasting, the ad hoc method of license distribution means that latecomers must make all the adjustments to avoid interference with incumbents, whatever the cost. The more crowded the AM spectrum becomes, the costlier these adjustments will be. For this reason in part, the marginal cost of AM spectrum utilization will tend to exceed its average cost.

In the VHF band, the pre-engineered Allocation Table precludes strictly comparable extra costs to latecomers. Nevertheless, entry costs have tended to rise over time because virtually the only way to enter is to buy a station at inflated prices. As in land mobile and AM broadcasting, then, once again the marginal cost to latecomers of using VHF spectrum exceeds the average cost to all users up to that point. Only in the underused UHF or FM bands is additional entry probable at little or no extra cost.

In short, the cost-savings derived from the allocation of additional spectrum in the same spectral region will probably be greater in land mobile, VHF television, and AM radio than in FM radio or UHF television. This is so because the marginal entrants into the first three services are more likely to raise costs against themselves than is true in FM and the UHF frequencies. Likewise, the loss of spectrum in the VHF, land mobile, or AM radio bands may have significant effects in raising entry costs there but loss in the UHF or FM band will have little if any comparable effect.

In the above context, the interchangeability of UHF, FM, and land mobile spectrum clearly suggests that the diversion of a marginal (unused) frequency from UHF and FM to land mobile would in fact increase aggregate net economic benefits. By the same token, it is by no means clear that any reallocation from land mobile to the UHF or FM bands, let alone to the VHF service, would have comparable effects.

The Costs of Nonspectrum Alternatives. For argument's sake, let us once again assume with Casselberry and Gifford that savings due to land mobile radio equipment are five to eight times that service's annual "cost of ownership."[16] Thus if "cost of ownership" is, as assumed above, some $1.6 billion, these savings would range between $8 and $13 billion. The precise figures are less important here than their theoretical implications. But it is still worth restating the underlying assumption: that three radio-equipped vehicles can do the work of four without radio.

Thus for 100 mobile units, if:

Amortization (over ten years) is	$8,000
Maintenance	8,000
Operating costs	9,000

then, according to Casselberry and Gifford, the annual "cost of ownership" is $25,000. And if the cost of operating 33 extra vehicles (in the absence of radio) is:

Per vehicle at 30,000 miles per year	$2,100
Cost of driver	5,000
Total cost per vehicle	7,100
Total cost for 33 vehicles	234,000

then net savings (after $25,000 annual ownership costs deducted) are	$209,300

The net savings are thus some eight times the ownership costs.

By way of further illustration, an alternative estimate of savings of $129,000 per 100 units can be derived from the increased productivity of radio-equipped vehicles which are assumed to handle eight service calls daily instead of seven, with additional profits of $1 and of labor charge of $6 for a service call normally billed at $10 ($4 parts, $6 labor). These savings are some five times as high as ownership costs— $7 × 100 units × 220 working days minus annual ownership costs of $25,000 producing net savings of $129,000. Hence annual savings due to radio would be some five to eight times the actual ownership cost of $1.6 billion, thus ranging from $8 to $13 billion.

This estimate has been further corroborated by a questionnaire survey and, in particular, by a study of two-way police radio. Without radio, the number of patrol cars must apparently be doubled to maintain the same quality of service, at an extra cost of some $6.1 billion. This

16 LMAC Report, Vol. 2, pp. 396–99, 421.

figure is derived by subtracting the current cost of operating the police radio service ($381 million) from the cost of doubling the service, leaving net savings of $5.7 billion due to mobile radio.[17] The estimate is broadly in line with the savings of $8 to $13 billion already noted.

How do these calculated cost-savings due to mobile radio (or extra costs incurred without radio) compare to the equivalent costs and savings for the broadcasters' use of spectrum space? That is, how much would it cost broadcasters to turn to *their* next-best alternative, say for television distribution? Let us assume with the LMAC Report[18] that a closed-circuit wire TV service costs $5 per month for the first set in each household and $1 per month thereafter, with connection charges at $20 per set. For 67,000,000 sets in 53,000,000 TV homes, estimated costs (excluding presently connected sets), would then be as follows:

Connection charges (67M × $20)	$1,340M
Amortization of connection charges over ten years	$134 M/yr
Connection charges on 7M new sets per year	140 M/yr
Total connection charge per year	274M
Service charge per year (53M × $5 × 12)	3,180M
Service charge per year (14M × $1 × 12)	168M
Total cost per year	$3,622M

This impressionistic cost estimate of $3.6 billion for a closed-circuit wire distribution alternative for the present broadcast-advertiser system clearly falls far short of the postulated cost-savings due to mobile radio, where they are no less than twice and probably as much as three to four times as great. That is, the $3.6 billion which broadcasters are assumed to save in this example by broadcasting instead of using wire are far less than the $8 to $13 billion which land mobile users are assumed to save by *their* present use of radio. The extra $3.6 billion cost broadcasters would incur if forced to their next-best alternative is far less than the land mobile users' extra costs were they forced to theirs. However, a diversion of occupied (let alone of unused) spectrum from broadcasting to land mobile will yield aggregate net benefits only if the marginal value of a unit of spectrum to the latter exceeds that to the former.

Stated otherwise, the reallocation of a single TV channel to land mobile would be in order if, but only if, the net cost-savings enjoyed by land mobile as a consequence (over the cost of their next-best alterna-

[17] Ibid., pp. 399–409; and critique by Lindow, pp. 5–11.
[18] Vol. 2, p. 420.

tive) exceeds the extra net costs incurred by TV after the reallocation. The illustrative data cited above are probably insufficient for any decisive answer in the case of VHF or AM broadcasting. But there seems little question about the excess of cost-savings in land mobile at the margin, over the extra cost-dissavings in much of the FM or UHF bands. For in the latter bands, outside the major urban centers, a diversion of bandwidth will presumably impose few if any cost-dissavings.

Whatever the net economic benefits of any hypothetical reallocation of broadcast spectrum to land mobile, broadcasters could of course still justify the status quo if their services were of demonstrably higher social value and widely accepted as such. The current allocations necessarily interfere with a market distribution of spectrum. To protect broadcasters against counterbidding by land mobile users, FCC and the broadcasting industry alike must demonstrate the return to the community for the valuable privileges granted. Free public service programming may constitute one such compensation, local live service another, and free popular entertainment a third. But the question is whether such benefits need be impaired by the loss of spectrum at the margin, and, if so, whether this impairment should be rated as more serious than any impairment of the land mobile service through congestion, delays, and rising equipment costs (due in part, of course, to zero spectrum costs).

Critique

So much, then, for two hypothetical examples where rival claims for spectrum could be evaluated better in the light of even crude estimates of shadow demand prices. Such shadow prices are not easy to calculate and will probably remain subject to a number of practical and conceptual limitations. Hence the illustrations offered, though related to real-world problems, serve mainly to indicate the kind of effort that will be needed and suggest no simple panacea. Because the practical difficulties are great, much careful effort is needed before proceeding with this approach.

Yet at least some of the alleged deficiencies may have been exaggerated. There is surely no reason in principle, for example, why shadow prices cannot be estimated for mobile as well as fixed services. The total value of spectrum used by the aeronautical-marine mobile services or space satellites is extremely high, of course, in view of their unique dependency on spectrum as such. But this is obviously irrelevant in any estimation of shadow demand prices where the relevant question is which of several alternative mobile systems to select, given the varying spectrum requirements of each and the dollar trade-offs between spectrum and nonspectrum inputs.[19]

A more telling deficiency may be that shadow pricing tends to favor the big established firm and firms that are high-cost producers. Surely where the big firm applies for more channels than the small firm, the cost-savings per channel to the former may well exceed those to the latter, even though the marginal cost-savings to the small firm (for a final channel) are relatively greater. Indeed this discrepancy between average and marginal cost-savings may be widened still more where the big firm is a relatively high-cost producer.

But here too the critic must be wary of exaggeration. Actually, this criticism confuses two separate issues. To be meaningful, shadow price estimates must clearly be made at the margin, and this is admittedly hard to do where the applicants themselves apply for different amounts of bandwidth. But does this more than underscore the need to devise some way to place the initiative with the manager-allocator (not the user) in: standardizing the size of spectrum parcels available and soliciting invitations to lease designated parcels, instead of awaiting bidder solicitations? Also germane here may be the present distinction between ad hoc licensing, as in AM radio, and licensing under a pre-engineered allocation table, as in FM radio or television.

The tendency to reward high-cost producers relative to efficient ones is another matter. Surely the value of spectrum is greater to a high-cost firm just because it has thus far substituted nonspectrum inputs for spectrum in an imperfect and inefficient manner. By the same token, the more efficient firm may be unduly penalized just because its use of nonspectrum factors has thus far been so efficient.

But the same imperfections hold true also in regard to nonspectrum inputs more generally. Suppose, for example, that both A and B want to buy a competitively priced factor x. Suppose also that firm A buys all its other factors in monopolistic markets, but that firm B buys its factors all in competitive markets. On these assumptions, firm A will clearly be willing to pay more for factor x as a substitute for its other factors (just because the latter are monopolistically priced), than firm B, which enjoys competitive pricing of its other factors.

The tendency to reward high-cost producers may well be a deficiency of shadow pricing. But so far as I can see, it is not a deficiency of any

[19] Superficially there may seem to be no next-best alternative against which to measure the value of spectrum to the mobile radio user. But see H. Levin, "There is Always a Substitute for Spectrum," *Telecommunication Journal* (January 1969), pp. 33–35.

different order than comparable imperfections in the demand for non-spectrum factors generally, under real-world conditions of competition and monopoly.

Perhaps the most telling criticism of shadow prices is that the relative strength of two users' claims for the same bandwidth will vary with what is accepted as their next-best alternative in either case. The TV broadcaster's case for extra spectrum will obviously look better where present facilities are compared with an expensive nationwide (or even citywide) wire system, than with hardware to transmit video signals in bandwidth of only 3 or 4 rather than 6 megacycles. Land mobile's claim for extra spectrum would likewise look better where its next-best alternative is an expensive set of call boxes or extra storage space, fuel, drivers, and vehicles rather than hardware to facilitate a simple move up into less-congested spectrum.

The determination of the "true" next-best alternative and the calculation of the extra costs incurred due to exclusion from the desired spectrum will themselves depend on the amount of extra spectrum any applicant has in mind. This too can be varied strategically to strengthen his claims. Presumably, then, the estimation and use of shadow prices by regulators will be subject to the same bargaining, negotiation, arbitrariness, and perhaps improper influence that now characterize the selection of licensees in comparative proceedings.

Before using shadow prices on any practical basis, a number of "bugs" will clearly have to be ironed out. As we shall see, the same is true of auctions. It therefore seems imprudent at best to dismiss any major technique to inject price incentives into spectrum allocation at this preliminary stage, considering the compromise that doubtless must be struck between economic relevance and strategic acceptability.

At the very least, substantial long-run discrepancies even in imperfectly estimated relative shadow prices may indicate a need for reallocation, sharing, borrowing, or lending. By the same token, the discrepancies would underline the need to exact a more tangible compensatory return in terms of regulatory priorities furthered or public service rendered, to justify any continuation of discrepancies in economic values.

RENTAL CHARGES

Once the shadow demand prices of spectrum for alternative services are calculated even crudely, the resultant values could be used to help design an appropriate rental charge schedule. The same is true also of values derived from auctions. Using occupied spectrum as the multiplicand, per unit charges could actually be set in at least four ways: (1) at some arbitrary flat rate; (2) at rates related to shadow demand prices for spectrum, as derived from the costs imposed by exclusion; (3) at rates that reflect auction prices on an ad hoc basis; or even (4) at rates geared to cover the costs incurred by a private concessionaire in acquiring, maintaining, and improving a band of frequencies for the government.[20]

The need for rental charges, as for shadow prices, should now be clear. At present, incumbents have no incentive to economize what is for them a free good, or they economize for the wrong reason. They do not benefit from releasing spectrum to others, even though the necessary cost of reducing occupied bandwidth may be considerable. Yet their reluctance to accommodate newcomers imposes substantial costs on the latter, who, unable to share, borrow, or buy spectrum, are forced to develop systems higher in the unused regions or to substitute transportation, storage, and personnel for spectrum.

The incumbents' preferred status is grounded on their "continuing interest" in spectrum assignments due to prior use, regulatory doctrine to the contrary notwithstanding. It is based also on the difficulty of overriding the facts of past performance with the paper promises of future possibilities and on incumbents' political leverage if the service is an old one geared to safety, security, education, or other public functions. However justifiable economically, the spectrum managers will rarely impose dislodgment costs. However, if they could raise rental charges when the opportunity costs of occupied spectrum rose, this might make incumbents less reluctant to vacate, lend, or share spectrum to accommodate new services. Long-term stockpiling would then be less necessary.

It is indeed hard to see why economists have so far dismissed the engineer's "spectrum usage measures"[21] as precise and operational but nonetheless irrelevant to the economic problem in allocational decisions. Economists have pointed out correctly the relation between spectrum value and the location of the bandwidth in spectral, geographic, and temporal terms. However, the true economic relevance of the spectrum usage measures, and of their contribution to physical dimensioning of the resource, lies in the valuable base they provide for setting user charges. Like the other options reviewed here, rental charges would surely provide incumbents with incentives to economize spectrum,

[20] Only option (a) has thus far been explicitly considered in the literature. See LMAC Report, Vol. 2, pp. 409–13.

[21] See Joint Technical Advisory Committee, *Spectrum Engineering: The Key to Progress* (New York: Institute of Electrical and Electronics Engineers, 1968), Supp. 8, pp. 83–93.

eliminate any tacit subsidy element in the present system,[22] and facilitate the rationing of spectrum within congested services and the transfer of spectrum as between different services.

Such charges could be imposed on the several dimensions of occupied bandwidth, with rebates allowed where users take steps to improve the efficiency of spectrum utilization. The more spectrum occupied in all major dimensions, the higher the rent. The less spectrum occupied, the lower the rent. Investment in new spectrum-economizing hardware would reduce the rent, but the spectrum user might prefer to keep his rent high by lax utilization in order to keep other costs low. He might thus trade spectrum for other factor inputs, or vice versa, just as he now strikes some balance among other factor inputs so as to maximize the net productivity of total dollar investment or to equalize the productivity of money spent on all factors. The only difference is that the price paid for spectrum would not be determined in any full-fledged market.

Dollar rental charges on a vertical axis should be related to some measure of efficiency in spectrum use on the horizontal axis. The relationship would also be affected by the quality of hardware, which is in turn affected by the volume of R&D investment. Hence, as technical performance in spectrum occupancy was improved, and less space thereby required for any given communication of information, the dollar charge would go down. In terms of information theory the user would have come closer to his maximum potential efficiency in using spectrum.

This concept seems close to that set forth by the Joint Technical Advisory Committee in expanding the "spectrum usage efficiency" concept. According to the JTAC, "efficient" spectrum usage can be defined as

$$E_s = \frac{S_i}{S_d} = \frac{V_i B_i T_i}{\sum_{jo}^{n} V_{dj} B_{dj} T_{dj}}$$

where E_s = technical efficiency; S_i = the total three-dimensional spectrum ideally required for the communication in question; S_d = the total three-dimensional spectrum denied to others; V_i, B_i, and T_i = volume of physical space, bandwidth, and time ideally required; V_d, B_d, and T_d = the same denied to others.[23]

Technically efficient spectrum usage may or may not be economically efficient in the largest sense. But for analytical purposes it should be possible to apply a rental rate to the total spectrum denied to others such that the greater the denial, the higher the total rental charge. Or the rate could be applied to technically ideal occupancy such that the further above the technical ideal a user's occupancy, the greater the total charge he must pay. Or the less the spectrum denied to others by the use in question, and the closer to the technically ideal occupancy, the lower would be the charge imposed. It might of course still not be economically worthwhile for any user to invest in equipment that reduced his rental charges below some minimal level. But technical inefficiency due to economic constraints is one thing; technical inefficiency which reflects the lack of economic incentives to conserve a valuable and scarce spectrum resource is something quite different.

Flat Token Rates

To continue the analysis, let us now consider the calculation of rental charges for representative installations in mobile radio, microwave, relay, and VHF television. Following Casselberry and Gifford again, we shall first use an arbitrary figure of $1 per standard unit of occupied spectrum (PODAF).[24] Rough estimates of rental charges for the three services would then be as follows:

	PODAF × $1	= Monthly rent	Annual rent
Land mobile*	$　　　1.94	$　　　2.00	$　　　24
Microwave	31.50	31.50	378
VHF television	11,400.00	11,400.00	136,800

* Includes base stations plus mobile units.

---

[23] See Joint Technical Advisory Committee, *Spectrum Engineering: The Key to Progress*, Supp. 8, pp. 84–93. This conception modifies and refines an earlier concept of occupied spectrum formulated by Gifford. See R. Gifford, "Maximizing Our Radio Resource," an address before the IEEE Group on Electromagnetic Compatibility, May 12, 1966, p. 6; "What is the Value of Establishing Spectrum Value?," 1967 EASTCON Convention, Oct. 18, 1967, pp. 10–12; and "Remarks at IEEE International Communications Conference," June 15, 1966, pp. 4–6. See also LMAC Report, pp. 409–13.

[24] By PODAF, Gifford means "Power Density exceeding a specified level over an Area within an assigned Frequency Band." Here occupied spectrum is classified "in terms of the amount of power which must be radiated from antenna of given heights to produce usable signals at the outer circumference of the land area served."

However one may question the flat per unit charge of $1, the relative rental charges calculated are clearly suggestive. At the least, relative charges of this sort would constitute a convenient way to introduce economic constraints into spectrum utilization.

Accepting these data for illustrative purposes gives further evidence that land mobile users would be willing to pay much more to retain their spectrum per megacycle than the broadcasters would pay to retain theirs. In this regard, Casselberry and Gifford derive the percentage of rent to annual savings due to radio as follows:

	Land mobile	VHF Broadcast TV
Annual rental, typical systems	$48*	$136,800
Assumed number of systems	1,870,000	600
Total annual rental, approximate	$90,000,000	$820,000,000
Annual cost of operation	$1.6 billion	$4.2 billion
Per cent rent to cost of operation	0.56	1.95
Annual saving, approximate	$10.5 billion	$3.6 billion
Per cent rent to approximate annual savings	0.1	2.3

* To make the comparison with TV conservative, assumed annual rental is set at double that calculated above.

According to these estimates, the rental charges which TV broadcasters must pay for occupied bandwidth run some 23 times larger than land mobile's rent payments relative to the cost-savings each service can expect from radio. With far greater dollar savings derivable per dollar rental outpayment, the land mobile spectrum would be worth more to mobile radio users than the VHF spectrum would be worth to TV broadcasters.[25]

Specifically, from spectrum which land mobile and television rent at $90 million and $820 million, respectively, they can expect annual cost-savings over their next-best alternatives of some $10.5 and $3.6 billion. Hence, for only one-ninth of TV's prorated rental payments, the land mobile users would enjoy some three times the cost-savings. But does this necessarily mean that mobile radio users would outbid TV broadcasters for any marginal parcel of spectrum available to both? Only if these wide discrepancies between assessed aggregate rental charges on total occupied bandwidth relative to anticipated cost-savings can be presumed to indicate relative values at the margin. Unfortunately, there is no way to know this from the data on hand.

[25] The inclusion of comparative cost-savings data clearly transforms the calculated index of "occupied spectrum" from a neutral physical quantity into a measure with potential economic content. Shadow prices or, even better, auction values for the occupied spectrum would move us still further in that direction.

It is conceivable that, notwithstanding their substantial but divergent average annual cost-savings, land mobile and VHF television both suffer from overinvestment. If so, they could both be characterized by declining marginal cost-savings already well below average cost-savings or by rising marginal costs well above average costs. In that case no reallocation might be justified at the margin unless one service's marginal cost-savings still exceeded those of the other and/or were declining less rapidly. But even then, some third party might merit the same bandwidth instead—say, a TV broadcast satellite.

From the above analysis, all one can probably conclude is that, if allocators had to require one service to vacate in toto for any reason, then the relative ratios of rental charges to cost-savings due to radio or the probable relative intraband auction values clearly point up the greater net benefits of switching all of TV to its next-best alternative (wire), than of turning all of land mobile to its next-best alternative. But this is quite different from saying that a marginal reallocation to land mobile would necessarily act to bring the marginal ratios of rental charges to cost-savings closer to equality for both services.

The relation between shadow demand prices, auctions, and rental charges should now be clear. In the above example the spectrum manager has four options. He could: (1) administer an open competitive contest between the two services; (2) set appropriate rental charges instead and thereby encourage the sharing, lending, or preemption of broadcast spectrum; (3) reallocate spectrum directly, without auctions or rental charges, towards a marginal equilibrium; or (4) maintain the status quo but exact greater public service in return for the opportunity costs of broadcast occupancy.

So far we have used an arbitrary flat per unit rate of $1, an option that has all the advantages of simplicity. Rental charges can thereby be easily calculated and the resulting sum kept below some appropriate fraction of annual gross earnings. However, assuming the perfection of some standard unit of spectrum occupancy, we could go further and explore the use of intraservice auction prices for a single appropriate service, to establish a unit rental rate for all services.

Auction Prices

There are at least two ways for competitive bidding to assist in the determination of rental charges for occupied bandwidth. Rights to enter a single service could be auctioned off and the resulting values used as a base from which to calculate the value of spectrum occupied elsewhere. Or new organizational entities could be created to bid for large blocs of spectrum from the government and subsequently sublet a variety of tracts for different classes of users at varying rental charges—total rental income being geared to cover the cost of administering the system, including the concessionaire's basic bid-price.

Adopting the first variant, auctions would be held in some single appropriate service, selected according to predetermined criteria. The values derived per unit of three-dimensional spectrum would then be applied to spectrum elsewhere. Where the resulting rental charges exceeded what some incumbent was willing to pay to retain his space, this would signify the need for reallocation, sharing, lending, or for some administrative technique to recover a larger quid pro quo than hitherto for maintenance of the status quo. Where the resulting charges fell short of what any other incumbent would be willing to pay, the reverse would be true.

One likely place to start would be in a congested service like land mobile. Here we would want to place some appropriate ceiling on the number of allowable entrants[26] and then auction off slots to the highest bidder. The resulting auction values for given bandwidth would then be used as the basis for annual rental charges per Kc/s bandwidth in land mobile. The next step would be to apply comparable rental charges to the competitively related service—broadcast television—using the initial auction values per Kc/s as a multiplier and the comparable volume of occupied spectrum used by, say, one TV station as the multiplicand. Monthly or annual rental charges could be designated for use at the managers' discretion in possible reallocations of spectrum at the margin. Comparable charges could then be calculated case by case for other pairs of services known to contest one another's grants, the most pertinent perhaps being:

> Terrestrial microwave—Space satellite
> Space satellite—Broadcast
> Common carrier fixed—Private fixed
> Common carrier mobile—Private mobile

It would of course be simpler and less likely to raise hostility to use a flat sum as a multiplier in both cases, instead of the auction values. But even on an ad hoc basis, auction prices would be invaluable for giving a feel for what the proper per unit rental charges should be.

---

[26] This is no easy matter in view of the technical difficulty of determining when a mobile radio frequency is really "saturated." See Joint Technical Advisory Committee, *Spectrum Engineering: The Key to Progress*, Supp. 5, pp. 1, 5–9.

Shadow Prices and the Costs of Exclusion

Equally pertinent would be some formula to capture per unit value as derived directly from the cost of replacing radio or from the cost-savings due to radio. In regard to value as derived from the cost of replacement or of exclusion, the question is simply what extra costs are incurred by being deprived of some small amount of bandwidth. This, of course, indicates the maximum price the user would presumably be willing to pay to retain it.

The economic effects of a set of charges based on such shadow prices should be considered in the following context:

1. Newcomers would presumably prefer to buy rights to share, borrow, or preempt spectrum directly, so long as these cost less than developing a new system or using some substitute for radio.
2. There is, however, no way at present for them to do so.
3. Incumbents normally have little economic incentive to accommodate newcomers now unless regulators compel or cajole them to do so.
4. De facto squatters' rights often strengthen the incumbents' hands immeasurably in exacting a monopoly rent before accommodating any newcomer.
5. The question is therefore how to articulate the opportunity costs of spectrum occupancy lest the incumbent's equities in his spectrum and his political leverage, plus the regulator's inertia, combine to make de facto squatters' rights determinative, whatever the economic or social merits of a new technique.

In utilizing shadow demand prices (i.e., exclusionary costs) to calculate rent in this example, we could formulate some such two-part rule as this: Newcomers (mobile radio) must reimburse incumbents (broadcasters) for any costs incurred in vacating, sharing, or lending space to accommodate them. However, should incumbents prefer not to accommodate, then they in turn pay "rent" to the spectrum manager equal to the extra costs imposed on newcomers through exclusion.[27] Had the FCC or the ODTM been empowered to impose rental charges in this manner over the years, some broadcasters might well have agreed to make adjustments which they have opposed as unwieldy or uneconomic.

Any such scheme must be judged partly on its enforcement costs

---

[27] This formulation differs from an earlier conception on one particular point. The rental payments would go to the spectrum manager, not to the newcomer himself (by way of defraying his exclusionary cost). See H. Levin, "New Technology and the Old Regulation in Radio Spectrum Management," *American Economic Review, Papers and Proceedings* (May 1966), p. 346.

and its net effect on economic efficiency. Enforcement costs will clearly be lower where incumbents must pay their "rent" directly to the spectrum manager, or even to the Treasury, than to the excluded newcomer. At the same time, the proposed formulation would minimize the likelihood of inefficient communications systems being financed out of the incumbents' monopoly rents, let alone being developed just because, as at present, there is no way for incumbents to sell sharing rights.

Under this proposal, the newcomer will at least have greater reason to cite his true low-cost alternative than where he can expect incumbents directly to reimburse his extra costs due to exclusion. In the latter case, he will have greater temptation to select his worst or highest-cost alternative. For not only could he thereby improve his chances of buying the sharing rights but he would have nothing to fear if incumbents decided to keep him out and pay rent instead. That is, assured of full reimbursement of all costs in excess of those he would incur via sharing, the newcomer would have special incentives to exaggerate the "excess" in regulatory proceedings that would thereby be made extremely complex and time-consuming.

My present proposal is different. Here newcomer may still be tempted to select some system other than his lowest-cost alternative in hopes of forcing incumbents to sell the sharing rights. But now he runs a real risk of being saddled with this alleged "second-best" option should incumbents refuse to accommodate him. Administrative policing will of course be needed to insure that newcomer follows through in the event of exclusion, so that the low-cost alternative provides the basis for calculating "rent" in other cases. However, newcomer's temptations to inflate these costs are obviously less, and the enforcement costs smaller, than where the incumbents must directly defray his extra costs due to exclusion. (See further discussion in Appendix D.)

The proposed rule might in any event have forced the broadcaster to choose between accepting full-cost reimbursement to accommodate land mobile users and refusing to accommodate them but paying "rent" instead—equal to the extra costs imposed by forcing land mobile to its next-best alternative. Likewise, land mobile could have chosen between the direct purchase of sharing, lending, or preemption rights and the development of a new system higher in the spectrum or the use of some substitute, such as more vehicles, drivers, and call boxes. While surely not ideal, such an arrangement might have helped articulate opportunity costs for spectrum managers and users alike.

The imposition of such charges on broadcasters might induce them to improve their old equipment in a more socially efficient way. For in the absence of alternative users, lax spectrum usage (e.g., the 6 megacycle TV channel) is economic. Broadcasters would merely economize on high-cost communications components by substituting low-cost frequency space. Rising opportunity costs of spectrum occupancy, on the other hand, when translated into rental charges equal to the costs imposed on next-best users, would raise the need for reallocation or for technical improvements which did not exist before. For it would be economically rational to invest in new equipment so long as the last dollar invested reduced one's bill for imposing extra costs on newcomers by an amount greater than this investment.

The mere quantification of exclusionary costs may not of course lead to any change in rules, regulations, or allocations. Every year the right-of-way legally provided for school buses probably costs the American motorist billions of dollars in wear and tear and wasted gasoline. Even an accurate accounting of costs may not lead the community to drop such rules, any more than an accurate measure of the costs imposed by drawbridges on motorists would lead to the end of drawbridges. But full knowledge of the costs may spark the community to consider other, less costly ways to accommodate school buses and motorists or motorists and barge owners.

It is conceivable that the costs which the school bus "right-of-way" now imposes on motorists would fall far short of the cost of building special off-street school bus boarding stations which did not require automobiles to stop and wait. If the community were faced with a hypothetical requirement to reimburse the motorists for their extra expenses due to the school buses, it might choose the less expensive option of constructing such stations. The costs imposed by drawbridge activity might also fall far short of the expense of building higher bridges, had these costs been better anticipated at the outset. Or in this case, a tax on the barge owner to reimburse the motorist might lead to rerouting or to modified ship design.

A community decision against the construction of new bus stations or against higher bridges is one thing when made in the full light of all the facts. So is the barge owner's decision against new routing or ship design. But these decisions are something quite different when made in the dark. Whatever the imperfections of the relevant decisional arena, one simply cannot predict the end results of fuller knowledge of opportunity costs until it is injected into the decision-making process.

In sum, an investment in communications hardware that is appropriate when opportunity costs are zero (and no one else is ready and willing to enter) is no longer justifiable when these costs are substantial. Opportunity costs of spectrum occupancy may rise over time and, in turn, raise new needs for reallocation or technical improvements.

The crucial question is how to relate shadow prices to the calculation of rent on occupied bandwidth. The extra costs a user incurs through exclusion and by having to replace his present equipment with some next-best substitute represent the spectrum's maximum marginal value to him. It is the difference between providing his communications capability with and without the additional bandwidth. Deriving the rental rate from this shadow demand price, the total rental charge would simply be "occupied spectrum times per unit rate."

So conceived, per unit rates derived from exclusionary cost might well exceed those derived from auction prices. Auction prices and shadow demand prices could in that case be used to fix minimum and maximum rental rates, and thus provide a base from which to calculate a reasonable flat rate.

STRATIFIED AUCTIONS

Under a stratified auction approach, market incentives and private valuations can be used within zones without necessarily using them throughout the whole spectrum. There is no reason why social values cannot be imposed over private values in specific areas. We would thus attempt to utilize market incentives within an overriding set of social constraints. But these overall constraints (the zoning rules) could themselves be modified later in light of the private valuations which emerge within predetermined zones.

The Problem of Small Units

One objection to any *unstratified* auction scheme is that the wealthiest bidders, those in the major urban centers, are likely to preempt most of the rights at the expense of rural areas where needs develop more slowly. It is feared also that local government, public safety, and educational or scientific users could never outbid private commercial entities in contests for spectrum.

But limits could certainly be placed upon the multiple ownership of rights by single entities as well as on their geographic location. Frequencies could also be set aside for smaller, less affluent users to bid on. Local government, public safety, and educational users could be charged for their rights too, but be required to bid only against like entities within common prescribed spectral zones.

In sum, stratified bidding would require a specification of who is qualified to bid, where, against whom, and for what.[28] Bidder qualifi-

[28] See H. Levin, "Regulatory Efficiency, Reform, and the FCC," *Georgetown Law Journal* (Fall 1961), pp. 29–33.

cations would be delimited in regard to geographic area, number of facilities already held, size of establishment, type of service, and the like. But there is no reason why price incentives could not be injected into the current regulatory framework in this way. In other words, social-administrative criteria would provide a matrix of constraints wherein economic incentives are reconciled with explicit safeguards against pricing out of the market the small unit, the developing nation, the government user, and the public user in general. Provision could be better made also to guard against monopolization, particularly of the broadcast spectrum.

At first glance, this approach differs somewhat from that endorsed by the Communications Task Force, whose proposal is to leave rights freely transferable within explicit broad service categories wherever substitution of spectrum among user classes is technically and operationally feasible.[29] Presumably this would mean that all mobile radio users could trade rights irrespective of the detailed license subclassifications now in force. The same would hold true for all TV broadcasters, all AM broadcasters, and presumably also for trading between space satellite and microwave relay systems.

My own approach envisions somewhat narrower constraints on all federally packaged rights up for sale or competitive leasing; namely, constraints based on social-administrative as well as technical standards. But the Task Force conception also requires that any buyer of existing licenses must meet all their original terms and that the FCC or OTM must approve and record all transfers.[30] Hence the difference may be more apparent than real.

The Problem of Cross-Band Bidding

Another problem in auctions arises from the intensification of interference where disparate uses (say, broadcast and point-point) are permitted within the same spectral region.[31] Adjacent and harmonic channel interference and intermodulation problems may all be commensurately greater. For this reason, auctions might better be limited to like users within the same bands, with interband or interservice reallocations made

[29] See Task Force Report, Ch. VIII, pp. 36–37.

[30] Ibid., Ch. VIII, pp. 37–38.

[31] The possibilities of efficient sharing in other cases may have been unduly minimized in the past. See Joint Technical Advisory Committee, *Spectrum Engineering: The Key to Progress*, Supp. 2, pp. 31–37. One can surely imagine situations where similar users, with similar peak loads and overall usage patterns, would cause much more interference among themselves than would different users who might be able to mesh peaks and troughs among themselves.

administratively in the light of relative intraband auction values but not uniquely determined by them. In land use, freedom to buy and sell does not mean freedom to buy residential land for industrial use, or vice versa. The market for land operates instead under the constraints of zoning laws, imperfect though they may be. Yet relative land values within zones can and do point up the economic need for reallocation as between zones, depending in the final analysis on legislative-administrative discretion wherein economic factors are tempered by sociopolitical considerations. The same could be done for the spectrum.

Purists contend, however, that bidding for rights across band or service lines is crucial for major improvements in frequency allocation. Indeed, the big conflicts today are less within than between current uses and bands. They lie in the heated contests between mobile radio and broadcasting, between military and nonmilitary or nongovernment users, between common carriers and private users. Without interband reallocation the really big problems might never be touched.

Yet auctions across band lines are far more difficult to administer than intraband auctions. Even assuming that intermodulation and harmonic or adjacent channel interference could be handled by the proper federal designation of rights, it would be awkward at best to administer an auction between a thousand land mobile radio users and a few TV broadcasters who want to lease the same unoccupied TV channel.

One way out is to authorize the numerous land mobile users to bid collectively for the TV channel, granting any necessary antitrust relief toward that end. One would presumably want (1) the broadcaster to hold out until the mobile radio users' offer just equalled the full discounted value of the spectrum to him, and (2) the mobile radio users to pay a sum equal to the extra costs imposed on them by exclusion. But a more cogent approach, would be to conduct intraband auctions within TV and land mobile and then to use the relative auction values per megacycle bandwidth as prima facie evidence for a reallocation from one service to the other. Any subsequent cross-band reallocations would in that case take into account all relevant social considerations.

The Parking Lot Concessionaire: An Analogy

If one were willing to consider radical organizational options, still another way to handle the interband problem would be to create new entities to rent spectrum. Such entities might themselves be regulated common carriers. Unlike present-day carriers, however, they would be expected to bid for franchises to radiate on whole bands of frequencies on the understanding that they might sublet or rent specific spectrum within these bands to some specified variety of services—broadcast, public safety, local government, military, industrial, land mobile, etc.

These concessionaires might be compared to parking lot operators who periodically bid for a franchise to occupy government land with rights to rent space to a variety of users. The spectrum concessionaire could of course be permitted to exercise discretion in determining the lessees, subject to overall constraints regarding the number of free (grandfathered) slots to be reserved for certain privileged users, the number of slots retained for second-level users at some token charge, and similar considerations. The rest could then be assigned, not first-come-first-served but through a market-clearing rental charge.

Competition would clearly figure in where competing applicants sought a given master franchise. The winning concessionaire's bid-price would presumably vary with the number of alternative bidders, the maximum bid-prices each applicant expected of others, the current value of the income stream each applicant expected to derive from renting his space, and the economic determinants of the rates which any and all users can and would pay. Rental charges would clear the market where the last slot would be taken up by a marginal applicant for whom the cost of occupying spectrum just equaled the benefits he expected.

Where the demand for spectrum exceeds the amount available at the going rent, charges would be raised. Should the realized rental income exceed the amount expected at the outset, the bid-price for the basic franchise would rise next time round. At some point, these payments might induce capital expenditures to develop the system at its intensive and extensive margins.

Some bands of frequencies could be designated exclusively for specified uses—commercial or noncommercial use, local or federal government use, etc. Or one might want to adopt the broad distinctions presently employed and allow franchise applicants to bid for rights to manage all spectrum for, say, the federal government or for all nongovernment users—or beyond this, for all spectrum divided along lines of the fixed, broadcast, mobile, or space services. Whatever the broad divisions used, provision could be made for alternative concessionaires to provide frequencies to given users. Here not only would applicants compete with one another for the basic franchises but operating concessionaires would compete for the rights to provide spectrum. Likewise users would vie for available space in meeting the market-clearing rental charges.

The critical points where economic incentives appear, then, would be in the concessionaire's bid-price for a master franchise and the rental charges any user must subsequently pay. Social priorities would constrain concessionaires and users alike in the manner already suggested.

The problem posed by distributing spectrum gratis as at present is that the occupant will necessarily be drawn at random and with little necessary relation to the relative economic value of the space to him. The exception, of course, is where uses are sufficiently well-developed to attract competing applicants from the outset, a situation that seldom obtains. When spectrum (or curb parking space) is priced competitively, on the other hand, users at the margin will be those who find it just worthwhile to pay. At a slightly lower price, newcomers will also pay, if given the chance, or incumbents may acquire more; whereas at a slightly higher price some users will withdraw in part or in whole. All of this contrasts with the situation where spectrum is awarded first come, first served.

Through trial and error, then, rental charges can be set which just result in all the spectrum being occupied, at which point all users are willing to pay for the opportunity costs of their occupancy. Once these spectrum rental values become established, proximity to the frequencies used for one purpose will come to determine the value for any use.

One final modification of the parking lot concessionaire analogy may offer a way to handle the sticky problem of spectrum for public safety, educational, scientific, or local government users. Whole spectrum concessions could be granted gratis to state or local school boards, or to other public agencies. That is, instead of taxing to finance police or educational use of privately rented frequencies, the community could award the concessions direct and permit the public service concessionaires to use their spectrum or to rent it and use the rental income as they see fit.

At present we do not know whether the block of frequencies reserved for education, police, or safety would in fact be so reserved if the country were fully cognizant of the opportunity costs. If a police department or a board of education were permitted to choose between using frequencies or renting them and using the money for alternative educational or policing inputs, their current organizational preferences for spectrum and nonspectrum inputs might be revised, perhaps considerably.

Of course, if police and education preferred to rent out their spectrum and use the proceeds for other inputs to further their respective missions, one might then ask whether they really should have had the frequencies in the first place. If they could not raise the money from their local or state governments because of some inability to demonstrate their needs persuasively, one could argue that making them a direct spectrum grant gratis circumvents the proper decisional arena.

This really takes us next to a third area of inquiry; viz., whether one should in fact force the cultural, scientific, and governmental users of spectrum to bid (or pay rent) for it under any circumstances.

The Rationale of Cross-Band Bidding

Although there are techniques to facilitate interband reallocations without reliance on direct cross-band bidding, it is still essential to consider the theoretical rationale of such bidding. This will help us determine whether public users merit special exemptions from auctions as such, or at least special priorities in any administrative evaluation of relative *intra*band auction values pursuant to an *inter*band reallocation. Specifically, how defensible is the oft-stated fear that, in any open contest, public, educational, or scientific users would lose to commercial interests, to the nonbroadcast private user in particular?

This fear is at least understandable. There is an important difference between auctioning off spectrum bit by bit in a zoned system and letting it out all at once, with or without zoning. In the former case, commercial users are virtually forced to pay a full producers' surplus at a price which is likely to outbid public safety, education, or local government. This is especially true if the total number of rights is not known by bidders at the outset. Where many rights are let simultaneously, on the other hand, commercial users might pay much less, and the going market rate would therefore be less likely to preclude successful bids by the public users too.

In conducting these auctions on a piecemeal basis, the FCC would actually behave like a discriminating monopolist. The danger of pricing the little fellow or the public user out would then presumably require greater reliance on carefully stratified intraband auctions, which would further operate to raise the auction prices, and so on. On this count, too, the supply of spectrum would be highly inelastic, much like that of essential materials in wartime. Competitive bidding for scarce spectrum under rigid constraints on short-run supply cannot but generate very high market-clearing prices. These prices might conceivably decline with long-run adjustments in technology or with cross-band bidding if a large enough number of rights were let all at once.

Much of the fear about open interband contests actually arises from the benefit externalities and public goods character of public safety, scientific, and educational radio services. Public users simply cannot collect direct payments for all the benefits they render. Neither can the present advertiser-supported, internally subsidized radio-TV broadcast service—not, at least without subscription arrangements or outside public service grants. By the same token, private nonbroadcast users are presumably better able to pay for spectrum sums that fully reflect its economic value to them and, in particular, to collect full payment for all the services they render.

The private user's bid would simply reflect his attempt to substitute radio for other factors until the economic productivity of all inputs, including spectrum, was proportional to their prices. Where investment in radio yielded a lower return than comparable investments in other resources, he would clearly turn to these other alternatives.

Yet to say that public users neither could nor would pay for spectrum the sums necessary to retain what they now utilize may simply mean one of two things: that the value of radio in implementing their organizational priorities is harder to measure accurately, or to demonstrate persuasively to legislative committees for tax purposes, than it is for private nonbroadcast users to do privately; or, even if radio's value could be measured with equal ease and accuracy in both cases, its value to the public users is simply less.

The public users' fear of private competition undoubtedly reflects their difficulties in demonstrating for budgetary purposes the economic value of virtually any productive factor. Yet this hardly means that all proposed public uses of spectrum are necessarily more efficient in implementing the goals of public agencies than private uses are in satisfying consumer preferences under competition. The fact that the public happens to own the spectrum and may choose to buy it from itself and give it to the public users should be a matter of conscious public choice, made in full knowledge of all the facts. Such public decisions would seem sounder if the community auctioned, or otherwise priced, the spectrum and gave the public users money to bid for it as for other factors.

My own view, then, is that the public goods argument clearly does apply to local government, educational, public safety, and related services, and it may well apply also to TV broadcasting. But this provides no persuasive reason not to charge for spectrum even in the former services, let alone in advertiser-supported TV. There are after all more efficient ways to subsidize them, if subsidies are indeed warranted, than by falsifying the relative price of their spectrum inputs. Nor indeed do we normally give such services any other factor inputs gratis.

Relative Intraband Auction Values in Cross-Band Contests between Different Services

Let us now return to the proposal for auctions within zonal constraints. Here the spectrum manager would consider relative intraband auction values along with other factors in interband reallocational decisions. Although relative interband values can clearly be overridden "for cause," it is still important to examine just what "winning" or "losing" the economic portion of these contests really signifies.

Towards this end, we shall very briefly consider hypothetical contests between three major classes of users, each in competition with the
private (nonbroadcast) services: public users, common carriers, and the
commercial broadcast service.

Public Users. Under an auction approach, spectrum managers and
public users of spectrum would both have to consider the full economic
benefits available in the resource's best-alternative use. Assignments
would be far less likely than at present to be made without careful prior
evaluation of all costs and benefits. If in the final analysis private users
generated higher intraband auction prices for spectrum than the public
users, this would simply mean that federal budgetary officials or public
users had rated appropriations for spectrum lower than for other factors
and lower also than private users had rated them.

Whether these "lower" governmental ratings reflect relatively deficient governmental knowledge about radio's value, compared to the
private user's knowledge, is immaterial. Budgetary constraints are a
major alternative to market constraints and, though neither mechanism
is perfect, actions or decisions that circumvent either are necessarily
suspect. Current spectrum allocation practice constitutes one such circumventing arrangement, insofar as spectrum managers do not normally
consider spectrum costs in their allocational decisions.

The Common Carriers. The failure of common carriers to outbid private (nonbroadcast) users would in principle reflect the rate regulator's
judgment as to a fair price for spectrum and on when that price represented "inflated costs." Such determinations are now made in reviewing
the admissibility of microwave hardware costs for rate determination
purposes. Where microwave costs-per-channel fall considerably short of
those for landlines or coaxial cable, the FCC authorizes such investments and includes them in the rate base. Indeed their inclusion presumably keeps common carrier costs lower than otherwise and gives the
consumer service at lower rates.

In setting maximum bid-prices for spectrum the common carriers
would presumably be constrained by: (1) the cost and availability of
open wire, coaxial cable, and radio equipment; (2) the FCC's judgment as to the reasonableness of prices paid for spectrum; (3) the
carrier's estimate of its own ability to negotiate successfully with FCC
for inclusion of spectrum costs in the rate base; and (4) the ultimate
consumer's willingness to pay any rate that reflected these spectrum
costs.

In short, a common carrier's successful contest with any other
spectrum user—say a manufacturer—would simply mean that the com-

posite judgment of regulatory and common carrier officials regarding the value of spectrum for common carrier purposes rate it "higher" than the private users did. A failure to bid enough would imply the opposite, as, for example, when budgetary officials fail to approve appropriations adequate to insure successful governmental bids against other users. Finally, to cite the complexities of cost analysis as any reason to short-circuit the whole budgetary process by simply handing out spectrum gratis on the basis of strictly administrative criteria is to meet the economic problem by ignoring it. For even now, the carrier is never really completely free of having to negotiate with the regulatory body regarding what it can or cannot include in its rate base.

The Broadcast Service. The commercial broadcaster's maximum acceptable bid-price would obviously depend on the income he expected to earn by using a dollar's worth of spectrum compared to what he could derive from his next-best alternative—wire broadcasting, for example. But these expectations will be modified in turn by the constraints the FCC imposes on advertising practices, network-affiliate relations, the degree of entry into any and all markets, the character and quality of programming, and the volume of relatively unprofitable public service that licensees are now required to carry during peak viewing hours.

The greater the regulatory constraints in these terms, the less the spectrum is worth to the broadcaster and the lower his maximum bid-price. The weaker the regulatory constraints, the higher the estimated economic value of spectrum and the higher his maximum bid-price. One might therefore challenge the social acceptability of any interservice contests as reducing the ability of "public-spirited" broadcasters to acquire spectrum for their public service function among others. Contrariwise, the "overcommercialized" broadcaster, in a position to milk every penny out of his assignments, would be in the strongest position to outbid other users.

Yet to say that public service requirements may reduce broadcast profits and thus the economic value of spectrum to broadcasters by no means implies that commercial broadcasters must be provided with only that amount of spectrum which their regulated operations make it worth while for them to acquire. Federal grants-in-aid to the arts, including mass media, are an obvious way out. Special public service grants would relieve the broadcaster from having to bear the full cost of this service and hence bring his net income-earning expectations for spectrum use back closer to where they might be without such public service responsibilities. His ability to acquire spectrum would improve accordingly.

Educational authorities would be able to bid for spectrum, only insofar as their sources of funding (governmental, private, nonprofit) could be convinced that radio-TV communication is as important for education as the more conventional facilities. The fact that educators now occupy a good deal of spectrum gratis by no means implies that the nation is not paying heavily in forgone economic benefits for the privilege of furthering its education this way. Nor does it follow that the present budgetary appropriations for broadcast equipment and pro-gramming represent the total economic investment therein.

The best alternative uses to which the occupied or unoccupied broad-cast channels could be put—the benefits they could produce in these uses and the costs that excluded users would save—must figure in any adequate accounting of costs and benefits. To short-circuit the budgetary process does not prevent the decision from being made. What it does is to shift the burden of costs inadvertently onto the general community in ways of which it may be largely unaware.

Critique

Although there is much to be said for stratified (zonal) auc-tions as a way to inject market incentives into allocational decisions, some serious problems still remain. Important merits notwithstanding, auctions cannot do their job efficiently in the face of collusion among bidders. Yet the very type of contest most likely to minimize such collu-sion by helping insure a large number of bidders is itself plagued by the most troublesome defects. Cross-band bidding in interband contests will doubtless be handicapped by the most intense problems of intermodula-tion and harmonic or adjacent channel interference. The reconstitution of rights may therefore be particularly complex and expensive. Yet many more bidders would appear in contests across band lines than within them, and the danger of collusion to hold down bid-prices would also be smaller.

Intraband auctions under careful zonal constraints would be freer of the interference problems but far more susceptible to bidder collu-sion. One has only to recall the small percentage of new TV grants issued to the "best" of several applicants after comparative hearings and the small number of candidates who compete even in those cases. Nor is it clear that dropping the minimal licensing standards would neces-sarily facilitate more applications, or more bidders.

Even today there is no limit on the type of institutions which can secure grants within given services, if otherwise qualified. Nor is it in any case clear that public officials would be willing to relax very far the standards used to qualify bidders. On the contrary, they will probably insist on specifying the minimal criteria more explicitly than heretofore, the better to reconcile market forces and regulatory priorities. Indeed the very possibility of effecting such a reconciliation has long been a major attraction of stratified auctions as such.[32]

By the same token, more explicit bidder qualifications and zonal constraints, with bidding limited to intraband contests, would operate to limit the number of effective bidders. The danger of bidder collusion would become commensurately greater. Safeguards would therefore be needed, such as the careful policing of auctions or the setting of minimum acceptable bid-prices wherever the number of bidders falls below some specified level. It is hard to see, moreover, how the manager could set minimum prices realistically without reference to shadow prices of some sort, since even crude shadow price values would be better than pulling the minimum values out of thin air. This latter point merely underscores our earlier conclusion that some combination of second-best options is the safest way to proceed during this formative period before all pros and cons have been carefully scrutinized.

One final problem arises from the special difficulties posed by the re-auctioning of existing licenses, in contrast with the initial auctioning of new grants. A careful demonstration of this point would take us far afield. But there is no question that competitive bidding for renewal rights is a far more complicated and potentially perverse matter than the letting of new grants for the first time,[33] so much so that public officials might well prefer to limit the auctions not only to applicants within the same bands but to new grants as well.

The most practical approach might be to combine auctions for the new grants with user charges to collect rentals during the subsequent license terms.[34] Here too the advantages of a composite multi-option package should be clear. For just as shadow prices can help in setting realistic minimum bid-prices so as to prevent bidder collusion, so auction values, shadow prices, and physical indexes of occupied spectrum could help to set realistic user charges over time.

Nor, finally, is there any reason why heavy reliance on an auction approach need rule out far less ambitious measures already being tested under the present management framework. It is to several of these new administrative techniques that we shall now turn.

---

[32] See the review of an auction scheme for broadcast licensing in H. Levin, "Regulatory Efficiency, Reform, and the FCC," pp. 22–33.

[33] For an analytical commentary on the special problem posed by renewal rights, see H. Levin, "Federal Control of Entry in the Broadcast Industry," *Journal of Law and Economics* (October 1962), pp. 58–62.

[34] Ibid., p. 63.

CHAPTER VI

NEW ADMINISTRATIVE TECHNIQUES

In Chapter V, it was proposed to articulate the opportunity costs of spectrum utilization through the use of direct price incentives. The spectrum manager could opt *against* any reallocation from one service to another for cause, even when relative shadow prices, rental charges, or intraband auction values indicated otherwise. But in so doing he would be compelled to justify his decision far more rigorously than under the present system.

New administrative techniques may also help the spectrum manager to take better account of opportunity costs in his allocational decisions. Far from the economist's ideal though they are, such techniques are important nonetheless because they may help improve the present nonprice system with a minimum of dislocation.

One good illustration is the so-called "frequency clearance" practice through which the Office of Telecommunications Management now urges that more comprehensive information be made available to all government procurement officers before any agency lets contracts for communications hardware or R&D. The terms and conditions on which the necessary frequencies will be forthcoming are becoming firm preconditions for procurement and systems development; spectrum can no longer be taken for granted.

A second regulatory technique to articulate opportunity costs is that of devising more rigorous administrative controls to recover a compensatory return for the differential economic values inadvertently conferred on favored classes of users. Rather than reallocate spectrum to equate its marginal value among alternative services, the spectrum manager tries to recover greater nonprice benefits for the community. This approach can be meaningful, however, only if the opportunity costs are first quantified, for "compensatory benefits" all too often elude objective measurement.

A third approach relates to the role of secondary rights in minimizing the net opportunity costs of frequency stockpiling. Here the question is how to use secondary rights to facilitate fuller usage of frequencies over time, consistent with overriding regulatory priorities and their periodic reexamination in the light of new facts.

All three techniques must be viewed as supplements to, not substitutes for, the pricing arrangements reviewed in Chapter V.

FREQUENCY CLEARANCE

Among government users, the longstanding failure to require procurement officers to secure formal frequency clearance before ordering hardware or committing funds to systems development, is well known. The spirited new attempts by OTM to alter this situation only attest to past deficiencies.

Hardware has too often been conceived in terms of engineering ideals alone. Budgeted items normally include materials, personnel, and R&D. But rarely has care been taken to determine: (a) whether the needed spectrum is available; or (b) if not, who is now using it and what it would cost to dislodge them; (c) whether value to newcomer sufficiently outweighs value to incumbent to warrant such dislodgment even if incumbent's adjustment costs are not reimbursed; (d) the relative suitability of the spectrum to the two services, and the relative availability of viable nonspectrum substitutes.

To insure that the above facts will be considered before procurement funds are committed, the OTM now asks all federal departments to institute frequency clearance procedures similar to those long used by the Navy. Such procedures would force the systems developer to examine the availability of spectrum. In so doing, they will clearly compel him to take account not only of his equipment and R&D costs but of the extra costs that his projected system would impose on others.

Knowledge of these exclusionary costs, acquired before new equipment is ordered or developed, may facilitate a more rational decision. The agency authorizing the equipment would at least have a clearer idea of all the costs incurred to develop and institute it. Where some technical-engineering ideal was found economically unsound, a compromise could be struck to reduce the exclusionary costs. To some extent, at least, frequency clearance would also keep all services informed of many of each other's parallel developments and thus help avoid duplication.

Frequency clearance is in any case part of an evolutionary process. Prior to World War II the military merely planned to use the amateur bands and certain high frequencies in wartime, though not to effect any general closure. They also counted on a long lead time to mobilize communications systems at home and abroad. In those days the military agencies in many nations planned unilaterally. But now they must live side by side with many civilian users. Long planning periods and explicit assurances are required to avoid costly errors and systems incompatibility. The new environment requires that all services be able to coexist. Increasingly, national planning and centralized coordination are the order of the day, and frequency clearance is part of this trend.

Because secrecy often shrouds new military systems development, even different military users may be unable to take one another's frequency requirements into account. Yet the military are very much concerned about interfering with each other. With enough advance planning, more compatible systems can be devised at far less cost than corrective hardware adjustments would require, once the mistakes are made. For such reasons, too, frequency clearance is needed to facilitate rational decision-making.

This new role for frequency clearance clearly implies modification of the traditional attitude towards spectrum as a free good. It may facilitate the procurement of better equipment at lower cost and avoid economic waste, for it is hard at best to turn a man down after he develops equipment, however costly the adjustments needed to accommodate him.

The need for some such procedure has been made clear on more than one occasion during the past decade. A few cases will serve as examples.

A National Distance-Measuring System for the Aeronautical Mobile Services

One episode grew out of the search in the early 1950s for a national distance-measuring system to provide en-route-terminal area navigational aids for aeronautical vehicles. The military and the Civil Aeronautics Administration clashed long and loud over whose system should be adopted. The CAA claimed its Distance-Measuring Equipment (DME) system was better and had been developed earlier. But the military had spent millions of dollars to develop its own model secretly. The problem arose mainly because the Air Force version (Tactical Air Navigation) totally duplicated the CAA's DME hardware, already installed though not yet widely used. The two systems would operate within the same band of frequencies.

On grounds of national security and a somewhat larger prior invest-

ment ($130 million) the military finally prevailed over the CAA and
the civilian air carriers. As a consequence, the CAA had to convert its
experimental DME hardware to maintain the common air-navigational
system—i.e., one usable by all civilian and military agencies. The choice,
hard at best, was between dropping one of two costly investments.
Eventually some 200 air-ground stations had to be scrapped, along with
certain airborne equipment.

In this case frequency clearance would have served as a convenient
device to eliminate a wasteful duplication of R&D effort. But the savings
would have been in hardware costs, not frequency space. And prior
clearance of all government R&D projects by some central board (regardless of whether spectrum was involved) could have performed a
comparable function.

Nevertheless, the spectrum dimension was important. The CAA
apparently cited its earlier start and the incompatibility of the two systems among the reasons for favoring its DME hardware. In retrospect,
it is not clear whether there was in fact any problem of technical incompatibility, or whether one can therefore say that the projected
benefits of spectrum utilization by two costly systems would have been
dramatically impaired if they were authorized simultaneously. The
wastes of parallel development are doubtless the key issue and these are
only indirectly related to frequency clearance as such.

But the uncertainties introduced by possible incompatibility make
the issues fuzzy. They needlessly complicate an already difficult decision.
The OTM should at least have been left free to weigh the merits of the
two systems and not forced at the final moment to determine their
compatibility in assessing the CAA's claims as the earlier venture. Prior
frequency clearance would have settled the frequency issue beforehand,
and done so in a manner less likely to compromise the OTM's position.
For, given OTM's latitude in making technical determinations, there may
well be suspicions in borderline cases that its rating of some systems as
compatible and others as not is somehow geared to undercut any claim
that a government user could mount on grounds of having made a prior
investment.

This is not to impugn the spectrum managers' integrity. But in a
field where even the technical determinations are subject to bargaining,
negotiation, and interpretation, the major contribution of frequency
clearance may well be to insure the most accurate and objective estimation of comparative spectrum costs of alternative communications systems.

In the present case, then, frequency clearance may simply have
served as a convenient device to prevent duplication of R&D invest-

ment. But its ramifications are obviously far wider. The military's failure to get clearance or to divulge its plans beforehand reflects a now outmoded conception. It is simply wrong to sweep opportunity costs under the rug even though the day of reckoning may be more remote in frequency budgeting than conventional budgeting. Lost in the annals of informal accommodation may well be other episodes where unused agency funds in one account were quietly used to cover the extra costs inadvertently incurred in another. For frequency management must at best operate in a world of bargaining, negotiation, attrition, political compromise, and cooperation, where only the really big conflicts ever go to the DTM and the President for resolution.

A related episode involves a government order during World War II for a $7 million communications system, which was found to be able to transmit signals on its assigned frequency over only part of the anticipated distance. Scientists with certain components on hand had come up with a system that simply did not take into account the limitations imposed by spectral location and by those who then shared the same frequency along its 3,000-mile range. A 30 per cent increase in outlays (for higher transmission power) would have enabled the government to salvage the investment this time. But frequency clearance would have required a propagation study beforehand. Trade-offs between spectral location, power requirements, and dollar costs would have been examined prior to systems development and costly corrective hardware adjustments would have been avoided. Here the neglected component in communications costs was the cost to the new system of having to offset the constraints imposed by a frequency low in the spectrum and interference due to spectrum sharing—costs which prior clearance would at least have identified at the outset.

Radio Astronomy on Channel 37

One of the best examples of the cost and inconvenience of circumventing frequency clearance involves radio astronomy and UHF television Channel 37.[1] In 1959, the Navy gave the University of Illinois a large grant to build a radio astronomy installation to operate in the spectrum then assigned to UHF Channel 37.[2] Neither the Navy nor the University seemed very concerned about the permanent availability of

---

[1] This account is based on interviews with officials at the Office of Telecommunications Management and the Federal Communications Commission.

[2] Report & Order in FCC Docket No. 15022 RM-18, FCC-63-901 41105, "Temporary Interference Protection to the University of Illinois Radio Astronomy Site on TV Channel No. 37," October 8, 1963, para. 25.

the needed spectrum. Those in charge took a calculated gamble. Once the radio telescope had been installed, the investment had grown, and the program's scientific value had been demonstrated, the FCC was expected to be virtually unable to dislodge the operation on three counts. First, the UHF channel had been unoccupied to that date and, though applicants might subsequently seek entry (and did so in 1963), there was ample spectrum to accommodate them elsewhere.[3] Second, radio astronomy, of great scientific value, was technically able to operate only in certain spectral regions, including Channel 37.[4] Third, because radio astronomy does not radiate or otherwise cause interference to others, it was not readily classifiable anyway as a "use" requiring prior FCC approval.[5]

Subsequently, the political influence of the National Academy of Sciences, backed by strong evidence on the unworkability of sharing Channel 37 with TV broadcasting, did in fact wrest from FCC an exclusive 10-year license for the University to use the frequency.[6] It is hard to know whether the University's (or Navy's) strategy was consciously to perpetuate a *fait accompli* or was the result of an untutored concept of the spectrum as a free good. As two FCC Commissioners aptly summed up:

> Whether a calculated judgment or a disregard of radio allocations was the factor which led the University of Illinois to choose Channel 37 for an investment in the installation of a radio telescope in Danville, Ill. is difficult to ascertain. Only a university, certainly not a commercial enterprise or a government entity, could have come out so favorably.[7]

Nowhere is reference made to the Navy's role in disbursing funds to create a $750,000 installation without first ascertaining the availability of necessary spectrum. Yet this is clearly the case of a politically sanctioned allocational decision made without full knowledge of opportunity costs whose measurement and divulgence might have undermined it.

As the radio astronomy investment in Channel 37 grew, the University explored the chances of staying on. Having first entered without formal authorization or from anticipation of a pending ITU assignment

---

[3] Ibid., paras. 31–33.

[4] Ibid., para. 26; *IG Bulletin of the National Academy of Sciences,* No. 81, March 1964, pp. 4–6; R. Smith-Rose, "The Protection of Frequencies for Radio Astronomy," *Journal of Research* (March–April 1963), pp. 99–104.

[5] *IG Bulletin No. 81*, p. 3.

[6] See account in *The Spectrum Window*, January 11, 1963, pp. 7–9; February 11, 1963, pp. 1–4; and October 18, 1963, pp. 1–3.

[7] Report & Order in FCC Docket No. 15022, dissenting opinion by Commissioners Lee and Cox, p. 1.

of that spectrum to radio astronomy, albeit spectrum unprotected from TV interference, the University now sought such protection against imminent entry of UHF TV applicants. As a passive system causing no interference to others, radio astronomy had in fact eluded Commission scrutiny at the outset. But since it is readily subject to interference by others on adjacent channels, the rigor of its demands on the spectrum was soon apparent.[8] Because radio astronomy can operate at certain spectral points only, the sole alternatives open to that service and the FCC were really: to preempt, share, or borrow Channel 37; to curtail the national radio astronomy program; or to relocate the telescope spatially, perhaps in the "quiet zone" in West Virginia or on some other frequency, possibly with reduced scientific value.[9] Without careful review of all the costs and benefits of these options it is hard to know whether the final decision was actually the one most consistent with integrity of the TV Allocation Plan, with prosecution of the national radio astronomy program, or with the projected international spectrum allocations.

What then is the frequency clearance issue? Frequency clearance simply assures that allocational decisions are made in the proper arena in full light of all evidence on costs and benefits, notwithstanding their uncertain parameters. In this case, the decision may well have been identical, for even without clearance, the temporary (10-year) license on TV Channel 37 for radio astronomy, with interim accommodation of UHF applicants elsewhere, would have enabled:

1. The Allocation Plan theoretically to remain intact with no impairment of the Commission's several regulatory priorities;

2. The uncertain future loss of TV service to be kept down to a remote minimum, unless the spectrum loaned to radio astronomy were finally preempted outright; and

3. Radio astronomy's unique spectral requirements to be accommodated with few if any exclusionary costs imposed on television, although the resulting scientific benefits remained uncertain.

Did it really make a difference then? When faced with the full facts including de facto occupancy of Channel 37, the Commission managed to find ways to reconcile the astronomers' needs substantially with TV's, with no one the serious loser. If the astronomers had raised the question before entering the field, the Commission might have turned them down merely to forestall any temporary partial abridgment of the Allocation Table. Wooden application of allocational criteria and the

[8] Ibid., paras. 33–34.
[9] Ibid.; see also J. Findlay, "Protecting the Science of Radio Astronomy," *Science* (September 14, 1962), pp. 832–35.

Commission's reluctance to lend frequencies are familiar enough. Perhaps some maneuver like this was therefore necessary.

Such reasoning, however, though possibly defensible in one case, could lay down untenable precedents and lead to real abuse on other occasions. The whole function of frequency clearance is to ensure that adequate attention be paid to the cost of borrowing, sharing, or pre-empting spectrum, *before* systems design and hardware development are approved and large investments made. In this case, the issue was not mere duplication of government R&D, the prevention of which could be achieved without reliance on frequency clearance as such. The issue is rather one of the misdirected use (malallocation) of spectrum where prior clearance would have helped. To be sure, the asserted benefits of radio astronomy, its unique requirements, and the minimal costs of exclusion with reference to TV broadcasting, might in fact have operated to produce a similar decision. But this is to confuse the probable end result in a single case with proper general procedure and the appropriate decisional arena.

However significant radio astronomy's scientific contributions, that program clearly lacks unlimited budgetary support. Presumably, in reviewing its claim on national, state, or university resources, the cost and benefits of alternative scientific programs are compared and a judgment then reached. Spectrum costs something, too, at least where it can be put to an alternative use. In the Channel 37 episode, the exclusionary costs were remote and could be kept to a minimum (i.e., equal to the cost of reassignments only) through computerized channel selection and careful temporal and spatial frequency sharing. But the precedent is bad on several counts:

1. One cost item in radio astronomy's budget is the cost of spectrum. To ignore this is to falsify the issues and obscure the true magnitude of resources which the nation must divert to promote this program.

2. Though these spectrum costs are low today, they could well become larger tomorrow. Yet what is ignored on the first round may be hard to weigh in adequately afterwards. Given the uncertain parameters of benefits, it is all the more important to be meticulous about costs. Spectrum costs are hidden costs in a real sense unless administrative practice requires that they be brought into the open.

3. However persuasive radio astronomy's case may be on the merits, one can never be entirely sure in retrospect that the Commission's paper approval was not to some degree an attempt to

rationalize a decision it felt compelled to make on political grounds in the face of an ongoing program and past investments.[10] By bringing all the evidence on anticipated costs and benefits out before the work on systems design and hardware development was under way, frequency clearance would have enabled the FCC to reach its decision with a freer hand.

In short, frequency clearance would have forced the radio astronomers and the Commission alike to review more carefully at the outset the full range of alternatives open to each in terms of comparative costs and benefits. One serious problem would assuredly have remained: newcomer's disadvantage relative to incumbent. But that is a limitation of the whole frequency management apparatus in the absence of price incentives and surely no reason to condone further circumvention of the apparatus.

Frequency clearance does leave us with the spectrum manager's traditional bias in favor of incumbents, a bias that makes at least understandable the strategic value of confronting the FCC with a *fait accompli*. But centralized clearance would help ensure the divulgence of costs imposed by incumbent's failure to accommodate, as well as the costs of such accommodation. By articulating and quantifying these costs, such a procedure might at least operate to reduce the Commission's normal bias against newcomers.

NEED FOR NEW REGULATORY TECHNIQUES IN THE BROADCAST AND COMMON CARRIER SERVICES

The techniques so far discussed purport to articulate opportunity costs either through direct price incentives or by requiring the government's procurement officers to take more complete account of spectrum costs before letting any hardware or R&D contracts. However, the spectrum manager may also try to recover a more adequate quid pro quo for the favors he unintentionally confers. That is, he may tolerate the high opportunity costs of his allocational decisions provided that "compensatory benefits" are then returned to the community.

Under present administrative practice, the incumbent's opportunity costs reflect the outputs which next-best users could generate if granted access to his spectrum. These opportunity costs may be virtually zero at

---

[10] Radio astronomers and their supporters emphasized the ongoing nature of the program at Illinois and the large investments already made. See *The Spectrum Window*, Jan. 11, 1963, p. 8; and Feb. 11, 1963, pp. 1–4 (*The Washington Post* and the Illinois State Senate Joint Resolution are cited).

the outset, but as alternative users appear the costs may well rise over time. The spectrum manager then has several choices. He can reallocate spectrum in light of its estimated value to the alternative users, or make incumbents more aware of their full opportunity costs by raising rental charges against them, or open up the coveted spectrum to competitive bidding on an intraband or interband basis. Finally, the manager can reject any such use of direct price incentives or of frequency clearance, and try instead to translate the opportunity costs into a more rigorous "burden of proof" on incumbents to show why they should not have to share, vacate, lend, or otherwise economize spectrum. Here the question really becomes how to justify the status quo in face of the costs it imposes on others.

Stated otherwise, the rising marginal value of broadcast and common carrier microwave spectrum to next-best users in land mobile and space satellites or private microwave, respectively, underscores the need to devise new techniques to recapture, or at least offset, the growing volume of riskless differential returns which economists call "economic rents." In the context of continued technical restraints on entry and output, for example, broadcast licensees now enjoy such rents both because they are spared having to bid against each other to retain their present assignments, and because they need not compete against non-broadcast users for the whole TV spectrum as such. In short, broadcast rents will vary with the level of opportunity costs across, as well as within, band lines.

If regulators fail to recover these rents in cash (by a tax or auction), there seems no alternative but to recover in kind. For, not being regulated on a cost-of-service basis, broadcasters do retain the rents incorporated in the prices which advertisers pay for access to their scarce public spectrum. The principal economic problem is not of course to recover rents per se, but to assure an efficient use of spectrum through user charges, auctions, or conceivably by leaving the rents intact in the prices which broadcasters charge their advertisers.

But the major regulatory or social task is different: to widen and diversify program choice almost irrespective of profit considerations by recovering the rents in kind. Presumably this will, under present arrangements, require greater rigor in defining and inducing company-subsidized public service programming for minority taste groups, an approach fraught with well-known dangers. Yet the need for subsidization of some sort (internal or external) is surely underscored by the tendency for additional commercial stations to duplicate the current pattern of program choice in their markets long after new entry has dissipated any monopoly rents. Barring direct subsidies of some sort, it will take a very large number of commercial stations indeed to make many programs for minority audiences economically attractive. Without trying to examine the various ways by which the rents could be collected and/or directed into public service,[11] suffice it to note simply that the rising marginal value of broadcast spectrum to next-best users increasingly dramatizes the hard choices which now confront regulators in this field.

In common carrier rate regulation, still other issues are posed. Because spectrum is free, the opportunity cost of spectrum usage does not enter into the carriers' cost of service or hence into their rates, so that the rates are really too low for economic efficiency. But that is quite different from saying that the economic rents are in any sense "recovered" for the community by rate-of-return regulation; they are simply passed on to the carriers' customers.

In the absence of user charges or auctions, then, growing spectrum scarcities for the carriers make an increasingly persuasive economic and social case for discriminatory rates as between commercial and public users. One modus operandi might be as follows. First, to set rates below the long-run marginal costs (LRMC), as currently measured, of servicing public users like educational, scientific, public safety, and national security services, where benefit externalities are large but the traditional sources of financing meager. Second, to insure that the carriers earn the minimum permissible return on their total investment anyway by charging commercial users more than the average total cost of serving them alone. This procedure would properly incorporate the economic rent (i.e., the opportunity cost of spectrum utilization) into the prices that commercial users pay, so that the subsidy implicit in the rates set below LRMC to the public users would be financed out of economic rents which the carriers collect by charging their commercial customers for the spectrum used to service them. (See further discussion in Chapter X.)

The dangers in following this route are well-known. The burden of proof in deviating from a marginal-cost standard is heavy. It must be

---

[11] One ingenious scheme to do both simultaneously is a proposal to finance a system of nonprofit public television largely out of (a) a gross receipts tax on commerical TV stations; (b) the cost-savings which result from new satellite (rather than conventional terrestrial) interconnection. In a modified version, all commercial spectrum users would also pay a user charge. See J. Dirlam and A. Kahn, "The Merits of Reserving the Cost-Savings from Domestic Communications Satellites for Support of Educational Television," Yale Law Journal (January 1968), pp. 494–96, 514–19; A. Kahn, "The Incidence of a Tax on Gross Broadcast Revenues," unpublished; and D. Netzer, Long-Range Financing of Public Broadcasting, a report for the National Citizens Committee for Broadcasting (New York: The Committee, 1969), pp. 20–21.

clearly demonstrated that forgone economic efficiency is carefully weighed off against expected social benefits and that no alternative technique could equally well generate the desired benefits.[12] Yet a serious problem in economic measurement could well frustrate this tactic. Without at least some rough idea of the magnitude of economic rents and spectrum costs, we will simply never know how far above or below LRMC to set the rates for private and public users. Indeed the vagueness and elusive character of the benefit externalities could well leave us with knowledge of no more than the direction to deviate from LRMC.

Two possible ways out can be mentioned. The first is to set the rates for public users precisely at LRMC; under present practice this means they will pay no spectrum costs anyway. The commercial users could then be charged rates that included spectrum costs (i.e., rates above the LRMC of servicing them alone), and the subsidy to public users thereby underwritten. As the carriers' overall return on their total investment rose above the permissible minimum, the pressures for generalized rate reductions would probably grow. The Commission would then have to justify its action under present Congressional mandate for reduced-rate interconnection for public broadcasting, a point to which we return in Chapter X. In so doing, FCC must face up more squarely to the need to accept the regulatory implications of the present nonprice spectrum system, unless we are willing to modify it.

This brings us to a second option: the introduction of auctions, user charges, or spectrum markets. If such mechanisms were available, the state would collect all rents direct and make a separate set of decisions as to which activities to subsidize. Public usage of spectrum would figure as only one set of decisions among many. Indeed, for that reason alone, students of public finance may prefer the latter approach.

Suffice it here mainly to point out the nature of this hard choice. The fact is that we simply cannot have our cake and eat it too. Without auctions or rental charges, Commission-induced carrier subsidization of public customers whose services have sizable benefit externalities appears as justifiable as in the broadcast case, and in some ways more so. Reduced communications rates for these public entities, financed out of higher charges to commercial users, are at least free of those unique definitional and political problems associated with any policy to encourage internal subsidization of particular program types by broadcasters.

[12] See A. Kahn, "Inducements to Superior Performance: Price," in H. Trebing, ed., *Performance under Regulation*, Michigan State University Public Utility Studies (Michigan State University Press, 1968), pp. 89–90, 100–1; J. C. Bonbright, *Principles of Public Utility Rates* (Columbia University Press, 1961), pp. 56–58, 112–14, 117–19.

By the same token, reluctance to sanction discriminatory rates toward this end underscores the need to recover the economic rents more directly.

One does not need to accept economic rents as an ideal source of support for public spectrum usage characterized by large benefit externalities, to recognize that the present nonprice spectrum system makes such rents a likely source, or to recognize that a market-type spectrum system would reduce the volume of economic rents and hence the significance of collecting or offsetting them.

Frequency Stockpiling and the Role of Secondary Rights

As loosely conceived, stockpiling refers to the retention of unused spectrum by individual grantees or by whole services. Because grantees do not legally "own" their assignments, the term more correctly refers to the spectrum manager's deliberate reservations of spectrum for future, rather than present, use by one class of users rather than another. In this case, the spectrum manager rather than the user withdraws the space, not because no one else is ready or able to enter but because certain preferred users are not yet ready.

For example, in regard to public safety and military users, the manager's decision to stockpile safeguards immediate and reliable access to the spectrum for purposes of internal and national security. At issue is the well-known reluctance of such users to surrender unused spectrum, notwithstanding "guarantees" of future access on request.

In regard to private commercial users, the manager's stockpiling decision is a technique to accommodate newcomers in the face of congestion, on the assumption, first, that once suboptimal use of a frequency is allowed, private and public investment in equipment become a prime factor preventing subsequent reassignment to a service that would utilize it more efficiently; and, second, that the relative value of different frequencies for different uses varies over time with changing technology and knowledge but that this rate of change does not necessarily coincide with the rate of obsolescence of equipment instituted at any earlier state of the arts. Insofar as these assumptions are valid, one might say that stockpiling is geared pragmatically to give the spectrum manager planning flexibility to minimize his blunders. That is, he may better strike a balance between full occupancy over time and underutilization today for the sake of accommodating new techniques that facilitate more efficient use tomorrow, with a minimum of costly dislocation and forced obsolescence.

In any case further distinction must be made between stockpiling and hoarding and the potential role of secondary rights must be considered in that context too. Stockpiling can be defined as the setting aside of unused spectrum by managers and users alike to prepare for the predicted growth of present uses and for contingencies. Hoarding is the setting aside of spectrum far beyond the amount needed for such projected future demands, even allowing for a generous safety margin. Hoarding may be deliberate, as when "excessive" set-asides are part of a bargaining strategy wherein nations claim far more newly available spectrum than they can possibly hope to use, for reasons of prestige or for leverage in attaining some other end. Or it may be inadvertent, as when stockpiling decisions are based on faulty projections of demand, faulty allowances for uncertainty, or deficient estimates of sharing and borrowing possibilities. Thus the greater the technical and administrative possibility of temporary interim usage by secondary grantees, the greater the danger that stockpiled spectrum is in fact being hoarded.

Spectrum managers must in any case plan for the future in the face of uncertainties. Above all, they must build in flexibility to cope with unexpected priority needs. When channels are reserved for such purposes it is hard to say exactly where rational stockpiling ends and hoarding begins. Moreover, some uses are intermittent, and yet it is essential for them to have spectrum immediately available when needed. Other uses make sharing very difficult technically and spectrum may have to be reserved for exclusive use. In these cases, too, stockpiling and hoarding may be hard to distinguish. The key economic test would seem to be whether a reservation does or does not maximize the discounted current use value of the frequencies in question. But there are also regulatory considerations where spectrum reservations, though uneconomic, may still be a rational means to maximize particular social priorities. Here too the reservation would constitute stockpiling rather than hoarding.

Perhaps the most we can hope for is that any stockpiling decision will be more accurate and defensible when made in fuller knowledge of its opportunity costs. At present, the costs imposed on next-best users through exclusion, the outputs forgone by stockpiling, and the possibilities of interim borrowing by secondary grantees are but imperfectly understood. Yet no stockpiling policy can really be intelligent unless discounted costs and benefits of alternative policies are adequately compared.

Without some rough idea of the opportunity costs of the reserved spectrum (minus any subsequent conversion costs), both managers and users may tend to stockpile far more frequencies than they otherwise would. The upshot would be an inadvertent hoarding in excess of projected demand or normal contingencies, a policy instituted out of sheer neglect of the possibilities for secondary rights.

On another count, potential borrowing or lending of spectrum casts a rather special light on the issues of stockpiling. The continued reservation of unused commercial and educational channels in UHF television seems defensible if, but only if: (a) the regulatory priorities, which the TV allocations were initially set up to further, will be furthered significantly within a reasonable time period and cannot be achieved in other ways (such as CATV) that are less wasteful of spectrum; (b) no techniques for lending or sharing this spectrum are available and no bandwidth reductions or reallocations conceivable to help congested next-best users without seriously impairing the projected TV structure; (c) none of the regulatory priorities in TV broadcasting is dispensable or, if dispensable, would facilitate release of spectrum without impairing the remaining priorities.

Similarly, the continued allocation of exclusive channels for public safety and military uses is economically justifiable only if there is no other way to guarantee instantaneous access to the spectrum in services characterized by intermittent usage where temporary grantees operate in the interim.

The continued underutilization of clear channels in AM broadcasting due to power limitations seems justified only if the Commission can demonstrate better than hitherto: (a) the danger to local community service that would allegedly ensue from outside clear channel competition in a situation where all stations are permitted to vary their power inputs freely; (b) the distinctive character of that local service in our present industry structure; and (c) the efficacy of present secondary grants to daytime broadcasters in reconciling fuller utilization of clear channel spectrum with the requirements of local live service. (For further discussion, see Chapters VII and XII.)

CONCLUSION

Frequency clearance will not in itself prevent all duplication and parallel systems development even within the government's spectrum sector. Yet any requirement that the full cost of frequency usage be considered before procurement officers commit funds to communications hardware or R&D is clearly a step in the right direction. The economic efficiency of spectrum utilization should improve.

On the nongovernment side in particular, the rising marginal value of one service's spectrum to some next-best user points up the need for new regulatory techniques in managing both. However, it is at best difficult to negotiate back a quid pro quo for allocated spectrum in the face of its rising opportunity costs. The use of auctions or rental charges would reduce the need to devise such new regulatory techniques but seems unlikely to dispense with them entirely.

Distasteful as they will doubtlessly find certain ramifications of this strategy, regulators and legislators have on balance opposed it rather less in the past than they have any concerted effort to introduce auctions, shadow prices, or rental charges. And far less indeed than they would have opposed any more radical movement towards a full-fledged market. Nevertheless, economic analysis still has an important role to play. It can above all help us clarify the relation between the rising opportunity costs of spectrum utilization by broadcast and common carrier users and the character of regulation to which each is rightly subject.

Use of secondary rights is another administrative technique that can help articulate opportunity costs, both on the government and nongovernment side. Because secondary rights offer an early opportunity for improving the performance of the present spectrum system—characterized as it is by congestion and squatters' rights in the absence of markets and prices—we shall now examine them in Chapter VII.

THE CASE FOR SECONDARY RIGHTS

This chapter will consider the extent to which temporary secondary rights to interim use of spectrum can operate to minimize the net opportunity costs of nonuse. Because dislodgment or conversion costs may be substantial where occupied spectrum is reallocated, the opportunity costs of nonuse are often smaller than may appear. The cost of interim nonuse is really the forgone benefits minus the dislodgment-conversion costs, including the cost of building extra technical flexibility into the hardware, the probable losses due to frequency sharing that result from unavoidable delays in conversion, and the cost of subsequent policing.

It would therefore follow that economically rational stockpiling would stop short of the point where net opportunity costs of nonuse exceed the calculated benefits of future use. The difficulty of quantifying all cost components simply implies that although the spectrum managers expect net opportunity costs to be zero when they stockpile, in fact these costs may exceed zero.

Thus within this context the questions are: Can secondary rights facilitate fuller and more nearly economic occupancy of allocated but unused spectrum by interim users otherwise excluded from all radio or subjected to costly congestion? Can secondary rights do so without disrupting the managers' social priorities, even inadvertently, as when temporary grantees refuse to vacate on request and employ political leverage to protect their spectral equities notwithstanding earlier promises to the contrary? What administrative safeguards could help prevent secondary grantees from entering into such risky, costly ventures that they would bring serious pressures to secure permission to stay on when ordered to vacate?

Before examining such questions, we must first review some aspects of the opportunity cost concept in radio spectrum management.

FORGONE BENEFITS AND NEXT-BEST ALTERNATIVES

Opportunity costs are the benefits forgone by using a limited resource in one way rather than in its next-best use. But since nonuse of the spectrum in any of its three dimensions—space, time, frequency—results in an unrecoverable economic loss, such losses must be weighed against future benefits which the nonuse could conceivably facilitate, as well as against the forgone benefits of foreclosed usage over time.

Interim users are not always easy to dislodge regardless of court decisions; illicit operations may be hard to shut down without continuous policing, once any temporary user has installed his hardware. There is also the further problem of fighting the political pressures which temporary users may generate, notwithstanding the waivers they have signed.

These are some of the costs or risks which might be avoided by holding spectrum idle before needed. The question is whether the losses due to stockpiling are greater or smaller than these subsequent net costs of dislodgment—that is, whether temporary use would generate sufficient economic benefits to offset all the costs and risks of displacement, including some rough allowance for deteriorating government-industry relations. This kind of question is simply not asked today.

Economics can help to formulate several propositions regarding the possible usefulness of "forgone benefits" or "second-best alternatives" in matters of spectrum management. A few examples follow:

1. Exclusive spectrum allocations have identifiable economic costs, though these costs may be hard to measure.

2. This is true both in the government and nongovernment sectors, although the case for nonuse varies as between the two.

3. The cost of nonuse is the next-best alternative use to which the spectrum could have been put had it not been reserved for some future use or for use by a present user at some future time.

These propositions can be illustrated as follows:

a. The cost of underused high frequency spectrum is the exclusion (under certain conditions) of underdeveloped countries that could put it to use domestically and internationally today, and for whom HF radio is probably an economically appropriate form of communications.

b. The cost of unused UHF or FM spectrum reserved for future commercial or educational broadcast service is clearly the economic benefits which could have been derived from opening up these frequencies for domestic land mobile, including industrial users, petroleum, the business user, railroads, taxicabs, local government, and police.

   c. The cost of underused or unused frequency bands allocated for police, public safety, aeronautical, or marine navigational use is clearly the benefits which could have been derived from opening up the reserved space for land mobile.

   d. The costs of unused government frequencies in large urban areas, especially military frequencies, are the benefits which could be derived from commercial use by turning them over to broadcasters, to mobile users, or even to the international services. Furthermore, the cost of unused military space may sometimes include the value of the services by, say, the Departments of Commerce, of Agriculture, or of State, which could have resulted from access to these frequencies even on an interim basis. In both cases, these costs will vary inversely with the degree of effective sharing.

Few would question the sincerity of those who defend such exclusive assignments, exclusionary costs notwithstanding. But exclusivity may not be the best approach. The costs it imposes on excluded users or users that cannot get all the space they could economically use are forced upon us all. These costs and the economic benefits we forgo may also exceed those really necessary to achieve the ends in view. Even if we accept the ends of educational TV, educational FM, a nationwide competitive TV service, or of channel reservations to promote safety in the air and internal security in the terms of the police function, there might still be a question about the *amount* of nonuse. Are the benefits forgone a higher price than we would agree to pay if we knew all the facts? Would such nonuse at least emerge as a higher price than necessary if we were only willing to take some limited risks in attempting a pragmatic accommodation to the problem?

My point is simply that no one has ever measured, and few have even thought seriously about, the magnitude of the benefits which a temporary release of reserved frequencies to next-best users might generate.[1] Hence we may have been overcautious in trying to avoid the risks and costs of dislodgment.

New efforts to reconcile regulatory priorities with fuller spectrum use may well be undertaken in response to the vigorous claims of parties who themselves represent the "next-best users" of unused spectrum today. As spectrum users, the manufacturer, power company, trucker and pipeline company represent viable alternatives to the future UHF (or FM) broadcaster and an immediate alternative to nonuse of broadcast spectrum. Ten years ago the private microwave user sought spec-

---

[1] Two exceptions are examined later in the chapter.

trum in the face of strong common carrier opposition.[2] In the broadcast case, the nonbroadcast user has so far been held at bay. In the common carrier case, immediate use by private systems has been favored over stockpiling to accommodate future space satellites.[3] But in both cases a review of the economic benefits of temporary use and the potential losses of long-run nonuse might have sharpened the issues considerably. The costs and risks of spectrum sharing might then have seemed less onerous, the use of secondary rights more appealing.

THE LOGIC OF SECONDARY RIGHTS FOR INTERIM USAGE

Reserved channels must be viewed in the context of spectrum congestion. Although only 1.3 per cent of the known spectrum is now used, within the usable segment certain bands are already congested, while others are reserved for exclusive use by selected priority applicants. Some of this earmarked space—EFM, ETV, commercial UHF—is totally unused. Other parts—aeronautical mobile and public safety— are far from intensively used. Hence, without systematic attempts to measure the interim benefits forgone, minus the displacement-conversion costs if interim users were allowed in, it can never be known how costly the channel reservations really are.

On the other hand, suppose the terms and conditions of temporary usage were clearly defined and the potential borrower allowed to occupy unused reserved space at his own risk. Borrowers could then balance the risks and costs of subsequent preemption against the risks and costs of reduced reliability and inconvenience in using their present congested band or the greater cost of moving up to some unoccupied region. Someone now excluded could enter as temporary user with secondary rights, perhaps banking on the chance that primary users will never try to claim their rights or that the spectrum manager would change the rules against them anyway. In that case, consistently with the allocational priority structure, we would secure additional outputs and possibly state-of-the-arts advances through increased usage. Because we can in no case recover the benefits lost through nonuse, the latter seems defensible only where current use is uneconomic or the costs of nonuse are more than offset by the subsequent resultant benefits.

In the international field, much business could not be conducted at

---

[2] See FCC Memorandum & Order in Docket No. 11866, Sept. 28, 1960, paras. 9, 40–46, 51.

[3] See FCC, Report & Order in Docket No. 11866, August 6, 1959, Issues 7, 8; Conclusions #20, 21, 24. Also Memorandum & Order, Sept. 28, 1960, paras. 23–24, 54–63.

all if a pragmatic arrangement had not been developed whereby unregistered communications users may operate temporarily on certain frequencies on the assumption that many registered primary users will not reclaim their rights at all. This pragmatic arrangement, combined with the rule of mutual forbearance, facilitates fuller use of the HF spectrum. The main problem is how to establish meaningful priorities for which all parties will have mutual respect.

Priority of registration is clearly inadequate, except in a head-on clash where the original registrant wants to come back in. Even priority of use is hard to invoke. Some users may stop using particular frequencies because of sunspot disturbances and yet not return afterwards because by that time their business needs have changed. Today, therefore, the would-be entrant merely determines whether some suitable frequency has been unused throughout a recent period. If so, he may enter, irrespective of someone else's priority in the IFRB Register. Indeed after six months the IFRB will give him a kind of secondary rights, and there is rarely any problem later. The question is whether spectrum managers can administer comparable temporary usage at home.

There are a number of practical difficulties. Temporary incumbents seem inevitably to gain equities in their grants, especially where a resource is publicly owned. Secondary rights might become more meaningful if property rights were privately held, with tenants allowed in for limited periods only on the explicit understanding that the property would be returned with all improvements on the termination date. But the original primary grantees could still threaten reentry to exact premiums from the temporary user. The question is how well the latter will recognize these blackmail threats and how good a policing job the spectrum managers can do afterwards, to make sure the original grantees had not been merely bluffing.

SECONDARY RIGHTS, INTERIM USAGE, AND THE SUPRAMANAGERIAL FUNCTION

One understandable reason that the FCC has granted secondary rights only with the greatest reluctance is that, prior waivers and promises notwithstanding, the temporary occupants have not always vacated on time. Indeed their demands to stay on are often realized through legislative intercession.

To remedy this, the spectrum managers might prevent even willing temporary grantees from entering in such numbers as to precipitate unusual economic distress. For example, the FCC might estimate aggregate market risks to prevent poor predictions by the applicants themselves and for fear that, no matter what they say, applicants really believe they can ultimately hang on through political influence.

There are of course many precedents for some such supramanagerial function. The Federal Power Commission has authority to disapprove pipeline applications in the absence of what it deems adequate evidence that projected traffic will materialize. That is, although the companies are willing to risk their venture capital, the regulatory authority may not allow them to do so, in part for fear that it may later be summoned to bail them out by raising rates at the consumers' expense.[4]

Still another example is found in air and motor transport where the regulatory authorities have also restricted entry notwithstanding applicants' willingness to risk venture capital. State regulatory authorities sometimes claim to act in this way for fear that, in risking venture capital under certain conditions and in subsequently competing to survive, applicants may debase their standards of service and reliability.[5]

In broadcasting, too, financial qualifications have sometimes been screened in ways that impose supramanagerial intervention on a broadcaster's willingness to invest. In the 1930s, the FCC feared that broadcasters who did not in fact make a financial go of it would waste the spectrum, presumably through sporadic or halting operations, before someone else could operate successfully. For a time, therefore, FCC imposed financial standards stricter than those imposed by the free capital market.[6] There is qualified evidence, too, that the Commission may limit entry where new competition might force incumbent broadcasters to debase their program service seriously or otherwise fail to discharge public service responsibilities.[7]

---

[4] See Kansas Pipe Line & Gas Co., 2 FPC 29 (1939). The FPC required adequate showings that applicants to build a pipeline had sufficient supplies of gas to service customers for whom the pipelines were being constructed, and adequate estimated demand to utilize pipeline capacity at the proposed rates. Construction costs were also required to be reasonable and sound financial resources available to complete the project.

[5] See D. Harper, *Economic Regulation of the Motor Trucking Industry by the States* (University of Illinois Press, 1959), pp. 91–98, 147–51, 265–72. See also L. Keyes, *Federal Control of Entry into Air Transportation* (Harvard University Press, 1951), pp. 80–100; L. Keyes, "A Reconsideration of Federal Control of Entry into Air Transportation," *Journal of Air Law and Commerce* (Spring 1955), pp. 195–200; and discussion in S. Richmond, *Regulation and Competition in Air Transportation* (Columbia University Press, 1961), pp. 154–58, 202–4, 250–56.

[6] See especially Paul R. Heitmeyer, 2 FCC 601, 603 (1936), rev. 95 F. 2d 91 (D.C. Cir. 1937). Also see review of other early cases in M. Edelman, *The Licensing of Radio Services in The United States, 1927–1947* (University of Illinois Press, 1950), pp. 62–64.

[7] See, e.g., *Carroll Broadcasting Co.* v. *FCC*, 103 U.S. App. D.C. 346, 258 F. 2d 440 (1958); also *FCC* v. *Sanders Brothers Radio Station*, 309 U.S. 470, 475–76 (1940).

Such precedents by no means justify the blanket rejection of secondary rights for licensees who now suffer inordinate delays and interference on congested frequencies or prohibitive costs in developing new equipment. The willingness of users in congested bands to borrow unused space on the explicit understanding that they will vacate upon request is hardly evidence that they should ipso facto be granted such rights. But entrepreneurs should presumably be permitted to assume investment risks at will, so long as they do not enter into a situation where, through bad judgment, they then have to prevail upon the Commission to alter its priority structure.

What the spectrum manager must avoid at all costs is being placed in a position where the courts may act to save the occupants from their own folly in having chosen between intolerably onerous options. For though they have theoretically waived all rights to do so, the temporary users may be allowed to stay on if the courts find that, though they consented, the conditions were too bizarre, too extreme, or that the managers' bargaining power at the time of consent far outweighed that of the would-be users. The question may well be raised also as to whether any temporary user did in fact really consent, notwithstanding a formal waiver of continuing rights.

Because the licensees have in some sense become the managers' wards, the key is to make a fair request of them. If the stakes are not too high, the bargain struck not too harsh, and the consequences not visited upon too many people, the arrangement may stand up in court. Whether it would stand up politically is another question, and here the small businessman with temporary status has in fact had considerable leverage.

The upshot may well be that the industry would like to take the risk of temporary occupancy but that the spectrum manager will refuse to sanction it. Because the Commission does not know who will replace you or what you will do when asked to vacate, it is not willing to let you take the risk you say you are willing to take. Yet this is really a lopsided articulation of risk. There are risks on the other side too—the risks of nonuse and of forgone benefits.

If the Commission is somehow forced to take account of the political liability of nonuse, of forgone benefits, and of imposing extra costs on excluded potential users, the decision on secondary rights might be made in a more rational manner. Dislodgment costs and risks in the absence of stockpiling would then be weighed against the costs of nonuse. Not as at present, where regulators seem overly sensitive to the risks on one side only, viz., that interim users will not vacate or that the managers' priority structure may be altered in the process. Unless the economic cost of nonuse is fully articulated, the political and administrative risks in not allowing potential entrants to assume the risks of temporary status may be obfuscated. In that case, the Commission will remain understandably hostile to arrangements that might conceivably facilitate fuller spectrum use consistent with its social priority structure.

This discussion has so far referred mainly to the nongovernment sector where business equities are crucial. On the government side, the military not only has the bulk of the spectrum today but also the power to regain whatever frequencies it allows other agencies to borrow or share. In principle, the military should be the ideal spectrum user to agree to extensive sharing or borrowing. Its unwillingness to do so more frequently may simply reflect its peculiar requirements and the difficulty outsiders have in protesting any national security argument.

As a practical matter, the military's access to the President may have served to constrain some of the DTM's formal power to institute greater borrowing and sharing. But if the IRAC is an arena where reasonable men seek reasonable decisions on these matters, albeit advisory ones, then a more systematic articulation of the opportunity costs of nonuse can only facilitate more rational spectrum utilization. Within the IRAC at least, a fuller knowledge of opportunity costs would place the burden of proof on incumbents to show why they should not lend unused spectrum to others under specified conditions; why others should not share it temporarily, or on a longer-run basis; or, in fact, why unused spectrum should not be completely reallocated. Rebuttable presumptions need not in every case force temporary use or sharing. But they could induce a more searching scrutiny of those presumably overriding considerations which now preclude such expedients.

ILLUSTRATIVE CASES OF SECONDARY RIGHTS

We now turn to two approaches to secondary rights: the FCC's proposal to experiment with secondary frequency assignments in California, pursuant to applying a similar arrangement more extensively elsewhere; and the Department of Transportation's proposal for a more comprehensive arrangement on a nationwide basis.

Proposals to Test the Principle of Secondary Frequency Assignments

The congestion of frequency bands now assigned to land mobile has led to a variety of remedial efforts. One of the most spectacular examples of private innovation has been the swift extension of the intensive and extensive margins of spectrum by Motorola and General Electric. But since such extension takes time, even partial temporary relief may be welcome by those now inconvenienced.

To provide temporary relief pending more fundamental developments, "secondary rights" have now been seriously proposed for the first time. In Docket No. 15399, the FCC considered granting no more than 500 such licenses under the following conditions:

1. All applicants for secondary rights must not only hold a valid primary grant on a frequency allocated to their service but must have operated on it for at least 90 days and have found such operation unsatisfactory due to frequency congestion.

2. Applicants must be able to revert to their primary assignment within 15 days after notice to vacate a secondary assignment. This requires that they retain a complete set of crystals for their primary assignment and that both primary and secondary frequencies be within tuning range of each other.

3. Holders of secondary assignments must waive all rights vs. any primary user present or prospective or vs. other secondary licensees.

4. Secondary licensees will be given 5-year grants, subject to normal licensing restraints, unless primary users seek to re-enter or suffer interference, in which case secondary grantees must vacate upon notice by FCC.

5. Secondary grants terminate with primary grants of the licensee.

6. Secondary grantees may not return to their primary assignments until they voluntarily relinquish their secondary assignments, or are directed to do so by FCC.[8]

The FCC was well aware that success of this proposal depends upon the positive cooperation of all licensees in question. In the Commission's own words: "[T]he Commission believes it to be unwise to 'lend' a frequency from one service to another without establishing the strongest of safeguards to assure its prompt return should it be required by a prospective licensee in the service to which it is allocated on a primary basis."[9] Nonetheless, FCC provided also that: (1) if interference is imposed on any primary user the Commission may request immediate vacating; (2) the secondary user waives all rights to any hearing in such cases; and (3) secondary licensees who fail to vacate with 15 days notice will not be permitted to hold any other secondary assignments.[10] In the Commission's words:

Although secondary operating authority will be withdrawn during the 5-year term of the experimental plan should the Commission determine

---

[8] See FCC, Notice of Proposed Rulemaking in Docket No. 15399, and FCC 64–267 48885, March 26, 1964, especially paras. 5–11.

[9] Ibid., para. 5.

[10] Ibid., para. 10.

that harmful interference is being caused by a secondary licensee to a primary licensee, the Commission cannot undertake to conduct formal proceedings whenever a dispute arises between the parties over the existence of harmful interference. If a hearing were to be required in such circumstances, the provisional plan could not, and would not, be undertaken. Consequently, it is proposed that the secondary licensee waives any right to a formal hearing to which he might otherwise be entitled.[11]

Crucial also in providing the cooperative and coordinated arrangements is the designation of a policy to determine when frequencies are available for secondary assignment in a particular area. In this regard: (1) applicants must have a frequency clearance from the area frequency advisory committee to which the frequency is allocated on a primary basis; or (2) their own statements that no primary assignments exist within some minimum distance of the secondary base station (or within some minimum frequency spacing); (3) prospective applicants should make their own frequency search before contacting their area advisory committee.[12]

The proposal pertained to applicants who sought temporary relief through interim usage in the bands 150.8—162 Mc/s and 450–470 Mc/s on any frequency now assigned to public safety, industrial, or land transportation radio service. Eligible for secondary rights were persons eligible to operate in power, petroleum, forest products, motion picture, special industrial, manufacturers', telephone maintenance radio, motor carrier, railroad, auto emergency, local government, police, fire, highway maintenance, and forestry-conservation services.

Clearly the Commission reserved discretion to determine when secondary assignments created undue interference for primary licensees. It did so wholly aside from its right to determine when an applicant should be accommodated and irrespective of clearance by any industry advisory committee or of the applicant's own frequency study. Where the Commission had reason to believe that the primary licensee would in fact soon return, the costs of temporary occupancy might be unduly high. Here, but nowhere else, it reserved the right to perform a supra-managerial function in excluding a willing potential applicant "for his own good."

The Commission's sensitivity to the many ways in which secondary grantees may interfere with primary licensees or refuse to vacate on request is clear throughout. What is less clear is how effective the proposed safeguards have been since the plan's adoption in 1965. In

[11] Ibid.
[12] Ibid., para. 8.

applying such a proposal across the board, moreover, the number of secondary grantees might have to be limited carefully to forestall undue economic distress and the consequent danger that, notwithstanding their waiver of rights, grantees would later use political leverage to stay on.

One major requirement for an efficient system of secondary rights is to select services and bands most suitable for them, economically and otherwise. One useful rule of thumb might be the availability of viable substitutes. Two-way radio for delivery trucks, transit radio for busses, or walkie-talkies clearly help facilitate business activity. But business could obviously proceed without them, so such users of spectrum are all probably good candidates for secondary rights. If their licensed frequencies are preempted suddenly by primary licensees, the mobile radio services in question could conceivably use call boxes instead or perhaps do without radio at all for limited periods.

Another rule of thumb might be the political or strategic power of any primary incumbent (and potential lender of spectrum) to recover the spectrum it does lend out from those that borrow it. Here the military seems an ideal candidate—with extensive spectrum allocations and the greatest strategic power among government users to recover from secondary grantees. Because security-related radio services require rigorous guarantees of instantaneous access, however, additional technical safeguards, such as lock-out devices, may also be necessary preconditions for any effective system of secondary rights.

A second and somewhat sketchy proposal for secondary rights was made more recently by Secretary Boyd of the Department of Transportation.[13] Briefly the DOT plan would:

1. create a pool of all unused land mobile frequencies;

2. distinguish between classes of primary and secondary users, granting priorities to the incumbents now assigned to particular frequencies;

3. henceforth permit mobile radio users to subscribe for "service" rather than apply for any particular frequency;

4. toward this end authorize a number of leasing companies to produce and lease equipment to interested subscribers, enabling them to operate on unused frequencies in various geographic areas. Whenever primary grantees invoked their rights to re-enter unused spectrum, the leasing companies would make the necessary equipment modifications to shift the secondary grantees elsewhere or, if necessary, exchange their equipment outright.[14]

[13] See Remarks by Alan S. Boyd to the Electronics Industries Association, Washington, D.C. March 6, 1968.
[14] Ibid., pp. 9–10.

New cooperative arrangements would also be needed to facilitate the trade-off of equipment no longer suited for secondary use in one area to an area where it would be usable. Improved records on effective frequency usage would also be necessary and perhaps also, though the secretary did not specifically mention it, some technical device to "bump" the secondary users once primary grantees invoked their priorities.

This proposal, like the FCC's California Plan, would facilitate fuller spectrum utilization consistent with the current priority structure. Exclusive grants to public safety users could still be made and protected. Unlike the California Plan, however, the DOT proposal would extend the principle of secondary rights beyond mere interservice lending and borrowing within land mobile to the large unused regions now allocated to television and presumably to those allocated to public safety and military spectrum as well. Even within the land mobile services alone, the DOT proposal would operate on a nationwide basis and not just in particular geographic areas or on particular frequencies.

More than the California Plan, finally, the DOT scheme recognizes the need for new supporting hardware.[15] The key to reducing the costs and risks of dislodgment as deterrents to potential spectrum lenders and borrowers may well lie in the development of suitable, and promptly modifiable, hardware and of a national secondhand market for such hardware when modifications do not suffice.

Even this latest conception of secondary rights, however, would not facilitate efficient utilization of intermittently used public safety or military spectrum. Here something more is needed. For example, domestic emergency power radio services, like the military, are supplied with surplus frequencies for the few times each year when service may be badly needed. But there seems no good reason why temporary users cannot be allowed in during the interim on the explicit understanding that they may have to be "locked out" without notice in an emergency. Nor does the fact that few parties may want temporary rights under these exacting conditions in any way alter the point. A lock-out device is clearly needed if the wide expanses of intermittently used public safety or military spectrum are to be lent at all to congested grantees, or even shared with them.

SECONDARY RIGHTS AND SPECTRUM BORROWING IN PRACTICE

One interesting case of temporary rights on an idle UHF frequency involves AT&T in its over-the-horizon transmissions from Florida to Cuba for multi-channel telephone. With enough power, the company

---

15 Ibid.

could have operated at 4,000 Mc/s. Lacking the needed power, however, and lacking a cable to Cuba with sufficient channel capacity, the
company "borrowed" an idle UHF channel with FCC approval. At
some future date it may be asked to vacate. But in view of the alternative (delay and eventual use of high-cost cable), the company was
willing to take its chances on the assumption that no UHF broadcasters
would be ready to commence operations for a long time; and by that
time AT&T would have developed the capability to transmit at 4,000
Mc/s or to utilize new broadband cable capacity.

Another example of cooperative lending of unused spectrum is that
now coordinated by the IRAC and the FCC in regard to the offshore
distance-measuring service known as SHORAN. This private nongovernment service is permitted to borrow government frequencies. But one
of the most promising areas for frequency lending by incumbents with
primary rights relates to the international high frequency bands. Here
the military, AT&T, and other carriers still have priority claims on spectrum which they rarely use, now that VHF, UHF, space communication,
and high-capacity cable have, to varying degrees, come of age. The
carriers are, of course, reluctant to give up spectral rights in the HF
band, even though they use these frequencies for back-up only. Among
other things, they cite the national security value of the HF space,
noting, for example, that the State Department can in fact take over idle
assignments for emergency purposes.

Another illustrative episode occurred a few years ago during the
Olympic Games in Japan. At that time, owing to a break in its cable,
AT&T had to use HF radio to transmit the voice signal that accompanied
Syncom's pictures, Syncom being unable to do both at that time. Even
though AT&T had not used its HF circuits for six months, it did finally
need them on a crash basis. But one wonders whether they could not
have been fruitfully loaned during the interim to Canada, where the
sparse population makes it a heavy user of HF radio. In this case,
Canada was the next-best user for HF circuits occupied by the United
States and AT&T, just as many developing nations are next-best users
of other U.S. or carrier-occupied HF circuits.

Frequency stockpiling may indeed perform some crucial national
security function, but it is sheer folly to ignore its costs in foregone
benefits even in the context of international spectrum negotiation. The
question is whether next-best users can at least be accommodated
through temporary access over protracted periods, even if we limit it
to so-called friendly nations to be sure that we can reoccupy the space
for cause. There may well be net economic benefits through some such
arrangement.

When articulated at the conference table, such benefits, conferred by incumbent nations on next-best users, could conceivably provide the basis for a whole series of concessions and accommodations in reaching international frequency agreements. Rather than endangering national security, the temporary loan of idle spectrum by incumbent nations could serve as a strategic bargaining device in its own right.

Temporary rights now figure in government spectrum too. In the 162–174 Mc/s band, just above public mobile, many of the frequencies in which the military services have priority are in fact borrowed by the Departments of Interior, Agriculture, and Justice. Here the government is tightly hemmed into one 12 Mc/s band and cannot easily go to FCC for relief. Hence, underused space is borrowed or shared through IRAC coordination.

Returning to the nongovernment side, an excellent example of what the FCC fears will happen when spectrum is "lent" is the case of daytime radio broadcasting. Here the Commission has had to balance between protecting the nighttime service of high-powered full-time clear channel stations geared to serving remote, presumably uneconomic markets, and extending the broadcast day of daytime-only licensees during the winter months so as to permit them to provide a more adequate and vital local service.[16]

Toward this end, some thirty years ago the Commission created a set of secondary rights for daytime licensees through which they could gain access to their assigned frequencies from 4 A.M. or 6 A.M. to sunrise under certain conditions. The temporary character of the pre-dawn rights was explicit and fully understood by all licensees in that they were permitted to operate before dawn only if the dominant clear channel station on or adjacent to their channel lay to the East, and the dominant station was not on the air at the same time.[17] Accordingly, a number of daytimers could in fact operate before dawn in 1950 when the Commission temporarily suspended all new daytime grants or modifications to safeguard its flexibility in reviewing the whole clear channel allocation.[18]

In accepting daytime status, then, the original daytime licensees had tacitly agreed to recognize primary rights of the dominant station and to limit their operations whenever necessary to protect the nighttime service offered by the dominant stations. Yet when the latter tried to invoke

---

[16] See Statement by FCC in House Commerce Committee, 87th Cong., 2d sess., *Hearings on Daytime Broadcast Stations*, 1962, sessions in July 1961 and April 1962, especially pp. 18–20.

[17] Ibid., pp. 19–20.

[18] See Senate Committee on Small Business, 85th Cong., 1st sess., *Hearings on Daytime Radiobroadcasting*, 1957, pp. 3–5, 18–20; *Report on Daytime Radio*, 1957, p. 7.

their primary rights in the 1950s, the daytimers balked on several counts and sought Congressional relief. According to the Daytime Broadcaster Association, the original daytime applicants had assented to daytime status under duress, no other grants being then available.[19] Since that time, potential market support for local service had grown substantially and the initial justification for clear channel service to remote rural markets was deemed far less persuasive.[20] The daytimers saw themselves as locked in a death struggle with the big clear channel licensees. They viewed with alarm any tendency for the Commission's technical expertise, conservative engineering bias, and extended suspension of new daytime grants to accentuate the "clears'" favored status under Rule 3.87 (now 73.87).[21]

After a heated review of the issues in 1957, the Senate Small Business Committee directed the FCC to expedite a solution which, if at all possible, should avoid removing the daytimers notwithstanding their original "agreement."[22] The Committee emphasized its concern over the protracted daytime proceedings and the suspension of new daytime grants. Both developments were attributed to a long-overdue revision of the clear channel allocation and the outdated record on which both proceedings were then based.[23] Five years later, the House Commerce Committee went still further in proposing that all daytimers be permitted to broadcast from 6 A.M. to 6 P.M. with some pre-existing operations being allowed to keep on starting at 4 A.M. The House passed a bill toward that end and, though it never became law, the Commission's policy appears to have eased somewhat thereafter.[24]

The text and tone of these proceedings make it quite clear that the political leverage of daytime licensees as small businesses was virtually irresistible, notwithstanding promises, waivers, and the Commission's authority to classify all licensees. For our purposes it is less important

[19] Senate Small Business Committee, *Hearings on Daytime Radiobroadcasting*, p. 284 (answer to question #1); and *Report on Daytime Radio*, p. 10.

[20] Senate Small Business Committee, *Hearings on Daytime Radiobroadcasting*, pp. 35–36.

[21] House Commerce Committee, *Hearings on Daytime Broadcast Stations*, pp. 112–14.

[22] Senate Small Business Committee, *Report on Daytime Radio*, pp. 29–31.

[23] See, for example, the Committee's barely veiled threat to provide legislative relief if the Commission did not proceed satisfactorily forthwith. (Ibid., p. 31.)

[24] See Federal Communications Commission, *Annual Report*, 1962, pp. 69–70, and *Annual Report*, 1963, pp. 77–78. The present accommodation of most daytimers in the pre-dawn hours clearly flows from the Commission's abandonment of its prior ad hoc approach in favor of a rule across the board. See FCC Report & Order in Docket No. 14419 RM-268, Amendment of the Rules with Respect to Hours of Operation of Standard Broadcast Stations; July 13, 1967, Appendix B, para. 2 (a) and (b).

that the above bill failed of enactment than that the FCC had been drawn into a proceeding lasting over twenty years, although the secondary rights it conferred on the daytimers in 1940 were explicitly temporary.

The economic distress cited in opposition to the Commission's order to stop pre-dawn broadcasts had provided the basis for a partly successful counter-strategy by the temporary grantees.[25] Once the daytimers had operated on an extended basis, the economic disruption associated with any curtailment of hours made it virtually impossible for the Commission to enforce its original rules on limited-time operations. In effect, secondary grantees challenged the whole Commission priority structure so far as it affected them, and, most important, used the equities they had gained in their "temporary" pre-dawn and post-sunset operations in so doing. Willy-nilly, the Commission became a party to having its allocational priorities altered despite itself.

In a less well-known but significant episode, the FCC granted the Navy and the Coast Guard temporary permission to use a device called RATAN to experiment in transmitting radar pictures of New York Harbor for reception on television receivers of boats. This was to be a limited experiment to determine whether the system was viable. If it proved to be usable, the service was then to be moved up into the microwave spectrum.

Although the Coast Guard had warned small boat owners not to count on continuation of the service, the latter found it highly attractive to secure radar services on TV without having to buy radar equipment. Magazines and newspapers picked up the issue. Pressure was effectively exerted on Congress (and thereby on the FCC) to continue the experiment on a regular basis. What was initially a temporary experimental authorization became extremely hard to terminate, although it finally was stopped.

Such episodes illustrate very clearly what the spectrum manager understandably fears will happen once the camel gets his nose under the tent.

A final case illustrates how thorny the issue can become when the would-be borrower is an educational entity, with a program geared to improve the quality of instructional service, and detailed study reveals virtually no likelihood that the borrowed spectrum would have been activated by other primary users during the period in question.

As a pioneering cooperative venture in bringing high-grade instruc-

---

[25] House Commerce Committee, pp. 123–27; Senate Small Business Committee, *Report on Daytime Radio*, pp. 18–20.

tion at low costs to sparsely populated areas, the FCC recognized the special educational value of the Midwest Program for Airborne Television Instruction (MPATI). There was no question about the value of a 6-channel MPATI system capable of providing six simultaneous programs to a full 12-grade school curriculum, or about the impossibility of operating such a system in the designated area over ground-based ETV stations only.[26]

But the FCC and MPATI diverged sharply on the appropriate spectrum to house MPATI. The Commission leaned heavily towards the Instructional TV Fixed Services (ITVFS) at 2,500 Mc/s in the microwave region. This had been earmarked specifically for point-point ETV systems by way of easing pressures on the more crowded VHF television band and to safeguard unused UHF frequencies for future broadcast use.[27] MPATI, on the other hand, questioned the technical and economic feasibility of operating its airborne system higher in the microwave and cited the "far greater" costs of doing so.[28]

As viewed by MPATI in 1964 the options were fourfold:

1. a system of ground-based, microwave-interconnected UHF stations;
2. a comparable non-interconnected grouping of UHF stations using video tape;
3. a ground-based, closed-circuit instructional system based on microwave stations and operating in the Instructional TV Fixed Service band; or
4. an airborne facility occupying six UHF channels outright or borrowing them for ten years with re-evaluation at that time.[29]

On technical and economic grounds, MPATI favored Option #4— an airborne facility in the UHF band—which it had in fact been operating experimentally on two UHF channels since 1961. Its request for

---

[26] FCC Report & Order in Docket No. 15201 RM-407 FCC 65-588 68750, July 2, 1965 (Use of Airborne Television Transmitters), para. 34, and also paras. 15, 17, 19, 22, 23, and dissenting statement of Kenneth A. Cox, pp. 1–2. Further, see "Petition for Reconsideration by Midwest Program for Airborne Television Instruction Inc. (MPATI)" in ibid., Aug. 2, 1965, paras. 2, 7; Comments by MPATI in ibid., April 3, 1964, pp. 14–22 and pp. 47ff., and Attachments 2–4.

[27] FCC Report & Order in ibid., July 2, 1965, paras. 22, 32, 35.

[28] Airborne transmitter costs at 2,500 Mc/s were estimated as 25 per cent higher than those at 800 Mc/s; receiving installation costs as 100 per cent to 120 per cent higher. See Comments by MPATI in Dockets No. 15201 & 14229, April 3, 1964, pp. 38–40, and Exhibit No. 2, Appendix VI–C. On relative technical feasibility, see Comments by MPATI, pp. 38–40, and Exhibit No. 2, Appendix VI–B. See finally Petition for Reconsideration by MPATI, Aug. 2, 1965, paras. 6–7, and attached engineering statement by T. A. Wright, pp. 2–8.

[29] Comments by MPATI, April 3, 1964, pp. 26–27.

six UHF channels in 1963 was defended in part as required by growing midwestern educational needs. However, a spectrum management problem still remained.

There was no question about the decisive cost advantages of an airborne system over any comparable ground-based option.[30] Yet the possibility remained that the extra costs incurred by having to run an airborne system at 2,500 Mc/s (in the ITVFS band) would compromise these advantages. MPATI presented preliminary evidence to the effect that it probably would.[31] Most important, MPATI showed that the extra costs it incurred due to exclusion from the UHF region were entirely avoidable. Specifically, MPATI demonstrated the feasibility of: first, temporal sharing (borrowing) of six UHF channels for a decade; and, second, spatial sharing via new techniques (alternating cross-polarization, antenna discrimination, precise carrier offsets) and a general relaxation of earlier, outmoded engineering taboos.[32]

Briefly, MPATI argued that the opportunity costs of its use of the six UHF channels would be virtually zero for the next decade under present allocational constraints, because there was little likelihood that any ground-based UHF station would be precluded.[33] Most of the apparent conflicts between the MPATI channels and the FCC Allocation Table for ground-based stations could be resolved with fairly minor engineering adjustments.[34] Those conflicts which remained, with one exception (a potential ETV station), were shown to be unlikely to emerge at all in the face of deficient market support for commercial UHF broadcast stations.[35] Accordingly, the net social value of MPATI's operation was estimated as virtually equal to the expected number of program hours it would generate over time, precluded ground-based UHF broadcast service being near zero.[36]

Basically, then, the MPATI studies showed that frequency sharing may be more feasible than first meets the eye, that new technical advances can readily facilitate such sharing through reduced channel

[30] Reply Comments by MPATI, June 3, 1964, pp. 15–17, and Exhibit No. 1 (cost comparisons of 6-channel UHF TV distribution facilities).

[31] See citations in fn. 28 above.

[32] Comments by MPATI, April 3, 1964, Exhibit No. 2, sec. V (review of engineering standards).

[33] The possibility of entry into the UHF band by nonbroadcast (mobile radio) users is irrelevant to any analysis of the opportunity costs of MPATI's proposal under the present TV Allocation Plan.

[34] Comments by MPATI, April 3, 1964, Exhibit No. 2, sec. IV (The conflict between MPATI and FCC or NAEB proposals is apparent but not real.)

[35] Ibid.; also see Exhibit No. 1 (Comments by P. Steiner and H. Barnett), pp. 57–63, and, on specific conflict cases, pp. 64–159.

[36] Comments by Steiner and Barnett in ibid., pp. 12–19.

spacing, that more efficient temporal sharing (borrowing) is much facilitated by the skillful use of economic prediction tools and cost-benefit analysis.

Why the FCC rejected the MPATI proposal still remains an intriguing question. Here we must return to the Commission's traditional sensitivity to secondary rights.

Ostensibly, the Commission rejected MPATI's plan on the merits. It questioned the technical feasibility of having airborne and presently allocated ground-based stations share the same UHF spectrum under current interference standards, while asserting the feasibility of airborne operations in the microwave. It challenged MPATI's economic projections as to the chances of ground-based UHF stations being activated during the coming decade without itself conducting comparable studies, and underscored the need to look far beyond that limited period in reaching a determination. It sought, finally, to forestall what it considered a real threat that other regional systems would "mushroom" should MPATI actually be granted any temporary rights.[37]

But a major factor appears to have been the Commission's fear that, once large investments had been made, temporary incumbents would be virtually impossible to dislodge. From sad experience the Commission had cause to fear that interim borrowers might not leave on request, and that they might gain political leverage to stay on. This would be true especially of an educational enterprise like MPATI. As noted, MPATI had indeed initially entered on a temporary experimental UHF grant and was now asking the FCC not just for its original two UHF channels but for four additional channels outright, or at least on a 10-year lease.[38]

Secondary Rights and Frequency Sharing

Secondary rights are of course not the only way to secure more efficient spectrum utilization. Further clarification is possible by contrasting them with schemes to facilitate greater interservice sharing.

---

[37] FCC Report & Order in ibid., July 2, 1965, paras. 24–31; FCC Memorandum & Order in ibid., Dec. 13, 1965, paras. 9, 11–16.

[38] A veiled allusion to subsequent dislodgment problems appears in FCC Memorandum Opinion & Order in ibid., Dec. 13, 1965, para. 9. The Commission was also well aware of the need to permit time to amortize investments. See Report & Order in ibid., July 2, 1965, para. 36. Finally, dissenting Commissioner Cox took note of the majority's sensitivity to lending MPATI the unused UHF spectrum in question. See Dissenting Statements in FCC Report & Order in ibid., July 2, 1965, pp. 3–4, and in Memorandum Opinion & Order in ibid., Dec. 13, 1965, p. 4.

Secondary rights and interservice sharing proposals have so far been largely limited to the several land mobile services, the objectives being to permit one mobile service to utilize another's unused frequencies under varying conditions. Proposals have also been made for comparable arrangements cutting across the land mobile and TV services, and in principal there is no reason why this could not be done under either approach.[39]

The main difference between interservice sharing and outright secondary rights, then, is not in determining whether users as different as broadcast and mobile radio can or cannot share the same spectrum but rather in defining the status of such users as do. Where primary and secondary rights exist, primary grantees would prevail in the event of any conflict. Unused spectrum is in that sense lent by the primary grantees and borrowed by the secondary grantees, for temporary renewable periods. The Commission's task is to create a framework where incumbents and borrowers will have adequate incentives to lend or borrow and adequate assurances that they may reenter when necessary or amortize their equipment. This is true whether we consider secondary rights within the mobile radio services alone (the California Plan) or secondary rights for mobile radio users on unoccupied TV frequencies as well (the DOT Plan).

In interservice sharing, on the other hand, all users have comparable primary status, the question being only whether specific groups of users are granted high-priority, and exclusive, channels, while others are limited to other groups of channels on a first-come-first-served basis; or whether all classes of users are permitted to share on a selective case-by-case basis, using unused frequencies in any or all bands. In no case, however, do the lower-priority users "return" frequencies shared with higher-priority grantees should the latter require more spectrum. So in that sense no frequencies are really "borrowed" or "lent."[40]

To understand the character of interservice sharing in land mobile we must first describe a few allocational alternatives. Two polar extremes would be the pure block or restricted block allocation on one hand, and the pure pool allocation on the other. In between might be varying

---

[39] It has been proposed that mobile radio be permitted to share VHF television channels by operating on alternate VHF frequencies in major metropolitan centers. Thus far the TV industry and the FCC have assumed that adjacent channel interference would preclude any such sharing. The question is whether this is true.

[40] The discussion of interservice sharing that follows is based on Federal Communications Commission, *Report of the Advisory Committee for the Land Mobile Radio Services* (U.S. Government Printing Office, 1967), Vol. 2, pp. 547–99.

degrees of interservice sharing within varied block-type or combined block-pool allocations.[41]

A pure block allocation would assign all like users to the same frequencies and permit no one to operate on frequencies outside his group's assigned channels. All police, public safety, business, or industrial users would operate on designated channels in all areas regardless of congestion and even if underused channels assigned to some other user group (say, forestry-conservation) are available in certain areas. A restricted block allocation is even more stringent, limiting access to certain priority users only, to designated channels only, and excluding some users from any access to spectrum at all. At the other extreme, a pure pool allocation would permit any type of user to apply for unused spectrum anywhere in the land mobile bands or geographically. Here all frequencies would be assigned on a first-come-first-served basis with no provision for priority users.

Our present allocation system falls somewhere in between, providing a modified block allocation with some interservice sharing.[42] Under it some twenty-five classes of mobile radio users are assigned to designated frequencies. (See Tables 25 and 26 below.) But users in certain classes, assigned to certain frequencies, are also allowed to share frequencies occupied mainly by other classes of users.

The attractiveness of interservice sharing can best be illustrated by a simple example. Today there are urban areas where frequencies assigned to forestry-conservation or forestry products lie idle, when users of congested public safety, industrial, or business frequencies who could use the forestry channels suffer delays and losses in reliability. Interservice sharing would permit some congested classes of users to use some of these unused forestry frequencies. Some such sharing goes on today under our modified block system, but there appears to be room and need for much more. The question is really which class of users should be allowed to operate on an exclusive channel assignment and for how long, before outsiders are authorized to share any of the assigned frequencies not adequately used. In reaching a determination it would presumably be necessary to know: (a) how soon the underused channels were likely to be needed by users to whom originally allocated; (b) how quickly the prospective "sharer" of said channels would be likely to need more spectrum which would be available through sharing; and (c) the extent to which temporary assignments might reduce the incen-

41 Ibid., pp. 558–61.
42 Ibid., pp. 575–76.

tives to develop other spectral regions higher up, if needed in any case.

Among the several options frequently proposed here, one in particular—greater sharing under the present modified block approach[43]—would require the fewest changes in rules. It purports to allow more congested users to file for rights to use underused or unused frequencies now allocated to certain groups without opening all frequencies to all groups. Contrariwise, the conception runs counter to any proposal to rule out all interservice sharing in the guise of protecting the priority users. Yet priority users could be protected better under this modified block approach than under first-come-first-served (pure pool) allocations.

While additional spectrum utilization is possible under this approach, it obviously fails to provide for more spectrum to accommodate new priority users who may arrive later when presently underused spectrum has been shared by users who now operate on congested channels. The same is true of all other sharing schemes cited, which at best offer only temporary palliatives. It is true also of the pool allocation, which could presumably facilitate the most intensive utilization of allocated land mobile spectrum. Since none of these schemes provide for the return of any borrowed spectrum by those authorized to share it, they can hardly help resolve the long-run problem of emerging spectrum needs.

A system of bona fide secondary rights, on the other hand, would not have comparable limitations. The Commission's priority structure could better be kept intact, since primary grantees who are not now using their allocated spectrum could invoke their rights at some future date to preempt frequencies from the secondary grantees who had operated there in the interim. Such a scheme could be readily applied also across major service lines (TV, FM radio, land mobile, government mobile, etc.) as well as among the several services within any single band. It would therefore make for greater flexibility than the sharing approach on at least two counts: first, by opening up wide reaches of stockpiled spectrum to temporary users, including the extensive military and broadcast regions; and, second, by protecting priority users better than most of the sharing schemes except, of course, the restricted block or pure block types.

SUMMARY

To keep the net opportunity costs of nonuse at a bare minimum, radio spectrum management must explore new economic-regulatory techniques. Granting secondary use rights subject to specified safeguards

---

[43] Ibid., pp. 576–78.

is such a technique. The task is twofold. First, we must facilitate fuller occupancy of allocated but unused spectrum by temporary interim users otherwise excluded from all radio or subjected to costly congestion. Second, we must do so without disrupting the managers' social priorities, as when temporary users refuse to vacate on request, or without making the managers party to inadvertent alteration of priorities, as when temporary users employ political leverage to protect equities in their grants notwithstanding earlier promises to the contrary.

Among the safeguards that seem appropriate are administrative measures to prevent secondary grantees from entering into such risky, costly ventures as to create serious pressures to grant them special relief to stay on when ordered to vacate. These measures may include: administrative limitations on the number of secondary rights, such rights to be distributed by lot or by auction to qualified applicants; and disqualification of applicants seeking temporary rights on used frequencies where primary grantees are expected to return very shortly. Still other safeguards might include: explicit waivers by secondary grantees of rights to a hearing in case primary grantees seek to reenter or suffer interference due to the secondary grants or in case the spectrum managers otherwise preempt the space for agreed-upon reasons; the requirement that secondary grantees retain the technical capability of reverting to their primary assignments upon notice; the use of industry advisory committees to help determine where and how many secondary users can technically be accommodated; the creation of companies authorized to lease radio equipment able to operate on unused frequencies nationally, such equipment to be modified (or exchanged outright) in the event that primary grantees invoke their priority rights; and the development of technical devices able to "lock out" secondary grantees of military or public safety spectrum, for cause.

PART THREE

THE LEVEL OF SPECTRUM DEVELOPMENT

CHAPTER VIII

SPECTRUM SCARCITY
AND TECHNOLOGICAL CHANGE

As noted in Part One, the federal government's promotional role in telecommunications is essentially twofold. The spectrum managers—the Federal Communications Commission and the Office of Telecommunications Management—permit or require the instituting of new technical standards in the wake of technological advance triggered by rising spectrum scarcities. But other government entities have traditionally dominated the underwriting of national telecommunications research and systems development.

Thus the spectrum manager works largely within the given state-of-the-arts, anticipating or responding to technical improvements of a spectrum-economizing, spectrum-developing sort which industry makes at the intensive and extensive margins. In a centralized nonprice spectrum system his task is to bring about what industry itself would do alone in any market-type system with prices. But there are serious impediments to discharging this promotional task under present constraints: de facto squatters' rights and the absence of price incentives for economy. The case for a market-type spectrum system is persuasive, therefore, not only for greater allocational efficiency, as indicated in Part Two, but also to relieve the manager of a fairly specific portion of his promotional function which at best he can now hope to perform only imperfectly.

In regard to the government's more general role in telecommunications R&D, there is no question of its longstanding importance. The past and present record amply attests to this. Here the growing dissatisfaction of high policy-makers is with the haphazard character of the several federal programs in telecommunications research and systems development. These programs are sponsored by several federal agencies

201

—Defense, NASA, AEC, and Commerce. Most of the R&D work is done under contract by private industry, though some of the most critical work is carried on in government-owned facilities too. The present patchwork of policies, programs, and disbursements has been criticized increasingly as no longer adequate, if ever it were, to meet the challenges and opportunities offered by the sustained development of telecommunications capabilities.

No really satisfactory understanding of the government's proper promotional function in electronic telecommunications is possible without careful prior review of two key sets of facts: the relation between spectrum scarcity and technological change in the present centralized nonprice system, where innovative activity at the intensive margins comes largely in response to recurrent spectrum congestion; and the historical record of the government's activity in telecommunications research and systems development (mainly at the extensive margin) in a field marked by the risks and magnitude of its capital outlays, the length of its planning periods, the divergence between its private and social returns, and the indiscriminate character of its benefits.

For that reason, this chapter and the chapter to follow will focus on these two areas and touch only in passing on some of their implications for a serious revamping of the promotional function. The proper organizational framework, important though it be for any effort to rationalize the government's role, lies well beyond the scope of this book. It should also be borne in mind that these chapters are at best exploratory studies in a field that badly needs far more systematic research and analysis.

In focusing first on the relation between spectrum scarcity and technological change, it is assumed that, wherever natural resources are bought and sold freely in a market, relative prices help us accommodate to scarcity. It is also assumed that in the centralized nonprice spectrum system today, differently sized spectrum shares function as prices do elsewhere to induce different users to economize on spectrum through innovation and substitution. However, these inducements will differ from those in an organized market in that different users are led to innovate or to substitute and different users are deterred from doing so. It is assumed, finally, that in the spectrum field the pattern of these inducements will more closely reflect the spectrum managers' than the consumers' preferences and, on that score, will probably diverge more from standards of economic efficiency and consumer welfare.

As noted in Chapter V, user charges and auctions may generate a distribution of incentives closer to the one which would flow from prices in a hypothetical market. But that is all the more reason to study the behavior of the present nonprice spectrum system whose operation we must understand if it is to be made more rational. Such knowledge is also essential to evaluating the case for any market-type system with prices, the system I believe to be best able to generate optimal technical standards in the wake of spectrum-saving innovative advance.

Spectrum Scarcity and Frequency Development

It is well known that natural resources do not become exhausted all at once. As superior sources run out, inferior sources are used at higher costs. This means that higher use rates today will impose higher costs on future users unless investment in new technology acts as an adequate offset. Business firms have an incentive to make such investments notwithstanding the risks of innovation. The greater the firm's expectations of future price rises and resource scarcities, the larger is its current inducement to invest in R&D or otherwise to develop and institute techniques which (a) permit the use of substitute factors; (b) permit the use of resource supplies hitherto unusable for technical or economic reasons; and/or (c) make possible more outputs per unit of resource used. Increased productivity would thereby help compensate for the rising supply price of the resource.[1]

At first glance one might therefore expect the absence of organized spectrum markets to blunt the nation's incentives for spectrum development. Yet frequency congestion and spectrum scarcity may provide inducements comparable to, if not identical with, relative prices in other resource fields. For decades we have distributed less spectrum to "deprived" users, and more to "favored" users than either might seek in a market. Theoretically, lush assignments would act to deter efforts to economize on or develop spectrum, whereas sparse assignments would have the opposite effect. Services or users hard-pressed to meet all their needs in the absence of a market would have special inducements to substitute more abundant factors, and to innovate new technologies that extend the intensive and extensive margins.

The constraints imposed by high relative prices in a spectrum market may be equally severe. But when users of spectrum are free to combine it with all other productive factors in minimizing their unit costs, they will tend to do three important things:

1. equate the value of the final units of all resource inputs, in terms of business or government objectives furthered;

---

[1] See generally, A. Scott, *Natural Resources: The Economics of Conservation* (University of Toronto Press, 1955), pp. 13–14: also R. Nelson, M. Peck, and E. Kalachek, *Technology, Economic Growth and Public Policy* (Brookings, 1967), pp. 28–33.

2. utilize a variety of low-cost substitutes for high-cost spectrum;

3. invest in developing new substitutes and new spectrum-saving techniques, so long as the extra R&D costs fall short of the extra economic benefits derived. In the process, the spectrum users would be freer to experiment at the margin in using a little more or a little less spectrum so long as they were willing to pay the price or the price of substitute inputs. Only their internal budgetary evaluation—not an externally imposed central allocation—would determine how much of each different resource was finally used. The overall market allocation would then come as the end result of these individual decisions; so, too, the flow of investment into spectrum-economizing, spectrum-developing R&D. Centrally allocated spectrum, on the other hand, while subject to reallocational decisions, imposes far more rigid outer limits on the user.

One critical difference between a market system and the present centralized nonprice spectrum system, then, is the latter's relative unresponsiveness to the decisions of individual users, and this cannot readily be otherwise. In evaluating the pattern of spectrum-economizing R&D in the two cases, therefore, one must distinguish carefully between the spectrum managers' preferences and consumer preferences in a market. Once one accepts a system of central allocation, one must willynilly accept also the pattern of inducements it generates. Even if the spectrum managers tried to distribute spectrum rights like a market (an unlikely eventuality), limitations of knowledge would result in a different pattern. Where the managers' priorities are consciously different from market priorities, the two patterns of innovative inducements are even more likely to diverge. Insofar as we accept the managers' priority structure as a desideratum there is nothing in principle "incorrect" about this tendency. The objection is rather that the frequency management establishment today seems so unaware of the secondary effects of allocation on technological change and, even when aware, operationally unable to take them into account.

To raise this problem is by no means to resolve it. But it must be raised explicitly to underscore a crucial oversight in the managers' newly emerging concern about the level of spectrum development. We raise it also to help explain the paradox of feverish innovative activity in the face of free spectrum grants, a phenomenon which too many economists still choose to ignore.

Within this broad context the remainder of the chapter will now focus on several bits of evidence regarding the innovative performance of radio services subject to different spectral constraints. Much more work is needed in this area, and what follows is offered only as a tentative perusal of a number of passing impressions of investigators in the field.

The following propositions are reviewed:

1. The differential innovative activity in land mobile and the TV broadcast service cannot be attributed entirely to differences in their spectral shares. But spectrum scarcity relative to demand under present allocational constraints may operate as one important factor among many.

2. In land mobile, relative scarcity of spectrum has set loose forces which have probably acted to extend the intensive and extensive margins of spectrum.

3. In TV broadcasting, technical "laggardness" in developing spectrum is associated with relatively generous spectrum allocations and the rigidities of a pre-engineered Allocation Table. The TV broadcast experience contrasts further with some evidence regarding intensive development of the relatively congested standard (AM) broadcast service.

4. A final contrast can be drawn between the technically static aeronautical-marine mobile field and the more congested land mobile and standard broadcast fields.

5. Additional analysis of the capitalization of scarcity rents in the market for broadcast stations is fully consistent with the above findings notwithstanding some superficial impressions to the contrary.

The Land Mobile Service

Frequency congestion in the domestic land mobile bands has produced increasingly long delays in two-way voice communication and a consequent loss of economic productivity. Faced with the specter of such losses if they stand pat, the land mobile users and their major hardware suppliers have in fact sought relief by other means.[2] First, they have devised equipment which would reduce the amount of spectrum needed to communicate at all, and also equipment that will enable them to operate at higher and higher frequencies, moving up from 150 Mc/s to 450 Mc/s or even higher. Second, they have sought to wrest spectrum now allocated to other services, some of which is occupied (the VHF)

[2] For an early historical account, see FCC Docket No. 11997: direct testimony of Motorola, Inc., March 30, 1959, especially by L. White, pp. 1–20; W. Weisz, pp. 25–60, including exhibits 2A, 2B, 3A, 3B; direct testimony of Electronic Industries Association, especially by R. Casselberry, March 1959, pp. 9–12, 24–36. Also see Motorola, Inc., "Future of Private Mobile Radio—A Synopsis of Motorola's Views" (company print, no date).

and some unoccupied (the UHF and FM). Third, they have sought rights to share occupied FM, VHF, or UHF frequencies with the present incumbents, or, short of that, to gain secondary rights in those bands, and elsewhere, on reserved frequencies which lie fallow for long periods before their primary users need them, as in the police and public safety services.

The pressure on land mobile has grown intense since 1945, when many industrial, transportation, and public utility users discovered radio after the so-called microwave breakthrough, which facilitated the narrow beaming of radio between fixed points, between fixed and moving points, and between moving points. Yet because other older services were already well entrenched in related spectral bands, the new land mobile users had to be accommodated in less congested but technically more demanding spectral regions.

In line with new economic needs and know-how, mobile radio users have repeatedly called for review of the FCC's allocations as between broadcast and nonbroadcast use below 890 Mc/s. In the absence of substitutes for mobile radio at least as viable as wire in the fixed (or even broadcast) services, they believe they have a powerful story to tell. Safety of life and property are emphasized first, valuable economic contributions next.[3]

The major accommodation to spectrum scarcities and congestion in land mobile has not come through the direct rationing of limited occupancy rights as in broadcasting, for all qualified applicants are allowed into many of the lower-priority mobile radio services. In contrast with the exclusive band allocations for police, safety, common carrier, and certain government services, the major facilitating factor in land mobile has been extension of the spectrum's dual margins.

Whether or not the final threshold has been reached in this approach is hard to say. The industry insists it has.[4] It contends that reallocation and more extensive sharing, or secondary rights, are now the only way out, short of leaving radio entirely. There is no doubt about the dramatic advances in spectrum resource development made by companies like Motorola and General Electric in past years. A brief review of the record dispels any doubt about just how effective private innovation can

---

[3] For a lucid review of the land mobile situation and its emergence over time, see address by R. L. Ransome, "The Land Mobile Problem," reprinted in *Industrial Communications* (February 9, 1968), pp. 8–14. Remedial options are appraised at length in Federal Communications Commission, *Report of the Advisory Committee for the Land Mobile Radio Services* (U.S. Government Printing Office, 1967).

[4] See "Comments of Electronic Industries Association Land Mobile Section" in FCC Docket No. 15398, March 31, 1965, pp. 1–9.

be in extending both the intensive and extensive margins of spectrum—in the face of the growing needs of radio users located in limited bands and hemmed in on either side by older higher-priority services. Hardware suppliers not only have developed systems to operate higher in the spectrum but also have successively reduced the amount of channel space they need for effective communication, in part by reducing transmitter deviation, by improving frequency stability, and by improving audio filters. The results are tabulated in Table 10.

TABLE 10. REDUCTIONS OF CHANNEL SPACING IN MOBILE RADIO, 1953–68

	Band	Channel spacing (Kc/s)		
		1953	1958	1968
Low	25–50 Mc/s	40	20	20
High	150–174 Mc/s	60	30	30/15
Ultra high	450–470 Mc/s	100	50	50/25

Source: Federal Communications Commission.

The sequence of events is well known. First, the low band filled up with early users. Congestion resulted in productivity losses and growing inconvenience. Mobile radio users eventually preferred to pay more for new equipment in the high band than to suffer delays, losses, and inconveniences with cheaper equipment in the low band. At this time, few would pay to risk the rigors and costs of developing the ultra high band, which is still far less populated today. Along the way, breakthroughs occurred also at the intensive margin. Needed bandwidth could consequently be halved and in some cases quartered. Accordingly, hundreds of eligible users who could not previously be accommodated could enter and/or secure better, more reliable service. State-of-the-arts advances over the years in the high band actually released 325 Kc/s of spectrum that formerly served as "guardbands" to separate the intelligence-carrying portions of adjacent channels from each other.

This high band is the most popular with mobile radio users today, although they were once as reluctant to operate there as they are now to acquire more expensive equipment for the ultra high band (450–470 Mc/s). On the other hand, the 450 Mc/s region may come to look increasingly attractive as 150 Mc/s becomes more congested, as the inconvenience of delays grows, and as technical advances reduce the cost of the new equipment.[5]

Although 600 Mc/s is now considered the highest frequency at which mobile radio can operate effectively, there has been talk of developing

[5] On the characteristics of all three mobile radio bands, see FCC Docket No. 11997, testimony of R. Gifford for EIA, March 1959, pp. 6–24.

systems that operate still higher—at 900 Mc/s or even at 2,000 Mc/s, or 3,000 Mc/s (tropospheric scatter systems adapted for mobile service).[6] The economic attractiveness of such innovative effort would depend not only on congestion and delays in the older bands but also on the possibility of borrowing unused FM or UHF space, sharing occupied VHF channels, or preempting spectrum on a long-run basis. The relative advantage of extending the spectrum's extensive margin must be determined also with reference to the chances for further intensive development (channel-splitting), whereas the economic viability of further channel-splitting must be determined with reference to the viability of all other options.

Whatever the future technical possibilities of further intensive development, the record of reductions in channel spacing since 1940 is dramatic as shown in Table 11.

TABLE 11. REDUCTIONS OF CHANNEL SPACING FOR MOBILE RADIO EQUIPMENT IN THE HIGH BAND, 1940–68

Year	Channel spacing (Kc/s)
1940	240
1945	180
1948	120
1953	60
1958	30
1968	30/15

Source: Federal Communications Commission.

A word next on the problem of testing the thesis that the rising demand for land mobile spectrum in the face of a fixed supply has resulted in growing congestion, growing access time, and diminishing reliability of service, and thereby acted to induce innovation of higher-cost equipment able to operate in the less congested higher spectral regions or in the lower more populated regions (with reduced channel bandwidth). This syndrome has been widely cited in recent years and bears directly on the general relation between spectrum congestion and innovative change.

The main obstacle to empirical analysis here is in preparing valid indices of "congestion" and "technological progress." What we should really like to have are (a) an index of changes in access time (that is, the time it takes any mobile radio service to put a call through) for particular services in particular cities and (b) data on the number of

---

[6] But see *Industrial Communications* (February 2, 1968), pp. 2–4, where EIA tells why land mobile needs can only be met by frequencies below 600 Mc/s.

frequencies available and channel spacing over time. The latter are fairly readily derived, but the data on access time are not.[7]

In their absence, we have sought instead to determine simply whether the demand for land mobile spectrum, rather than its supply, is mainly responsible for the number of licensed transmitters in major mobile radio services. That is, in the face of stable overall spectrum allocations, has transmitter growth come in response to the growing demand for mobile radio generated by a growing population? If so, have the accuracy of the allocator's initial projections and his careful long-range planning kept the supply of land mobile spectrum roughly in line with this demand? Or, despite a recurrent divergence between short-run supply and demand, has technological progress in the form of channel splitting simply been sufficient to keep congestion and degradation within manageable bounds?

In this regard, Tables 12 and 13 reveal that the demand for spectrum is relatively more important than the supply in explaining the number of licensed transmitters. Presumably, the relative power of population as a proxy for demand and the relative insignificance of number of channels reflect the fact that allocators did not make accurate predictions in the early 1950s as to where the transmitters would be needed by 1963. Had their long-run predictions been better, the distribution of transmitters among the leading 25 communities would presumably have coincided more closely with the distribution of mobile radio channels, as well as with population.

In Table 12, population always has greater explanatory power than the number of channels in all services studied. In no case is number of channels *also* significant. Accordingly, the degree of spectrum utilization may well vary among the different services and mobile radio bands. So, too, the inducements for spectrum-economizing technical advances. For the likelihood of encountering underutilization (or congestion) is obviously greater where the distribution of channels and licensed transmitters diverges significantly than where it coincides, assuming that transmitters and population are similarly distributed.

Additional evidence on the degree and pattern of spectrum utilization takes the form of "channel-loading" statistics (see Appendix B). Here the question is whether the number of transmitters per land mobile chan-

[7] The delay will vary with the number of other users trying to communicate on the same frequency at the same time. These data are widely considered a more direct and refined measure of "congestion" than mere estimates of transmitters per channel. For a recent exposition of the concept and a detailed application to urban area spectrum usage, see Joint Technical Advisory Committee, *Spectrum Engineering—The Key to Progress* (New York: Institute of Electrical and Electronic Engineers, 1968), Supp. 5.

TABLE 12. MULTIPLE REGRESSIONS ON LAND MOBILE TRANSMITTERS IN SELECTED SERVICES, FOR THREE BANDS AND 25 POPULATION CENTERS, 1963

Service/Variable	Regression coefficients (b)	Standardized regression coefficients (Beta)	Constant term	R^2 adjusted for degrees of freedom ($\bar{R}^2$)
1. Special industrial (Average number of transmitters per band per center = 1,307)				
X_2 Population	0.3442[b]	0.4052[b]		
X_3 Number of channels	40.8942	0.2342		
X_4 Channel type[a]	848.1026	0.3617	−1,153.6628	0.48676[b]
2. Business (Average number of transmitters = 2,707)				
X_2 Population	0.7414[b]	0.6215[b]		
X_3 Number of channels	9.2586	0.1284		
X_4 Channel type[a]	2,118.1545[b]	0.6433[b]	−1,767.8919	0.65613[b]
3. Power (Average number of transmitters = 705)				
X_2 Population	0.1695[b]	0.3223[b]		
X_3 Number of channels	11.4277	0.1883		
X_4 Channel type[a]	445.9452	0.3078	−488.2291	0.31671[b]
4. Fire (Average number of transmitters = 820)				
X_2 Population	0.3029[b]	0.4949[b]		
X_3 Number of channels	−41.4587	−0.1354		
X_4 Channel type[a]	646.6935[b]	0.3835[b]	819.5572	0.39520[b]
5. Local government (Average number of transmitters = 296)				
X_2 Population	0.0741[b]	0.5411[b]		
X_3 Number of channels	2.1418	0.1079		
X_4 Channel type[a]	194.4933[b]	0.5158[b]	−171.3448	0.61041[b]
6. Motor-interurban property (Average number of transmitters = 387)				
X_2 Population	0.1247[b]	0.5936[b]		
X_3 Number of channels	5.8829[c]	0.1932[c]		
X_4 Channel type[a]	228.7715[b]	0.3953[b]	−337.2493	0.61055[b]

Source: See Appendix B.
Note: N = 75.
[a] Dummy variable (three bands).
[b] Significant at 1 per cent level in two-tailed test.
[c] Significant at 5 per cent level in two-tailed test.

nel, by service and market grouping, varies significantly with the level of economic activity. Does it at least do so when differences in channel type are taken fully into account? Accordingly, the postulated syndrome of rising spectrum demand, congestion, and reduced channel spacing is examined further in a set of regressions on transmitters per channel (see Table 13). The independent variables are population density, value added by manufacturing (or median family income), and channel type.

In all six services, transmitters per channel vary significantly with population density ($P = .01$), though not with median family income. In virtually all six cases, too, transmitters per channel vary significantly with either population density or value added by manufacturing. Hence, while median family income is a consistently poor proxy for demand

TABLE 13. MULTIPLE REGRESSIONS ON LAND MOBILE TRANSMITTERS PER CHANNEL IN SELECTED SERVICES, FOR THREE BANDS AND 25 POPULATION CENTERS, 1963

Service/Variable	Regression coefficients (b)	Standardized regression coefficients (Beta)	Constant term	R^2 adjusted for degrees of freedom ($\bar{R}^2$)
PART A				
1. Special industrial (Average number of transmitters per channel per band per center = 61)				
X₂ Median family income	−0.0016	−0.0136		
X₃ Population density	0.0366[b]	0.5320[b]		
X₄ Channel type[a]	40.8200[b]	0.4891[b]	−10.4789	0.49757[b]
2. Business (Average number of transmitters per channel = 120)				
X₂ Median family income	0.0001	0.0003		
X₃ Population density	0.0533[b]	0.3837[b]		
X₄ Channel type[a]	115.1000[b]	0.6642[b]	−58.4285	0.57109[b]
3. Power (Average number of transmitters per channel = 22)				
X₂ Median family income	0.0020	0.0431		
X₃ Population density	0.0019[b]	0.4521[b]		
X₄ Channel type[a]	13.2400[b]	0.4131[b]	−16.9261	0.36246[b]
4. Fire (Average number of transmitters per channel = 25)				
X₂ Median family income	0.0029	0.0414		
X₃ Population density	0.0181[b]	0.4507[b]		
X₄ Channel type[a]	19.0800[b]	0.3991[b]	−32.2001	0.34206[b]
5. Local government (Average number of transmitters per channel = 8)				
X₂ Median family income	0.0009	0.0476		
X₃ Population density	0.0050[b]	0.4798[b]		
X₄ Channel type[a]	5.3800[b]	0.4203[b]	−8.4565	0.39882[b]
6. Motor-interurban property (Average number of transmitters per channel = 12)				
X₂ Median family income	0.0024	0.1039		
X₃ Population density	0.0062[b]	0.4606[b]		
X₄ Channel type[a]	8.1200[b]	0.5009[b]	−18.6208	0.48702[b]
PART B				
1. Special industrial (Average number of transmitters per channel per band per center = 61)				
X₂ Value added	[c]	0.1098		
X₃ Population density	0.0307[b]	0.4461[b]		
X₄ Channel type[a]	40.8200[b]	0.4891[b]	−21.3420	0.50326[b]
2. Business (Average number of transmitters per channel = 120)				
X₂ Value added	[c]	0.3114[b]		
X₃ Population density	0.0217	0.1563		
X₄ Channel type[a]	115.1000[b]	0.6642[b]	−62.7337	0.61821[b]
3. Power (Average number of transmitters per channel = 22)				
X₂ Value added	[c]	0.2323		
X₃ Population density	0.0077[d]	0.2914[d]		
X₄ Channel type[a]	13.2400[b]	0.4131[b]	−5.3903	0.38562[b]
4. Fire (Average number of transmitters per channel = 25)				
X₂ Value added	[c]	0.1538		
X₃ Population density	0.0140[d]	0.3481[d]		
X₄ Channel type[a]	19.0800[b]	0.3911[b]	−15.0240	0.35135[b]
5. Local government (Average number of transmitters per channel = 8)				
X₂ Value added	[c]	0.1582		

TABLE 13.—Continued

Service/Variable	Regression coefficients (b)	Standardized regression coefficients (Beta)	Constant term	R² adjusted for degrees of freedom (R̄²)
X₃ Population density	0.0039[b]	0.3758[b]		
X₄ Channel type[a]	5.3800[b]	0.4203[b]	−2.8551	0.40812[b]
6. Motor-interurban property (Average number of transmitters per channel = 12)				
X₂ Value added	[c]	0.4841[b]		
X₃ Population density	0.0018	0.1358		
X₄ Channel type[a]	8.1200[b]	0.5009[b]	−4.4434	0.58502[b]

Source: See Appendix B.
Note: N = 75.
[a] Dummy variable (three bands).
[b] Significant at 1 per cent level in two-tailed test.
[c] Due to machine limitations the value of regression coefficients did not register, but their significance in two cases is indicated by partial r's of 0.3314 (Business) and 0.4549 (Motor-interurban property).
[d] Significant at 5 per cent level in two-tailed test.

for land mobile spectrum, population density is a fairly good one, except where value added is more pertinent in business radio and motor-interurban property.

Given the concordance between transmitters and population, then, the divergence between channels and transmitters logically implies the existence of differing degrees of spectrum utilization and hence of pressures for reduced channel spacing, at least within certain bands and services. Where transmitters cluster in the more densely populated areas irrespective of the number of channels therein, some bands and services in some areas are almost bound to be far more intensively utilized than others (see Table 13).

The pattern just described is corroborated by data in Table 14 based on an EIA ranking of population centers. The urban-type services—the several classes of motor carriers, citizens, taxicab, auto emergency—emerge at the top of the list. Rural-type services are most clearly at the bottom—forest products, forestry-conservation, common carrier-rural, petroleum, and special emergency. The remainder fall somewhere in between. Hence, one would indeed expect distinctly higher channel loading and congestion in the urban-type group than the rural-type group, with the others falling in between.

These computed results are broadly consistent with the thesis that: (a) land mobile users tend to enter the field, or to multiply transmitters in use, as population grows; (b) they have done so irrespective of marked stability in their total allocated spectrum, by service, in the period 1950–64; and (c) their continued influx has been made possible partly by technical progress reflected in the steady reduction of channel spacing and partly by the toleration of increased delays and service degradation.

The results are further consistent with the related thesis that the influx of new transmitters in response to a rising demand for land mobile service may, in the face of fixed overall spectrum allocations, at some point result in greater interference, rising equipment costs, growing access time, and a move upward to higher frequencies at higher costs. Contrariwise, where the demand for additional transmitters can be ac-

TABLE 14. PERCENTAGE OF LAND MOBILE TRANSMITTERS LOCATED IN COMMUNITIES CONTAINING VARYING PORTIONS OF U.S. POPULATION, BY TYPE OF SERVICE, 1963

Service	In communities with 50 per cent of U.S population		In communities with 70 per cent of U.S population		In communities with 90 per cent of U.S population	
	Per cent of service trans- mitters	Rank among serv- ices	Per cent of service trans- mitters	Rank among serv- ices	Per cent of service trans- mitters	Rank among serv- ices
Motor carrier-urban property	91.47	1	98.01	1	99.85	2
Motor carrier-interurban passenger	82.21	2	94.63	2	95.81	8
Motor carrier-urban passenger	79.33	3	85.19	7	95.05	9
Citizens	75.57	4	87.05	6	95.87	7
Motor carrier-interurban property	71.44	5	87.46	5	96.18	6
Common carrier-domestic public	67.71	6	74.15	13	83.70	17
Relay press	67.66	7	90.43	4	99.30	3
Auto emergency	66.87	8	80.44	9	98.35	4
Taxicab	62.91	9	81.56	8	96.41	5
Telephone maintenance	62.57	10	78.09	11	90.45	12
Motion picture	58.29	11	90.91	3	100.00	1
Railroad	55.93	12	68.45	14	73.19	21
Manufacturers	55.35	13	78.66	10	94.22	11
Fire	49.95	14	75.27	12	95.15	9
Business	46.64	15	68.22	15	90.20	13
Police	44.53	16	60.91	17	84.51	16
Local government	40.50	17	62.07	16	85.50	14
Power	33.88	18	54.47	20	83.39	18
Highway maintenance	33.49	19	54.87	19	75.06	20
Special industrial	32.31	20	57.36	18	85.21	15
Special emergency	26.77	21	53.13	21	77.70	19
Petroleum	13.08	22	29.57	22	54.46	22
Common carrier-rural	7.14	23	23.52	23	25.02	25
Forestry-conservation	6.16	24	19.96	24	38.94	24
Forest products	2.84	25	11.74	25	51.03	23

Source: Derived from Electronic Industries Association's *Land Mobile Study*, Vol. II, Exhibit K, pp. 292–95.

Illustrative note on reading the table:

In a study of 2,938 population centers defined by EIA and ranked in descending order, 2.84 per cent of land mobile transmitters licensed to the forest products service were located in communities with 50 per cent of the U.S population, while 91.47 per cent of the transmitters licensed to motor carrier-urban property service were located in these communities.

commodated in some part by more spectrum, the number of licensed transmitters can grow with far less congestion and delay and with lower equipment costs.

The land mobile story makes an interesting contrast with various parts of the broadcast field. But first a brief comment on the situation in its counterparts in air and at sea.

Aeronautical-Marine Mobile Radio

In aeronautical-marine mobile radio, a relatively generous spectrum allocation is associated with an apparent dulling of incentive to tighten technical standards or otherwise economize spectrum. At issue in aeronautical mobile in particular is the political power to retain relatively large allocations which might not be needed if the technical improvements already available were instituted.

This political power derives in part from the overriding safety requirements of ships at sea and airplanes in flight. But it derives also from aeronautical-marine's dependence on foreign partners whose technological development often lags considerably behind ours and the consequent need to install two sets of equipment if our users are to improve their hardware at home.

Technical "laggardness" is notable in civil aviation's reluctance to go to a single sideband modulation as the ITU Panel of Experts recommended several years ago.[8] Such a conversion would involve substantial outlays which the industry appears unwilling to make. As elsewhere, the question for spectrum management is how someone can be induced to do something which provides him no more capability for a reliable, efficient communication service but would help someone else by releasing spectrum for alternative uses. How, that is, can any incumbent be induced to extend the intensive margin of allocated spectrum by converting to single sideband when he stands to gain nothing himself, notwithstanding the costliness of the adjustments?[9]

It is hard to see why civil aviation should resist any wholesale switch over to single sideband on mere cost grounds alone. By the recom-

---

[8] On the issues discussed in the rest of this section see International Civil Aviation Organization, *Report of Special Communications Meeting* (Montreal: ICAO, 1963), Items 1.4–1.5; 3.2–3.5, 3.7–3.12; 4.1–4.6; 9.1–9.8. See also, FCC *Annual Report* for 1966, pp. 135–36, FCC *Annual Report* for 1965, pp. 139–40, and Interdepartment Radio Advisory Committee, *Report*, January 1–June 30, 1966, sec. 1, paras. 10.23–10.25.

[9] Presumably, the licensees are already operating in line with prescribed safety standards and resent any extra (conversion) cost to end up doing the same thing no better.

mended date of 1975, most of its equipment will have been replaced anyway, except perhaps in Alaska. The sore point seems to be rather a fear as to the disposition of the released HF spectrum, none of which aviation would retain and which might go to government users. The industry sees this insistence on conversion to single sideband as a "cloak" for the Federal Aviation Administration's plans to "take over" air-ground stations in the international services, as it has already done at home.

In land mobile, on the other hand, hardware suppliers have had direct financial incentives to devise techniques and equipment that facilitate the accommodation of more transmitters in the older congested regions, and licensees have had incentives to use them. The more transmitters and base stations accommodated in this way, the greater the potential hardware market.

At first glance, the demand for new equipment may seem likely to vary inversely with the level of spectrum congestion, access time, and losses in reliability. But this is a superficial conclusion. Other things being equal, demand should actually grow just as soon as the value of a dollar spent on old equipment, reduced by delays and diminished reliability, falls short of the current value of income anticipated by instituting the new costlier types.

Finally, the expected benefits of reduced access time and greater reliability in land mobile, though evanescent, may make marginal spectrum-economizing hardware investment there seem worthwhile for a time. As noted in Chapter II, mobile radio users apparently believe that no single user can gain from staying out when technical improvements facilitate entry and when his withdrawal merely lets some other competitor in.[10] However imperfect this economic logic, it does help explain why land mobile has continued to invest so much more heavily than aeronautical-marine mobile in spectrum-economizing R&D.

The TV Broadcast Service

Frequency allocations to television and FM radio have been more generous than in land mobile. There has also been a marked indulgence of the broadcaster's failure to activate many of his assignments. Indeed,

---

[10] Compare discussion in Ch. I, fn. 21 and associated text. Aside from their imperfect knowledge of the long-run results of new hardware investment and development, the mobile radio users would also lack the means to act collectively on more accurate knowledge even if they had it. Hence their greater relative willingness to economize and develop spectrum along the aforementioned lines than users in aeronautical-marine mobile, where controlled entry makes an outright reallocation of any released spectrum more likely.

so marked has this indulgence been that the relatively deprived mobile radio users have registered increasingly vociferous demands for rights to share, borrow, or preempt specific channels in the UHF and VHF television bands and the FM band.

The pre-engineered allocation tables in FM and television necessarily preclude the kind of congestion found in nonexclusive bands like AM broadcasting or in bands such as business radio where virtually any eligible user can enter. The upshot is that broadcasters have not been adequately motivated to develop (let alone institute) spectrum-economizing, spectrum-developing techniques comparable to those in domestic land mobile. Industry spokesmen frequently cite the FCC's resistance to changes which would seriously or suddenly make obsolescent the public's huge investment in TV receivers. Yet these changes could be phased in gradually enough to minimize such costs. Meanwhile, television channels continue to occupy the same 6 Mc/s per station that they did 15 or 20 years ago. FM radio also retains its orginal bandwidth.

This static situation in television must be considered from the viewpoint of the technical possibilities of reduced channel spacing. Although opinions differ as to how signal quality would fare, several techniques do exist to reduce drastically the amount of occupied spectrum. One such technique would store video images and transmit only the changes in consecutive pictures, not the whole picture. This is estimated as potentially able to reduce TV bandwidth requirements by a factor of five, ten, or even 100 to one.[11] Such bandwidth reduction would of course facilitate a commensurate increase in the number of TV channels available and the number of station assignments that could be made.

Two developments in communication theory since the initial definition of TV technical standards provide the basis for such potential breakthroughs: Shannon's theory of communication in the presence of noise as summarized below; and the development of digital techniques which, through appropriate encoding of information, provide the physical basis to implement the theory.[12]

Summarizing the current state of affairs in both areas, the Telecommunication Science Panel states:

> Effective tranmission . . . can be achieved by (1) maximizing the capacity of the link for given bandwidth and signal-to-noise ratio, and by (2) compressing the information to be transmitted.
> Insight into "channel capacity" has grown profoundly since Shannon's

---

[11] W. Coombs, "Communications Innovations Affecting Television Standards," National Bureau of Standards PM-85-36, March 30, 1960, especially pp. 1–6.
[12] Ibid., pp. 3–9.

introduction in 1948 of the concept and basic theorem of bounds on information capacity for transmission related to limiting noise. Many practical applications have been stimulated, and are showing capabilities of several-fold increase of capacity and/or accuracy of transmission in given channel widths as compared to present day radio operating practices. . . .

In "source encoding," statistical characteristics or redundancy in picture and speech (or even teleprinter) transmission can be exploited to reduce the bandwidth or time required for transmission. Advantage can be taken of the "activity statistics" in multiplexing an ensemble of transmissions. "Vocoders" (speech bandwidth compressing techniques) have achieved some success. . . .[13]

Although there has been little actual progress in either area in regard to TV transmission, there is reason to believe that, in principle at least, substantial bandwidth reduction could ultimately be facilitated here too. Present TV signals transmit a rate of information many times greater than the observer's capacity to perceive it. As Coombs puts it, the occupied TV channel has "an information rate capability that exceeds the human visual perception capability by a factor of many hundred thousand times."[14] Furthermore, the information transmitted in typical TV pictures may be as much as 95 per cent redundant. By storing selected video information and transmitting only the portions of consecutive TV pictures that change, considerable reduction in needed bandwidth could be effected. In this regard, we have learned increasingly more about practical techniques to encode information, techniques based on applied digital principles developed in defense-oriented computer systems, telemetry, space communication, air navigation, and other data-processing systems.

To apply these two basic developments to TV, then, requires research: first, on a more suitable relationship between television's rate of information transmission and human standards of information perception; and, second, on the proper encoding of TV picture signals (via digital conversion) for more efficient transmission.[15] It is not clear that any individual broadcaster could conduct such research single-handed, and present spectrum management arrangements unquestionably act to reduce his incentives to do so anyway.

[13] Telecommunication Science Panel, Commerce Technical Advisory Board, *Electromagnetic Spectrum Utilization: The Silent Crisis* (U.S. Government Printing Office, 1966), pp. 23–24.

[14] W. Coombs, "Communications Innovations," p. 4.

[15] See also W. Coombs, "Communication Theory Aspects of Television Bandwidth Conservation," National Bureau of Standards Technical Note No. 25, August 1959.

Perhaps the most dramatic evidence of broadcasting's failure to develop its spectrum extensively lies in the laggard development of hardware, including inexpensive converters, to help activate the UHF band and until very recently much of the FM band as well. Of course, the nonuse of UHF and FM space for protracted periods is also the result of many nontechnical factors, including economic and administrative ones.[16] But the speedy innovation of a cheap, efficient converter of all-channel receivers and of equipment to equalize the quality of VHF and UHF signals could undoubtedly have tipped the balance towards earlier, speedier activation.

The mere existence of such potential breakthroughs by no means makes them economically justifiable. However, the broadcast industry's failure to seize more vigorously upon any of them cannot really be evaluated without careful reference to its rent-free occupancy of broadcast spectrum.[17]

Conceivably, the excluded nonbroadcast services might have been willing to pay, in return for spectrum thereby released to them, the whole cost of developing and instituting one or more of the above innovations. The value of the released space to government users might also have exceeded the development costs to the nation. Under present frequency management arrangements, there is simply no way to facilitate such cross-service financing. Yet clearly, the incumbent broadcast service will not finance by itself spectrum-economizing, spectrum-developing innovations that can only increase the number of rival stations and networks or enrich the rival nonbroadcast services.

A suggestive contrast can be drawn between the relatively static technical experience in TV and the sustained extension of the intensive margin in standard broadcasting. An explanation of the different levels of spectrum utilization lies at least partly in differences in acceptable frequency congestion and signal deterioration and the different consequences of licensing by rule and by the ad hoc approach.

The TV Allocation Plan of itself rules out the kind of frequency congestion that results under the ad hoc approach used in the standard

---

[16] An excellent early account of factors initially at play appears in Senate Commerce Committee, *Report of the Ad Hoc Committee on Allocations*, 1958, especially Supporting Brief by Edward L. Bowles.

[17] Television's technical laggardness in particular is often attributed to the FCC's sensitivity to Congressional intransigeance in opposing all technological changes that would make obsolete the public's billion-dollar investment in broadcast receivers. Nor do most broadcasters normally have hardware capabilities of their own, comparable say to Westinghouse, General Electric, RCA–NBC, or the research facilities of CBS Labs. But the question remains as to why one has not found greater advances at the intensive margin in view of well-known redundancy in TV bandwidth.

broadcast band, congestion which could in fact help induce technical advances of the sort already indicated. Not only is the ad hoc approach more likely to tolerate congestion and degradation, but it is also better able to incorporate new proposals for channel sharing and reduced channel spacing without further degradation. In television, such proposals might well require modification of the whole Allocation Table.

To be sure, new computer techniques promise to facilitate the rapid evaluation of alternatives on a case-by-case basis and thus the possibility of amending an Allocation Table without disrupting its overall priority structure.[18] New technologies to reduce channel spacing may also help narrow the gap between pre-engineered plans and the case-by-case approach. Nevertheless, this gap has been considerable in the past. There is no small irony in the fact that the preplanned Allocation Table has failed to meet initial expectations by not working better than the less orderly case-by-case approach in implementing FCC priorities in the face of spectral constraints.

The Standard (AM) Broadcast Service

Congestion in the standard broadcast band has normally generated the development of improved antennas. Unable to enter any other way, newcomers have invested in more precise directional capabilities. At higher dollar cost, these capabilities have almost from the start facilitated the accommodation of more radio stations within the same time-space-frequency dimensions.

This process of accommodation is by no means ideal from an economic viewpoint. Latecomers have borne the bulk of the extra entry costs; incumbents have enjoyed a valuable protection right. The costs of greater directionality, and of congestion more generally, may have exceeded the sums that AM broadcasters would have had to pay for extra frequencies in this country—say, below 550 Kc/s—had they been available for sale.

As the AM broadcast spectrum has become more intensively utilized, a number of other important FCC priorities have also been furthered: maximum area coverage, local service, and multi-station service. Hence extension of the intensive margin, precipitated by spectrum congestion

---

[18] But selective amendments of a pre-engineered table are far less significant in facilitating new entry than the full-fledged ad hoc approach used in AM broadcasting. See W. Baker, "Policy by Rule or Ad Hoc Approach," *Law and Contemporary Problems* (Autumn 1957), pp. 658–71. Compare with "Comments by Midwest Program for Airborne Television Instruction" by P. Steiner & H. Barnett in FCC Docket No. 15201 RM-407, April 3, 1964, Ex. No. 1, pp. 7–11.

TABLE 15. INCREASE IN NUMBER OF AM RADIO STATIONS, BY CHANNEL TYPE, 1947–67

Size of increase in number of stations	Type and number of channels with specified increases		
	Clear channel	Regional channel	Local channel
Loss or no change	8	0	1
1–5	24	0	0
6–10	4	4	0
11–15	4	4	0
16–20	3	0	0
21–25	4	1	0
26–30	2	2	3
31–35	4	4	0
36–40	1	2	2
41–45	1	3	0
46–50	1	9	0
51–55	0	6	0
56–60	1	4	0
61–65	2	2	0
Total number of channels	59	41	6

Source: Derived from Broadcasting Yearbooks, 1947 and 1967

and facilitated by the Commission's ad hoc licensing practice, has helped promote several regulatory goals.

As early as 1939, for example, the whole standard broadcast band of one megacycle bandwidth (550–1,550 Kc/s) was deemed "saturated" by the FCC. Ten years earlier the Federal Radio Commission had actually removed some 150 stations from the air to maintain or restore tolerable signal standards. Yet the number of AM radio stations grew steadily throughout the depression and postwar years, "saturation" notwithstanding. After falling from 733 in 1927 to 591 in 1934 (mainly to reduce electrical interference), the number of stations rose to some 764 by 1939 (the year of "saturation"), to 1,520 by 1947 and 2,086 by 1950. Today over 4,200 standard broadcast stations are on the air.

Looking at the 13-year period 1950–62, to be sure, we find considerable variations in the number of stations added on different standard broadcast frequencies. But the growth pattern still indicates a more intensive use. A survey by the National Association of Broadcasters reveals that, between 1950 and 1962, nine AM frequencies had increases of 40–50 stations each; 19 frequencies, increases of 30–40 stations; nine frequencies, increases of 20–30 stations; and the remaining 70 AM frequencies, increases of 0–19 each.[19] More details on changes in channel loading during the longer period, 1947–67, appear in Table 15.

[19] National Association of Broadcasters, "Frequency Loading between 1950 and 1962," unpublished compilation pursuant to AM Allocations Conference, January 1963.

Without far more refined data it is hard to determine whether such increases in channel loading mainly reflect, as with land mobile, population growth and hence an increase in the demand for spectrum, or technical improvements that facilitate closer co-channel and adjacent channel spacing. Both factors have doubtlessly played a role. So too, in some cases at least, may alterations in the classification of channels as between clear, regional and local, limited and unlimited time, as well as in authorized power and antenna heights.

Some further evidence on the above issues appears in Table 16, based on an NAB study of a six-state Southeastern Region rated by NAB as "representative" of problems elsewhere as well. The percentage of the Region's area, communities, and population receiving at least 1, 2, 3, or 4 radio services rose sharply between 1940 and 1960—indeed, the sharpest rise was between 1940 and 1950. It also rose more sharply the larger the number of services involved—the area served by four or more stations rose from a mere 0.6 per cent in 1940 to 43.4 per cent in 1950 and 87.1 per cent in 1960. Clearly, technical constraints did not impede the multiplication of daytime services over time, however measured. The FCC's regulatory goals—maximum area cover-

TABLE 16. CHANGING PROPORTIONS OF SOUTHEASTERN REGION SERVED BY STANDARD BROADCAST STATIONS (DAYTIME), 1940–60

	Number of daytime broadcast services	1940	1950	1960
		(. . . . . . per cent . . . . . .)		
Area reached by	1 or more	60.9	96.7	99.4
	2 or more	20.3	82.8	98.0
	3 or more	3.6	62.3	94.6
	4 or more	0.6	43.4	87.1
Communities with	1 or more	38.0	87.4	97.3
	2 or more	9.9	48.9	80.0
	3 or more	1.8	26.9	48.6
	4 or more	0.7	13.7	30.6
Population reached by	1 or more	70.2	97.8	99.7
	2 or more	33.9	86.1	96.7
	3 or more	11.3	71.6	89.6
	4 or more	3.7	57.7	81.6
Area reached by	none	39.1	3.3	0.6
Communities with	none	61.9	12.6	2.7
Population reached by	none	29.8	2.2	0.3

Source: Adapted from National Association of Broadcasters, Standard Broadcast Frequency Usage Study, 1940–1950–1960, December 1962.
Note: Region consists of Alabama, Florida, Georgia, North Carolina, South Carolina, and Tennessee and, in 1960, 300 cities therein.

age, competing services, and local stations—have all been strikingly furthered, in contrast with the TV situation.[20]

Table 17 underlines these generalizations in the sharp growth indicated in the number of smaller communities with two or more local radio outlets. Small communities have normally lacked competing local stations. Hence, a rise in the number of those where competition has increased since 1940 is good evidence that the Commission's goals have been furthered.

Table 18 illuminates the Commission's success and the process of intensive frequency development in still another way. Here we see the changing intensity of usage of one high and one low frequency—600 Kc/s and 1,300 Kc/s—between 1940 and 1960. Once again, the data reveal increasingly effective frequency utilization, probably in response to an interaction between technical progress (and signal degradation) on one hand, and growing population and income on the other.

Notwithstanding cries of "spectrum saturation" as early as 1939, then, at least four factors help explain the sustained growth of AM radio stations since 1946: first, the growth of market support in small communities which had little or no service before 1940;[21] second, more efficient directional antennas and related technical advances; third, the Commission's acquiescence to debased signal standards; and fourth, the greater flexibility of ad hoc licensing than of pre-engineered Allocation Tables.

Economic Rents in the TV Broadcast Service

Wherever access to spectrum is artificially restricted and the resultant demand for space exceeds its supply, economic rents accrue to the favored occupants. Such rents are capitalized at the time physical properties are bought and sold, even if the transactions are subject to regulatory approval. Markets as organized and active as those for broadcast properties do not exist widely among spectrum users. However, evidence in the broadcast field may help indicate how they would operate to capitalize the rents more generally if ever given the chance.

It is well known, for example, that TV broadcast applicants have frequently paid sizable premiums to (1) reduce the potential losses of

[20] In television, maximum area coverage has virtually been attained, with most Americans living within the range of at least one TV signal and only a handful lacking TV receivers. But progress has been more modest on the local station and multiple service goals.

[21] See in particular, FCC *Annual Report* for 1950, pp. 115–16 (tabulation of number and percentage of communities with one or more authorized AM stations, by community size, October 8, 1945, December 31, 1948, June 30, 1950).

TABLE 17. COMMUNITIES WITH TWO OR MORE LOCAL STANDARD BROADCAST STATIONS IN THE SOUTHEASTERN REGION, 1940-60

Population	1940		1950		1960	
	Total communities	With two or more stations	Total communities	With two or more stations	Total communities	With two or more stations
5,000–9,999	61	0	110	4	119	10
10,000–49,999	53	2	66	30	96	49
50,000–99,999	10	6	10	10	12	12
Above 100,000	6	6	8	8	9	9

Source: Derived from testimony by National Association of Broadcasters at AM Allocations Conference, January 7, 1963.

Note: See definition of region in Table 16.

TABLE 18. USAGE OF SELECTED STANDARD BROADCAST FREQUENCIES IN THE SOUTHEASTERN REGION, 1940–60

	600 Kc				1,300 Kc			
	1940	1950	1960	1960/40 (per cent)	1940	1950	1960	1960/40 (per cent)
Daytime								
Number of stations	5.0	14.0	22.0	440	6.0	23.0	48.0	800
Population served (millions)	6.5	14.4	19.6	302	2.5	16.8	23.9	956
Area served (thous. sq. mi.)	103.0	276.8	389.7	378	25.5	108.5	220.7	866
Nighttime								
Number of stations	5.0	12.0	14.0	280	5.0	14.0	20.0	400
Population served (millions)	2.3	6.3	9.3	404	1.8	5.6	7.5	417
Area served (thous. sq. mi.)	14.8	35.3	38.1	257	6.2	10.5	12.0	194

Source: Derived from National Association of Broadcasters, *Standard Broadcast Frequency Usage Study, 1940–1950–1960*, December 1962.

Note: See definition of region in Table 16.

income anticipated in extended comparative hearings or rule-making proceedings subject to judicial review; (2) narrow the range of Commission discretion in choosing between specific qualified applicants; (3) reduce the general uncertainties of Commission behavior. In the past they have paid these premiums to rival candidates in contested licensing cases, to induce them to withdraw or to merge applications; to other broadcasters in transfer cases, to secure their licenses and physical assets promptly, with only token FCC screening; and/or to lobbyists to influence regulatory decisions. Applicants will prefer to pay premiums for old stations (with licenses) so long as their combined price falls short of the expected cost of getting a new license gratis through regular channels and then building from scratch.

The premium now offered for an old license will range between the anticipated cost of acquiring a new one gratis (including legal fees, ex parte contacts, payments for rivals to withdraw, and the capitalized value of the income forgone during the negotiation-construction period) and the discounted current value of earnings expected from using the license during the probable period of its retention. (This period depends on the licensing authority's behavior at renewals as well as on the legal length of the license term). Within this range, the effective premium the buyer can be forced to pay will be higher: (1) the fewer the number of new licenses available gratis; (2) the greater the current value of the seller's expected earnings if he stayed on; (3) the more elusive the character of the service standards to which buyer will be subjected; and (4) the more certain he is of pro forma renewals. In any case, it may be noted that the trading of TV stations does operate to capitalize the rents inherent in spectrum occupancy under the present regulatory system.

Postponing for a moment the actual effects of inflated station sale prices, how would hypothetical rental charges[22] imposed by the government compare with the premiums which TV station buyers now pay the station owners? Are the rents collected by a station owner in trading his station strictly comparable to the rental charges which might be imposed under the illustrative rules developed in Chapter V?

In both cases, any would-be newcomer's willingness to pay for spectrum will clearly depend on the expected value of the additional end service it helps him provide and the cost of his next-best factor inputs. The more costly these inputs and the greater his expected marginal revenue product, the larger is the sum a newcomer will be willing to pay

---

[22] Throughout this section and the next it will be convenient to limit the discussion mainly to rental charges only. Similar points could be made about auctions if space permitted.

an incumbent to share, borrow, or preempt his spectrum under Rule I.[23] However, incumbent can only collect these reimbursement costs, an amount which may well fall short of the full value to him of the space in question. The reason he is unlikely to hold out for more is that, under Rule II,[24] his rejection of reimbursement costs would force him to pay the spectrum manager for any additional costs which exclusion imposes on newcomer, and these may be substantial.

In short, incumbent may accept reimbursement and share, lend, or vacate—going to or developing new substitutes or moving to spectrum elsewhere. Or incumbent may refuse to adjust and then pay "rent" to the manager equal to the net incremental costs which newcomer incurs by having to go to a substitute, to develop one, or to move higher into the spectrum. In either case incumbent will retain far less than the full value of the space to him—specifically, that value minus the costs imposed on newcomer.

In the case of TV's economic rents today, on the other hand, the seller would be in a better position to hold out for the full rent. As already noted, this will be true the fewer and more costly the buyer's alternatives, the vaguer the service standards to which he will be subject, and the more certain he is of pro forma renewals. The original owner will normally not sell unless paid a price no less than the discounted value of the income he could have earned by retaining his rights. Any failure to regain the full rent will be due either to his incorrect estimate of future income or to having to sell under duress.

It is conceivable, then, that the premiums which a TV station buyer pays for physical assets and good-will far exceed the imaginary payments under Rule I of a hypothetical newcomer to an incumbent for access rights. Whatever the actual difference in the rents paid (or collected) in either case, the main point stands: the inflated TV station sale prices (with the scarcity rents incorporated in them), no less than explicit rental charges, will provide significant inducements for incumbents or newcomers to economize and develop spectrum and nonspectrum substitutes, *if permitted to do so*.

With the few exceptions noted, however, we have actually encoun-

---

[23] As formulated in Ch. V (and Appendix D), under Rule I a newcomer could buy access to spectrum by reimbursing a willing incumbent for the cost of sharing, lending, or vacating his assignments. Thus a newcomer would be able to choose between buying access directly or developing a new system that could operate in unused higher spectrum which he could obtain gratis.

[24] Under Rule II, an incumbent who refused to accommodate a newcomer under Rule I (notwithstanding reimbursement of his adjustment expenses), must instead pay "rent" to the spectrum manager equal to costs imposed on excluded newcomers. See Ch. V above and Appendix D.

tered strikingly static technical standards in the TV broadcast field. Nothing comparable to the channel-splitting, spectrum-economizing achievements of land mobile has occurred here. The artificially lush channel assignments in FM and TV that result from their pre-engineered Allocation Tables, plus the FCC's reluctance to encourage (let alone force) reductions in channel bandwidth comparable to those in land mobile, may well have precluded any such tendencies.

Nevertheless, the bidding up of AM radio sale prices to several times their original costs between 1939 and 1947 doubtlessly *did* contribute to the early interest of regulators and potential entrants in developing the FM band. The reluctance of the then existing AM licensees to open up spectrum to a potential competitor, and of set manufacturers to render obsolete their older hardware investments, merely underline the vital role of industrial structure in shaping spectrum development.

More recently, comparable incentives to develop unused UHF space extensively have presumably flowed from the inflated VHF sale prices. But once again, the pre-engineered Allocation Table has virtually ruled out intensive development of the channel-splitting or spectrum-sharing variety. And once again, the underlying economic organization has acted to dampen any price inducements for spectrum economy or spectrum development.

Hardest to account for here is the fact that the inflated standard radio sale prices of the late 1930s and early 1940s did not facilitate a speedier development of unused FM space. And the added fact that the comparably inflated VHF prices in the 1950s have not been followed sooner by technical breakthroughs in converters and cheap all-channel receivers to develop the unused UHF space. Within standard radio, on the other hand, congestion has traditionally precipitated technical improvements to accommodate new entrants in ways comparable to those in land mobile.

As indicated, an explanation must consider (a) the special administrative constraints implicit in the Commission's pre-engineered TV Allocation Table, in contrast with the ad hoc approach used in AM radio allocations; (b) the Commission's alleged political sensitivity to rule changes that could render obsolete the public's billion-dollar investment in radio-TV sets; (c) the incentives of set manufacturers to preserve their investments in older sets and hardware; (d) the broadcaster's desire to preserve himself against new competition; (e) the FCC's failure to discriminate in the degree of access granted to different bands.

The FM band, on the other hand, was developed in part to escape from the crowded conditions of AM broadcasting and so, ipso facto, represents an extension of the extensive margin at least partly responsive to spectrum scarcity. In TV although the problems posed by the public's investment in sets is no reason not to phase in rule changes gradually in line with normal set replacement patterns, the aforementioned administrative constraints remain.

Under what conditions might an active market for broadcast or other radio properties be expected to induce the same spectrum-economizing, spectrum-developing responses on the part of users and suppliers as we find in other natural resources? The inflated sale prices charged to buyers of radio properties would produce the above responses if, but only if:

1. the broadcaster holds property rights in his spectrum and may sell to others whatever portion technical improvements render superfluous for himself; or

2. broadcasters own their spectrum space, are liable for the damage which transmissions impose on others, and can reduce these damage claims substantially through new spectrum-economizing techniques; or, short of this,

3. a principle of first-come-first-served governs frequency assignments (as in standard broadcasting) and the would-be newcomer has to bear the whole burden of proof in demonstrating his ability to operate without interference with any existing grantee.[25]

In the first two cases one would expect the pressure of high sale prices and the desire of buyers to offset the high resultant capital charges, to reinforce any ordinary incentives to improve technical standards. In the third case, incumbents who have bought their entry rights at inflated prices, if granted "standing" in a licensing proceeding, would make all the more vigorous attempts to screen the technical acceptability of the proposed grant. In broadcasting, they are obviously motivated to prevent entry to preserve their market position. However, they must couch their opposition in terms of "inadmissible" technical interference and dangers to the public interest, not in bald terms of economic injury to their broadcast investments.

TOWARD A GENERAL ROLE FOR RENTAL CHARGES

A final word is now in order on the possible role of general rental charges on spectrum occupancy. As noted, spectrum managers have set aside relatively large spectral blocks for broadcast television and FM radio but only small bands for the land mobile service. Likewise, the military have spacious bands, whereas newcomer government users like

[25] On this point see FCC, AM Rules & Regulations, para. 73.24.

NASA have relatively limited allocations. One burning question today is therefore whether the social priorities and general philosophy which underlie the relative size of spectrum allocations to different user groups can be reconciled with greater economic efficiency. In Chapter VII we explored the potential value of secondary rights and interim usage in this regard. Here the question has been broadened to include the spectrum-developing incentives inherent in different-sized spectrum shares and the problems these present.

There is no reason for spectrum managers not to allocate abundant space to high-priority services and make only niggardly grants to low-priority ones. Or not to formulate special criteria to guide these allocations, giving higher ratings, say, to safety, security, or education than would presumably result from a strict market allocation. But to allocate space to public services is one thing; to fail to institute adequate incentives for such favored user groups to use and develop their allocated space optimally is something quite different.

The earlier discussion of rental charges and competitive bidding in Chapter V is equally relevant here. A comparable analysis can be made of the effects of such arrangements on decisions to develop spectrum intensively and extensively, and on the development and use of substitutes.

Whatever the user group in question, and however abundant or stringent the allocated space, appropriate rental charges[26] can be instituted to guide the investment decisions. Where newcomer prefers to pay for sharing privileges rather than to develop a new system or to use a substitute (wire), incumbent's reimbursable expenses (under Rule I) may well be his costs for installing the superior costly equipment that makes sharing possible. Should these reimbursements exceed the costs for newcomer to develop a new system to utilize unused spectrum higher up, one might expect the imposition of rental charges on newcomer (equal to incumbent's cost in accommodating him) to induce newcomer to develop such unused spectrum. He would then have a chance at least to choose between frequency sharing and the development of new hardware. The result would be an economically more rational distribution of the burden of spectrum development as between newcomer and incumbent.

Likewise, under Rule II, incumbent would have the option of rejecting newcomer's offer to reimburse him for developing and instituting frequency sharing techniques—provided that he in turn stood ready to pay "rent" (to the spectrum manager) for the extra costs imposed on

[26] Once again, though we limit our comments mainly to rental charges, they also apply to auctions. This is obviously the case where auction values assist in setting rental charges, but it is also true of competitive bidding more generally.

newcomer in *his* next-best alternative—say, the development of a new system to operate on unused frequencies. Depending, then, on who paid "rent" to whom, a balance would be struck in the *amount* of development effort and in the distribution of its financial burden.

The point to remember is that occupancy of spectrum that is rational at one time may no longer be rational at another. Occupancy when no one else can readily use a frequency may well be economic, even if far less spectrum could serve the same needs with superior (though more costly) equipment. When next-best users grow in number and needs, however, economic rationality will require additional investment to facilitate more intensive and extensive use of spectrum and development of viable substitutes. Without some such rental charge the spectrum manager will be forced to reduce permissible occupancy by fiat, with little chance for newcomer or incumbent to participate directly in the decision except at an engineering level. The use of rental charges (or some other price equivalent) would at least leave newcomer and incumbent—within all user groups—free to arrange between them the best distribution of the financial burden of spectrum development.

The same reasoning applies to the institution of available substitutes and the development of new ones. Newcomer will prefer one of these options when the cost of moving incumbent elsewhere, or of equipping him to share, exceeds a certain level. Likewise, incumbent will choose to pay "rent" to the spectrum manager equal to the extra costs he imposes on newcomer when the value of incumbent's present space to him exceeds these extra costs. Both the decision to use presently available substitutes (wire, labor, transport) and the decision to develop new ones (new call-boxes, lasers, wave-guides) would be made within the context of expected rental charges. Wherever these charges exceeded a certain level (due to the costs imposed on others), newcomer, incumbent, or both, would have adequate incentive to turn to available substitutes or conceivably (though improbably) to develop new ones. This presumes, of course, that these substitutes constitute the spectrum user's next-best alternative—i.e., a better option for him than further development of his spectrum at its intensive or extensive margins.

The reader interested in exploring some of these issues further in a concrete example is referred to a Special Appendix below on the problems posed by narrower channel spacing in the VHF television band. Here it will suffice to conclude by remarking that the institution of user charges or auctions in a market-type spectrum system would relieve the spectrum manager of one of his most onerous tasks today: that of inducing incumbents to accommodate newcomers or otherwise innovate spectrum-saving, spectrum-extending technological improvements in the wake of recurrent spectrum congestion.

APPENDIX TO CHAPTER VIII
NARROWER VHF SPACING

The purpose of this Appendix is to illustrate the potential role of market-type incentives in changing the level of spectrum development in the TV broadcast service.

For analytical purposes only we shall examine the Norton Plan for narrower spacing in VHF television[1] and accept as fact its predicted effects on the TV broadcast structure. Without passing judgment on the Plan's actual validity, we focus rather on impediments to its implementation under the current management framework.

The Norton theory states simply that signal noise should be permitted to set the limits on any station's service range and that the areas in between the stations should suffer the interference. Applied systematically throughout the country, this principle is predicted to provide more service for some 80 per cent of the people resident in major urban centers, at the possible expense of the 20 per cent living in rural fringe areas. Under the narrower VHF spacing, the FCC's several allocational priorities would ideally be achieved more fully in 12 VHF channels than in all 82 VHF–UHF channels as presently spaced. The unused UHF spectrum could then be released for next-best users in radio astronomy and presumably in a variety of other nonbroadcast services clamoring for it.

The Norton Plan is based on technical improvements that could facilitate more intensive use of the VHF band, much as directional antennas have already done in standard broadcasting. These technical

---

[1] The following account of the Norton Plan is based on K. Norton and R. Kirby, "Optimum Frequency Assignments to VHF Television Broadcasting Stations," Draft of NBS Technical Note, April 22, 1963, appearing as Appendix 18 in K. Norton, *The Five-Dimensional Electromagnetic Spectrum Resource* (Boulder, Colo.: Environmental Science Services Administration, Institute of Telecommunication Sciences, multilith, rev. Dec. 12, 1967).

improvements, which would facilitate greater spatial (not temporal) sharing of key TV frequencies, include: (a) use of alternating vertical and horizontal cross-polarization in adjacent communities and precise carrier offsets, innovations already adopted in Europe; (b) use of computer programming for allocational decisions wherein all significant variables are fed in as needed inputs; (c) the consequent reduction in minimum geographic separation between co-channel stations from 170 to 100 miles; (d) reduction of spatial separation of adjacent-channel stations from 60 to 40 miles.[2]

One serious source of opposition to the Norton Plan has come from those who fear the political consequences of any reduction of service to fringe rural areas, although the Plan could presumably be tailored to minimize such losses. A second problem has arisen from the Plan's expected economic consequences: a flood of new station entries due to the sharp reduction of technical entry barriers. The FCC will itself not limit new entry merely because incumbent broadcast licensees foresee economic injury. The probability and magnitude of such injury and its necessary effects on program service must also be demonstrated. Nonetheless incumbents' fears do figure importantly in Congressional circles at this stage and may help explain the Commission's reluctance to move. A related criticism is that terrain was not adequately taken into account by Norton[3] and that the technical requirements of optimal spacing would place TV stations in sparsely populated areas where outlets would never be activated. But the answer presumably lies in the proper use of computer programming to introduce economic and topographical as well as technical constraints.[4]

A careful weighing of costs and benefits of the appropriate form of some such plan, adjusted for population, topography, and market constraints, and evaluated also for the value of the spectrum that would be released to next-best users, might well produce a more rational implementation of the Commission's several priorities. For argument's sake, however, we shall accept as fact that an optimal version would result in:

    a. more services for more people by educational as well as commercial stations;

    b. more interstation competition in more markets, more local stations and local services per market, and perhaps more networks too;

[2] Ibid., Appendix 18.1–18.5.

[3] The several sources of opposition are conveniently illustrated in ibid., Appendix 17, especially at 17.30–17.73 (exchange of correspondence).

[4] See, e.g., more recent statistical analysis in ibid., Appendix 18, 18.44–18.116.

    c. little if any serious loss of actual service in any fringe areas where people now reside;

    d. the release of unused UHF space for next-best users (e.g., land mobile radio and radio astronomy), with no disruption of the FCC's priority structure.[5]

Let us further include among the Norton Plan's predicted costs:

    a. cost of alternating polarization and precise offset carrier frequencies;

    b. cost of relocation of transmitters possibly in areas outside the major urban centers.

The question for radio spectrum management would then be whether the value of the UHF space to the land mobile users in fact exceeded the cost of instituting the new VHF Plan and hence the sums which would suffice to reimburse the incumbents for adopting it. Or, if the broadcasters preferred to stay put, whether they would want to do so if they had to pay rent for their occupancy equal to the extra costs imposed on land mobile by keeping them out. In this regard, each TV station's *potential* service area is 2.5 times as large under the old as under the new Plan, although the *actual* service areas are comparable. There is some question as to whether incumbent broadcasters would want to retain the current Plan if they would then have to pay rental charges 2½ times as large.

There are thus two ways to look at this new VHF Plan. One issue is whether the next-best user of the idle UHF band (land mobile) can use that space economically and without impairing the FCC's TV broadcast allocational priorities. This really depends in turn on whether the unused frequencies are worth more to land mobile than it would cost the broadcaster or the nation to institute the new VHF Plan as a whole and thus to implement the Commission's priorities in that way.

A second issue is that the proposed plan would facilitate a far more intensive utilization of the VHF spectrum. As such it clearly brings to mind the greater utilization of AM frequencies facilitated by directional antennas and the role of innovative activity and channel-splitting in the land mobile service.

Narrower VHF spacing would not relieve congestion in any ordinary sense because this is virtually precluded by the pre-engineered Allocation Table. Nor would such spacing offset any rising costs of spectrum utilization, except insofar perhaps as the cost of acquiring new TV stations (or the processing line for rights to build new ones) has grown sub-

[5] Ibid., 18.1–18.23.

stantially. However, the cost of very precise offset carriers, of alternating cross-polarization, and even of relocating transmitters elsewhere, can be viewed as an alternative to the cost of implementing the FCC's TV Allocation Plan of 1952—and in particular its commitment to maximum area coverage, local stations, and competing services—through steps to activate the UHF or to promote CATV.

The question is whether the value of the released UHF space to the best alternative user will exceed the cost of instituting the new VHF system and thereby the cost of further implementing the Commission's major priorities. In this regard, broadcast occupancy would clearly be "excessive" and technical standards "laggard," if we found that: (a) the Commission's priorities in television could be furthered through the new VHF Plan just described; and (b) to institute this Plan would cost at most a sum less than the price that land mobile users would be willing to pay to gain access to the idle UHF. For in that case, present TV allocations would not be justified even for the ultimate furtherance of the stated priorities. The more intensively used VHF would suffice for this. In a word, the VHF spectrum could be used more intensively and the idle UHF space *also* put to immediate and productive use.

If, on the other hand, the cost of adjustment exceeded the value of the UHF frequencies to the next-best user, we might say then that the broadcasters' share of spectrum is not "excessive" and their technology not "laggard," again provided that we accept as desirable the FCC's priorities. What we would really be saying in that case is that the present FCC Allocation Plan is relatively more efficient than the Norton Plan, or than still other arrangements to further the ends in view.

Finally, the stockpiling of unused UHF space would be needlessly costly if (a) the land mobile service were willing to reimburse existing stations to institute new equipment to facilitate narrower VHF spacing; and (b) the FCC could administer its television priorities with 12 VHF channels only, releasing the UHF spectrum and thus generating increments to the GNP only, the tax returns on which could compensate for any dislodgment or adjustment costs. In that case we could say that adoption of the Norton Plan was rational. Indeed even if spectrum managers could gradually activate the whole UHF band for television use through an all-channel receiver law (the FCC's present hope), a truly rational decision must still weigh interim losses due to underuse and the fact that these too could have been avoided under the proposed plan.

We can now turn in conclusion to the question of financial implementation. That is, suppose the new VHF Plan does constitute a way to achieve the FCC's priorities more fully than the present plan, at the same time releasing the unused UHF space once and for all. Just as private financial incentives have led hardware suppliers to extend the intensive margins of land mobile spectrum, so here the cost of the new VHF plan can be viewed as offset by the income and output generated by turning the idle UHF space over to next-best users. The main difference would lie in the relative automaticity of private innovative activity in land mobile, in contrast with the far more deliberate and comprehensive action required from TV spectrum managers here. However, if land mobile users had the option of reimbursing TV incumbents for instituting the new Plan, or could themselves expect reimbursement for costs they incurred through exclusion by a TV industry unwilling to budge, the chances for instituting the rather far-reaching allocational changes described would be considerably better.[6]

Two options emerge. The first, already suggested in the preceding discussion, would be to give land mobile a chance to reimburse TV incumbents for the cost of installing the new Plan. By the same token, land mobile could itself expect reimbursement for the costs it incurred through exclusion should TV be unwilling to budge. This would be one way to provide the incentives for change.

Another approach would presumably be that of competitive bidding. As more recently and very sketchily indicated by Norton,[7] a new Allocation Table could be instituted as follows: (a) advertise all outlets made available thereinunder in all relevant communities; (b) advertise a second set of grants under some alternate plan, like the present one;[8] (c) qualify all bidders carefully in each case in terms of prevailing regulatory criteria; (d) clarify beforehand the exact differences in service range of stations under each plan; (e) permit incumbents to bid for two types of grants, one generated under the present plan, the other under a new plan; and (f) conduct the auctions region by region, nationally.

---

[6] The cumbersomeness of the central allocation approach is nowhere clearer than in the fact, amply apparent here, that comprehensive changes must be acted on all at once, in contrast with the more gradual trial-and-error adjustments of normal market processes. Even with the present national allocational framework, however, the injection of cost-price incentives into frequency management practices could help facilitate difficult reallocational decisions.

[7] See K. Norton, "A Flexible Dynamic Scientific Procedure for Achieving More Efficient Use of the Electromagnetic Spectrum Resource" (Boulder, Colo.: Environmental Science Services Administration, Institute of Telecommunication Science, multilith, July 15, 1968), pp. 15–16.

[8] Norton does not consider the problems posed by phasing out an old system while phasing in a new one. His conception is aimed rather at a choice between two new systems. A more difficult task would be to open up bids on a community basis, nationally, between grants under an existing Allocation Table and grants under an alternative hypothetical table.

One would of course expect bidders to bid less on the average for the narrow-spaced outlets (given their more limited service range and smaller potential audiences), than for renewal rights under the present plan. However, a choice could be made by announcing beforehand that the plan generating the largest total sum of all bids would be selected. The question would then be whether the larger number of VHF assignments under the new plan would more than compensate for the lower average-bid price per assignment than under the old plan, even taking into account the bids for UHF grants as well.

The choice between the two would presumably reflect the relative economic preferences of broadcast applicants. Insofar as these preferences reflect the ultimate viewers' valuations (albeit imperfectly under an advertiser-supported system), the choice between the two plans would further correspond at least roughly with relative consumer preferences.

CHAPTER IX

GOVERNMENT'S ROLE IN SPECTRUM DEVELOPMENT: THE RECORD

Although there is need for more systematic scrutiny of optimality criteria for public investment in telecommunications R&D, the present chapter will stop far short of that. Nor will it contain speculation about the conceivable or desirable changes in administrative organization for mounting a more potent governmental promotional effort. Rather, it will focus on the federal government's actual role, with special reference to the historical record, the current underwriting of private R&D, and the federal program in atmospheric research.

The federal goverment's traditional role lies in its longstanding activity in defense- and security-related communications R&D. But it has more recently taken the form also of noncommunications breakthroughs in rocketry, missilry, and nuclear-powered orbital components. Two of the government's major contributions have been its wartime development of radar and microwave and the postwar space program. Electronic communications figure in all these areas, but the space program is characterized also by advances in military noncommunications technology.

Risky and costly at best, the process of spectrum development appears increasingly dependent on the close coordination of new sources of power and new metal alloys, as well as improvements in antennas, transmitters, receivers, and other communications components. Development-by-inadvertence is familiar enough in the history of spectrum utilization since 1900. But the possibility of a more rational basis for telecommunications R&D has emerged with the new interest in estimating the value of spectrum to alternative users and to the nation as a whole.

THE HISTORICAL RECORD

One crucial dimension of spectrum resource development is extension of the extensive margin—i.e., of the ability to transmit intelligence

237

with the equipment that utilizes higher and higher frequencies. To develop electronic equipment with such capabilities is costly and risky. It has been done mainly by government agencies—military for the most part—contracting out to private hardware–laboratory facilities or to comparable facilities of the federal government. This contrasts broadly with the intensive development of spectrum—i.e., of the ability to transmit a growing volume of messages within the same frequency space— where private industry has played a more extensive part. Among government agencies, the U.S. Navy has figured dramatically from the outset while, more recently, NASA and the Department of Defense have also played key roles.

The record shows that the major spectrum-developing breakthroughs have occurred at the turn of the century, with the Navy's early development of radio systems[1] during the two World Wars, especially with the accelerated development of radar in the second, and during the postwar years, with the further opening up of microwave frequencies and the development of communication satellites. In each instance, the military figured largely in R&D and systems development; in each case also, the breakthrough was subsequently taken up by the private electronics industry and made the basis for swift, extensive development of the spectrum resource. Actually, over four-fifths of today's spectrum uses emerged during or after World War II. Radar, television, satellites, and measurement and control devices in industry and science are only a few of the new technologies generated by our defense-related federal programs in telecommunications.[2]

The development of radar epitomizes the government's traditional role. Primarily military in origin, radar generated technical breakthroughs that later helped facilitate the commercial utilization of extensive spectral regions. When combined more recently with the development of booster-tracking-launching capabilities and orbital communications components, microwave, which grew out of radar, was probably the single most spectacular development of spectrum at its extensive margin in all of communications history.

Stated very simply, the key element in terrestrial or space microwave communication is line-of-sight beaming. As it moves up into the microwave region (above 890 Mc/s), communication requires ever

---

[1] From the outset, military factors naturally underlay the Navy's activity, including the attempt to develop capabilities to use higher and higher frequencies. See L. Howeth, *History of Communication-Electronics in the U.S. Navy* (U.S. Government Printing Office, 1963), especially pp. 330–31, 386–87.

[2] Telecommunication Science Panel, Commerce Technical Advisory Board, *Electromagnetic Spectrum Utilization: The Silent Crisis* (U.S. Government Printing Office, 1966), pp. 1–2.

narrower and sharper beams. In transmitting a pulse and measuring the time it takes to get back—the time lapse that indicates the distance of an object—radar helped to develop this capability.[3]

The higher the frequencies used, the narrower the beam required. The narrower the beam, the lower the power needed, and hence the lower the hardware costs for any fixed service (point-point microwave), although the harder to track any moving object and the higher the costs on that score (as in land mobile). The longer the distance from the point being tracked, the greater the power needed at any frequency. Thus in radar, as in microwave relay and space communication more generally, there are trade-offs between the frequencies used, distance, power, breadth of beam, and, of course, dollar costs. Knowledge of the technical trade-offs and the capability to capitalize on them in systems design emerged in the Navy's long and costly in-house radar program during the thirties and the war years.[4]

The Navy's role is well attested by the response of Bell Laboratories to the Navy's early documentation of radar's capabilities. A high Bell official said that "private industry would never have undertaken the development of radar because it promised so little in commercial return."[5] Impressive peacetime uses have emerged from the work on military radar which took $20 billion in World War II. Among these are uses for maritime and aeronautical navigation, weather surveillance, and studying the propagation of electromagnetic energy through the atmosphere, the ionosphere, and the space between earth and moon. Radar also generated such civilian by-products as the improved cathode ray tube, klystron, and magnetron, each of which figured in subsequent development of television and the whole microwave region.

Pinpoint electronic beaming was also crucial in the more recent development of communications satellites. But here the government's most visible and dramatic contribution has unquestionably been its creation of booster-launching–tracking capabilities and a basic role in supporting R&D. High capital requirements, great risks, long planning periods, the indiscriminate character of benefits, and the difficulty of private financing would presumably impede any unaided private venture which sought to provide all three major components of a global satellite system: terminal stations, satellites, and boosters. The United States has

[3] R. Page, *The Origin of Radar* (Doubleday, 1962), pp. 15–18, 36–37.

[4] Ibid., pp. 33–40, 168–71 and, more generally, Chs. 1–2, 7, 10. American radar development in World War II is also reviewed briefly in M. Peck and F. Scherer, *The Weapons Acquisition Process* (Harvard Business School, 1962), pp. 31–37.

[5] Page, *The Origin of Radar*, p. 179.

therefore broken down the job thus far by: (a) assigning the boosters
entirely to the government; (b) permitting ComSat and the carriers
jointly to establish all U.S. terminal stations; and (c) permitting ComSat
to collaborate with numerous foreign entities in establishing the space
satellite segment but leaving these entities to build and operate all
foreign earth stations. More than the earlier case of radar, then, the
satellite episode suggests new possibilities for a partnership between
government and industry.[6]

If radar and satellites are good examples of the government's traditional role in spectrum development for military and security-related
purposes, one index of just how significant the wartime surges have
been appears in Table 19, based on ITU allocation tables and frequency lists. Except for the first two ITU Conferences (in 1906 and
1912), when only the lower limit of allocated spectrum was adjusted
downward, all ITU Conferences have extended the ceiling upwards. But
the rate of extension has varied considerably over time.

Thus the first postwar conference in 1927 raised the ceiling from
1 Mc/s to 23 Mc/s, at the same time lowering the bottom limit from
150 Kc/s to 10 Kc/s. This represented an increase in added bandwidth
of some 2,600 per cent, compared to increases of 70 per cent in 1912,
and 30 per cent in 1932. Further allocations at Cairo in 1938 raised
the ceiling to 200 Mc/s, an increase in new bandwidth of some 570 per
cent. In contrast, the first postwar conference in 1947 pushed the ceiling up to 10,500 Mc/s, adding new bandwidth at the rate of 5,000
per cent, or 50 times more than all the spectrum allocated between
1900 and World War II.[7]

In one sense, Table 19 understates the relative impact of World
War II. During the war, a U.S. military allocation plan extended up to
30,000,000 Kc/s, and clearly paved the way for the subsequent push

[6] This is not to minimize Bell's critical contribution to microwave: first, its
wartime development of AN/TRC-6 for the Signal Corps and, second, its postwar
development of the TD-X and TD-2 systems. Bell appears to have moved swiftly.
(See F. Scherer, "The Development of the TD-X and TD-2 Microwave Radio Relay Systems in Bell Telephone Laboratories," Harvard Business School, October
1960, unpublished, pp. 35–74.) Bell's haste may have come from efforts to meet
competitive hardware threats by Raytheon, General Electric, and Philco, and otherwise to stake out claims in the new microwave spectrum. (Ibid.) Also see D.
Beelar, "Cables in the Sky and the Struggle for Their Control," *Federal Communications Bar Journal* (January 1967), pp. 26–32; A. Dickieson, "The TD-2
Story," *Bell Laboratories Record* (October, November, and December 1967), pp.
283–89, 325–31, 357–63. However, the government's direct contribution through
earlier radar development may have been unduly discounted. (See, e.g., account
in Dickieson, "The TD-2 Story," pp. 284–85.)

[7] See Office of Telecommunications Management, "Expansion of Radio Services
and Radio Spectrum Allocations," February 28, 1968.

TABLE 19. RADIO FREQUENCY SPACE ADDED BY ITU FREQUENCY ALLOCATIONS, AND NUMBER OF NEW RADIO SERVICES ADDED, 1906–67

Year	Conference	Total allocated spectrum (Kc/s)	As per cent of known radio spectrum	Additional bandwidth allocated (Kc/s)	As per cent of spectrum previously allocated	Number of new radio services added	Total radio services
1906	Berlin	500–1,000					1
1912	London	150–1,000					1
1927	Washington[a]	10–23,000	0.0007	350	70.0	4	5
1932	Madrid	10–30,000	0.0010	22,140	2,604.7	2	7
1938	Cairo	10–200,000	0.0066	7,000	30.4	8	15
1947	Atlantic City[a]	10–10,500,000	0.3550	170,000	566.9	8	23
1959	Geneva	10–40,000,000[b]	1.3330	10,300,000	5,150.0	8	26
1963	Geneva (Space)	10–40,000,000		29,500,000	281.0	3	27
1967	Geneva (Maritime)	10–40,000,000				1	

1967 { Known radio spectrum: 0–3,000,000,000 Kc/s
Magnitude: 3,000,000,000 Kc/s
Unallocated: 2,960,000,000 Kc/s
Per cent unallocated: 98.66

Sources: International Telecommunications Union; U.S. Office of Telecommunications Management.
[a] First postwar conference.
[b] In the U.S., radio astronomy is allocated to 88,000,000–90,000,000 Kc/s. Experimental services also operate as high as 300,000,000 Kc/s.

to 40,000,000 Kc/s at Geneva in 1959. Accordingly, if we consider the de facto capability in 1947 as 30,000,000 Kc/s, then the added spectrum bandwidth allocated at that time would be 15,000 per cent, or 150 times, more than all the spectrum allocated before World War II. More new radio services, too, were initiated in 1947 than at any other time.

A second index of wartime and related impact appears in data on the number of authorized users in key radio services over time. "Authorized stations" are of course not comparable for all services, but there is still some value in observing their separate growth rates. Aside from the nonavailability of data on access time, the only other comparable index of spectrum usage must be derived from licensed transmitters anyway, and these are equally plagued with problems of interservice comparability. The latter would also be less complete for our purposes, and for that reason too, authorized stations have been used.

Table 20 records the number of public safety stations for selected years when new bands were added. It is well known that wartime developments facilitated the utilization of Band B (152–162 Mc/s) for public safety, frequencies well suited for this service. The wartime impact is clear in the far greater growth before 1949 than after.

A distinction can also be drawn in Table 21 (and Figure 2) between services whose sharpest growth culminates in 1947 (marine, aviation, public safety, industrial, broadcasting) and those where the swiftest growth occurs after that date (common carrier, land transport, citizens). The technical breakthroughs and pent-up demand of the war years help explain the surge between 1935 and 1947; in the other cases, the full wartime impact was apparently delayed until the 1950s. In citizens radio, for example, the band was formally established only in 1949, the same year that land transport assumed its present form (it got its main new allocations a few years before). Without drawing too sweeping

TABLE 20. PUBLIC SAFETY SERVICES: NEW BANDS ADDED AND NUMBER OF STATIONS OPERATING, 1931–63

Year	New bands added (Mc/s)	Total stations	Percentage increase
1931	1.5–3	62	
1935	30–40	252	306.5
1949	152–162	5,700	2,161.9
1954	450–470	15,697	175.4
1963		43,168	175.0
1935–49			2,161.9
1949–63			657.3

Source: Adapted from H. Booker and C. Little, "Atmospheric Research and Electromagnetic Telecommunication—Part I," IEEE Spectrum (August 1965), p. 47.

TABLE 21. AVERAGE ANNUAL RATES OF GROWTH OF AUTHORIZED STATIONS AND GRANTEES IN SELECTED RADIO SERVICES, 1935–66

(per cent)

Service	1935–66	1935–47	1947–53	1953–60	1960–66
Citizens	92.3[a]		170.0	64.4[b]	37.8
Amateur and disaster	6.5	4.5	8.3	10.7	3.8
Marine	23.1	37.8	22.7	13.4	5.5
Aviation	79.6	188.0	18.0	13.1	2.6
Public safety	55.4	120.8	20.0	13.4	9.0
Industrial	52.9	93.6	46.5	20.8	15.4
Land transport	17.3[a]		25.8	19.0	6.7
Common carrier	10.8	0.2	29.7[c]	18.0[d]	15.4
Broadcasting	21.1	39.2	7.5	11.0	10.5

Source: Derived from statistics in annual reports of the Federal Communications Commission.

[a] 1947–66. [c] 1947–50.
[b] 1955–60. [d] 1954–60.

conclusions, these growth rates are broadly consistent with the other evidence already cited on the wartime impact.

Older bands tend to be lower in the spectrum and more intensively developed than the higher bands. Broadly speaking, this tendency would be consistent with the government's role in moving upward for new systems development. Room for new services is more readily available in the higher, sparser spectral regions which are less developed and normally more costly to use.

Indicative of the government's role in the higher spectral regions today is its rising relative share of frequencies (in the United States) as we move from the lower to the higher ITU Bands. Table 22 shows the federal government's share of spectrum to be notably less than the nongovernment share in Bands 6–9 (below 3,000 Mc/s), but substantially greater in Bands 10 and 11 (above 3,000 Mc/s). Specifically, the ratio of exclusive government to nongovernment spectral shares rises gradually in Bands 6–8, declines slightly in Band 9, and then rises very sharply in Bands 10 and 11. Stated otherwise, although Bands 4–7 (0–30 Mc/s) are largely shared, the portion used on an exclusive basis is mainly nongovernment, whereas Bands 8 and 9 (30–3,000 Mc/s) are also used relatively more by nongovernment. Government usage, on the other hand, prevails in the regions still higher up. The same pattern holds true when all the spectrum shared by both is attributed to either separately.

In the evidence thus far reviewed, the government's security-related role in spectrum development is clearly associated with a physical movement upward and a chronological movement forward. A further piece of evidence on the general tendency of older spectral regions to be more

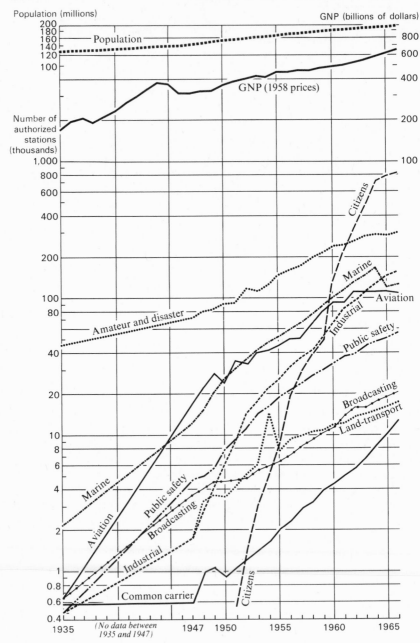

Figure 2. Number of authorized stations by major radio service, 1935–66. (For source, see Appendix A.)

TABLE 22. GOVERNMENT AND NONGOVERNMENT SHARES OF SPECTRUM, BY ITU BAND, 1967

ITU Band: Megacycles:	Band 4 0.01 to 0.03	Band 5 0.03 to 0.3	Band 6 0.3 to 3	Band 7 3 to 30	Band 8 30 to 300	Band 9 300 to 3,000	Band 10 3,000 to 30,000	Band 11 30,000 to 40,000	Total 0.01 to 40,000
Shared[a]									
Mc/s	0.0199	0.268	1.605	19.365	33.275	1,006.9	5,955.0	2,100.0	9,116.4
Per cent	99.5	99.3	5.9	71.7	12.3	37.3	22.1	21.0	22.8
Government[b]									
Mc/s	0.0001	0.002	0.025	2.065	107.010	645.1	12,290.0	5,200.0	18,244.2
Per cent	0.5	0.7	0.9	7.7	39.6	23.9	45.5	52.0	45.6
Nongovernment[c]									
Mc/s	*	*	1.070	5.570	129.715	1,048.0	8,755.0	2,700.0	12,639.4
Per cent			39.6	20.6	48.0	38.8	32.4	27.0	31.6
Total government[d]									
Mc/s	0.0200	0.270	1.630	21.430	140.285	1,652.0	18,245.0	7,300.0	27,360.6
Per cent	100.0	100.0	60.4	79.4	52.0	61.2	67.6	73.0	68.4
Total nongovernment[e]									
Mc/s	0.0199	0.268	2.675	24.935	162.990	2,054.9	14,710.0	4,800.0	21,755.8
Per cent	99.5	99.3	99.1	92.4	60.4	76.1	54.5	48.0	54.4

Source: K. Norton, *The Five-Dimensional Electromagnetic Spectrum Resource* (rev., December 12, 1967, unofficial multilith), Appendix 16.60 (adapted).

* No spectrum allocated to nongovernment users on an exclusive basis.
[a] Shared = used by government and nongovernment.
[b] Government = federal government users only.
[c] Nongovernment = all FCC licensees, including local or state governments.
[d] Total government = "shared" plus government.
[e] Total nongovernment = "shared" plus nongovernment.

fully utilized (and congested) than the newer ones appears in Table 23, which records data on economic usage of the spectrum in 1962. Two broad patterns emerge.

1. The older the allocated band in 1962, the lower its spectral location and the larger its economic value per megacycle of bandwidth. In short, spectrum utilization tends to be more intensive and productive of greater value per unit of bandwidth in the older segments, even though the development of the wider, higher spectral regions can and often does generate far greater aggregate value, at sharply reduced rates per megacycle used.

2. The role of wartime breakthroughs is apparent in the rising absolute magnitude of the spectrum's economic value as the higher spectral regions have gradually opened up. The large relative share of telecommunications product value which the 30 Mc/s–3,000 Gc/s region accounted for in 1962 clearly indicates this. So, too, does the fact that most of this value occurs below 20 Gc/s in the extensive regions allocated since World War II, especially at Atlantic City in 1947.

Because these estimates of economic product value are vitiated by heterogeneity and double-counting,[8] it is of additional interest to examine data on broadcast revenues alone, by spectral region, data which are free of the above deficiencies (see Table 24). Even recognizing the multiplicity of factors at play here, the intra-radio and intra-television comparisons underscore the importance of both age of effective utilization and spectral location. Thus the older radio band (AM broadcast) generates almost $850 million per Mc/s compared to $2 million for FM radio, whereas VHF television generates over $29 million per Mc/s, compared to only $352,000 for the UHF band. The contrast between the oldest of all broadcast bands (AM radio) and the newest band (UHF) is even more dramatic.

It is of course true that FM radio and television as such require more spectrum than AM radio for any acceptable transmission at all. But the spectrum's imputed economic value productivity in each case is still relevant to our general thesis. To say that an acre of residential land would be worth much more if the zoning laws permitted the construction of tall office buildings hardly denies all economic significance to relative land values in the current framework.

Nevertheless, the postulated importance of age and spectral location must not be exaggerated as factors in spectrum utilization. Other elements must also be weighed in.

Returning to the safety and special radio services, according to our

[8] See discussion in Ch. V.

TABLE 23. ESTIMATED ECONOMIC VALUE OF ELECTROMAGNETIC TELECOMMUNICATION BY SPECTRAL REGION, 1962

Frequency band (1)	ITU allocation date (2)	Economic usage, 1962[a] ($ million) (3)	Per cent of total (4)	Usage per megacycle[b] ($ million) (5)	Propagation mechanism (6)
0–30 Mc/s	to 30 Mc/s = 1932 to 200 Mc/s = 1938	2,940	17.3	98.0	ground wave; ionospheric; VLF, LF, MF, HF
30–1,000 Mc/s	to 30 Gc/s = 1947 to 40 Gc/s = 1959	9,090	53.5	9.4	tropospheric; line-of-sight; VHF, UHF
1–3,000 Gc/s		4,370	25.7	0.0015	tropospheric; beyond horizon; SHF, EHF, TR
Over 3,000 Gc/s		600	3.5	—	infrared; visible light near ultraviolet
Total		17,000	100.0		

Source: Adapted from H. Booker and C. Little, "Atmospheric Research and Electromagnetic Telecommunication—Part I," IEEE Spectrum (August 1965), p. 46.
[a] Activities included are: manufacturing (value of shipments); government expenditures for installation operations and maintenance; annual revenue or expenditures in broadcasting, common carriers, and safety and special services; allocable R&D expenditures by industry, government and nonprofit; wholesale and retail trade in hardware and components; radio–TV and commercial installation and repair services.
[b] Column (3) divided by column (1).

247

TABLE 24. BROADCAST REVENUES PER MEGACYCLE BANDWIDTH, BY SERVICE AND SPECTRAL REGION, 1967

Service	Revenues in 1967 ($ million)	Number of mega-cycles	Revenues per megacycle ($ million)	Spectral region	Date of entry	
					Official	Effective
AM	907.3	1.07	847.9	535–1,605 Kc/s	1923	1926
FM	39.8	20.00	2.0	88–108 Mc/s	1941	1945
VHF–TV	2,127.5[a]	72.00	29.5	174–216 Mc/s	1941	1945
UHF–TV	147.9[a]	420.00	0.3	470–890 Mc/s	1952	1952

Source: Federal Communications Commission.
[a] Includes allocated share of revenues of networks and their stations (93.5 per cent VHF, 6.5 per cent UHF).

theory the newest Band C (450–474 Mc/s) should be the least congested. In Table 25, Band C does consistently contain by far the smallest proportion of transmitters of any service recorded. But Band B (at 150–174 Mc/s), chronologically "younger" than Band A (at 50–74 Mc/s)[9] and higher in the spectrum, often contains a *larger* share of U.S. transmitters today. The question is—Why is this so?

One explanation may be simply that the nationwide data obscure forces at play in the major metropolitan centers known to be subject to the greatest congestion. The degree of channel loading is also more suitably characterized by transmitters per channel than by percentage of total transmitters in band. Before qualifying age as any determinative factor, therefore, we have tabulated in Table 26 per channel transmitter data by spectral band and by service, for 25 leading metropolitan centers.

Deriving the basic data once more from the EIA Land Mobile Study, we have calculated the median (and mean) number of transmitters per channel for each of 20 safety and special radio services. For comparative purposes, we also calculated the median and mean percentage of transmitters in each band.

Once again, the newest Band (C) consistently has far fewer transmitters per channel than the older Bands (A and B), but the oldest

[9] Land mobile began at 1.5–3 Mc/s around 1930, and gradually moved up to the 30–50 Mc/s region (Band A) later in the decade. Then, mainly after World War II, came further shifts to the 152–162 Mc/s region (Band B); and still later, to the 450–474 Mc/s region (Band C). In short, Band A is clearly the oldest in continuous use, and Band C the newest. See Direct Testimony of Motorola Inc., in FCC Docket No. 11997, March 30, 1959, especially exhibits No. 1 and 2A; and statement of L. White at pp. 1–4. Also see FCC Annual Reports for 1947, pp. 39–50; for 1948, pp. 60–72; for 1949, pp. 70–82; for 1950, pp. 77–92; for 1959, pp. 88–100; for 1960, pp. 75–91.

TABLE 25. TOTAL U.S. LICENSED TRANSMITTERS, LAND MOBILE SERVICE, BY BAND, 1963

Service and band	Total trans- mitters	Percentage of transmitters in service and band
Motor-urban property	9,719	100.0
B	5,814	59.8
C	3,905	40.2
Motor-interurban passenger	596	100.0
A	596	100.0
C	0	0.0
Motor-urban passenger	4,104	100.0
A	4,002	97.5
C	102	2.5
Citizens	37,529	100.0
A	37,529	100.0
Motor-interurban property	47,711	100.0
A	29,181	61.2
B	17,407	36.5
C	1,123	2.3
Common carrier-public	896,283	100.0
A	242,528	27.0
B	586,133	65.4
C	67,622	7.6
Relay press	2,238	100.0
B	2,238	100.0
Auto emergency	11,065	100.0
B	10,188	92.1
C	877	7.9
Taxicab	122,663	100.0
B	108,996	88.8
C	13,667	11.2
Telephone maintenance	14,895	100.0
A	2,392	16.0
B	8,627	57.9
C	3,876	26.1
Motion picture	425	100.0
B	425	100.0
Railroad	200,030	100.0
A	24	0.0
B	199,685	99.8
C	321	0.2
Manufacturers	19,432	100.0
A	18,428	94.8
B	1,004	5.2
Fire	111,083	100.0
A	51,981	46.8
B	58,306	52.5
C	796	0.7
Business	391,975	100.0
A	143,878	36.7
B	206,997	52.8
C	41,100	10.5
Police	366,678	100.0
A	170,606	46.5

TABLE 25.—Continued

Service and band	Total transmitters	Percentage of transmitters in service and band
B	187,973	51.0
C	8,099	2.5
Local government	56,339	100.0
A	13,464	23.9
B	39,617	70.3
C	3,258	5.8
Power	141,399	100.0
A	88,408	62.5
B	49,921	35.3
C	3,070	4.2
Highway maintenance	74,109	100.0
A	50,426	68.0
B	19,122	25.8
C	4,561	6.2
Special industrial	275,483	100.0
A	187,068	67.9
B	84,772	30.7
C	3,643	1.4
Special emergency	23,787	100.0
A	17,171	72.1
B	6,616	27.9
Petroleum	49,134	100.0
A	34,827	70.9
B	13,790	28.0
C	517	1.1
Common carrier-rural	20,088	100.0
B	12,621	62.8
C	7,467	37.2
Forestry-conservation	106,578	100.0
A	31,397	29.4
B	75,107	70.5
C	74	0.1

Source: Electronic Industries Association, *Land Mobile Study*, 1963. See Appendix B.

Band (A) does not always outclass the next-oldest Band (B).[10] Other factors than relative age are also at play.

By way of explanation,[11] Band A offers the longest range and is most useful in rural areas but is far more subject than Band B to interference from man-made noise and long-distance "skip." But Band B,

[10] The fact that the means generally substantially exceed the medians for most services studied, particularly in Band C, simply underscores the higher relative channel loading in the largest cities.

[11] See generally, FCC Docket No. 11997, prepared statement of R. Gifford for Electronic Industries Association, March 30, 1959, pp. 6–9. See also the characterization in the EIA Land Mobile Study, Vol. I, pp. 21–27; and in President's Commission on Law Enforcement and Administration of Justice, *Science and Technology* (U.S. Government Printing Office, 1967), pp. 116–18.

TABLE 26. MEDIAN AND MEAN NUMBER OF TRANSMITTERS PER CHANNEL AND OF PERCENTAGES OF TOTAL TRANSMITTERS IN THREE LAND MOBILE BANDS, SELECTED MOBILE SERVICES, IN 25 METROPOLITAN AREAS, 1963

Service and band	Number of transmitters per channel		Percentages of all transmitters in each band	
	Median	Mean	Median	Mean
Motor-urban property				
B	3.0	4.320	55.8	56.7
C	12.0	13.320	39.8	35.3
Motor-urban passenger				
A	2.0	3.800	100.0	84.0
C	0.0	0.360	0.0	8.0
Motor-interurban property				
A	14.0	20.640	55.6	55.0
B	6.0	10.400	37.5	41.0
C	4.0	4.400	2.8	4.0
Press relay				
B	7.0	10.760	100.0	96.0
Auto emergency				
B	16.0	31.200	92.4	87.4
C	4.0	7.400	3.6	8.6
Taxicabs				
B	152.0	237.080	95.4	91.7
C	5.0	25.760	4.6	8.3
Telephone maintenance				
A	0.0	4.040	0.0	22.3
B	4.0	26.520	44.4	41.6
C	0.0	2.360	0.0	28.1
Railroads				
B	10.0	48.520	100.0	99.0
C	0.0	1.960	0.0	1.0
Manufacturers				
B	21.0	32.640	100.0	89.1
C	0.0	1.320	0.0	6.9
Fire				
A	7.0	36.800	26.5	39.0
B	29.0	38.880	67.8	59.6
C	0.0	0.720	0.0	1.8
Business				
A	87.0	107.880	31.4	30.3
B	180.0	240.960	56.6	56.0
C	6.0	10.760	7.7	13.7
Police				
A	22.0	43.680	29.5	33.9
B	34.0	51.5	64.9	61.9
C	1.0	7.7	0.8	4.2
Local government				
A	9.0	13.4	26.1	27.5
B	9.0	9.320	60.0	63.7
C	1.0	2.680	5.9	8.8
Power				
A	14.0	27.120	63.1	60.2
B	24.0	33.000	34.1	36.8
C	1.0	6.520	1.5	3.0
Highway maintenance				
A	26.0	71.480	51.1	58.9
B	7.0	7.280	30.3	30.8
C	1.0	3.840	3.8	10.4
Special industrial				
A	57.0	84.320	68.1	65.7

TABLE 26.—Continued

Service and band	Number of transmitters per channel		Percentages of all transmitters in each band	
	Median	Mean	Median	Mean
B	80.0	89.640	30.7	31.7
C	2.0	8.000	0.7	2.6
Special emergency				
A	11.0	14.240	77.7	73.7
B	4.0	8.960	22.3	26.3
Petroleum				
A	3.0	5.400	71.9	66.9
B	2.0	7.600	21.4	23.5
C	0.0	0.520	0.0	1.6
Forestry–conservation				
A	2.0	25.960	34.1	40.5
B	1.0	8.400	43.2	38.6
C	0.0	0.240	0.0	4.9
Forestry products				
A	1.0	1.680	53.1	46.3
B	0.0	1.440	0.0	13.3
C	0.0	0.240	0.0	4.5

Source: Derived from Electronic Industries Association, *Land Mobile Study* (1963). See Appendix B below.

providing a more reliable medium-range service (adequate for all but the longest-distance requirements), is better suited than Band A for combined rural-urban (or suburban) needs. Finally Band C, initially used because other spectrum had grown scarce, now qualifies more on the merits in meeting special urban needs, with the shortest range and the signal freest from interference.

The technical characteristics of Band B, in sum, favor it for suburban-type services even though Band A developed earlier and is admittedly better for extensive rural coverage. Band C, potentially as useful for shorter-range urban needs as Band B, developed much later and is still subject to substantial cost barriers. It would seem, then, that the postulated importance of "age of band" as a factor in radio spectrum utilization must be qualified. The special characteristics of the several bands may also play a key role. (See further discussion in Chapter VIII and Appendix B.)

Finally, the magnitude of the government's impact as spectrum user and promoter is indirectly suggested by general data on the electronics product market[12] and specifically on the distribution of government, industry, and consumer demand for communications hardware and components since 1950.

[12] The electronics product market refers largely to communications and data-processing equipment, electronic components, and precision instrumentation. See *Electronic Industries Yearbook for 1969* (Washington: Electronic Industries Association, 1969), pp. 91–92.

Insofar as electronic product sales value is both reflective of and conducive to further development of telecommunications capability and know-how, Figure 3 indicates the rapidly rising value of spectrum for electromagnetic communication. The data plotted in Figure 4 further trace the changing relative growth rates of government, industry, and consumer factory sales of electronic products, 1923–65. Specifically, Figure 4 underlies the large absolute and relative contribution of the

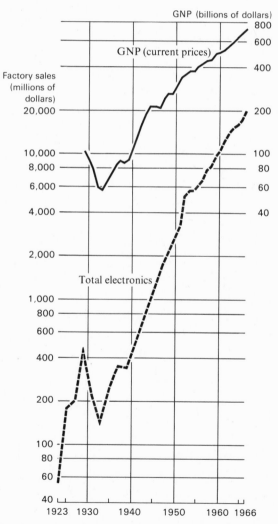

Figure 3. Total electronics output and Gross National Product, 1923–66. (For source, see Appendix A.)

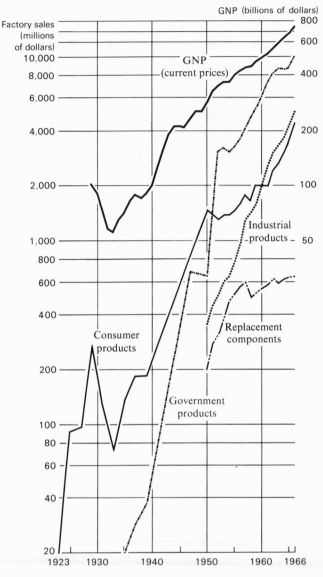

Figure 4. Electronics output by product type and source of demand, 1923–66. (For source, see Appendix A.)

government electronics demand, as well as the rising magnitude of industrial demand, and the declining relative demand for consumer products.

In sum, government electronics products actually grew relative to GNP through most of the period 1935–65, but their growth rate has now started to slacken, at least as compared with industrial electronics. Nonetheless, the government's share of total electronics factory sales remained more than double that of industrial electronics in the years 1950–64, as well as in the EIA projections for 1965–70.[13] In 1968, the government's share actually stood at 51.0 per cent of total electronics sales value, industrial electronics at 27.3 per cent, and consumer electronics at 19.0 per cent.[14] The quantitative importance of the government's electronics demand, then, reveals it to be the major source of such demand and hence the major user and promoter of new telecommunications capabilities.

The Federal Role in Telecommunications R&D

The efficacy and defensibility of government R&D programs will to some extent depend on the economic structure of communications equipment and electronics components, including its vertical relation with the operating carriers and electronics research laboratories. That is, whether in-house or extramural, public R&D is geared basically to correct deficiencies in private innovative performance which in turn reflects vertical and horizontal structure.[15]

Of special import here is the performance of regulated carriers under a profit constraint,[16] and in particular the alleged preference for their own hardware and research subsidiaries as suppliers. Pertinent also are the preclusive effects of tariffs that prohibit the interconnection of customer-owned and carrier-provided facilities and, more generally, of commonly owned communications lines and equipment production facilities.

Because any detailed examination of vertical or horizontal structure and conduct is beyond our present scope, we cannot reject the possibility that the same volume and pattern of federal R&D expenditures might generate greater productivity increases under an alternative structure; for instance, one where the carriers had less vertical control over equipment, manufacturing, or procurement.[17] It is at least conceivable that

---

[13] See Electronic Industries Association, *Forecast of the Electronic Industries, 1965–70* (Washington: EIA, November 1, 1965), pp. 28–33.

[14] *Electronic Industries Yearbook for 1969*, p. 3.

[15] R. Nelson, M. Peck, and E. Kalachek, *Technology, Economic Growth and Public Policy* (Brookings, 1967), pp. 154–58, 177–89.

[16] On the investment behavior of regulated carriers, see H. Averch and L. Johnson, "Behavior of the Firm under Regulatory Constraint," *American Economic Review* (December 1962), pp. 1052–69. Also see Ch. X, citations in fns. 26–34 and associated text.

[17] See M. Irwin and R. McKee, "Vertical Integration and the Communications Equipment Industry," *Cornell Law Review* (February 1968), pp. 452–57; and Beelar, "Cables in the Sky," pp. 26–41.

better safeguards against foreclosed access would help enhance the efficacy both of government-supported programs and private innovative performance. So too might the wider use of competitive bidding, arm's-length bargaining, or competitive negotiation arrangements in government and common carrier procurement practice.[18]

In regard to the R&D efforts most pertinent to spectrum utilization, we are concerned with the limits imposed by artificial and natural atmospheric noise. The knowledge of these limits that is essential to overcoming them is expensive to develop and hard to exploit. Like much basic scientific research it is therefore best suited for public/nonprofit sponsorship. Limited though the federal government's atmospheric research program has been thus far, a brief review here will indicate the character and magnitude of government's participation in a crucial phase of spectrum resource development.

The capacity to communicate is also governed by "larger research efforts in such activities as the design of materials, components, antennas, etc."[19] Hardware design and supporting R&D are presumably closer to applied than to basic research and even more likely to involve development than research. Although this hardware development operates within the more fundamental parameters set by atmospheric research, the largely applied R&D programs in communications equipment and electronics components are important in their own right as factors in spectrum development.

Two kinds of data will be analyzed below: first, the National Science Foundation surveys of R&D expenditures in major American manufacturing industries; second, estimated expenditures on atmospheric research derived from recent findings of the Interdepartmental Committee on Atmospheric Sciences. In reviewing them, it must be remembered that R&D expenditures of themselves neither produce new ideas nor guarantee their effective use. Even when combined with the separate cost of product design, R&D costs are but a small fraction of the total costs of successful product innovation.[20]

The magnitude of federal support for R&D is dramatically larger

---

[18] Irwin and McKee, "Vertical Integration," pp. 457–72.

[19] H. Booker and C. Little, "Atmospheric Research and Electromagnetic Telecommunications—Part II," *IEEE Spectrum* (September 1965), p. 100.

[20] The typical distribution of costs in successful product innovations has been estimated to include: (a) research and advanced development, 5–10 per cent; (b) product design, 10–20 per cent; (c) tooling—getting ready for manufacture, 40–60 per cent; (d) manufacturing—start-up expenses, 5–15 per cent; (e) marketing—start-up expenses, 10–25 per cent. See U.S. Dept. of Commerce, *Technological Innovation: Its Environment and Management* (U.S. Government Printing Office, 1967), pp. 8–10.

than support for atmospheric research. In 1962, some $2.1 billion was spent for R&D on all communications equipment and electronic components products, and a full $0.9 billion within the electronic components industry alone, whereas estimated expenditure on atmospheric research was only $39 million. Nevertheless, this need not imply any comparable difference in relative contributions to spectrum development, for such contributions depend also on the different objectives and results of basic research, applied research, and development.

Because atmospheric research is almost entirely federally funded basic research, the more relevant comparison is with similar basic research in the communications equipment and electronic components industry—a sum of $40 million in 1963—not with total R&D in that industry or even with the $748 million which the government spent there on development alone. (The government's $39 million investment in atmospheric research was about one-fourth of the total of federally funded basic research in 1963.) Furthermore, in assessing the government's promotional role, research sponsorship, rather than performance, is obviously the key, and here the preponderance of federal financing is indisputable.

Federally Financed R&D in Communications Equipment and Electronic Components

As already suggested, the nation's defense and space programs seem likely to continue to make major contributions to our telecommunications capabilities. Vital breakthroughs have occurred as incidental by-products of efforts in both défense and space. Radar and other war-stimulated advances have opened up hitherto unused spectral regions. The Department of Defense plays a major role in atmospheric research, generally. In space exploration, new hardware components are needed, new propagation problems must be solved, and major breakthroughs in booster and tracking capability also figure in developing the spectrum resource.

Between fiscal 1960 and 1968, NASA and the DOD together provided about four-fifths of all federal R&D outlays. But NASA's share of this total rose from 4.5 per cent to 31.4 per cent, while DOD's fell from 76.3 per cent to 46.6 per cent.[21] Stated otherwise, of some $20 billion spent on all R&D in the United States in 1965, over three-fifths

---

[21] The Defense Department's share of the government's total electronics market also fell between fiscal 1963 and 1968 from 89.5 per cent to 85.4 per cent while NASA's rose from 8.7 per cent to 13.7 per cent. By fiscal 1969, the figures stood at 88.4 per cent DOD and 10.7 per cent NASA. *Electronic Industries Yearbook for 1966*, p. 39; *Electronic Industries Yearbook for 1968*, p. 47.

came from the federal government, and NASA and DOD provided about four-fifths of this amount. Two industries alone—aircraft and missiles, and electrical equipment and communication—accounted for two-fifths of the U.S. total, almost three-fifths of the R&D in all manufacturing industries in 1965, and over four-fifths of total federally funded R&D in manufacturing.

Further indicative of the importance to U.S. telecommunications R&D of federal funding in electrical equipment and communication and aircraft and missiles are data in Table 27. Most striking here is the large portion of total R&D money and of research scientists and engineers that is accounted for by these two industries, and the still larger portion of federally funded R&D. In 1965, the two industries had almost three-fifths of all R&D funds in the manufacturing industries, over one-half of all scientists and engineers working there, and over four-fifths of the federally funded R&D.

In each case, the proportions were somewhat greater in 1965 than in 1957. In each case, also, electrical equipment and communication outclassed each of the other industries reported except aircraft and missiles, often by a significant margin. Its share of federally funded R&D is particularly large. Finally, communications equipment and electronic components, the subindustry probably most relevant to our discussion here, also rated higher than all other comparable subindustries reported and generally higher also than the major industry groupings.

Turning next from the general distribution of R&D funding and of scientists and engineers among the several manufacturing industries, Table 28 sets forth data on federal funding relative to total R&D funding and net industry sales in the six most "research-intensive" industries, 1957–65. Clearly, a far larger share of R&D in the aircraft and missiles and electrical equipment and communications industries is federally financed than of any other industry reported, and this holds true throughout the period. Furthermore, both total R&D and federal R&D loom significantly larger as percentages of net industry sales for these two industries than for any other, and this too holds true over time.

In regard to electrical equipment and communication, then, not only does it account (in Table 27) for a significantly larger share of total R&D and federally funded R&D over time than all other industry groups except aircraft and missiles but federally funded R&D in that industry is also a larger fraction of its total R&D (in Table 28) and a higher fraction of its net sales than is true elsewhere, again except for aircraft and missiles.

TABLE 27. DISTRIBUTION OF TOTAL R&D FUNDS, FEDERAL FUNDS, AND NUMBER OF SCIENTISTS AND ENGINEERS AMONG SELECTED MANUFACTURING INDUSTRIES, 1965 AND 1957

Industry and class	Total R&D ($ million)		Per cent[a]		Number of scientists and engineers		Per cent[a]		Federally financed R&D ($ million)		Per cent[a]	
	1965	1957	1965	1957	1965	1957	1965	1957	1965	1957	1965	1957
Research-intensive industries:												
Aircraft and missiles	5,120	2,574	36.1	33.3	100,700	58,600	28.1	24.0	4,500	2,275	58.0	52.5
Electrical equipment and communication	3,167	1,804	22.3	23.3	91,200	47,900	25.4	19.6	1,978	1,196	25.5	27.6
Communications	1,912	748	13.5	9.7	58,000	22,300	16.2	9.1	1,253	518	16.1	11.9
Other	1,255	1,056	8.8	13.6	33,200	25,600	9.3	10.5	725	678	9.3	15.6
Chemicals	1,377	705	9.7	9.1	41,400	31,000	11.5	12.7	190	89	2.4	2.1
Industrial	928	503	6.5	6.5	26,300	18,800	7.3	7.7	147	80	1.9	1.8
Drugs and medicines	268	104	1.9	1.3	8,200	5,100	2.3	2.1	*	*	*	*
Other	181	98	1.3	1.3	6,800	7,100	1.9	2.9	*	9	*	0.2
Motor vehicle and other transp. equip.	1,238	707	8.7	9.1	24,700	15,000	6.9	6.2	326	190	4.2	4.4
Machinery (nonelectric)	1,129	669	8.0	8.7	34,100	27,400	9.5	11.2	258	272	3.3	6.3
Prof. and scient. instr.	387	249	2.7	3.2	11,300	11,000	3.1	4.5	125	109	1.6	2.5
Scient., mech. meas. instr.	76	139	0.5	1.8	3,700	6,500	1.0	2.7	18	80	0.2	2.7
Optical, surg., photo., etc.	311	110	2.2	1.4	7,600	4,500	2.1	1.8	107	29	1.4	0.7
Subtotal (research-intensive)	12,408	6,708	87.5	86.7	303,400	190,900	84.5	78.3	7,377	4,131	95.0	95.4
Nonresearch-intensive industries:												
Petroleum refining and extract.	435	211	3.1	2.7	10,000	7,400	2.8	3.0	69	11	0.9	0.3
Primary metals	216	108	1.5	1.4	5,700	5,200	1.6	2.1	8	5	0.1	0.1
Primary ferrous	131	64	0.9	0.8	3,300	3,000	0.9	1.2	1	1	—	—
Nonferrous and other	85	44	0.6	0.6	2,300	2,200	0.6	0.9	7	4	0.1	0.1
Rubber products	166	107	1.2	1.4	6,000	4,700	1.7	1.9	25	37	0.3	0.9
Fabricated metal products	145	135	1.0	1.7	6,400	8,300	1.8	3.4	17	38	0.2	0.9
Food and kindred products	150	74	1.1	1.0	5,800	4,800	1.6	2.0	1	*	—	*
Other industries	667	388	4.6	5.1	21,600	22,500	6.0	9.3	262	113	3.5	2.6
Subtotal (nonresearch-intensive)	1,789	1,023	12.5	13.3	55,500	52,900	15.5	21.7	382	204	5.0	4.7
Total all manufacturing industries	14,197	7,731	100.0	100.0	358,900	243,800	100.0	100.0	7,759	4,335	100.0	100.0

Source: Derived from National Science Foundation, Basic Research, Applied Research, and Development in Industry, 1965 (U.S. Government Printing Office, 1967).

— Less than 0.1 percent.

[a] Because of rounding, subindustry percentages exceed or fall short of those of the parent industry. Percentages may also exceed 100.

* Not available separately but included in total.

260

TABLE 28. FEDERAL R&D AS PERCENTAGE OF TOTAL R&D AND OF NET SALES FOR SELECTED MANUFACTURING INDUSTRIES, 1965, 1960, AND 1957

Industry and year	Total R&D ($ million)	Federal R&D ($ million)	Per cent federal	Total R&D as per cent of net sales	Federal R&D as per cent of net sales
Aircraft and missiles					
1965	5,120	4,500	87.9	28.0	24.6
1960	3,514	3,150	89.6	23.2	20.8
1957	2,574	2,275	88.4	16.8	14.8
Electrical equipment and communications					
1965	3,167	1,978	62.5	9.4	5.9
1960	2,532	1,685	66.5	11.2	7.4
1957	1,804	1,196	66.3	7.6	5.0
Chemicals					
1965	1,377	190	13.8	4.2	0.6
1960	980	171	17.4	4.5	0.8
1957	705	89	12.6	3.5	0.4
Motor vehicles and transportation equipment					
1965	1,238	326	26.3	3.1	0.8
1960	884	216	24.4	3.0	0.7
1957	707	190	26.9	2.9	0.8
Machinery, nonelectric					
1965	1,129	258	23.0	4.1	0.9
1960	949	391	41.2	4.7	2.0
1957	669	272	40.7	3.4	1.4
Professional and scientific instruments					
1965	387	125	32.3	6.2	2.0
1960	329	153	46.5	6.3	2.9
1957	249	109	43.8	7.0	3.1
Total all manufacturing industries					
1965	14,197	7,759	54.7	4.3	2.3
1960	10,509	6,081	57.9	4.2	2.4
1957	7,731	4,335	56.1	3.4	1.9

Source: Derived from National Science Foundation, Basic Research, Applied Research, and Development in Industry, 1965.

Looking further at the broad distribution of basic research, applied research, and development (in Table 29), over four-fifths of the funds spent in aircraft and missiles and electrical equipment and communications were clearly for "development," as was also true for machinery. Yet once more, the fraction of each of these three categories of research activity that was *federally funded* was greater for the first two industries than for any other group. (See Table 30.) Jointly, the two industries account for only about one-third of all basic industrial R&D, two-fifths of all applied research, and two-thirds of all development in 1965. But their combined share of federally financed programs is in each case significantly higher: 49.2 per cent, 73.7 per cent, and 86.1 per cent, respectively.

However viewed, then, there is no question about the quantitative importance of federal funding in electrical equipment and communications or, for that matter, in the subindustry of communications equipment and electronic components, which is not fully traced here. The only other research-intensive industry even remotely approaching its importance at any point is chemicals—insofar at least as its share of federally funded basic research in 1965 was 20.9 per cent, compared to 20.4 per cent for aircraft and missiles, and 28.8 per cent for electrical equipment and communications.

In sum, the government's pivotal role in the R&D funding most closely associated with spectrum utilization is unmistakable. However, a final qualifying word is in order on industry-product classifications. How relevant to telecommunications capabilities are the data for the communications equipment and electronics components industry alone? In 1966, the total R&D performance in the communications equipment and electronic components products within all industries totalled some $2.5 billion, including $1,314 million from that subindustry, $251 million from "other electrical equipment," and $417 million from aircraft and missiles. Hence, while one-half of all the money spent on electronics products R&D came from outside that industry, roughly four-fifths was accounted for by two major industry groups—electrical equipment and communications, and aircraft and missiles. We can probably assume, therefore, that the R&D expenditures in these two industries also include most of the R&D outlays on all communications equipment and electronic components products, as well as expenditures on other products. Accordingly, the general pattern of trends reviewed earlier does broadly reflect the relative importance of those government- and company-supported R&D expenditures which bear most directly on spectrum utilization.

TABLE 29. FUNDS FOR BASIC RESEARCH, APPLIED RESEARCH, AND DEVELOPMENT AS PER CENT OF TOTAL R&D FUNDS, SELECTED INDUSTRIES, 1965

	Total R&D ($ million)	Basic research ($ million)	Per cent basic research	Applied research ($ million)	Per cent applied research	Development ($ million)	Per cent development
Aircraft and missiles	5,120	68	1.3	739	14.4	4,314	84.3
Electrical equipment and communications	3,167	147	4.6	437	13.8	2,583	81.6
Chemicals	1,377	172	12.5	534	38.8	672	48.8
Machinery, nonelectric	1,129	26	2.3	144	12.8	959	84.9
Total (all manufacturing)	14,197	607	4.3	2,673	18.8	10,918	76.9

Source: Derived from National Science Foundation, Basic Research, Applied Research, and Development in Industry, 1965.

262

TABLE 30. DISTRIBUTION OF TOTAL FUNDS AND FEDERAL FUNDS FOR BASIC RESEARCH, APPLIED RESEARCH, AND DEVELOPMENT AMONG SELECTED MANUFACTURING INDUSTRIES, 1965

	Basic research				Applied research				Development			
	$ million		Per cent		$ million		Per cent		$ million		Per cent	
	Total	Federal	Total	Federal	Total	Federal	Total	Federal	Total	Federal	Total	Federal
Aircraft and missiles	68	39	11.2	20.4	739	566	27.6	53.8	4,314	3,895	39.5	59.8
Electrical equipment and communications	147	55	24.2	28.8	437	209	16.3	19.9	2,583	1,714	23.7	26.3
Chemicals	172	40	28.3	20.9	534	47	20.0	4.5	672	103	6.2	1.6
Machinery, nonelectric	26	2	4.3	1.0	144	44	5.4	4.2	959	212	8.8	3.3
Total (all mfg.)	607	191	100.0	100.0	2,673	1,052	100.0	100.0	10,918	6,516	100.0	100.0

Source: Derived from National Science Foundation, Basic Research, Applied Research, and Development in Industry, 1965.

The Government's Role in Atmospheric Research

What of the government's more limited but strategically important role in atmospheric research? We noted earlier the limits imposed on telecommunications by various properties of the atmosphere and the consequent need for greater knowledge of these properties. As stated in the report of the Interdepartmental Committee for Atmospheric Sciences:

> The final limit to the information-carrying capability of an electromagnetic telecommunication system is the existence of unwanted signals and noise. These may be man-made or of natural origin; they may originate in the system itself or may be signals that originate elsewhere and are picked up by the receiving system. In any discussion of the effects of the atmosphere on telecommunication systems, the atmospheric noise level in which the system is immersed must therefore be considered.[22]

In addition to the atmospheric noise levels, then, special limits are imposed by man-made interference. The Joint Technical Advisory Committee reports:

> Below about 20 Mc/s, the limiting noise is usually natural or man-made noise. Man-made noise can be controlled; however, in many areas, especially near large urban settlements, usually atmospheric or man-made noise will be the limiting noise against which systems must compete. Atmospheric noise (in this region) can be propagated over great distances . . . Since there are large numbers of atmospheric storms . . . at all times, the background noise level is a composite of contributions of many storms . . . At about 20 Mc/s the predominant concurring noise changes from atmospheric to extraterrestrial origin. Solar noise and radio stars become the principal sources of noise. As frequency is increased, thermal noise . . . becomes predominant. . . . Cosmic and thermal noise are quite predictable. . . . Atmospheric and man-made noise are much less predictable. . . .[23]

It should come as no surprise that radio noise, whether natural or man-made, should be generally viewed as the "ineluctable limit from which wanted signals can be extracted."[24] It is also understandable that the prediction (and even control) of noise levels should be viewed increasingly as part of the R&D effort needed to facilitate a more efficient and extensive use of the radio spectrum. The predictability of noise levels

---

[22] H. Booker and C. Little, "Atmospheric Research and Electromagnetic Telecommunication—Part I," *IEEE Spectrum* (August 1965), p. 49.

[23] Joint Technical Advisory Committee, *Radio Spectrum Utilization* (New York: Institute of Electrical and Electronics Engineers, 1965), pp. 43–44.

[24] Ibid., p. 43.

and interference fields is actually vital both for efficient civilian and military users. Indeed, the atmosphere's varying telecommunications capabilities as between different spectral regions further underscore the need for greater knowledge of its electromagnetic properties. Such knowledge bears on our ability to extend the intensive and extensive margin and thereby to generate greater contributions to the GNP, in particular to safety, security, public information, and education. It bears also on forestalling or correcting any malallocation of frequency use as between alternative users.

According to the ICAS report, deficient knowledge of propagation characteristics has resulted in costly mistakes, in regard to the early design of radar systems in World War II, the initial allocation of FM and TV channels (at 42–50 Mc/s), and the cessation of all new TV grants between 1948 and 1952.[25] Without tracing the details here, the main claim is that more comprehensive knowledge of propagation characteristics of various spectral regions would have avoided costly reallocations and facilitated the release of frequencies for alternative uses. By enabling pioneer TV licensees to entrench themselves in the choicest network and advertising affiliations, the so-called TV freeze has had an impact on industry structure that is felt to this very day.

Of great relevance here are: (1) some picture of the nation's present state of knowledge of the propagation properties of different spectral regions and of the limits imposed by artificial and natural noise levels; (2) the magnitude and distribution of atmospheric research currently designed to enhance this knowledge; and (3) the distribution of such research among sponsoring agencies, spectral bands, and propagation mechanisms. We shall then be in a better position to draw some conclusions as to the government's present and potential promotional role.

In regard to sponsoring organizations, Table 31 indicates that the federal government, particularly the Department of Defense, plays a major role in supporting atmospheric research directed towards electromagnetic propagation. Looking next at the spectral regions where most of the research occurs, Table 32 reveals some two-thirds of it to be concentrated on the ionosphere (10 Kc/s–30 Mc/s). Yet it is unclear how economically significant further advances here will be. Only one-third of the research occurs in frequencies above 30 Mc/s where fruitful breakthroughs *are* expected.

The ratio of research outlays to telecommunications usage is generally higher in the upper, "newer" spectral regions (i.e., the optical-light spectrum above 3,000 Gc/s), than in the lower, "older" regions

[25] Booker and Little, Part II, p. 103.

TABLE 31. DISTRIBUTION OF EXPENDITURES FOR ATMOSPHERIC RESEARCH, BY SPONSOR, 1964

Sponsor	$ million	Percentage
Department of Defense	33.9	86.9
ARPA	5.8	14.9
DASA	5.1	13.1
Army	2.9	7.4
Navy	9.5	24.4
Air Force	10.6	27.1
Government: Nonmilitary	4.8	12.3
NASA	1.6	4.1
Commerce	2.2	5.6
NSF	0.8	2.1
USIA	0.1	0.3
FAA, AEC, HEW	0.1	0.3
Nongovernment		
Industrial laboratories and nonprofit institutions	0.3	0.8
Total	39.0	100.0

Source: Atmospheric Research Required to Facilitate Electromagnetic Telecommunication—An Analysis Prepared for the Interdepartmental Committee for Atmospheric Sciences by the Central Radio Propagation Laboratory (Boulder, Colo.: National Bureau of Standards, Boulder Laboratories, October 1964), Figure 3.1.

(at 30–1,000 Mc/s, and 1–3,000 Gc/s). But the highest ratio actually occurs in the oldest, most fully developed region of all (below 30 Mc/s). Whether this reflects an imbalance due to the peculiar needs of particular military users or a fundamental failure of industry and government to capture the full economic ramifications of the higher frequencies is hard to say.

One could of course argue that the older, more fully developed bands permit more hardware investment. But we are talking here about the most basic R&D on atmospheric effects. Furthermore, the region between 30–1,000 Mc/s was developed much earlier than the optical-light spectrum and does show a smaller research effort relative to telecommunications usage. Hence the military's special needs below 30 Mc/s, and the more general failure to grasp the full potential of spectrum above 1 Gc/s, may both be partly at issue.

In Table 33 the distribution of atmospheric research by benefiting ITU frequency band shows the same pattern. The highest levels of research efforts mainly occur in the older bands, allocated and developed earlier. As we rise into the higher, newer frequencies, the research then generally tapers off, though not consistently.[26]

This shows up clearly also in the share of total atmospheric research located within each ITU Band, ranging between roughly 10 and 25

[26] As we rise from the ionosphere to the lower troposphere and thence to the optical light spectrum.

TABLE 32. RELEVANT ATMOSPHERIC RESEARCH AND TELECOMMUNICATIONS EXPENDITURES, BY SPECTRAL REGION, 1962

Spectral region	U.S. expenditures on telecommunications		Propagation medium	Relevant atmospheric research		
	$ million	Per cent of total		$ million	Per cent of total	Per cent of total telecommunications expenditures column (1)
10 Kc/s–30 Mc/s	2,940	17.5	Ionosphere	25.6	66.1	0.870
30 Mc/s–1,000 Mc/s	8,890	52.9	Troposphere	5.7	14.7	0.064
1 Gc/s–3,000 Gc/s	4,370	26.0	Troposphere	4.2	10.9	0.096
Over 3,000 Gc/s	600	3.6	Troposphere	3.2	8.3	0.533
Total	16,800	100.0		38.7	100.0	0.230

Source: Adapted from H. Booker and C. Little, "Atmospheric Research and Electromagnetic Telecommunication—Part II," IEEE Spectrum (September 1965), p. 103.

267

TABLE 33. DISTRIBUTION OF ATMOSPHERIC RESEARCH, BY BENEFITING ITU BAND, 1962

Spectral region	ITU band	Frequency band	Telecommunications expenditures ($ million)	Propagation medium	Relevant atmospheric research ($ million)	Research as percentage telecommunication expenditures	Research as percentage all atmospheric research
Radio spectrum							
10–30 Kc/s	4	VLF			7.3		18.9
30–300 Kc/s	5	LF			4.1		10.6
300–3,000 Kc/s	6	MF			3.9		10.0
3–30 Mc/s	7	HF			10.3		26.6
Subtotal			2,940	Ionosphere	25.6	0.87	66.1
30–300 Mc/s	8	VHF			4.8		12.4
300–3,000 Mc/s	9	UHF			1.8		4.6
3–30 Gc/s	10	SHF			2.5		6.5
	11	EHF			0.6		1.6
300–3,000 Gc/s	12	Terracycle			0.2		0.5
Subtotal			13,260	Troposphere	9.9	0.07	25.6
Optical, infrared spectrum							
300–500,000 Gc/s		Infrared			1.2		3.1
400,000–800,000 Gc/s		Visible			2.0		5.1
800,000–1,000,000 Gc/s		Near ultraviolet			0.03		0.1
Subtotal			600	Troposphere	3.2	0.53	8.3
Total			16,800		38.7	0.23	100.0

Source: Adapted from H. Booker and C. Little, "Atmospheric Research and Electromagnetic Telecommunication—Part II," *IEEE Spectrum* (September 1965), p. 102.

per cent in the lower atmosphere (Bands 4–7), some 4 to 12 per cent in the next three bands (8–10), and down to a mere 1.6 per cent and 0.5 per cent in Bands 11 and 12. However, our generalization must be qualified insofar as the ratio actually rises somewhat in the optical, infrared spectrum, where it is 3 to 5 per cent of atmospheric research outlays. In other words, the newest, highest spectral region (optical, infrared) accounts for a larger share of atmospheric research effort than the highest portion of the radio spectrum (30–3,000 Gc/s). This may in part reflect new military and space use of lasers and new needs for surveillance, detection, satellite tracking, ground-space, space-space communication, and navigation.

How does the atmospheric research effort relate to gaps in our scientific knowledge of atmospheric effects of different propagation mechanisms and the significance of these effects? The ICAS report is worth reviewing here for some notion as to how these cost-benefit ratios might look if we could in fact construct them. (We may well be a decade or more away from developing such data as a guide to public investment.)

In reviewing the present state of knowledge about atmospheric noise and the significance of the limits it imposes on our telecommunications capabilities, the ICAS report identifies several pertinent facts and relationships:

1. Some 70 per cent of the $17 billion value of telecommunications usage in 1962 was generated in the lower atmosphere—below 1,000 Mc/s—another 25 per cent in the remainder of the radio spectrum—up to 3,000 Gc/s—but only some 5 per cent in the optical spectrum beyond. This rough breakdown seems likely to continue for the foreseeable future.

2. By and large, the higher the radio or light frequency, the greater the importance of atmospheric limitations on our telecommunications capabilities and the lower the degree of understanding of these limits. And this holds true for the several different propagation mechanisms.

3. The predictability of atmospheric effects on the main electromagnetic propagation mechanisms tends to decline as we rise in the radio and optical spectrum, although the rate of decline in predictability varies among the different mechanisms. In the lower reaches of the radio spectrum, developed earlier and studied more fully, this knowledge is in general greater than that in the higher reaches.

4. Nevertheless, it is at these very high radio frequencies that relatively little is being spent on R&D. The upshot is that the large

tracts of frequency space above 1 Gc/s are only sparsely used; and those in the optical and infrared spectrum (above 3,000 Gc/s) are utilized even less (a mere $0.6 billion compared to $4.4 billion). Yet the limits on our telecommunications capabilities, the problems of predictability, and the chances for significant technical breakthroughs are greatest in the higher reaches.

5. Perhaps the only mild qualification of these generalizations regards the ratio of atmospheric research to telecommunications usage. This ratio is higher in the newest optical-light spectrum (0.53 per cent) than in the older portions of the radio spectrum —being only 0.064 per cent in the 30–1,000 Mc/s band. However, the ratio is actually highest (0.87 per cent) in the very oldest segment, 0–30 Mc/s. This fact in part reflects special defense needs and presumably in part a lagging general response to the challenge and potential of new technology. Nonetheless, the share of total atmospheric research devoted to the optical-light spectrum is at best only 56 per cent as large as that devoted to the economically attractive region lying between 30 and 1,000 Mc/s. And this is true even though the expanse of frequency space which the optical-light spectrum occupies is several hundred times greater than the entire radio spectrum.

How then may we explain this lack of concordance between needed knowledge and research efforts? Such a situation might be more understandable if the bulk of this R&D were privately financed. But the government, not private industry, is the prime generator of the atmospheric research as well as of R&D on communications equipment and electronics components more generally. Hence we must look elsewhere for an explanation.

For one thing, in the last resort the military's special needs are for a simple, rough-and-ready communications service. The lower frequencies—especially HF radio at 3–30 Mc/s—still provide such a service for the Navy, the Air Force, and the Army. Insofar as national security may depend on the ability to communicate a very simple message at the precise moment needed, it is understandable that the predictability of ionospheric propagation and knowledge of the lower atmosphere (Bands 4–7) should continue to account for much of total atmospheric research.

Second, the relative shares accounted for by lower and higher frequencies may in some cases also reflect the failure to grasp the dramatic new potentialities of the higher reaches.

Third, there has undoubtedly been a lag in adjusting the organizational structure of research programs in certain key government facilities. Until recently, for example, the Institute for Telecommunication Sciences

(ITS) of the Commerce Department was simply not authorized to explore the higher reaches of the radio or light spectrum. ITS is still the major federal facility actively involved in both basic and applied atmospheric research, the source of advisory and consultative services to industry and government, and the center of scientific liaison abroad. But ITS is largely limited to the lower atmosphere, even though its mission has been extended into the upper reaches.[27] As yet there has been relatively little budgetary reflection of this change.

Fourth, and partly related to the above, is the continued failure to organize governmental research efforts on a coherent, integrated basis. ITS, for example, might conceivably develop such a research program, balanced in regard to degrees of understanding and predictability of frequency usage on one hand, and the possibility of significant breakthroughs on the other. Instead, some three-fifths of ITS's work in 1967 was for other federal agencies, and only two-fifths on its own research and technical services. Research for outside agencies was actually a somewhat higher proportion than this for the ionosphere and troposphere, and somewhat lower for space environment and aeronomy.[28]

As a consequence, systematic R&D geared to a basic development program for spectrum has been hard to mount. The best ITS can manage has been to pick up useful fallout from work done for its major sponsors—the Department of Defense, which contributes two-thirds of all outside funds, and NASA, which contributes about one-fifth. Although the needs of these two entities are obviously vital to security and national well-being, they are also fairly specialized. To fill them does not necessarily produce the kind of systematic basic effort that is needed to develop the spectrum resource extensively. Nor, according to ITS at least, does the sum of its separate tasks for outside agencies really add up to anything near what an integrated program of atmospheric research must include. Apparently, the sponsored research is too often geared to the solutions of particular problems which may be retarding the development of a particular telecommunications system.

CONCLUSION

This review of the historical record has shown that military factors have figured in the major spectrum-opening breakthroughs, their impact being clearly revealed in radar and satellite development and in the

[27] National Bureau of Standards, *The Central Radio Propagation Laboratory* (Boulder, Colo.: March 1965, mimeo.), p. 2.
[28] Institute for Telecommunication Sciences, *Resources and Management Information* (Boulder, Colo.: February 1967, mimeo.), pp. 12–13.

surge of allocated spectrum after the major wars. One key source of spectrum development at the intensive and extensive margins lies in basic and applied research and development in the electrical equipment and communications industry, and in aircraft and missiles. Though federally financed, the bulk of this R&D is privately performed. A second source of greater innovative advance lies in the nation's still limited but growing research in the atmospheric sciences, largely funded by the Department of Defense. A growing awareness of the limits imposed by atmospheric noise has led to new interest in the less-developed, less-utilized spectral regions and in those deemed most likely to respond to new knowledge of propagation characteristics.

Some observers believe that the major room for progress still remains at the intensive margin. However, extensive development, dramatic in the past, continues to attract the attention of private and governmental innovators notwithstanding the rigorous physical constraints that operate in the upper spectral regions.

Badly needed now, but outside the scope of this book, is systematic analysis to determine the proper criteria for federal support of telecommunications R&D. It will then be possible to suggest the organizational changes needed to ensure more effective promotion of telecommunications R&D by the federal government.

PART FOUR

ALLOCATION, REGULATION, PRICES, AND SERVICE

CHAPTER X

THE RATIONALE
OF COMPETITIVE ALTERNATIVES
IN COMMON CARRIER RATE REGULATION

Having examined the framework of the present centralized nonprice spectrum system, alternative techniques to inject economic factors more effectively, and the government's promotional role in the preceding parts of this book, we now turn to certain regulatory implications of spectrum scarcity today.

Practically speaking, short of a full-fledged spectrum market, many spectrum users will continue to enjoy sizable economic rents. Indeed the special obstacles to efficient cross-band bidding for rights make this particularly likely. Therefore the rising marginal value of broadcast and common carrier microwave spectrum to next-best users in land mobile and space satellites or private microwave, respectively, underscores the need to reexamine present regulatory techniques. The remaining chapters serve as a very modest beginning toward this end.

To give so much attention to industry structure and the regulation of business conduct at this point may seem to be straying far from the central issues of spectrum management. But this is not so. The relation between spectrum allocation and entry barriers in the several interrelated segments of the communications field has too long been neglected. The private microwave allocation surely opened up entry for a new class of users who would otherwise have been forced to pay more for their communications inputs from the common carriers. A comparable allocation of spectrum to private domestic satellites could have comparable effects. The allocation of 70 UHF channels to television broadcasting opened up entry there too, though, as it appears in retrospect, at costs far higher than the initial VHF allocation.

It is altogether fitting and proper, then, for spectrum managers to consider the end effects of these allocational decisions on common carrier rates (via greater intermode or intersystem competition) and/or

275

on the performance of the broadcast service. It is indeed hard to see how any really rational decision is possible in these cases without projecting the probable end results in some such fashion. The manager, *qua* manager, cannot escape scrutinizing the ultimate impact of his allocation decisions on price, quality, reliability, and diversity. And at that point the line between strictly regulatory and allocational responsibilities becomes slim indeed.

One reason for the manager's reluctance to consider these linkages more explicitly is a rather provincial belief that the task of regulating industry must be distinguished from that of managing a natural resource. The organizational separation of allocational and regulatory functions at the Federal Communications Commission reveals some such philosophy. And the predominant role of engineers in spectrum management, as thus narrowly viewed, may further explain the manager's uneasiness about inquiring into the interrelations of industry structure, conduct, and performance—obviously the economist's domain.

However, one does find cogent links between allocation and regulation, as the discussion of microwave and satellites in the next two chapters will clearly show.

The present chapter will analyze the case for administering these new technologies so as best to promote competition in long-distance communication. The argument is mainly applicable to domestic communications where actual and projected telecommunications demands are sufficiently large to accommodate numerous common carriers and private systems. In the international field, projected demand is much smaller and the cost advantage of satellites over submarine cable may in fact be more decisive than their advantage over the long-distance overland microwave radio relay. Nevertheless, the potential role of competition in international telecommunications must also be considered.

In examining the role of competitive alternatives it is necessary to focus on the current satellite-cable rivalry. But suggestive episodes are found also in the well-known domestic contests between private, independent specialized, and common carrier microwave radio systems. Although these domestic and international case studies are not necessarily fully predictive of future developments in either field, they serve nonetheless to illustrate the potential contributions of, and characteristic problems posed by, any concerted attempt to utilize competitive alternatives in Commission rate regulation.

In the domestic communications market, the case for a procompetitive policy—i.e., one that promotes competition—flows first from the Commission's endorsement of private systems despite the fact that their spectrum costs are higher than those of a carrier-owned system. The private microwave allocation recognized the big user's right to build his own system where this would act to reduce his nonspectrum communications costs and better enable him to tailor his communications inputs. Having opened up the spectrum for these reasons, the presumption can hardly be that it was done to prevent the carriers from competing in price and service to offer the potential private user comparable advantages unless, of course, the carriers acted in a punitive, coercive, or discriminatory way. Or unless the diversion of private line business to the big private systems or the independent specialized carriers were seriously to harm the small general user, notwithstanding the large benefit externalities which the whole nation derives from having available a basic common carrier switched network.

The case for domestic competition flows secondly from the cost-savings enjoyed by space satellites as newcomers in sharing spectrum with incumbent terrestrial microwave systems, instead of having to move up above 15 Gc/s on an exclusive basis. These cost-savings and the FCC's decision to permit spectrum sharing will act to reduce entry barriers for the satellite newcomer, perhaps substantially. Another such clearly procompetitive step would be to permit the new entrants to compete with the older terrestrial radio relays, provided the carriers do not reduce their rates below long-run marginal cost, and that the adverse distributional effects of "cream-skimming" by the specialized for-hire carriers or big private systems are not intolerable. "Cream-skimming" refers to the private or specialized carrier's competitive inroads on the common carrier's most lucrative traffic, which is generated by big corporate entities. At some point this diversion of business may compel the common carriers to raise their rates against the small general users whom they must also legally serve, but who have no alternative options and will thereby be saddled with more of the carriers' common costs than hitherto.

Satellite-cable rivalry on the transoceanic links poses still more difficult regulatory problems. But here too, under certain assumptions at least, there is a case for more competition, especially to induce cost-reducing innovations.

A third factor in the case for competition is the known inadequacy of direct regulation in delimiting the broad range of managerial discretion relative to common carrier rates and service, and competitive alternatives can be justified as reducing the magnitude of any such tendency. Furthermore, such alternatives would reduce the basic theoretical predisposition of firms subject to a profit constraint toward inefficiency and overinvestment in capital-intensive technology.

On all four counts, the case for spectrum allocation geared to facilitate greater competition merits serious consideration largely, though not exclusively, in the domestic field. Before examining these propositions in greater detail, however, some attention needs to be given to the character of telecommunications structure and new communications technology.

INDUSTRY STRUCTURE AND NEW COMMUNICATIONS TECHNOLOGY

The point-point telecommunications structure includes common carriers permitted to handle voice traffic, record traffic, and the growing demand for alternate voice/record service. With one major exception (AT&T), the operations of these carriers are either domestic or international but not both. The principal services provided include local and long-distance telephone, telegraph, teletypewriter, telephoto, dataphone, facsimile, and broadcast program relay by cable, microwave, or satellite. In the domestic field, a further major distinction is between the common carriers, the private systems, and the independent specialized for-hire carriers. In the international field, AT&T is largely (though not entirely) limited to voice communication and the record carriers largely excluded from voice. All common carriers are however permitted to handle some part of the lucrative alternate voice/record service.[1] The sole authorized American entity to provide international satellite facilities is the Communications Satellite Corporation, 50 per cent of whose stock the carriers held until recently and 6 of whose 15 directors they elected. As yet there are no domestic satellites, but some such system may presently be authorized.

Communications equipment for both fields is provided by the equipment manufacturing industry, made up of a number of large common carrier hardware affiliates as well as of independent companies. This industry provides a major source of innovative advance for telecommunications but, as seen in Chapter IX, the federal government (in particu-

---

[1] For a brief description of telecommunications structure and identification of major public policy issues, see President's Task Force on Communications Policy, *Final Report* (U.S. Government Printing Office, 1968), Chs. II, VI (cited below as *Task Force Report*); and Intragovernmental Committee on International Telecommunications, *Report and Recommendations to the Senate and House Committees* (U.S. Government Printing Office, 1966), cited below as *Intragovernmental Committee Report*. See also W. Jones, "Electronic Communications, Public Policy Issues and Research Activities," report to the Ford Foundation, October 1967, unpublished, Ch. 3; C. Phillips, Jr., *Economics of Regulation* (Irwin, 1969), Ch. 17; M. Irwin, "The Communication Industry and the Policy of Competition," *Buffalo Law Review* (Winter 1964), pp. 256–73.

lar the Defense Department) is also an important source of funds for related electronics R&D.

In the domestic sphere, the Bell system provides some 85 per cent of the nation's local telephone service through a number of locally franchised and state-regulated monopolies. The remainder is handled by about 2,100 independent telephone companies which operate under exclusive local franchises and interconnect with Bell's long-distance microwave and cable networks. Thus local telephone service is provided under exclusive local franchises and state regulation, whereas AT&T's Long Lines Division handles virtually all of the long-distance telephone service and most of the interconnection of national radio-TV network companies with their affiliated stations. All interstate service is regulated by the FCC. The Western Union Telegraph Company, with annual revenues less than 3 per cent of Bell's, operates the sole public message telegraph service, while competing against Bell in providing a switched teletypewriter exchange service.

The domestic structure has remained relatively stable for the last 35 years, but at least minor changes have now begun. Special-purpose microwave carriers provide end-link relay of TV signals from Bell's key transmission routes to broadcast stations and to CATV systems in the smaller communities. A number of private microwave systems currently meet the special requirements of certain classes of users. Finally, the Commission not only licenses private and specialized for-hire systems towards this end but also permits the cooperative sharing of private systems by certain groups of users.

Carrier-owned affiliates loom large in the production of communications hardware and in the necessary R&D performance, paramount here being the Bell&AT&T-Western Electric complex, GT&E, RCA, and ITT. (Western Electric accounts for about 85 per cent of the domestic equipment market.) However, independent suppliers like General Electric, Lockheed, and Bendix account for a large share of the remaining hardware business. The federal government not only underwrites the bulk of the underlying telecommunications R&D but is also the largest single user of leased channels (i.e., private lines) for overseas alternate voice/record services and a major customer at home too. The DOD's special requirements for reliability have led it to endorse continued maintenance and expansion of cable as well as satellite facilities, notwithstanding evidence that this policy may be uneconomic.

The kinds of problems posed and opportunities offered by new communications technology are well illustrated by the introduction of terrestrial microwave relays now operated by both the common carriers and the big private users. The issues at stake here are clearly suggestive of those already encountered with the advent of cable/satellite rivalry internationally. The same problems doubtlessly will be posed by any future domestic space satellite system, whether carrier-owned, private, or both. Because the transoceanic case may be less familiar to many than that of the microwave relays, we shall spell out in greater detail just how a satellite system fits into the present international telecommunications structure.

The basic structure into which the transoceanic satellites are now integrated[2] includes several key components—mainly the communications common carriers but also such private users of long-distance transmission facilities as television networks, newspaper associations, data-processing companies, and other interests in business, industry, and finance. The federal government is also a major user of these facilities, though the DOD and NASA will operate their own satellite systems for military and experimental purposes, respectively. Finally, satellite hardware, like communications hardware generally, is supplied by numerous equipment manufacturers, some but not all of whom are affiliated with the common carriers, whereas R&D is underwritten in large measure by the military and space programs.

The international carriers still see satellites as a potentially inexpensive form of long-distance communication in the face of crowded spectrum and limited cable capacity. AT&T, which is by far the largest carrier,[3] virtually monopolizes international voice communication and provides some mixed voice/record service too, using submarine cable on high-density routes and radiotelephone on low-density routes or as a back-up for cable. With its subsidiaries, AT&T has pioneered in experimental satellites and components for earth station facilities.

Present regulations and technology have left AT&T with a substantial competitive advantage over its main rivals. The three major international record carriers—RCA Communications, ITT Worldcom,

---

[2] On satellite structure, its emergence and related regulatory constraints, see generally H. Schwartz, "ComSat, the Carriers, and the Earth Stations: Some Problems with 'Melding' Variegated Interests," *Yale Law Journal* (January 1967); and H. Levin, "Organization and Control of Communications Satellites," *University of Pennsylvania Law Review* (January 1965).

[3] In 1968, AT&T's assets were $40.2 billion, its gross sales and revenues $14.1 billion, and its net profits after tax roughly $2.1 billion. The parent companies of the three next largest carriers—GT&E, RCA Communications, and ITT Worldcom—had combined assets of only $12.6 billion (less than one-third of AT&T's) and combined gross revenues of only $10.1 billion (less than three-fourths of AT&T's). Indeed AT&T's net profit after tax of $2.1 billion in 1968 was one-half to two-thirds of the gross revenues earned separately by each of these three companies. See "Directory of 500 Leading Industrials and 50 Largest Utility Companies for 1968," *Fortune* (May 15, 1969).

and Western Union International—favor permissive merger policies to facilitate a two-carrier duopoly in the communications business as a whole instead of the present unbalanced competitive situation. A major source of their competitive inferiority to AT&T is their continued dependency on the latter's voice-grade cable without which they could handle none of the newer combined voice/record services. Until recently, the record carriers have had to lease AT&T circuits paying rates comparable to those the latter would charge its own end customers. The FCC has tried to equalize the record carriers' competitive position by permitting them to acquire "indefeasible rights of use" in the first three transatlantic cables and explicit rights of joint ownership in the others. (The only transmission facilities they still own outright themselves are standby radio-telegraph facilities which are also used to service remote areas.)

These message carriers initially saw communications satellites as a source of even greater competitive imbalance for them unless they were guaranteed participation on a basis equal to that of AT&T. In their view, too, the increasingly blurred line between voice and record communication required that each carrier be authorized to provide a full range of service—record, voice, condensed data, television, and facsimile—unless, of course, AT&T could be limited to voice only. Therefore, they have urged Congress to permit them to combine their assets with those of the Western Union Telegraph Company to create a single integrated carrier which would (1) compete with AT&T domestically as well as internationally in both voice and record communication, and (2) participate in the joint ownership of a global satellite system.[4]

Under more recent intragovernmental scrutiny a different formulation has emerged. Suggested alternatives are (a) that ITT Worldcom, RCAC, and WUI be merged; (b) that the three companies be merged further with Western Union Telegraph; (c) that the three overseas record carriers be merged with AT&T's overseas operations; or (d) that the record carriers be merged with ComSat alone.[5] Still another option, proposed by the President's Task Force on Communications Policy, is (e) that the record carriers be merged with ComSat and AT&T's overseas facilities for long-haul transmission, while retaining their separate identities as "freight forwarders."[6]

---

[4] See Senate Judiciary Committee, 87th Cong., 2d sess., *Hearings on S. Res. 258,* 1962, pp. 390–92, 409, 449–50, 456–64; Senate Space Committee, *Hearings on S. 2650 and S. 2814,* 1962, pp. 78–79; and Senate Commerce Committee, *Hearings on S. 2814 and S. 2814 Amendment,* 1962, pp. 282–84.

[5] *Intragovernmental Committee Report,* pp. 28–30.

[6] See *Task Force Report,* Ch. II.

Options (a) and (b) purport to eliminate the duplication of facilities, encourage R&D, and strengthen the record carriers relative to AT&T and also vis-à-vis the foreign administrations. With AT&T's overseas facilities added in too, in (c), even greater scale economies, research, bargaining leverage abroad, and more effective cable/satellite competition are predicted. But the past pattern of intercarrier rivalry will be ended.

In (d), a joinder of ComSat with the record carriers is said to facilitate still more vigorous competition with AT&T and further relax the need for present restrictive FCC policies. To the Task Force proposal (e), which is in some ways the most radical, we return later in this chapter.

At the time of the Satellite Act, Congress had not yet acted on any merger proposal and, indeed, had traditionally opposed such proposals in the international field.[7] Consequently, the problem was (and so far still is) how to guarantee to all the carriers assured, equitable, nondiscriminatory access to a satellite facility affiliated in some fashion with the industry's most powerful member. The need to determine the precise form of earth station ownership best suited to this goal has assumed imperative importance today.

The problems posed by uneven intercarrier relations have also emerged, in the controversy over AT&T's eligibility to provide circuits for international television. As sole carrier authorized to operate both domestically and internationally and the sole supplier of domestic TV circuits, AT&T would have a substantial competitive advantage in servicing any future international TV market. A basic question is whether TV is in fact a voice-only or combined voice-and-record service.

Besides the federal government, the major potential noncarrier users of satellites include the TV networks, data-processing companies, press associations, and various transport and business groups. A key question is whether such users should have access to ComSat directly or only through common carrier intermediaries and, if the former, the most appropriate form for earth station ownership. A second issue is whether the noncarrier users should be permitted to create their own domestic satellites individually or jointly, in ways comparable to their private microwave systems. The common carriers are well aware of the threat to their revenues and future status posed by these developments. For

---

[7] Shortly thereafter, the FCC, in a landmark decision, authorized the record carriers to share in joint ownership of a fourth transatlantic cable capable of handling combined voice-record services of the sort previously open only to AT&T. See FCC Public Notice No. 48671, March 17, 1964; FCC Memorandum Opinion and Order (on TAT-4), mimeo 64–217 48006, March 18, 1964.

that reason they have sought (with some success) to block such moves at every possible point in the Commission's proceedings, including earth station ownership, location of the interface, Early Bird rates and temporary noncarrier access to ComSat, the Thirty Circuit case.[8]

The present joint venture format of ComSat may have been justifiable at the outset. Its broad-based ownership, the limits placed on common carrier participation, the appointment of government directors, and the provision for competitive procurement, were designed to insure nondiscriminatory access by all users and suppliers. They were geared also to reconcile speedy growth and wide diffusion at a time when more than one global system was opposed as a technical and economic impracticality.

Yet the changing character of communications technology, costs, and systems options has led some observers to emphasize the feasibility of a more competitive structure, at least at home. Increasingly, the question asked is whether present or proposed satellite organization is at least consistent with the evolution of viable "competitive alternatives"[9] in Commission rate regulation, or may itself impose avoidable constraints on the operation of such alternatives. There is no question that the Commission has on occasion sought to limit competition between ComSat and the carriers, or that since 1962 the carriers' interests have frequently prevailed against those of ComSat and the private users in major organizational decisions. This was surely true on authorized users, ground station ownership, and location of the interface. Domestic satellites will soon provide another and perhaps more important testing ground.

The Case for Competitive Alternatives

The case for competitive alternatives can best be set forth with reference to the domestic long-distance communications structure and therein the past and potential threat posed by the private and independent specialized for-hire microwave systems. The principles at issue, however, bear also on the future potential threat of satellites to terrestrial systems generally, assuming both to be separately owned. The principles are relevant whether the newcomer systems are big private or specialized for-hire satellite carriers or a ComSat-operated system. For in either

[8] See Ch. XI.

[9] As used in this chapter and the next, the term refers to private microwave or private satellite systems, specialized for-hire carriers, and also to the FCC's discretion to permit ComSat to compete directly with the common carriers for governmental or other leased circuit business.

case, the competitive impact is of newcomer satellites on incumbent terrestrial carriers.

In the international field, the comparable rivalry is now between newcomer ComSat satellite links and incumbent common carrier submarine cable. However, other organizational options are also conceivable. Competition could, for example, be between private and ComSat-operated satellite systems or between both of these and carrier-owned cable.

The Domestic Market

From the viewpoint of spectrum management today, the case for a procompetitive policy in domestic telecommunications can be briefly stated as follows. Once the FCC allocates and licenses spectrum—say, to private user or specialized noncommon-carrier for-hire systems—it virtually must permit the carriers to cut private line or other bulk usage rates down to long-run marginal cost. And it must do so notwithstanding (a) the higher spectrum costs of private systems; (b) the adverse distributional effects of cream-skimming on small users; and (c) the further failure of big private users to pay for the public goods component of the basic switched common carrier network.[10]

At present, because rates are set uniformly according to systemwide costs, the rates of new entrants, while often below common carrier rates, may still exceed the carriers' costs. New entrants may therefore have artificial, uneconomic incentives to enter the low-cost high-density routes, "cream-skimming" in ways that impair the service on high-cost routes. To safeguard the integrity of the basic switched public message voice networks, the FCC must set rates at the "specific costs of serving specific routes."[11] By the same token, the carriers must bear the burden of proof in defending their tariff proposals in light of cost and demand characteristics which prevail in specific markets.[12] However, to facilitate

---

[10] Much of the argument that immediately follows is adapted from L. Johnson's incisive analysis in "Technological Advance and Market Structure in Domestic Telecommunications," *American Economic Review, Papers and Proceedings* (May 1970). See also *Task Force Report*, Ch. VI.

[11] See *Task Force Report*, Ch. VI, pp. 16–20, 59–60. Kahn further elucidates the cream-skimming problem by noting the carriers' inability, under present "unrealistically low" depreciation allowances, to price at current costs. Part at least of the competitive advantages of private or independent specialized systems over common carrier microwave, like the advantages of ComSat over cable internationally, may thus simply reflect the fact that the carriers are perhaps understandably compelled to recoup historic, embedded costs from their subscribers. See Comments of Alfred E. Kahn on "Issues in National Communications Policy," *American Economic Review, Papers and Proceedings* (May 1970).

[12] *Task Force Report*, Ch. VI, pp. 59–60.

greater competition between the user-owned or for-hire private line services and the common carriers, some provision must also be made for
compulsory interconnection between the two. Otherwise, the costly duplication of parallel transmission facilities would be economically wasteful
if not actually preclusive of new entry.[13] Competition would also be
helped by arrangements that enable customer-owned terminal equipment
and private systems to interconnect with the switched public telephone
network.[14]

For present purposes, the case for competition is really five-fold.
First, the carriers' reduction of private line or other bulk usage rates
down to long-run marginal cost (LRMC) is essential to forestall uneconomic entry of private or specialized systems. This is true even
though, lacking any market for spectrum today, there is no ready way
to include spectrum costs in estimating carriers' cost of service for rate
determination purposes. Second, the rate reductions are necessary notwithstanding the presently higher spectrum costs of private than of
common carrier systems, which mean that seemingly economic entry
may not in fact be so. "Spectrum costs" mean any communications system's spectrum requirements per two-way voice channel, calculated
irrespective of the spectrum's value or of the dollar costs its utilization
imposes on others. Private systems are known to have decisively higher
spectrum requirements in the above terms than the common carriers.[15]
(See Table 34, especially Items 3, 4, and 6.)

Third, the reasons that spectrum costs should in any case be disregarded in setting common carrier rates in the wake of new entry are
as follows. The carriers' long-run marginal *nonspectrum* costs are hard
enough to measure accurately. To include spectrum costs at this time
would simply be impractical, whereas ignoring such costs would, in
borderline cases, favor the new entrant. Though seemingly uneconomic,
such competitive entry may lead to a rationalization of the spectrum
management framework itself. By intensifying the interference problem,
uneconomic entry can force a revamping of spectrum management practice such that newcomers and incumbents are permitted to negotiate a
mutually acceptable degree of interference and thus jointly to maximize
the economic value of spectrum used in common.[16] To deter such competitive entry on the hazy grounds that private systems have higher

[13] Ibid., pp. 22–23.
[14] Ibid., pp. 26–28.
[15] See also L. Johnson, "New Technology: Its Use and Management of the
Radio Spectrum," *Washington University Law Quarterly* (Fall 1967), pp. 528–32.
[16] See Johnson, "Technological Advance and Market Structure," pp. 11–12;
and "New Technology," pp. 524–28.

TABLE 34. COMPARISON OF PRIVATE AND COMMON CARRIER MICROWAVE SYSTEMS, 1968

Item number	Stem, by frequency band	Private microwave	Common carrier microwave (Bell System)	
1.	Route-miles:	110,000	All Carriers	79,000
	3,700–4,200 Mc/s		Bell TD-2, TD-3	59,000
	5,925–6,425 Mc/s		Bell TH, TL	13,000
	6,575–6,875 Mc/s			
	10.7–11.7 Gc/s		Bell TJ, TM	
	12.2–12.7 Gc/s			
2.	Channel-miles:	2,500,000	Bell Total	150,000,000
	3,700–4,200 Mc/s		Bell TD-2, TD-3	
	5,925–6,425 Mc/s		Bell TH, TL	
	6,575–6,875 Mc/s			
	10.7–11.7 Gc/s		Bell TJ, TM	
	12.2–12.7 Gc/s			
3.	Voice equivalent channels per route-mile (average)[a]	22.7		2,080
4.	Voice equivalent 2-way channels per route:[a]			
	3,700–4,200 Mc/s		Bell TD-2, TD-3	12,000
	5,925–6,425 Mc/s		Bell TH, TL	11,000
	6,575–6,875 Mc/s	240		
	10.7–11.7 Gc/s		Bell TJ, TM	240
	12.2–12.7 Gc/s	240		
5.	Radio frequency bandwidth-Mc/s:			
	3,700–4,200 Mc/s		Bell TD-2, TD-3	20
	5,925–6,425 Mc/s		Bell TH, TL	30
	6,575–6,875 Mc/s	10		
	10.7–11.7 Gc/s		Bell TJ, TM	40
	12.2–12.7 Gc/s	20		
6.	Voice equivalent 2-way channels per Mc/s:[a]			
	3,700–4,200 Mc/s		Bell TD-2, TD-3	600
	5,925–6,425 Mc/s		Bell TH, TL	367
	6,575–6,875 Mc/s	24		
	10.7–11.7 Gc/s		Bell TJ, TM	6
	12.2–12.7 Gc/s	12		

Source: Office of Telecommunications Management.

[a] The spectrum requirements of any communications system per two-way voice channel are calculated irrespective of the spectrum's value or the dollar costs its utilization imposes on others.

spectrum costs than common carriers would simply forestall powerful inducements for the carriers to introduce cost-reducing innovations.

This brings us to a fourth reason for competition. The carriers' pre-emptive innovation of cost-reducing technology will help offset any adverse distributional effects of "cream-skimming" as between big and small users, since both types will benefit from the rate reductions that are thereby made possible.[17] Indeed, these cost- and rate-reducing innovations should help safeguard the integrity of the whole switched net-

[17] Compare with Johnson, "Technological Advance," pp. 8–9.

work, over and beyond the above-mentioned effects of a policy to equate rates with "the specific costs of serving specific routes."

Finally, once private systems are authorized, any loss of common carrier business will force the general users to pay a greater portion of the network's common costs. That is, general users will have to pay more than the average total cost (ATC) of serving them alone. But this is true whether the carriers are permitted to meet the threatened diversion by reducing rates to LRMC or are kept from doing so by a policy that purports to protect the private systems by keeping minimum rates *above* LRMC.[18] The economic advantage of the former approach lies in the probability that general users will then be spared having to pay as much of the common costs as they otherwise would—that is, as much as if the big users were not retained and hence could make no contribution to common costs.

Stated otherwise, the carriers' rate adjustments down to LRMC will force the users on protected routes to pay more of the common costs than they actually generate. But the newcomer cannot be charged the fully allocated costs (the ATC of servicing them alone), including a fair share of common costs, without seriously impeding new entry. Willynilly, the common costs will be shifted and the only question is "how much" and "onto whom."

Many of the most strenuous objections to "cream-skimming" appear to overlook the possibility that the amount of cream available for skimming raises serious questions as to the defensibility of the carriers' general rate level in the first place, as well as the particular structure of their costs and rates. Furthermore, the fact that only some 15 per cent of Bell's business and 30 per cent of Western Union's are subject to such competition further underscores the case for permitting it. So too, finally, does the waning importance of the public goods element in the basic switched network. Because the established core network is now large and viable, the old argument that it must be protected against private system competition seems far less compelling.[19] And this is true notwithstanding the indirect benefits which accrue to the big specialized private line customers who do not actually use the public message switched network at all.

Returning to the more strictly management dimension of the case for competition, a further word should be said on the intensification of

[18] Ibid., pp. 6–7.

[19] Ibid., pp. 8–9. Granted, however, that the big users might find their low-cost low-reliability systems economically less attractive even today if they had no basic switched voice network to turn to in case of a breakdown. See Comments of Alfred E. Kahn, p. 5.

interference by new entrants and its eventual effects on current management practice. At present, because a newcomer must pay his own sharing costs to prevent such interference, he may stay out because these costs are prohibitive or moving up higher is still more costly. Yet he might be quite willing to compensate incumbents, as the price of entry, for all their losses due to interference. To forbid the newcomer to reimburse the incumbents toward this end precludes competitive new entry that is in fact "economic" and perpetuates a currently inefficient use of the spectrum besides.

Following the line of analysis in Chapter V (and Appendix D), all three options should ideally be opened up to the newcomer, permitting him to pay his own sharing costs; to reimburse the incumbents for accommodating him; or to move up to another, higher spectral region at higher costs. Newcomer would then select his low-cost option, which may well be the second.

But we must also consider incumbent's incentives to negotiate. At present, he will prefer to foreclose entry to newcomer. Either he exaggerates the costs of sharing and the degree of inacceptable interference that is likely, or he exaggerates the ease of moving up and minimizes the cost of so doing. But suppose incumbent must choose between accommodating newcomer (and being compensated for doing so), and paying to the spectrum manager a "rent" for spectrum equal to the difference between newcomer's sharing payments and the cost of newcomer moving up to a next-best spectral location. The incumbent could still squat but only at a price, paid not to newcomer but to the spectrum manager. He would thus have greater incentive to negotiate fair compensation for accommodating the newcomer on the merits. That is, calculated economic value to incumbent of keeping newcomer out entirely by manipulating the spectrum management apparatus to raise entry barriers to outsiders would be largely eliminated from consideration.

A final word on the special issues raised by the legal provision that the FCC may require free or reduced-rate common carrier interconnection for public television.[20] The question here is whether spectrum costs should on this count alone be excluded from the LRMC of servicing these public users, where benefit externalities are large but the traditional sources of finance meager. Would this facilitate their subsidization out of the economic rents inherent in the spectrum which the carriers use to service public television? And could this "subsidy" best be financed by

[20] Public Broadcasting Act of 1967, sec. 396(h).

permitting the carriers to charge private commercial broadcast users more than the ATC of servicing *them* alone?

As noted in Chapter VI, in meeting Congress's mandate for free or reduced-rate interconnection for public TV, common carrier rates could presumably be set at the LRMC of serving it or, better still, at the long-run marginal nonspectrum costs of so doing. By the same token, private commercial users of the common carrier interconnection service would have to be charged the common costs of servicing the public users too. This premium charge would presumably include the spectrum costs incurred to service the commercial users alone, and possibly more. Hence the subsidy implicit in the rates set at the LRMC of servicing the public users would be paid out of the economic rents the carriers collect by charging commercial broadcast users for the spectrum used to service *them*; i.e., by charging them above the average total nonspectrum costs of servicing them alone.[21]

Before moving on to the international market and its special problems, a word about two general factors in the case for competition wherever it is found in communications: first, the need to delimit the range of carrier managerial discretion in rates and service; second, the need to offset the tendency to overinvestment and inefficiency in regulated firms subject to a profit constraint. Both factors operate in the international as well as the domestic communications market.

The Range of Managerial Discretion. Competitive alternatives can operate to delimit the broad range of managerial discretion still retained by the communications common carriers. As a practical matter, public utility commissions can most readily regulate the general rate level and, through that, the rate of return. But even that kind of regulation has been far from rigorous. For example, imprudent expenses can theoretically be disallowed in calculating the return that remains after expenses are subtracted. Imprudent capital investment or R&D, or excessive investment not used to provide a service, can also be excluded from the rate base in calculating an admissible rate of return. But little progress has been made on either count.

By far the main problem is the laxity of public utility commissions in controlling costs, laxity due largely to their inability to determine which inputs of capital and labor will be most efficient, or otherwise to correct the deficiencies with remedial techniques for so-called incen-

---

[21] The argument made in the paragraph above stems largely from correspondence with Alfred E. Kahn.

tive regulation, audits of internal efficiency, etc.[22] As a practical matter, it is extremely hard to determine the cost of equity capital and hence to set a fair rate of return. Quality deterioration may in any case operate to offset any rate reduction. According to one observer:

> Many close questions of judgment arise in deciding which assets should be included in the rate base; in valuing those assets; in determining depreciation allowances; and in separating costs between regulated and nonregulated services and between different regulatory jurisdictions (some of which may be very lax). Moreover, where services involve joint or common costs a rational allocation is impossible even in theory.[23]

Combined, such factors "can easily emasculate the profit ceiling. . . ."[24]

Even assuming general use of any original cost method of rate base valuation, a satisfactory empirical standard to set a proper rate of return is hard to find. The unregulated industries provide only a faulty comparative standard. Unregulated competitive industries can be criticized as riskier than the regulated utilities, whereas unregulated noncompetitive industries are likely to earn monopoly profits. Admittedly the price-earnings ratio may tighten the fair return component of the cost of service and provide a more useful standard in determining the true cost of capital. As such, it takes us beyond the older comparative standards. However, price-earnings ratios are subject to deficiencies of their own, in particular their disincentive effects on improved utility performance.[25]

As already suggested, commission regulation has been unable to delimit managerial discretion with regard to a great many dimensions of common carrier performance other than the general rate level, such as service standards, the volume of R&D and capital investment, operating procedures, and operating efficiency. A commission can theoretically question excessive R&D, capital investment, or deteriorating service standards, but as a practical matter this has been hard to do. In practice, new services are introduced irrespective of the prior availability of like service options.

Finally, special problems are posed in determining the proper structure of rates—that is, in the pricing of particular services. This is especially noteworthy in allocating the economies due to new communications technology and more generally in allocating between individual services

[22] See generally R. Posner, "Natural Monopoly and its Regulation," *Stanford Law Review* (February 1969), pp. 592–99, 617, 627–34. On past and current regulatory practice and problems, see W. Jones, *Cases in Regulated Industries* (Foundation Press, 1967), pp. 102–86.
[23] Posner, "Natural Monopoly," pp. 594–95.
[24] Ibid., p. 595.
[25] See discussion in ibid., pp. 625–27.

the joint or overhead costs common to all services. The satellite technology has posed this particular problem in a most vivid manner, but it applies more generally to the terrestrial carriers as well.

Among the questions at issue are: whether new technology should be priced separately at cost or averaged with older technologies; whether special new media uses should be favored with special rates to facilitate their special social functions; whether rates should be held to cost or made to reflect fully any cost savings due to new technology or perhaps set even below minimum cost. Here too managerial discretion remains in the absence of clear-cut criteria. Once again, insofar as the new technologies can be administered as credible competitive alternatives, they may provide both a comparative standard for rate setting *and* also a catalyst to precipitate common carrier rate adjustments.

The Tendency to Overinvestment and Inefficiency. The tendency to overinvestment and inefficiency is being increasingly attributed to economic forces inherent in the facts of rate base regulation. Many academic economists believe that regulated utilities subject to a profit constraint have a theoretical predisposition towards overinvestment and inefficiency.

The regulated firm's response to a profit constraint has been variously described as follows:[26]

1. Such a firm has little reason to keep cost expenditures down insofar as:
   a. it can recoup any cost increase by simply raising the rates on those services it sells to users with inelastic demands; and/or
   b. it has managerial goals other than profits, whose pursuit can be furthered by a variety of "unprofitable" cost-increasing outlays.
2. The tendency of such firms to overinvest in capital-intensive technology is grounded in:
   a. the higher earnings level they are currently allowed with a larger rate base;
   b. their relative uncertainty of earning the allowable returns, again by raising their rates to users with inelastic demands for particular services; and
   c. the regulators' practice of permitting rates of return higher than the cost of capital.

[26] See, e.g., W. Baumol, "Reasonable Rules for Rate Regulation: Plausible Policies for an Imperfect World," paper presented at Brookings Rate Base Symposium, June 7, 1968, pp. 3–6. See further discussion in H. Trebing, ed., *Performance under Regulation*, MSU Public Utilities Studies (Michigan State University Press, 1968), pp. 42–47, 74–78.

3. The regulated firm has a related incentive to engage in short-run predatory price-cutting to eliminate rivals on product lines sold under competitive conditions, and thus improve its own long-run chances for expanded investments and a larger rate base.

4. The regulated firm can also augment its rate base by having its own hardware subsidiary raise equipment charges against it. In this case, its older machines are automatically revalued at the replacement cost (under a reproduction cost standard of rate base regulation), and allowable earnings will rise proportionately.[27]

Although firms that operate under a profit constraint are generally agreed to have the above theoretical predispositions,[28] there is less agreement on the magnitude of any such tendencies in fact.[29] Such empirical behavior would presumably have to be sought out in a more subtle fashion than utility management traditionally does in its attempted rebuttal. The distortions, if they exist, might conceivably take such forms as excessive back-up service, redundant facilities, or unusual safeguards of reliability.

The several major probable manifestations of these postulated predispositions of regulated carriers are said to include:[30] service reliability standards higher than those that are socially optimal; a tendency to forward integration with utility ownership of terminals as well as lines; a comparable tendency of operating carriers to integrate backwards into equipment manufacturing and electronics laboratories; the carriers' normal preference for owning rather than leasing any needed facilities;

[27] This fourth postulated response must be strongly qualified on two counts. First, it implies a far more general use of reproduction cost valuation than is currently true. Second, it wrongly presumes a lack of supervision by regulators of the subsidiary's charges. On the latter point, see Jones, *Cases in Regulated Industries,* pp. 186–98.

[28] The original Averch-Johnson formulation emphasizes items #2 and #3 in the preceding paragraph, i.e., the tendency for regulated firms to (a) substitute between factors in an uneconomic way, thereby failing to minimize social cost at any selected outputs; and (b) to expand into other regulated industries even at a long-run loss, engaging in predatory competition toward that end. See H. Averch and L. Johnson, "Behavior of the Firm Under Regulatory Constraint," *American Economic Review* (December 1962), pp. 1052–68. A. Alchian and R. Kessel have stated item #1 explicitly in their distinction between firm behavior (and corporate preference maximization) under monopolistic and competitive conditions, with reference also to a regulatory constraint. ("Competition, Monopoly, and the Pursuit of Money" in Universities—National Bureau Committee for Economic Research, *Aspects of Labor Economics* [Princeton University Press, 1962], pp. 157–68.) For the original source of item #4 see F. Westfield, "Regulation and Conspiracy," *American Economic Review* (June 1965), pp. 424–43.

[29] But see affirmative evidence cited in Trebing, ed., *Performance under Regulation,* pp. 48–53.

[30] Comments by Johnson at Brookings Rate Symposium, June 7, 1968.

and lastly, their provision of some services at non-compensatory rates. Some of these developments may in their own right produce anticompetitive structural results.[31] Logically, therefore, the tendencies to over-investment and inefficiency might require a commission to be more rigorous in evaluating new capital-intensive investment projects; more committed to devising measures of LRMC by way of identifying predatory price-cutting; more sensitive to the possibilities of adjusting the fair-rate-of-returns approach to regulation by taking proper account of operating ratios where firms face risks in areas of declining sales.

There are doubtless a number of ways to cope with such phenomena,[32] assuming them to be empirically valid and identified more systematically than hitherto. Without questioning the importance of exploring several remedial options simultaneously, including new ways to average returns over time and to institutionalize the so-called regulatory lag,[33] the thrust of this chapter is different. It is simply that greater reliance on competitive alternatives (through the necessary revamping of the FCC's policies on authorized users, ground station ownership, private domestic satellites, etc.) is at the least a necessary precondition of any significant improvement. It is, moreover, an approach likely to reduce tendencies to overinvestment, inefficiency, and predation, and hence the need to devise drastically new regulatory techniques to deal with them directly.[34]

There would of course still be room for the FCC to screen new capital-intensive investment projects more carefully in the light of leasing alternatives. And room also to devise new ways to ascertain LRMC for purposes of determining where and when services are provided on a noncompensatory basis and hence where pricing may be preclusive. Special steps might still be taken to institutionalize the regulatory lag or to institute periodic management audits on a regularized rather than ad hoc basis.

[31] See M. Irwin and R. McKee, "Vertical Integration and the Communications Equipment Industry: Alternatives for Public Policy," *Cornell Law Review* (February 1968), pp. 446–51, 472.

[32] A suggestive range of possible approaches is identified in Trebing, ed., *Performance under Regulation*, pp. 54–67, 80–87.

[33] By "regulatory lag" is normally meant the lapse of time between an initial change in carrier costs, demand, etc., and the subsequent change in rate regulation warranted thereby. In seeking to contain the uneconomic side-effects of regulation mentioned above, some writers propose new ways to utilize the regulatory lag. See three unpublished papers presented at the Brookings Rate Base Symposium, June 7, 1968: W. Baumol, "Reasonable Rules," p. 11; A. Matthews, "Problems Posed by Current Regulatory Practices to the Rapid Introduction of Communications Satellite Technology," pp. 6–13; and J. Scanlon, "Is Rate-Base of Return Regulation Obsolete?," pp. 4–5, 15.

[34] My analysis here seems closest to views set forth by Kahn at the Brookings Rate Base Symposium. This section has benefited from his formulations there.

But greater reliance on competitive alternatives in telecommunications is particularly germane in view of the recognized difficulties in the above approach,[35] to say nothing of devising ways to take operating ratios into account. Competitive alternatives are of value also in view of the complexities and subjectivity of any commission evaluation of comparative efficiency of alternative systems, some of which are capital-saving and others capital-intensive.

To reduce the magnitude of any distortion, then, we need to create competitive, self-regulating structures. We might still face an irreducible core of inefficiency. In that case we would want techniques to observe directly, albeit with a minimum of subjective judgment. Here we could institutionalize the prodding and let managerial professionalism take over. Competitive alternatives offer at the very least a way to avoid having to make judgments about things of which we are ignorant. At the same time, they help the regulator do what is expected of him without undue direct intervention.

The International Market

A number of additional problems arise in the international field. First, critical foreign policy objectives may override the economic case for competition, even if one were to grant its validity here too, for argument's sake. Second, there is the even more fundamental question of whether the economic structures of international and domestic communications differ sufficiently to raise serious doubts about the viability of competition in the former field.

Overriding Foreign Policy Constraints. If the United States remains committed to a single global system and to sustaining ComSat's managerial role therein, a number of delicate negotiations will periodically confront the FCC, the State Department, ComSat, and other Intelsat members. Is the policy of competitive alternatives fully consistent with overriding foreign policy requirements? Or would it exacerbate the tensions posed by including rich and poor nations in the same intergovernmental consortium? Would it worsen the tensions posed by European members who insist on a prorated share of ComSat's hardware con-

---

[35] To cite one example, the regulatory lag should ideally be of uncertain duration. On that score alone it is hard to conceive of it as operating on a strictly mechanical basis. Considerable Commission discretion would also presumably be needed in defining norms of expected behavior in regard to service reliability, acceptable earnings, etc. Nor is it easy to see how inefficiency would be punished where general cost levels are declining for other reasons.

tracts (for their $80 million equity investment) and counterpressures from the developing nations who favor the lower cost of American hardware companies?[36] What of the further clash between the Europeans, who benefit from older conventional routings, and the newer nations, who seek direct links between one another? Between ComSat's fiduciary obligations to its stockholders and its contractual commitments to Intelsat?

Finally, some form of value-of-service pricing by ComSat is virtually dictated by the peculiar legislative history of the Satellite Act. Because Congress appears unwilling to relax its insistence for a self-sustaining entity, ComSat's sizable joint costs will presumably have to be allocated on the thinner routes between the developing nations, or between them and the advanced nations.[37] However, the high-capacity routes between, say, the United States and Europe will presumably enjoy lower unit cable costs than the low-capacity routes which involve the developing countries. Therefore, the former will also enjoy lower satellite charges. Otherwise, the diversion of users from satellite to cheaper cable modes would act to increase the whole system's unused capacity and result in still higher satellite charges for the developing nations. Yet the latter will doubtless lodge serious complaints that ComSat had met competition in the wealthier countries, where conventional facilities are convenient and inexpensive, by exploiting links subject to weaker competition.[38]

The question for national policy is how big a price we are willing to pay to underwrite the telecommunications development of Asia, Africa, and South America. And second, whether direct money grants to them are economically and politically preferable to protecting ComSat against global (or domestic) competition to facilitate its internal subsidization of the developing countries. Such issues are very complex and could conceivably preclude any general procompetitive policy. In any case they should not be prejudged here. The analysis and evidence that follow in Chapter XI are for consideration on the merits as part of the "whole picture" but not necessarily determinative alone.

The Economics of Natural Monopoly. A major area untouched in this discussion as yet is the thesis that economics and technology militate strongly in favor of a natural monopoly in international telecommuni-

[36] The pressure on ComSat to distribute procurement and research contracts outside the U.S. has continued to mount. See *Electronic News* (October 16, 1967), pp. 1, 23; also (November 6, 1967), pp. 1, 37.

[37] See Levin, "Organization and Control of Communications Satellites," pp. 349–54.

[38] See generally L. Johnson, "Joint Cost and Price Discrimination: The Case of Communications Satellites," *Journal of Business* (January 1964), pp. 44–46.

cations. The President's Task Force on Communications Policy recently proposed that all international traffic be handled by a single entity.[39] As noted, this would entail a merger of overseas AT&T transmission facilities with those of ComSat and the international record carriers, and explicit exclusion of that entity from domestic communications carriage, hardware manufacturing, or related research. The proposal was grounded on two major factual premises: that cable/satellite cost and demand characteristics plus important reliability/security considerations make it very difficult to establish effective cable/satellite competition; and that scale economies alone would preclude unsubsidized competing bimodal entities, each using both technologies.

In its affirmative case the *Task Force Report* made five points.[40] Lacking any vested interest in cable or satellite, the single entity is seen able to facilitate systems optimization, full realization of scale economies, and more objective choices as between the competing technologies. It would, secondly, permit the U.S. carriers to bargain with foreign entities in unison and facilitate a more consistent U.S. position in Intelsat than ComSat can now provide while its management is being increasingly internationalized. Third, it would eliminate serious conflicts of interest issuing from carrier participation in ComSat, representation on its board, and divided earth station ownership. Fourth, it would facilitate ending the current FCC protectionist policy towards the overseas record carriers, and do so in a manner both equitable and responsive to national security requirements.

On balance, far from posing more onerous regulatory responsibilities, the proposal is seen on several counts to simplify the task of regulation.[41] The overseas record carriers would no longer require special protection. Lacking their domestic and hardware ties and their terminal service functions, the single entity would also have more readily identifiable costs and a simpler rate structure. Regulation would be simplified further by breaking out the relatively small international segment of the telecommunications business. The special problems posed by regulating a single-firm monopoly would allegedly be met in part by AT&T's great bargaining power as a domestic carrier in search of low-cost international transmission from an entity in a position to exploit full-scale economies. Independent competitive hardware and research entities would provide another safeguard of low transmission costs by providing low-cost factor inputs.

---

[39] See generally, *Task Force Report*, Ch. II.
[40] Ibid., pp. 27–33.
[41] Ibid., pp. 35–37.

To consider even the economic dimensions of such a far-reaching proposal would take us far afield. The inefficiency of FCC practice today in allocating market shares between rival cable and satellite companies must be granted. So must the inadequacy of adversary proceedings as a mechanism for optimizing cable/satellite investment. But this hardly rules out the possibility of structuring competition more effectively. There is some advantage also in keeping this door open in view of the political obstacles to any more fundamental restructuring. The Task Force itself indicated as much in recognizing the steps that might be taken should the single entity not materialize.[42]

The question is how far to go down this other path. Should we now repeal outright the FCC's Authorized User Policy, which now normally limits ComSat to dealing directly with the communications common carriers alone? Should we authorize a merger of the three record carriers with AT&T's overseas facilities? Would the prospect of limiting ComSat to the international field induce the AT&T to part with those assets voluntarily? Could the record carriers then survive without special FCC protection? Even so ingenious a trade-off would presumably raise political opposition similar to that which confronts the single-entity proposal today and has long forestalled repeated attempts to merge the record carriers. At this juncture, therefore, a more modest strategy may still merit exploration.

Within the current framework steps could be taken to insure the continued credibility of ComSat's competitive threat to the carriers, mainly by easing the conditions under which direct dealings between it and the ultimate users are possible. In the far larger domestic market the door would be left open to a variety of terrestrial and satellite systems—private, cooperative, common carrier.

It is in any case important to distinguish between regulated competition as it is today, with parallel expansion of cable and satellites and allocated market shares, and regulated competition as it might be with: (a) drastic revision or repeal of the Authorized User Policy and at the least its rejection wherever satellite economies are not adequately reflected in common carrier rates; (b) relocation of the satellite-terrestrial interface at the gateway cities; (c) ComSat ownership of overland links from earth station to interface; (d) some exclusive ComSat-owned earth stations to facilitate the direct servicing of end customers and (e) compulsory interconnection of transoceanic satellite traffic with domestic AT&T facilities. The last consideration is important not only if the

---

[42] While noting the obstacles to effective cable/satellite competition today, the *Task Force Report* also recognizes a role for procompetitive regulatory changes in the present framework, in last resort. See ibid., pp. 21–29, 47–50.

carriers are excluded from some earth stations but also if they are excluded from the ComSat board or from ComSat entirely.

This stops short of having AT&T spin off all cable holdings on overseas links, but the steps proposed would help insure the continued credibility of ComSat's competitive threat to the carriers. The resultant competition in rates and service, restrained though it be, might help avoid both the probable stalemate of a two-firm duopoly[43] (one handling satellite and the other cable facilities) or the waste of the bimodal duopoly, each handling both satellite and cable facilities.[44] Yet there would still be some competitive pressure to limit the tendencies to over-investment and inefficiency in regulated firms subject to a profit restraint; induce competitive rate adjustments down to the carriers' LRMC; and induce cost-reducing innovations by the carriers and by ComSat in light of one another's applications for new authorizations, especially if new satellite systems should eventually appear on the scene.

In regard to the pressures for parallel expansion, ComSat and the cable owners both want to enter the growing lucrative international market and, with the DOD's endorsement of the national security interest in cable expansion, the FCC has generally acquiesced.[45] Given the consumers' inelastic demand schedule, the Commission has accommodated both cables and satellites, with some savings to the consumer but far less than if all the new investment were limited largely to satellites.[46] As noted above, moreover, the carriers have special incentives to own cable rather than to lease satellite circuits. Because they earn profits on their actual capital investment, they will tend to expand it until the incremental cost of capital exceeds the allowable rate of return. My point is simply that competitive structuring would help reduce some of this excessive capital investment.

On the other hand, technological progress under the present system, let alone under a modified competitive option, might help offset some of the higher costs and excess capacity of today's economic structure and regulatory practice. In the growth of new telecommunications capabili-

[43] See M. Peck, "The Single Entity Proposal for International Communications," *American Economic Review, Papers and Proceedings* (May 1970).

[44] See *Task Force Report*, Ch. II, pp. 21–25.

[45] See Peck, "The Single Entity Proposal," pp. 7–9. The argument that follows here is much indebted to that paper, though it differs on a number of counts.

[46] Ibid., pp. 3–8. Kahn attributes the rate at which users enjoy the economies of new communications technologies to the carriers' "unrealistically low" depreciation allowances. Given past "errors and distortions" here, regulators understandably permit the carriers to recoup from subscribers embedded costs "far higher than the costs of the newest facilities . . ." Rates are therefore set on "the average cost of a composite of new and old facilities." (See Comments of Alfred E. Kahn, pp. 1–2.)

ties, the preemptive competitive strategies of regulated carriers could well play some role over and beyond that of the present military and space programs.

This may be of critical importance because even large military/space expenditures on electronic communications have only limited civilian spillover effects. Moreover, the degree to which basic know-how or components are applied depends on the structure and incentives of the common carrier and equipment manufacturing industries, wherein active competition is an affirmative factor. This role for competition seems at least comparable to, or perhaps greater than, the role enumerated by the Task Force for AT&T in ensuring the adequate progressiveness and efficiency of a single overseas carrier entity excluded from domestic carriage and equipment manufacturing.[47]

In other words, there may be some role in international communication for cost-reducing innovations by ComSat and the carriers, geared to preclude new competitive entry by each other or by eventual private cooperative systems. These innovations would help big and small users alike, thus offsetting any adverse distributional effects of cream-skimming, and would also safeguard the integrity of the basic switched network notwithstanding the diversion of private line business. The stimulus of cable/satellite rivalry to technical progress on both sides has in fact been recognized as helping to offset the excess capacity and added costs of parallel expansion plus rate base expansion on the cable side.[48] But the preemptive competitive strategies of the cable companies to keep big users from switching to ComSat or to eventual private satellite systems could play a crucial role in their own right. Indeed the advent of such satellite systems, international or domestic, could one day induce ComSat and the cable companies to try to introduce new technology and more attractive tariffs.

Two spurious factors sometimes cited in support of an otherwise uneconomic competitive system (with parallel expansion of cable and satellites) can now be discussed briefly: the zero spectrum costs of cable transmission; and the national security contributions of a mixed system.

Whatever other reasons may exist for subsidizing relatively uneconomic cable expansion, the comparative spectrum costs of the two modes seem largely irrelevant.[49] Total satellite delivery costs will of course rise

[47] See *Task Force Report*, Ch. II, pp. 38–42. Compare with Comments of Alfred E. Kahn, p. 4.

[48] See Peck, "The Single Entity Proposal," pp. 12–13.

[49] See generally Johnson, "New Technology," pp. 537–38; and Peck, "The Single Entity Proposal," p. 5.

if earth stations are relocated in remote rural areas and satellite traffic is brought into the gateway cities over cable links. But there are other options too. Overland connecting microwave links between earth station and interface at the gateway cities might be much cheaper, and hence preferable, unless of course the satellites cause excessive interference to the connecting links themselves. The real question is whether satellite operators could afford to reimburse other spectrum users for losses due to interference (or for the hardware adjustments needed to minimize them) and still show a net advantage over cable. If so, any qualitative advantage of submarine cable on this aspect could clearly be dismissed.

If the scale economies of satellites over cable are as decisive as a National Academy of Engineering panel suggests, even sizable spectrum costs alone need not alter the case against competing cable/satellite entities, or for a combined single entity. However, the third-party effects of satellite transmission may underscore the need to consider trade-offs between physical location of earth stations, costs of relaying the satellite traffic to the gateways, and the costs of otherwise eliminating (or compensating for) intolerable interference with the conventional microwave systems.

In regard to the national security value of a policy of parallel cable/satellite expansion, it has been very persuasively argued that the DOD, as major beneficiary of new cable investment, ought to pay directly for it.[50] If general users of the domestic long-distance network now paid for new submarine cable investment too (via rates set on a composite rate base), a switch to direct DOD payment would improve equity but little. For the number of all these general ratepayers is almost indistinguishable from the mass of the population who will benefit from any extra national security that results from more cables. Today, however, only the users of the international communications facilities themselves pay (in higher charges) for the new cable investment.

Accordingly, equity does require that the DOD pay direct for that portion of new cable investment (or for the maintenance of existing cables) of which it is the major beneficiary. Indeed, imposing these costs squarely on the DOD will force it to evaluate cable and noncable inputs in the defense budget more rigorously. In borderline cases noncable options might then be more seriously considered.

In short, the national security value of added cable investment is no more reason to sanction parallel cable/satellite expansion than are the comparative spectrum costs of the two modes. In both cases, rational

---

[50] Peck, "The Single Entity Proposal," pp. 6–7.

account of the economic issues can be taken without necessarily justifying, on those counts at least, further growth of a mixed system.

To recognize the spurious character of these two arguments in favor of cable/satellite rivalry, however, by no means implies that the case against such rivalry (and for a single entity) is self-evident. The viability of any modified competitive international option, like that described above, would vary inversely with just how decisive a cost advantage satellites have over cable. In view of the uncertainties on future cost comparisons,[51] some such modified approach might merit consideration during what could be a protracted interim period. It would at least act to infuse greater market incentives into the present economic-regulatory framework. Since it requires far less basic restructuring than any other plan, it is not surprising that the Task Force Report should make at least passing reference to this modified approach as "second best."

Finally, the greater maximum realizable scale economies of a single entity may, conceivably, be offset by what some observers still believe would be the greater difficulty of regulating a single-seller monopoly in practice.[52] Even granting for argument's sake the smaller potential economies of competing modes, they may at least be more readily realized. Without prejudging these important issues, one may state that they constitute still another reason for continued research on a possible role for competitive alternatives in rate regulation.

[51] National Academy of Engineering, Committee on Telecommunications, *Report on Selected Topics in Telecommunications* (Washington: The Academy, 1968), pp. 5–20.

[52] See e.g., Comments by W. Jones and W. Meckling on "Issues in National Communications Policy," *American Economic Review, Papers and Proceedings* (May 1970). Jones would permit AT&T to maintain present cable capacity, but not to increase it without divesting all such facilities to a separate cable company. Should such a separate company not be viable, the market would then have determined that no net new cable investment was economically justifiable.

CHAPTER XI

COMPETITIVE ALTERNATIVES IN PRACTICE

Against the backdrop of Chapter X, we may now turn to more detailed evidence on just how competitive alternatives have worked in practice, and what potential obstacles are posed by conflicts of interest in present or potential satellite organization, with special reference to vertical ties between users, suppliers, and owners of the satellite system. The possibility of still more radical changes along lines developed in the last chapter should not be ruled out. But whatever the validity of their major economic premises, the political hazards of any plans which require a basic restructuring of the industry underscore the continued need for research on the more modest conception that follows.

COMPETITIVE ALTERNATIVES IN ACTION

Big private users can help, as big government users have helped, to induce the wide diffusion of satellite economies. They can do so by securing the benefits of cost-savings directly for themselves by gaining direct access to ComSat, under unique and exceptional circumstances. Or their mere threat to do so may operate to jar loose more extensive and speedier general rate adjustments from common carriers anxious to forestall such developments at all cost. The advent of private domestic satellite systems could also strengthen the FCC's hands in bringing rates down, just as the rapid growth of private microwave systems has done in the past. In either case, it is less important that big users actually gain direct access to ComSat or create their own systems than that these possibilities remain credible to the carriers.

The theoretical point can best be illustrated as follows. Let newcomer private (or specialized for-hire) service B threaten to divert significant revenues from incumbent common carrier service A, thereby

303

reducing A's plant utilization and raising his costs and rates. Let A respond either by innovating new cost- and rate-reducing technologies or by competitive adjustments in rates and service without changes in technology.

In the first case, discussed in Chapter X, A's preemptive strategy is to innovate a cost-reducing technology and then to propose tariffs reflective of the economies it makes possible, with benefits conceivably enjoyed by big specialized and small general users alike.

In the second case, the result of competition might well be (1) lower rates for the big users who would otherwise have turned to B, and who now pay less than the ATC (average total costs) of serving them alone but a sum at least equal to the long-run marginal cost (LRMC) of so doing; (2) a shift of the common costs of serving these big users onto the small general users of A's switched network service; (3) higher charges for these general users, but not as high as if A's big customers had in fact turned elsewhere.

On this last point, reference is made to the ideal prototype of value-of-service rate discrimination, where some sort of discrimination (and excess of price over marginal cost) is inevitable if total costs are to be covered without a subsidy. The character and defensibility of the competitive response that B elicits will depend specifically on whether: (1) rates must in fact exceed marginal costs if total costs are to be covered; (2) rates will be lower even for users discriminated against, due to the otherwise unavailable contribution of the favored users to total revenue requirements beyond mere incremental costs; (3) even the preferential rates the big user enjoys will cover long-run incremental costs (including capital cost), not merely short-run incremental costs due to temporarily redundant plant capacity; (4) no serious disadvantages will be suffered by businesses discriminated against in competition with those favored, even though all may enjoy lower rates due to discrimination.[1]

The three episodes briefly examined next are germane to these issues. First, we shall consider AT&T's domestic rate adjustments in response to the private microwave allocation; and second, its more recent response to the proposals for private or cooperative TV satellites. We then turn to the international record carriers' response to the Defense Department's tentative purchase of circuits direct from ComSat as low bidder in the Thirty-Circuit case. We offer these episodes to illustrate the kind of intermodal rivalry in rates and technology which a modified economic-regulatory structure might promote. It contrasts with

[1] J. Bonbright, *Principles of Public Utility Rates* (Columbia University Press, 1961), pp. 383–84.

both the more radical restructuring outlined in Chapter X, and the Commission's present practice of allocating traffic between cable and satellites. But it clearly works within the present organizational framework.

In this, our analysis is as much of competitive conduct within the current industry structure as it is of the longer-run prospects for altering that structure. That is, the carriers' adjustments in rates, service, and innovative activity may well preclude new entrants. But if the threat of such entry can somehow be kept credible, and if it does in fact materialize on occasion, the incumbent carriers' competitive response would still enhance the industry's economic performance.[2]

The Private Microwave Threat

In the Above-890 case, in the face of concerted carrier opposition, the Commission proposed to authorize private users to construct their own microwave systems instead of buying common carrier service direct. Unable to stop the Commission, the carriers then sought to meet the competitive threat by selective rate reductions for bulk users.[3]

Thus far, the Commission has disallowed many of these selective concessions as discriminatory. But the need remains to devise acceptable adjustments in rates and costs. For the practical situation is one where the alternative to selective rate cuts may well be no cuts, at least in the near future. A requirement that rate reductions be generalized would presumably provide greater incentives for general cost adjustments. But applied to the whole rate base, such cost adjustments, however desirable, would take a very long time to benefit users of all sizes substantially. On the other hand, a number of selective rate reductions in response to private microwave may at least raise questions about the defensibility of the general rate levels of carriers which, after all, also utilize the new microwave technology.

Once the FCC decided to authorize the private microwave service,

---

[2] Compare with Melody's contrary argument, that the carriers' competitive response to potential entry has been, and will continue to be predatory, preclusive, grounded on interservice subsidy, and mainly geared to safeguard the existing industry structure. See W. Melody, "Market Structure and Public Policy in Communications," unpublished paper presented at the 82nd Annual Meeting of the American Economic Association.

[3] A decade earlier, AT&T actually had to meet the threat of other for-hire systems planned or operated by such companies as Philco, Raytheon, General Electric, and Dumont. Crucial in AT&T's effective domination of the field by 1951 was its refusal to interconnect any TV broadcast user of non-AT&T microwave links with the AT&T system generally. See D. Beelar, "Cables in the Sky and the Struggle for Their Control," *Federal Communications Bar Journal* (January 1967), pp. 27–33.

the Bell Telephone Company, fearful of a growing diversion of revenues, promptly proposed a number of new bulk-line tariffs. First, Bell offered special multi-channel private line rates, meeting the private microwave threat by citing discounts of 28 per cent to big customers over what nonvolume users could get. Second, Bell proposed special Telpak rates, again competitive with private microwave, in offering bulk users discounts of 51 to 85 per cent of preexisting private line rates. Telpak also offered the customer greater latitude and flexibility in the size of channels he selected, whether voice or nonvoice, to accommodate telephone, teletype, control, signalling, facsimile or data.[4]

Of major concern to the FCC each time was the tariff's alleged discriminatory character. In Telpak, the Commission found the "new" service to be essentially the same as that provided by private line;[5] and costing the carriers per voice circuit no less than the private line service would.[6] Hence the Telpak rate differentials were deemed to be without any justification in cost differentials.[7] The Commission also found insufficient evidence to establish AT&T's major argument; namely, that the Telpak discounts, by meeting potential private microwave competition, would retain the business of big users at rates covering incremental cost[8] plus some of Bell's joint costs, and hence keep the rates to small general users lower than otherwise.[9]

In the earlier multiple-channel private line tariffs, the Commission found very similar deficiencies. Again, the differential rates to big and small users were said to be for a service, largely similar to regular private line, that cost AT&T no less to provide per voice circuit.[10] Nor did the Commission find the revenues likely to be retained through bulk discounts so large that all users would stand to gain from the lower rates facilitated by the fuller utilization of common carrier plant.[11]

The question is whether any acceptable competitive response in

[4] In addition, Bell has instituted wide area telephone service (WATS), wide area data service (WADS), and data-phone service. In each case the competitive threat of private microwave was an issue.

[5] FCC, Tentative Decision in Docket No. 14251, March 20, 1964, hereinafter called Telpak Decision, paras. 10–13.

[6] Ibid., paras. 15–21.

[7] Ibid., paras. 14, 21.

[8] Ibid., paras. 43–53.

[9] Ibid., paras. 21–42.

[10] See FCC, Final Decision in Docket No. 11645, January 28, 1963 (hereinafter called Private Line Decision), paras. 179, 183. Indeed the parties do not go so far here as in Telpak in failing to compare private microwave costs and multiple-channel private line costs to demonstrate their competitiveness. In Telpak there was a showing (albeit an unsatisfactory one) on this point. See Private Line Decision, para. 183 and Telpak Decision, paras. 25–35.

[11] Private Line Decision, paras. 183–85.

rates is conceivable, one that is neither unduly discriminatory nor limited to general overall rate adjustments which the carriers will in fact never make (or the FCC order) before very great reductions in overall costs due to microwave investment have occurred. After all, Bell's response to private microwave was competitive in intent. Having tried, and failed, to stop a potential rival in the Above-890 case through entry restrictions, it then sought to meet competition by rate concessions instead.[12] To say that private microwave systems cannot be produced profitably in the face of Telpak or multiple-channel private line tariffs, and that such tariffs discriminate in favor of big users, does not speak to the more fundamental question of whether virtually any bona fide competitive response in rates is conceivable in the present communications structure. Nor does it speak to whether pricing practices which preclude procompetitive changes in that structure via new carrier entry are ipso facto unacceptable.[13]

To test the relative benefits of permitting AT&T to institute Telpak-like tariffs for the big users, Coase would simply have us compare the added cost of providing any given volume of service by common carriers and by private microwave systems.[14] Where a common carrier can provide service for some user for less than it would cost him to provide it himself through private microwave, efficiency requires that the carriers be permitted to charge a price as low as long-run incremental cost. Indeed any price lower than the private microwave costs (so long as it does not fall below incremental cost) will produce a more efficient use of national resources than is likely where the Commission keeps the former's rates artificially above private microwave costs. Any adjustment of particular rates downward toward long-run incremental cost will, in short, enhance resource allocation though it may deter the growth of private microwave.[15]

What the Commission would do well to consider is whether proce-

---

[12] In bargaining for special charges closer to the actual cost of the common carrier service provided, some big users have explicitly cited their private microwave option. Whatever else one may say, Telpak and multiple-channel private line rates cannot be understood without reference to the private microwave threat. Telpak Decision, para. 54, fn. 7; Private Line Decision, para. 179; Proposed Findings & Conclusions of Bell System in Docket No. 11645, January 15, 1960, pp. 156–58.

[13] Compare the position set forth in this section with an argument to the contrary (on the inacceptability of such practices) in Melody, "Market Structure and Public Policy."

[14] R. Coase, "Theory of Public Utility Pricing," in "Economics of Regulation of Public Utilities," paper presented at Conference at Northwestern University, June 19–24, 1966.

[15] Ibid., pp. 104–6.

dures can be devised under which the carriers' selective rate reductions to big users could help generate benefits for *all* users. If the Telpak type of selective rate reduction will actually increase carrier revenues and facilitate greater scale economies through fuller plant utilization, one might conclude that the private microwave threat too will not only jar loose special rate concessions for big specialized users, but also make possible more general rate adjustments for all.[16]

One problem here will of course be how to keep the threat of private systems "credible" where, if the big common carriers are always permitted to meet the lower prices of private microwave systems, the latters' manufacturers will soon leave the field entirely or refrain from new entry. A second task is to measure incremental costs more accurately especially where, as in Telpak, the company's discriminatory pricing is found to be noncompensatory on a fully allocated cost basis. Third, we will need to mount far more extensive quantitative studies of price elasticity of demand by class of service to test the theory of defensible value-of-service rate discrimination.

Judging from Telpak and Private Line, a common carrier seeking to meet private microwave competition other than through an across-the-board rate reduction can meet one of three tests. It may demonstrate that:

1. The new service is essentially different from private line service, constituting a competitive product innovation of sorts for which a separate rate can justifiably be set;

2. The new service, while essentially no different from private line, enjoys demonstrable cost-savings and therefore warrants a rate differential reflective of the cost-differences, a proposition that takes us into the whole difficult area of allocating the cost-savings of new communications technologies;

3. The new service, while basically similar to private line and supplied at the same per-voice circuit costs, will fail to retain the big user at the old private line rates in the face of a private microwave option. The loss of bulk users would be such as to reduce general plant utilization to a point that overall rates for the small user must be raised. Hence, if the common carrier can demonstrate that its special bulk rates will retain or promote business otherwise lost to private microwave, thus covering joint costs otherwise charged to the small general user, then the rate

---

[16] In Above-890, to be sure, AT&T and the other carriers had argued to the contrary, i.e., that any substantial diversion of revenues from them to the private systems would eventually saddle with higher rates the smaller users unable to afford their own systems. (See Brief of AT&T in Docket No. 11866, December 13, 1957, pp. 30–37, 38–46.)

differential is not unduly discriminatory and can be presumed to be the least injurious way to cover total costs.

The question, then, is not whether these particular tariffs are discriminatory so much as what Telpak and Private Line tell us about the conditions that must presumably be met before *any* tariff differentiating between big and small users qualifies as acceptable competitive response.[17] The sheer complexity of the cost relationships, the nonadditive character of costs allocated to particular services, and the difference between historical costs and the expected avoidable costs relevant to designing a rate structure—all tend to make some sort of price discrimination virtually unavoidable.[18] And this is true whether or not rates are kept proportional to marginal costs, or rate differentials equal to cost differentials.[19] Therefore, the question is whether the discrimination has the least possible injurious effect on allocative efficiency for the full-cost-covering revenues it generates. Insofar as value-of-service pricing will repress demand against the high-value service less than would be true of all services were they priced above marginal costs but with no reference to demand elasticity, it may in fact be the least harmful way to cover total costs.[20]

Within this context, the key function of competitive alternatives is to set loose a whole series of competitive responses by common carriers otherwise uninterested in rate adjustments, where costs may not have been fully allocated. The competitive impact moves the carriers and the FCC in the right direction and starts them thinking about the form for an acceptable rate adjustment. Because the carriers will now tend to initiate the rate adjustments, such adjustments may be more easily brought about than if the Commission itself had to work through formal rate proceedings and bear the burden of proof accordingly.

Private Domestic Satellites

The advent of private domestic satellites raises comparable issues and some different ones. Even though such systems are not in operation today, the mere threat has already elicited proposals for significant rate adjustments. Silberman has observed that: ". . . had it not been for the Ford Foundation proposal [for a cooperative domestic TV satellite sys-

---

[17] The only alternative is to look to competitive cost adjustments, which would figure mainly in long-run generalized rate reductions. But this is no reason to stop the search for acceptable selective responses as well.

[18] Bonbright, *Principles of Public Utility Rates*, pp. 296–301.

[19] Ibid., pp. 372–77.

[20] Ibid., pp. 88–90, 383–84.

tem in August 1966], the application of satellite technology to TV distribution would have been delayed by at least several years, and the costs of conventional TV distribution would have gone up instead of down."

It is known also that:

> just three days before the Foundation filed its plan . . ., AT&T formally asked the FCC for permission to *raise* its TV transmission rates. The rate increase was necessary, AT&T told the Commission, because its revenues from TV distribution were not large enough to cover the incremental costs in providing the service. (The company explained that it would have liked to raise its rates still more, but felt unable to do so because a growing number of television stations—177 at the end of 1955—have found it cheaper to get their network programs from private microwave systems than from the Bell System.) In discussing the increase, the company made only a vague reference to a "preliminary investigation of the use of satellites for domestic communications service" on its part that indicated "that there may be possibilities for cost reductions when a combination of satellites and landlines is used for longer hauls." Just five months later—in response to the Ford proposal—the phone company was proposing a combined satellite–land line system that would cut TV distribution costs by $19 million—more than 25 per cent—in 1969.[21]

The Ford Plan is crucial here, not as a device to strengthen the finances of public television or to recover the nation's "equity" in satellites without exclusive reliance on general rate reductions but rather in its role as a catalyst generating competitive counterproposals for attractive TV interconnection rates. The scheme's competitive impact is all the more revealing when one recalls that this was hardly an explicit objective; i.e., reduced terrestrial rates would obviously reduce the sums the plan would otherwise make available for public television. For present purposes, the episode simply indicates that the competitive alternative now most likely to assist the Commission in bringing domestic rates down is that of the threat or actuality of a private or cooperative special-purpose satellite for TV program transmission.

Pivotal as the Ford Plan has been, moreover, one must not lose sight of the American Broadcasting Company's role at the outset. It is well known that ABC's initial application for permission to establish its own private TV satellite system in September 1965,[22] based on the Hughes synchronous technology, started the chain of events whose rate-reducing

---

[21] Silberman, "The Little Bird That Casts a Big Shadow," *Fortune* (February 1967), p. 224.
[22] Application by ABC for Satellite Authorization in the Auxiliary Radio Broadcast Service for TV Program Distribution Purposes, September 1965.

effects have yet to be fully realized. Aside from the subsequent status of ABC-Hughes relations,[23] ABC's original contribution is clear.

Nor does the fact that the Ford scheme is really sui generis in any way blunt its relevance here. Organizational classifications must not blur the fundamental competitive fact: that a credible competitive alternative to conventional terrestrial TV interconnection and to general multipurpose satellites has so far elicited important cost-saving counterproposals —at least two from AT&T and another from ComSat.[24]

A final word of comparison on the form which the carriers' response has taken in the private microwave and domestic satellite cases. During the domestic satellite proceeding, Bell offered lower rates for big and small users alike, whereas in private microwave it offered concessions to the big users alone. But one basic difference was in the timing of the private threat.

In domestic satellites, Bell's offer came before any system, private or common carrier, had been authorized. As a preemptive strategy against the proposal for as yet unseen private systems, Bell proposed a cost-reducing technological innovation, the multipurpose relay satellite. The projected cost-savings for big and small users were highly visible and offered simultaneously.

In the earlier microwave case, Bell had already gone some way toward incorporating the new technology into its intercity plant before any private systems were authorized. The FCC reported that microwave relays represented over one-half those intercity investments in fiscal 1957, two years before the private microwave decision. So Bell's subsequent selective rate reductions to the big microwave users came after the small general users had already received at least some generalized benefits.[25] Had initial access to the microwave region somehow been

[23] During the ABC–ITT merger proceeding, a Hughes official stated that "the increasing likelihood of merger between ABC and ITT had a retarding effect upon the working relationship between Hughes and ABC." See FCC Docket No. 16828, Specification of Issues by Justice Department, February 15, 1967, App. B, pp. 17–18.

[24] See Comments of AT&T in Docket No. 16495, December 15, 1966, Attachment #1 (Integrated Space/Earth Communications System), pp. 25–27; Attachment #3 (evaluation of Ford proposal). A useful comparison of satellite systems proposals by AT&T, ComSat, and the Ford Foundation, including comparative cost estimates, appears in Supplemental Comments of Ford Foundation in Docket No. 16495, Vol. I, April 3, 1967, pp. 29–37. The competitive interplay between the Ford special-purpose system and the multipurpose systems models of AT&T and ComSat is set forth in ibid., pp. 38–52 (a report by Hammett and Edison).

[25] The Commission estimated that Bell's cost per intercity telephone circuit had decreased from some $70 to $51 between 1952 and 1956, due "principally to microwave." See FCC Annual Report for 1957, p. 46. On the subsequent rate reduction of $50 million annually on intercity public message toll service, see Annual Report for 1959, p. 108; Annual Report for 1960, pp. 94–95; and Annual Report for 1961, pp. 91–92.

handled simultaneously for all parties (as in domestic satellites), the carriers might have responded similarly, with fewer subsequent problems of acceptable and unacceptable rate discrimination.

The Thirty-Circuit Case

In the international field, the Defense Department's procurement of thirty satellite circuits in the Pacific a few years ago offers another illustration of competitive alternatives in action. The Defense Communications Agency awarded a contract for thirty satellite circuits to ComSat as low bidder. To forestall the loss not only of the thirty-circuit contract but of future leased-circuit government business, the record carriers made hurried counteroffers to reduce their composite cable/satellite rates throughout the whole region.

As *Fortune* reported the episode:

> Before it contracted with ComSat, the Defense Department had opened the bidding to others; the three U.S. international record carriers . . . quoted prices ranging from $10,000 to $12,500 a month per half circuit. The department then decided to lease the circuits directly from ComSat at a cost of $4,000 a month, only slightly more than what the carriers would have had to pay ComSat had the Defense Department leased the circuits from them. The carriers made a counterproposal to cut rates about 40 per cent on *all* leased circuits in the Pacific if the thirty-circuit satellite contract were assigned to them.[26]

Subsequently, the Director of Telecommunications Management advised the Commission that the national interest did not after all require any direct purchase from ComSat of circuits by the Defense Department beyond some limited initial period. But substantial savings to government and private users[27] in the Pacific region have resulted from rate adjustments through which the carriers sought to meet ComSat's initial winning bid. The Commission must, of course, still determine how far the big users' satellite rates should reflect the cost of servicing them. But once again, general rate reductions have been facilitated in the interim. This time the "credible threat" was that of a big government user dealing direct with ComSat.

The Thirty-Circuit episode is revealing on at least three counts.

[26] Silberman, "The Little Bird That Casts a Big Shadow," p. 225. A fourth (voice) carrier, Hawaiian Telephone Co., also entered into the bidding. See footnote 28.

[27] See House Committee on Government Operations, 89th Cong., 2d sess., *Report on Government Use of Satellite Communications*, 1966, pp. 50–55.

1. *It yields a useful initial index of just how large the potential savings due to satellites may be.* The spread between ComSat's initial bid of $4,200 and the next-best opening carrier bids was impressive: ITT Worldcom, $10,000; RCA Communications, $11,000; Western Union International, also $11,000; and Hawaiian Telephone, $12,500.[28] The initial projected savings to the DCA from leasing the 30 channels for 36 months direct from ComSat were estimated at $8,640,000.[29] In the negotiations that followed, RCAC finally offered a nonprofit bid of $4,000 to prevail against the winning ComSat bid,[30] whereas all three carriers later proposed, as an alternative, rate reductions of some 25 to 40 per cent across the board on *all* their Pacific cable and satellite circuits.[31]

2. *The episode reveals the strategic importance of a big government user not only in wresting savings for itself (as it did in this case notwithstanding regulatory constraints), but, under the Authorized User policy, as a vehicle for bringing down rates for all users.* In this case, the small user of conventional facilities was not left saddled with higher rates as a consequence of government business diverted elsewhere. The Commission's Authorized User policy prevented this. But the composite rate adjustments which have now benefited government as well as nongovernment users are generally agreed to have come as speedily as they did only because the DCA's initial contract with ComSat joined the issue so squarely.

Under its Authorized User policy, the FCC normally permits only the communications common carriers to have direct access to ComSat. Where common carrier rates do not adequately reflect the cost-savings derived from satellite circuitry, the Commission can also authorize private users, including government users, to deal direct—i.e., without any common carrier intermediary.[32]

---

[28] House Committee on Government Operations, Hearings on Government Use of Satellite Communications, 1966, pp. 113, 489–90. ComSat first bid $4,200 per half-circuit per month but revised this to $4,000 by subtracting the cost of the lease proper and service charge. ComSat's charge to the carriers was $3,800. Ibid., pp. 113–15. (Hawaiian Telephone Co. is formally classified as a voice not a record carrier.)

[29] Ibid., p. 132.

[30] Ibid., pp. 114–18, 551–52. RCAC was finally turned down in part because it had proposed a $1.1 million higher maximum liability than ComSat in case the government cancelled the contract. Its "no profit, public service" bid was also viewed as discriminatory in favor of the government.

[31] Ibid., pp. 571–72, 632–34, 666–67, 749–59. Also *Report on Government Use of Satellite Communications*, pp. 9–10.

[32] See FCC Memorandum & Statement of Policy in Docket No. 16058, FCC 66–677, July 21, 1966, paras, 23–27, 34, 36, 38c; also FCC Memorandum Opinion and Order in Docket No. 16058, February 8, 1967, paras. 5–6.

In Thirty Circuits, what happened was in fact a kind of limited, regulated competition between ComSat and the carriers, subject to restraints of the Authorized User policy.[33] To meet the initial ComSat low bid when notified they were all "high," the three carriers responded differently. Only RCAC offered a series of alternate bids within the permissible time period, varying its bids successively, in response to the DCA's continued preference for ComSat as the most economical supplier, until the "nonprofit" bid was submitted.[34] As still another alternative, all three carriers offered substantial reductions in their composite cable/satellite rates on all Pacific area circuits and not just on the Thirty Circuits. The Commission's directive that satellite economies be reflected in overall rate schedules was cited in this regard.[35]

Subsequently, the Commission solicited the DTM's judgment as to whether unique and exceptional national interest considerations required direct access to ComSat.[36] Except for a temporary initial period of direct service, the DTM found otherwise.[37] But in finding otherwise, the magnitude of savings the government could expect from the composite rate adjustments was doubtless weighed.[38] Hence, while ComSat could not in the final analysis retain the contract, it has in retrospect provided a competitive stimulus of sorts, a kind of yardstick from whose rates the carriers could not afford to diverge too far without risking the loss of business.[39]

[33] This appears to be the kind of limited competition advocated by such big private users as IBM and CBS. See Statement of IBM in Docket No. 16058, October 6, 1965, pp. 5–9; Legal Brief of IBM in ibid., October 6, 1965, pp. 17–21; Comments of CBS, ibid., November 1, 1965, pp. 2–4.

[34] See ibid., pp. 550–607.

[35] Ibid., pp. 571, 636, 666.

[36] Memorandum Opinion in File No. T-C-2014, FCC 67–173, Feb. 9, 1967, paras, 2, 4–7.

[37] Ibid., para. 6.

[38] Ibid., paras. 6–7. In the final analysis the DTM ruled that the national interest required no such long-run authorization. However, the response might well have been different in the absence of: (a) RCAC's successively lower counteroffers after the ComSat bid of $4,000 per half circuit per month; (b) the composite cable-satellite rate reductions offered in response by all carriers; (c) FCC's estimates of the savings that DOD could expect from such composite rate reductions; (d) the ComSat bid which clearly served as a catalyst to trigger off the rate adjustment that followed. Once these adjustments had occurred, moreover, all users, private as well as government, small as well as large, stood to enjoy the cost-savings.

[39] See Hearings on Government Use of Satellite Communications, pp. 577–78. RCAC insisted that it could in fact have met ComSat's low bid without giving up its whole profit on the business, if the Commission had approved its application for a ground station in Hawaii and thus had made it possible for RCAC to include the hardware in its rate base. Ibid., pp. 550–52. Nonetheless, a review of the bidding clearly shows that the availability to the DCA of a ComSat alternative operated as a catalyst to bring the rates down. (Ibid., pp. 113–19.)

3. *The Thirty-Circuit episode inferentially points up the role of the big private user, too, even under the current policy on authorized users, in helping to bring down the carriers' general rates.* In the Thirty-Circuit case, the noncarrier user was the DCA(DOD). But private noncarriers with substantial financial stakes in satellite circuitry can play a comparable role in pressing for direct access to ComSat.[40] For the "appropriate steps" which the Commission will take should satellite economies not be fully reflected in common carrier rates could well include the actual or threatened authorization of direct access.[41] In that case, ComSat would provide a potential competitive check on the carriers, to be invoked at the Commission's discretion.[42] The Commission could further the speed and magnitude of rate adjustments, using ComSat as a yardstick.[43] Of course, on some few occasions at least, ComSat must actually get the business if the mere threat of its doing so is to remain credible.

The big private users are in any case the key link here. They would clearly be the parties to challenge the adequacy of existing service and rates and to seek more substantial savings due to satellites, much as the DCA did in the Thirty-Circuit case.

The preconditions for mounting this case seem clear. The magnitude of available savings over carrier charges must be substantial. Unique and exceptional requirements must be demonstrated. And other national interest considerations may be relevant. As entities involved in the dissemination of news and comment, the TV networks and press associations would qualify as likely parties to mount a persuasive case.[44] To

[40] Under the Commission's Memorandum and Statement of Policy, July 21, 1966, ComSat can legally service noncarrier users direct (para. 38a), but is *primarily* a common carrier's common carrier, and normally limited to dealing through the carriers as intermediaries (para. 38b). However, ComSat may be authorized to provide direct services to noncarriers in unique and exceptional circumstances (para. 38c). Pertinent facts here (under para. 39) would include evidence on the availability of needed facilities from the carriers and on special public interests that cannot otherwise be served. Under para. 36, however, the Commission goes further in defining what may constitute a unique or exceptional circumstance: "refusal or failure of the terrestrial carriers to provide, upon reasonable demand, satellite leased circuit facilities, otherwise available. . . ." Elsewhere, the Commission also notes the potential economies realizable through satellite circuitry and the potential cost and rate reductions these should facilitate. Failure of the carriers to make suitable adjustments promptly will "require the Commission to take such actions as are appropriate" (para. 34).

[41] Ibid., para. 38a.

[42] Ibid., para. 36.

[43] See fn. 32.

[44] Such valuable privileges carry with them special public service responsibilities which the media are often criticized for not discharging adequately. Having already secured and long retained these public grants, broadcast and newspaper media can be expected to press hard for direct access to ComSat for themselves at least. See Comments by ABC in Docket No. 16495, August 1, 1966, pp. 19–22.

forestall any such likelihood of losing business to ComSat, the carriers could then come forth with more attractive tariffs. If successful, the mere availability of direct ComSat service, and the credibility of the big users' threatened diversion, would have operated to facilitate rate adjustments and cost-savings possibly for all users, big and small, depending on the kind of bargain the Commission can strike. Any such competitive threat would presumably work better if the carriers no longer held ComSat stock or at least were excluded from the ComSat board.

The TV Networks as Noncarrier Users

The special potential role of the TV networks in bringing down transmission rates is evident in their current status as the major prospective private noncarrier user. ComSat estimates that TV's demand for domestic circuits will actually exceed the demand by all other users (including telephone, data, and telegraph) until the mid-1970s.[45] Afterward, TV appears likely to remain the principal private user, although its share of circuits may then be increasingly exceeded by other uses. Even in the global system, ComSat estimates that during the years 1967–71, an average of 10 per cent of all Intelsat circuits will be allocated to TV,[46] leaving it still the major private user.

The TV networks therefore have a major financial stake in lower transmission costs and rates. They would want to bring them down in any way they could, whether through continued advocacy of a new policy on authorized users or by invoking the Commission's present escape hatch (para. 38-c) in case carrier rates were not adequately responsive to satellite economies. The networks are also among those most likely to establish their own private domestic systems; to continue to press for permission towards this end and for multipurpose carrier-operated systems with tariffs that afford them comparable savings.

What the government has done in the Thirty-Circuit case, then, the big private user, and especially the TV networks, could do in the domestic arena.[47] One final question is whether their potential rate-reducing

[45] See Technical Submission of ComSat in Docket No. 16495, December 16, 1966, pp. 12–17, 43 (Fig. 4); 1966 Report of ComSat to the President and Congress, p. 12. The Ford Foundation contrasted AT&T, ComSat, and its own projected demand estimates in its Supplemental Comments in Docket No. 16495, Vol. I, April 3, 1967, Figure 1.

[46] See ComSat Revised Report on Rates and Revenue Requirements, 1967–71 (November 1966), pp. B–12, and exhibit B–4. This refers to allocated capacity and is not a prediction of actual usage.

[47] Big users of multipoint voice-data service in business and industry may also become sizable satellite customers. But they have not yet come forth with plans for their own private systems, and there is little evidence that their satellite needs will approach television's in the near future. See Supplemental Statement of ComSat in Docket No. 16495, December 16, 1966, pp. 8–12; also ComSat Technical Submission in ibid., December 16, 1966, pp. 12–17.

contributions are as likely to materialize if they are vertically associated with the communications carriers.

SATELLITE ORGANIZATION AND THE EMERGENCE OF COMPETITIVE ALTERNATIVES

The question just raised is really part of a larger issue: Will conflicts of interest in the current or potential satellite structure impede the wide diffusion of satellite economies in the form of lower prices?

Present Conflicts of Interest

The recent proceedings on authorized users and earth station ownership provide good examples of how potential competition may be forestalled. The carriers have strongly opposed ComSat's right to service the private users direct. Locked out of the satellite business except through their ComSat shareholdings, the carriers fear serious inroads if ComSat is permitted to compete for their conventional business at home and abroad. For this reason they also oppose ComSat-owned ground stations and location of the terrestrial-satellite interface at the gateway cities.

The carriers' past strategy in curbing ComSat inroads was at least partially grounded on their ComSat shareholdings. The present close corporate ties between ComSat and the carriers would make conflicts of interest inevitable in the event of any open competitive rivalry for the noncarrier traffic. Carrier-elected directors would frequently have to absent themselves from board meetings and deliberations, thereby reducing the carriers' hoped-for contributions in know-how and experience, and compromising their satellite investments as well.[48] Even without a truly competitive situation, such abstentions have already become commonplace in the sharp conflicts over authorized users, earth station ownership, and domestic satellites. Any such withdrawal from fundamental policy-making might further frustrate the Act's several goals. The carriers have therefore pressed the FCC on all these counts to consider their ComSat participation as good reason to limit cable-satellite competition.[49]

Of course, one could equally well conclude that the carriers should

[48] See H. Schwartz, "ComSat, the Carriers and the Earth Stations: Some Problems with 'Melding' Variegated Interests," *Yale Law Journal* (January 1967), pp. 475–76 and associated citations.

[49] See FCC Docket No. 16058, especially Brief of Western Union International, November 1, 1965, pp. 9–12; Brief of ITT Worldcom, October 29, 1965, pp. 3–4, 19–21; Statement of RCA Communications, November 1, 1965, pp. 22–23; December 30, 1965, pp. 10–12.

be excluded from ComSat outright in order to further cable/satellite rivalry.[50] And there is in any case no explicit reference to this issue in the Authorized User proceeding. The Commission appears actually to have other reasons (and to it more persuasive ones) for keeping ComSat on a close leash: to follow the Act's directive not to restructure the telecommunications industry; to safeguard competitive alternatives for small general users of conventional facilities; to maintain a diversity of communications modes for national security purposes; to guarantee the carriers a hand in shaping the future of satellite technology, lest they be doubly jeopardized through technical obsolescence of the predominantly cable component of their rate base with no offsetting gains via inclusion of earth station investment. Opponents of this last objective fear for technological retardation if the carriers *are* allowed in.

The international record carriers actually stand most to lose if ComSat can "skim the cream" in diverting from them the business of a few big private users, including the federal government. Their inevitable disadvantage in competing against ComSat, their major supplier of leased satellite circuits, is underlined by an earlier inability to compete successfully against AT&T, using AT&T's leased circuits, for the lucrative federal voice-record business.[51]

In short, the carriers have shielded themselves against a serious competitive threat, although one which may have led them to saddle their smaller private or general customers with higher rates. However, they have done so not through their internal voting power, dwindling ComSat stockholdings, or limited representation on ComSat's board, but through FCC action, which the carriers say they support in part to reduce conflicts of interest inherent in the joint-venture framework. Although the Commission did not actually base its decision on the above issue, the "internal safeguards" can hardly be said to have promoted a viable cable-satellite competition in this case.[52]

Potential Conflicts of Interest

Further conflicts of interest appear likely in any extensive joinder of common carriers and private users. The divergent interests of such

[50] See Schwartz, "ComSat, the Carriers and the Earth Stations," pp. 451–52 and associated citations.

[51] See Docket No. 16058, especially Brief of Western Union International, November 1, 1965, pp. 9–11; Reply Comments, December 31, 1965, pp. 27–30; Brief of ITT Worldcom, October 29, 1965, pp. 21–24; Statement of RCA Communications, November 1, 1965, pp. 20–22.

[52] For a somewhat different account of deficiencies in the "internal safeguards" and of factors impeding competition between ComSat and the carriers to date, see H. Schwartz, "ComSat, the Carriers, and the Earth Stations," pp. 455–75.

entities are nowhere more evident than in the satellite proceedings discussed earlier. In each case, the private users were either allied with ComSat in opposition to the carriers, or, on domestic satellites, opposed both to ComSat and the carriers.

These conflicting interests suggest that any joinder of common carriers and the TV networks would operate to silence one or the other entity in the Commission's adversary proceedings. The emergence of competitive alternatives would therefore seem more likely in the absence of such joinders.

The assumption here is that the Commission is largely limited in its adversary proceedings to the plans, proposals, evidence, and interests of the contesting parties. It must admittedly go beyond these parties in evaluating all options in light of the national policy goals in the broadcast, satellite, and general communications fields. But judicious judgments, at best no easy matter, are far harder to reach where the TV networks are removed from militant advocacy on such delicate basic matters as the relative merits of single and multipurpose systems, private and carrier-owned systems, and the diffusion of satellite economies through composite rate adjustments or special tariffs for specialized users.

Let us now conclude by sifting out the basis for these general propositions in the record of major recent satellite proceedings.[53]

Common Carriers and Private Users: The Global Proceeding. In the Authorized User proceeding, the private users' demand for direct access to ComSat was crystal clear. Here, in one of the most important episodes since passage of the Satellite Act in 1962, the divergence between the common carrier and private user positions could not have been more dramatic.

Almost as a group, the common carriers sought to preserve their status as sole authorized users. They did so not only in the Authorized User proceeding, but also in opposing sole ComSat ownership of all U.S. ground stations and in urging location of the interface between satellite and terrestrial facilities near the remote earth stations instead of near the traditional "gateway" (coastal) cities. (See Table 35.)

A common carrier's chance to get TV network business simply looks better where (a) ComSat owns no earth stations (or none exclusively);

---

[53] Detailed documentation for the analysis that follows to the end of the chapter appears in my testimony, "Carrier and Noncarrier Interests in Satellite Organizational Structure," introduced as evidence in FCC Docket No. 16828 (ABC-ITT Merger). See Justice Department Evidentiary Document J343.

TABLE 35. POSITIONS TAKEN IN MAJOR SATELLITE PROCEEDINGS BY SELECTED COMMON CARRIERS, PRIVATE USERS, AND OTHER ENTITIES: AUTHORIZED USERS, EARTH STATION OWNERSHIP

Entity	Authorized users of ComSat		Early Bird circuits			Earth station ownership				Location of interface		
	Common carriers only	Private users, too	Temporary private access	Carriers only	But not AT&T	ComSat only	Carriers after ComSat builds	Joint carrier/ ComSat, ComSat manages	Case-by-case	Near gate-ways	Near earth stations	Direction and control of terrestrial links
American Telephone and Telegraph	x			x		(x)		x			x	Carriers
Western Union Telegraph	x			x								
General Telephone and Electronics	x										x	Carriers
ITT World Communications	x			x	x		x		x		x	Carriers (Jntly.)
RCA Communications	x			x	(x)		x	(x)	x		x	Carriers
Western Union International	x			Jnt. Venture				x				
Hawaiian Telephone	x						x	x			x	HTC (in Hawaii)
U.S. Independent Telephone Assn.	x	x						x	(x)			
ComSat	x					x				x	x	Carriers
Westrex Communications						x				x		ComSat
Philco Corp.						x						ComSat
National Broadcasting Co.	----NO FILING----		x (then withdrew)									

Organization			
Columbia Broadcasting System	x		
American Broadcasting Co.	x	x	(x)
International Business Machines	x	x	
National Assn. of Manufacturers	x		(x)
American Petroleum Institute	x		
Aeronautical Radio, Inc.	x		
Air Transport Assn.	x		
American Trucking Assn.	x		
American Assn. of Railroads	x		
Eastern Airlines	x		
Merrill Lynch	x		
Dow Jones	x		
Associated Press	x		
United Press	x		
American Newspaper Publishers Assn.	x		
Washington Post	x		
International Educational Broadcasting	x		
U.S. General Services Administration	x		

Source: See Appendix A.

( ) Denotes position was implied but not stated explicitly.

321

(b) where the interface is far from the gateway cities (where the networks have their main headquarters); and (c) where direct noncarrier access to ComSat is permitted anyway only in unique and exceptional cases. To meet the threat of AT&T competition, on the other hand, the record carriers could (and did) seek to keep it entirely out of international satellite TV and to contest AT&T's and ComSat's exclusive ownership and operation of terrestrial links between the gateways and the earth stations, wherever the interface was located.

The private users took the reverse position in strong support of direct access to ComSat and, by implication, of ComSat-owned ground stations. For without its own stations, ComSat would be dependent on its carrier rivals and as disadvantaged competitively as the record carriers have been vis-à-vis AT&T. Even where ComSat and the carriers must share ownership, the procompetitive role of ComSat may be blunted by the carriers' veto power in station design and general management. Exclusive ComSat ownership of stations is probably the best way to preclude those subtle advantages of self-preference the carriers might otherwise enjoy in dealing with their own stations, especially when the demand for circuits exceeds the supply. Earth stations can obviously be designed to tie in more readily with the carrier-parent's facilities than with ComSat's.

Thus ComSat and the private users have favored—and the carriers opposed—ComSat ownership both of stations and ground links. The Commission's reluctance to authorize direct access to ComSat (except under special circumstances) has been accompanied by earth station-interface decisions close to the carriers' position and likely to shield them further from ComSat.

Among the private users which endorsed the above strategy in the Authorized User proceeding were the data-processing and newspaper interests, truckers, manufacturers, oil companies, aeronautical interests, the U.S. General Services Administration and two TV networks (NBC did not file). But the TV networks' role is of particular importance in view of their dominant position as the major private users of satellite circuits for the foreseeable future.

Therefore something needs to be said about the contrasting behavior of NBC and the two other national networks. NBC did not participate at all in Authorized Users. In this first major confrontation of carriers and noncarriers over their future relations with the emerging satellite system, the RCAC (and not the NBC) component of the RCA conglomerate clearly prevailed and argued against direct noncarrier access. RCAC's militant position throughout the recent Thirty-Circuit episode further underlines the magnitude of its stake in meeting the threat of

ComSat competition. On the other hand, ABC and CBS filed in support of direct access, along with 17 other noncarriers ranging from newspaper and aeronautical interests to companies with data-processing requirements and the National Association of Manufacturers.

A similar episode had occurred a year earlier in the maneuvers over Early Bird circuitry and rates. At that time, the carriers first came in with separate applications for circuits which exceeded in number those anticipated for U.S. use in Early Bird. However, they disagreed on who could or could not handle TV, some question being raised about AT&T's eligibility as a voice carrier. AT&T threatened to protest the other carriers' applications if they protested its applications. For such reasons, the Commission on its own motion granted temporary special authorization to the TV networks to deal directly with ComSat. Special pains were taken, of course, to ensure that this temporary authorization would not compromise any future decision on authorized users.

What had happened, then, was that the carriers' initial failure to resolve their differences (and to keep their total requests for circuit rentals in line with circuits available) led the Commission to proceed without them. Notably, RCAC was among the carriers who first applied for circuits. When the Commission rejected these applications and acted instead on its own motion to authorize the networks to deal with ComSat direct, NBC was of course among those so favored. Subsequently, the carriers, including RCAC, returned with a joint petition for reconsideration, having at least suspended their differences over AT&T's eligibility. They requested the Commission to rescind its special temporary authorizations to the networks and ComSat and approve instead the carriers' original applications for permission to lease ComSat circuits. Rebuttal came from ABC and CBS, but not from NBC. Once the carriers had ironed out a joint position sufficiently to persuade the Commission to respond favorably, the RCAC end of the enterprise once more prevailed.

A third example of divergent carrier and TV network interests occurred in the deliberations over ComSat's first proposed tariff. On one hand, each network protested the "prohibitive" and "discriminatory" character of the tariff and the unduly long minimum time period of usage required, in contrast with the shorter, more flexible time periods needed for effective news coverage. They also protested the subjection of all TV network requests for TV circuits to prior approval by the carriers' regular customers of leased voice-grade circuits.

There was, however, one major difference between the protest of NBC and those of CBS and ABC: NBC failed to raise the authorized user issue. Thus, ABC and CBS not only questioned the level of the

ComSat rates as then quoted but also criticized ComSat for failing to make allowances for TV networks' special status as authorized users. They noted that the quoted rates were not only high, but would necessarily be even higher once the carrier intermediaries had cited their tariffs. As ABC stated:

> Taken alone, ComSat's proposed rate would inhibit the use of satellites by broadcasters. However, they cannot be considered alone. The Europeans are also imposing charges for the use of their connecting facilities. Moreover, since the domestic common carriers have not filed their tariff, ABC has no means of ascertaining what those costs will be. Presumably the common carriers will not operate at a loss so that ABC must regard this tariff as indicative of what the rockbottom rates to common carriers will be. The upper limits of the carrier rates could be ascertained only by speculation.
>
> The tariff filed makes no reference whatsoever to authorized or qualified users. ABC has no information about rates which would be applicable to that class to compare with the common carrier rates contained in the tariff. The ComSat tariff should include rates applicable to common carriers and to authorized and qualified users, and it is severely deficient in this respect. ABC's position, as previously reported to the Commission, is that it is a qualified user and that it qualifies as an authorized user of the satellite.[54]

Now NBC was also deeply concerned about rates. But it remained silent about the bearing on satellite rates of the emerging telecommunications structure and of the potential eligibility of TV networks, among others, to buy their circuits "wholesale." Again, the RCAC end of the enterprise prevailed as it, in contrast with NBC's silence, joined with ITT Worldcom, WUI and AT&T, first in applying for permission to rent Early Bird circuits and then in requesting the Commission's reconsideration and approval of its application irrespective of AT&T's eligibility and the authorized user issue.

Of interest also are other criticisms which ABC alone made regarding ComSat's failure to cite rates on the delivery of TV service not just from the Andover earth station to the satellite, but from "points within the U.S. to points in Europe and vice versa . . . similar to AT&T and other carriers' present cable practice." It further cited ComSat's failure, contrary to prevailing carrier custom, to allow "promotional" bargain rates to stimulate the development and use of the satellite facility in its "experimental and early use."

---

[54] See Petition by ABC for FCC Suspension of ComSat Tariff No. 1, June 17, 1965, paras. 4–5.

These three instances are cited only to illustrate what is meant by saying that a joinder of TV networks and common carriers may "silence" the TV networks as a vigorous factor in adversary proceedings. But three points should be kept in mind.

First, there was obviously no "conspiracy" to silence anyone. It is perfectly rational business strategy for a joint enterprise to advocate a position in regulatory proceedings most likely to benefit the enterprise as a whole. The question is whether one end of the enterprise stands to benefit more than enough to offset what the other end may lose. And here there are really three interrelated components—TV network, common carrier, and hardware entities.

Second, the question is not merely what difference it would have made for the positions advocated before the Commission in past adversary proceedings had NBC not been owned by RCA, but also what difference it would now make should all present and future networks have comparable associations with common carriers and/or hardware companies, insofar at least as the proposed merger of ABC and ITT might have emerged as a decisive step in that direction.

Third, the fact that other noncarriers were available to argue the case in most of these proceedings is not really satisfactory. As noted, the TV networks will be one of Intelsat's major private users for years to come. They clearly have the kind of stake that could impel them to mount a case for direct access under the current policy on authorized users, to say nothing of working hard for an easing of that policy. Their stake in the domestic TV satellite market would of course be even greater.

Common Carriers and Private Users: Domestic Satellites. The case of private domestic satellites works out somewhat differently. Here the carriers have all favored carrier-operated domestic satellite systems and opposed private systems, at least for the foreseeable future when carrier-owned systems are fully accommodated in the face of alleged spectrum scarcities. Private noncarrier users generally urge the Commission to authorize without delay the establishment of both private and common carrier systems. In this they seek rights to choose between competing alternatives domestically as well as internationally. (See Table 36.)

The carriers and noncarriers generally diverge also in their positions on multipurpose and single-purpose (dedicated) systems. No carrier favors the latter, whereas most noncarrier users do, irrespective of whether they are operated by a specialized noncommon carrier or by the user itself. The TV networks, for example, generally favor a single-

TABLE 36. POSITIONS TAKEN IN MAJOR SATELLITE PROCEEDINGS BY SELECTED COMMON CARRIERS, PRIVATE USERS, AND OTHER ENTITIES: DOMESTIC SATELLITES

Entity	Type		Private systems	Single or joint carrier venture in sats or stations	Integrated sat/terrest system	ComSat monopoly of sats	ComSat role in space segment/carrier-owned stations
	Multiple purpose	Single purpose					
American Telephone and Telegraph	x		Later?		Yes	Yes	Yes
Western Union Telegraph	x		No	Possibly	Yes	Yes	Yes
General Telephone and Electronics	x		No		Yes	Yes	Yes
ITT World Communications	x		Later		Yes	No	No
RCA Communications				——NO FILING——			
Western Union International	x		No		Yes	No	Yes
Hawaiian Telephone	x		No			Yes	Yes
U.S. Independent Telephone Assn.	x		No	(Possibly)		Yes	
ComSat	x		No		Yes	Yes	
General Electric		x	Perhaps	New Carrier	No	No	No
JFD Electronics			Now				
National Broadcasting Co.		x	Possibly	Possibly	Possibly	No	Possibly
Columbia Broadcasting System		x	No	No	No	No	No
American Broadcasting Co.		x	Now	Possibly	(No)	No	No
National Assn. of Manufacturers			Yes			No	Possibly
American Petroleum Institute			Later	Possibly			
Aeronautical Radio, Inc.	x		No				(No)
American Trucking Assn.		x	Later				
American Assn. of Railroads		x	Now				
Dow Jones			No				
American Assn. of Newspaper Publishers	x		Now	Possibly			(No)
Ford Foundation	Possibly		Now		No		(No)
Joint Committee on Educational Telecommunications		x	Now			No	(No)
National Education Assn.		x	Now			No	(No)
U.S. Department of Health, Education, and Welfare			Now				

( ) Denotes position was implied but not stated explicitly.

Source: See Appendix A.

purpose system as more economical for them. Somehow, they fear, their combined usage of a multipurpose system, while making it more economical for them. Only a factual determination of relative costs and efficiency could persuade them otherwise. Short of a full pilot program involving both types of systems, the networks would like to ensure either (a) special tariffs for television on any carrier- or ComSat-operated multipurpose system set up to forestall the networks' single-purpose option; or (b) institution of the single-purpose system. Indeed, even if the AT&T/ComSat multipurpose systems are in fact more economical for all users, one can say that it took the threat of a private, special-purpose system to jar them loose as cost-saving proposals with special TV tariffs.

Closer examination reveals a greater diversity of positions on each side. Some carriers and ComSat question the Commission's legal right to authorize private noncarrier systems (GT&E, Hawaiian, WUTC). Others grant that right but oppose private systems for the foreseeable future, until the carriers have had time to service the needs of general users and private specialized users alike (AT&T, ITTWC, WUI). Paramount here are alleged spectrum scarcities and higher rates for small users as a result of the loss of substantial private business. In opposition to any single-purpose system for TV program distribution only, the carriers all favor a multipurpose system instead. (See Table 36.)

For example, AT&T proposes an integrated multipurpose satellite-terrestrial system whose space segment would be run by ComSat and whose earth stations the domestic carriers would operate. ComSat has also favored a multipurpose system. Supported by GT&E, Hawaiian, and Western Union Telegraph, ComSat presents itself as the sole entity legally able to create any domestic space segment and, jointly with the domestic carriers, to build any necessary ground stations. Finally, Western Union International has endorsed some such ComSat system, whereas ITT Worldcom still opposes any ComSat system and has endorsed the AT&T model.

The TV networks also vary in their support of private single-purpose systems. ABC and CBS favor such systems outright, whereas NBC favors them only after the Commission has determined, case by case, the relative efficiency and spectrum requirements of private and carrier-owned systems and the speed with which either could be established.

Specifically, NBC has reserved judgment as to whether private domestic TV satellites are in fact in the public interest at this time and, in contrast with ABC and CBS, has left the door open instead to a carrier-owned system. While emphasizing the need to establish some TV satellite system at once to replace the costly terrestrial interconnection,

NBC urges the Commission to proceed with the technical-physical groundwork even before all organizational details have been ironed out. The range of organizational options which NBC would accept is much wider than that proposed by the other networks.

ABC's latest formulation, like NBC's, continues to endorse a special-purpose TV system. ABC also appears willing to have a specialized noncommon carrier create such a system on behalf of the TV networks. But ABC still opposes any role for ComSat and the carriers, presumably out of suspicions of common carrier control and for fear of AT&T-ComSat laggardness in capitalizing on the new satellite technology in ways that favor television.

In contrast with the Authorized User proceeding, then, NBC did file on domestic satellites whereas RCAC did not. Thus one might say that the value to RCA of lower interconnection costs for NBC (via a possible private satellite) was worth more than the mere principle of endorsing outright carrier-owned domestic systems from which RCAC would be excluded anyway as an international carrier. Beyond the value of a private satellite to the NBC network, moreover, and probably of greater economic significance, was the apparent value to RCA hardware capabilities of a favored position in the potentially burgeoning domestic satellite hardware market. Here the NBC filing figures as sound business strategy for RCA. Obviously, the more numerous the satellite systems, the larger the hardware requirements and the larger the market. As sole hardware company with a TV network (as well as communications carrier) subsidiary, RCA would stand to gain more from the authorization of private domestic systems than from its limited stockholdings in ComSat (still insufficient for Board representation). RCA might conceivably benefit more also from selling hardware to numerous private systems, especially those where a TV subsidiary gave it entrée, than from sharing on an FCC-allocated basis in the ground stations of a single ComSat-operated domestic system.

In sum, the NBC end of the enterprise prevailed throughout the Authorized User proceeding and Early Bird tariffs in the global proceeding. This may seem reasonable insofar as RCAC is an international and not a domestic carrier. But ITT Worldcom and WUI, subject to similar constraints, have done otherwise, at least entering the domestic proceeding as proponents of multipurpose, carrier-operated systems on the merits and opponents of private special-purpose systems. They thus provided the Commission, in the ITT Worldcom case, with an additional, distinctive organizational alternative.

What difference for policy formulation it may make for one end of a joint enterprise to speak for the whole in proceedings where both ends might appear on different sides if they were independent, is hard to state categorically. However, anything that narrows the Commission's range of choice among competing options must be suspect at this formative stage of satellite organization.

Without prejudging the desirability of any single option, and regardless of any sponsor's motives, a range of competing alternatives will virtually compel the FCC to develop and evaluate the welfare implications of each proposal in reaching a decision. Furthermore, corporate entities prosecute their interests in the regulatory arena as well as the marketplace. Regulators and legislators will as a practical matter be better able to negotiate some particular organizational option when located in a range of options reflective of the varying business strategies of various industry members.

As a matter of principle, no international carrier that strongly opposes the private users on direct access to ComSat internationally can readily condone it domestically or give blanket endorsement to the more probable domestic equivalent, private domestic systems. For that reason, ITT Worldcom might well give only qualified approval to private systems "in the future," and RCAC, NBC and ITT Worldcom positions reveal them to be at least consistent with the hardware interests of their parents.

Without going too far afield, suffice it to note that NBC left the door open to a future TV network joint venture that bought satellite circuits from AT&T, ComSat, or the other carriers. In this it took a position between unqualified endorsement of independent private TV satellites unrelated to ComSat or the carriers (as ABC and CBS did), and the blanket opposition to such systems shown by ComSat, GT&E, and WUTC. NBC also stopped short of opposing private systems "for the foreseeable future at least," as AT&T and ITT Worldcom had done. That is, NBC steered carefully between outright endorsement of a private TV network system unrelated to ComSat or AT&T and routine endorsement of one of the carriers' multipurpose options. One consequence is that RCAC was spared the dilemma of being the sole carrier to condone a private TV satellite system unless it were willing to oppose it publicly against ABC, CBS, and others.

An independent ABC and ITT Worldcom behaved quite differently in the same proceedings. They opposed each other as to proper policy for authorized users and domestic satellites and, by implication, also on ground station ownership and location of the interface. But both the NBC compromises on domestic satellites and the ITT Worldcom position ("no private systems today, perhaps tomorrow") are strategies to keep these two companies from diverging too dramatically from the positions of other firms in their respective industries. At the same time, each company to varying degrees endorsed the future advent of private satellite systems.

As noted, one factor underlying these compromise positions may be the advantages a hardware parent could derive from a TV network subsidiary in selling satellite hardware therein. Without examining the evidence here, suffice it to state that the hardware parent would presumably have information about key decisions on systems design long before the contracts were let and even before bids were called for. Satellite and ground station design could be tilted to favor the parent's special capabilities. In fields where early contracts generate the skills and expertise needed to win subsequent contracts (and where major ComSat suppliers are at best few in number), these seemingly modest advantages could become determinative. This danger is even more likely to emerge in the continued absence of special procurement safeguards.

Conclusions and Implications

A twofold dilemma now confronts the FCC. On one hand, there are cogent economic reasons to use competitive alternatives in the regulation of long-distance communications rates, service, and reliability. In Chapter X, spectrum allocation for private or specialized for-hire systems was shown to create one such alternative. As such, that decision was analytically very hard to reconcile with any deliberate comprehensive policy to restrain all competitive response on the common carrier side.

As a technique to lower entry barriers, moreover, spectrum *sharing* between newcomer satellite and incumbent microwave systems further underscored the case for a procompetitive FCC policy. And it did so irrespective of the relatively higher spectrum costs of private communications systems under present management arrangements. There was also much to be said for competitive alternatives in order to narrow managerial discretion among the common carriers, to curb possible tendencies towards overinvestment and inefficiency where regulated firms are subject to a profit constraint, and, generally, to simplify the task of regulation. The rebuttable presumption in favor of competition appeared strongest in the domestic market but was also germane internationally.

Nevertheless, the present chapter suggests that the FCC has tended to constrain competition between the private and common carriers and between cable and satellites generally, and might well do likewise in the event of private domestic satellites. By forcing the carriers to average costs of service by old and new technologies over the whole rate base, the FCC clearly limits the degree to which the big communications users may enjoy the savings that accrue to specialized use. The carriers' resultant inability to make selective rate adjustments reduces the likelihood of virtually any reductions, in the near future at least. To safeguard the integrity of the basic switched network for the sake of the small general user, moreover, the Commission still seems predisposed to blockade new system entry. Yet the well-known political obstacles to any radical restructuring of industry underscores the need to capitalize on competition wherever we find it.

Well short of any basic restructuring, there is already evidence that the current economic-regulatory framework can be sufficiently revamped to permit the FCC to capitalize better on competitive alternatives in bringing the rates of major services down closer to their long-run marginal nonspectrum costs. (The resultant increase in interference, and in spectrum costs generally, can be disregarded, or even harnessed, on a number of counts specified in Chapter X.) Most promising is the possible use of new system competition to induce the incumbent common carriers to introduce cost-reducing technology which makes possible tariff adjustments that benefit general and specialized users alike.

Towards both these ends, there is a strong presumption against pro forma FCC approval of new vertical associations between the common carriers, the equipment manufacturers, and the TV networks or other big private users. At least, the chances for new competitive alternatives to emerge in the current formative stage of telecommunications structure seem notably greater in the absence of more such vertical links.

The two major benefits of competition today, then, include: the stimulus to innovative advance; and the search for new procedures wherein the carriers' fear of losing business from the big users can be harnessed for the good of all. In regard to hardware development, the independent manufacturers will doubtless fare better where private systems are also authorized, whereas the carriers' response to the prospect of private domestic satellites further reveals their alertness to the advantages of a preemptive strategy of cost-reducing innovations. The Private Microwave decision demonstrates awareness of these facts on the part of the Commission itself.

As for new procedures, the most hopeful sign to date is the role of the Authorized User policy in the Thirty-Circuits case and the carriers' counterproposals in Domestic Satellites. Although the peculiarities of these episodes make sweeping generalizations risky, there is every reason to try to devise or to improve on comparable procedures elsewhere too. The practical problem today is to learn how to live within the present economic-regulatory framework for what could be a protracted interim period. No opportunity must be overlooked to structure and strengthen viable competitive conduct among the principal users and suppliers of telecommunications services at home or abroad.

One such opportunity would be to create a scheme whereby newcomer and incumbent users of spectrum could negotiate between them (subject to FCC approval) an optimal level of interference in their joint maximization of the value of frequencies used in common. Another approach would be to revamp the satellite structure modestly so as better to facilitate international competition between ComSat and the carriers and also the advent of private systems at home. A third avenue that merits exploration relates to a procedure whereby new spectral regions are opened up to private and common carriers simultaneously, and not on widely separated occasions.

CHAPTER XII

BROADCAST ALLOCATIONS
IN THEORY AND FACT

In the area of broadcast regulation, it is clear that the rising marginal value of broadcast spectrum to its next-best users underlines the urgency of recovering a tangible return for the valuable privileges conferred there too. The extra costs imposed on next-best users, the forgone benefits of unused UHF, the creation of sizable economic rents in television, and the valuable policing of signal standards are all bases for the improved discharge of longstanding responsibilities of the Federal Communications Commission as regards program service. Among the policy options available are techniques to impose greater internal subsidization of cultural-informational-educational programming; to increase the number of markets with competing services and of communities with competing local stations; to enable the viewer to choose between local and national programming directly, via pay-TV and CATV; and techniques to finance public television as an alternate service in markets of varying sizes.

These options for benefit-diffusion are not all mutually exclusive, but neither are they fully consistent. Factual inquiries are therefore needed here to determine whether:

1. unlimited entry of new stations will reduce the economic rents, and hence the revenue available for higher standards or programming for minority audiences, long before additional outlets provide structural incentives for greater program diversity;

2. CATV (community antenna television) could be used as a vehicle to diversify service and otherwise improve program balance in areas far from the main urban centers that are now deprived of full network coverage and, if so, how far CATV can be so used before jeopardizing local TV revenues and particularly new UHF entry;

3. some combination of pay-TV and CATV can permit viewers to choose more explicitly between national and local programming than is now possible under the current system of advertiser-

supported national networks and, if so, the spectrum requirements of these alternative systems; and

4. comparable choices must be made between encouraging the more
vigorous growth of multiple national service and the protection
of local live service, with special reference to the limitation of
power used by clear channel radio stations and to the antitrust-
regulatory status of several key network trade practices, as well
as the spectrum implications of these decisions.

The following chapter will take up one relationship in particular,
viz., that between the licensing-allocation function and the character
and magnitude of its economic effects. A second critical relationship,
between the number of stations in the market, by market size and type
of station, though closely linked with the other, can only be mentioned
in passing in this book, for empirical inquiry into the several major
determinants of program diversity would require a study in its own right.

First, however, let us touch briefly on the industry's basic framework,
with special reference to the allocation plans by which the Federal Communications Commission now purports to guide an emerging broadcast
structure. This will provide a backdrop against which later to analyze
the pressing problems of competition and regulation.

THE ECONOMIC AND REGULATORY FRAMEWORK

The broadcast industry's structure includes several major components. Hardware companies make the sets. Set owners view the programs
and buy the products advertised thereon. Stations transmit the programs supplied by national or specialized network companies, by independent program producers, or by the station itself. National, regional,
and local advertisers sponsor whole programs and/or buy time for inter-
spersed commercial "messages" from the networks for delivery on
chains of stations, or from the national "spot" representatives (for
reaching specified markets only); these advertisers ultimately support
all other components. Network organizations integrate stations into
nationwide systems, selling the time of affiliated stations to network
advertisers, supplying commercial and sustaining public service programs
to the affiliates, and leasing from AT&T the coaxial cable and microwave
facilities to link together the chains of stations that advertisers order.[1]

---

[1] Brief descriptions of TV broadcast structure appear in House Commerce
Committee, 85th Cong., 2d sess., *Report on Network Broadcasting*, 1958, pp. 37–
52; H. Blake and J. Blum, "Network Television Rate Practices," *Yale Law Journal*
(July 1965), pp. 1340–47; and J. Peterman, "The Structure of National Time
Rates in the Television Broadcasting Industry," *Journal of Law and Economics*
(October 1965), pp. 77–93.

The Federal Communications Commission allocates spectrum to the several broadcast services and enfranchises all stations according to a variety of administrative-regulatory criteria geared to widen program choice consistent with standards of signal clarity.

To further program diversity, broadcast regulation purports essentially to (a) free the individual station from constraints by the industry's most powerful components (the networks and advertisers) and (b) leave the station management better able to choose between program suppliers and advertisers in ways that discharge public service responsibilities consistent with economic viability. The ultimate goal is to widen program choice both by diversifying program sources and by encouraging the internal subsidization of cultural-informational-educational programming for admittedly minority audiences.

Specifically, broadcast stations must operate under licenses granted by the FCC for three-year periods to applicants whose technical, legal, and financial qualifications, program plans, past experience, and involvement in the community appear to qualify them to service the public interest. Under the Communications Act they are expected to serve as informational and instructional media as well as disseminators of entertainment and advertising. Although the networks are not licensed, the Commission affects their operations by what it requires the affiliated stations to do and not to do in executing their public service responsibilities. One major aspect of the public interest is that of securing diversity of programming in terms of cultural, political, social and economic viewpoints expressed therein.

Broadcast stations discharge their public service responsibilities mainly through decisions on program content, format, and scheduling. The two critical inputs here are advertiser support and the programs themselves. Affiliation contracts with a national network company provide one invaluable source of both inputs in the TV field, though far less frequently now in radio. However, broadcast stations can also deal with the nonnetwork system of independent program producers, film syndicators, and local or national spot advertisers. In effect only 122 commercial TV stations lack a network tie today, and they are of course located in markets with more than three stations on the air. In the smaller markets where the number of available network affiliations exceeds the number of stations, stations may gain relative bargaining power in securing a preferred network tie.

Radio broadcast stations now operate in the AM band on assignments 10 Kc/s wide (at 535–1, 605 Kc/s), and in the FM band on assignments 200 Kc/s wide (at 88–108 Mc/s). Television broadcasting, where each channel occupies 6 Mc/s of bandwidth, is in the VHF band (at 54–72, 76–88, and 176–216 Mc/s) and the UHF band (at 470–608 and 614–890 Mc/s). On May 1, 1970, commercial broadcasters operated almost 4,300 radio stations in the AM band and some 2,100 in the FM band. There were 500 commercial television stations in the VHF band and 181 in the UHF as well as 413 educational FM stations.

The AM stations vary considerably in authorized power, service range, and length of broadcast day. Nonetheless AM, FM, and TV stations are all licensed according to similar social priorities. The Commission's allocation criteria are: (1) to provide all people in all markets with at least one service; (2) to provide each community with at least one local station; (3) to provide all persons in all markets with at least two services; (4) to provide each community with at least two local stations; (5) to provide larger communities with additional facilities depending on population, geographic area, and number of TV services available.[2] In addition, a virtual sixth priority in the TV and FM bands, at least, has been the reservation of several hundred channels for noncommercial educational use in major metropolitan centers and in "other educational centers."[3] A final FCC commitment, which its TV Allocation Plan reflects in at least a general way, is often said to be that of a nationwide competitive broadcast system.

The major question in this chapter and the next is whether the licensing-allocation function is a useful, efficient mechanism for widening and enriching program choice with special reference to the balance struck between local and national service, between majority and minority tastes, and between entertainment, news, and information. A second question is whether small advances in program diversity are more than offset by losses in competition and the conferral of sizable economic rents on favored classes of licensees.

Because the technical, economic, and social consequences of allocational and regulatory arrangements often intermesh, the remainder of

[2] See Sixth Report & Order, in re Amendment of 47 C.F.R. para. 3.606, FCC Docket No. 8736, 17 Fed. Reg. 3905, 3906, 3912 (1952) (applied to TV Broadcasting); Report & Order, in re Amendment of Part 3, Daytime Broadcasting Rules, 25 FCC 1135, 1137–38 (1958) (applied to AM Broadcasting); Further Notice of Proposed Rule Making, Clear Channel Case, FCC Docket No. 6741, 23 Fed. Reg. 2612 (1958) (applied to AM Broadcasting). To resolve conflicts between the maximum area coverage, local community station, and multiple station's objectives, the Commission's priorities may be applied as illustrated in Senate Commerce Committee, 85th Cong., 2d sess., *Staff Report on the Problem of Television Service for Smaller Communities*, 1958, pp. 3–5, 37–43, 47–54. Compare Report & Order, in re Amendment of Part 3, Daytime Broadcasting Rules, 25 FCC 1135 (1958).

[3] On the original reservation of TV channels for noncommercial educational purposes in major metropolitan areas and elsewhere, see 17 Fed. Reg. at 3911–14.

this chapter will examine some effects of the FCC allocation plans on spectrum utilization as such, and some further effects on economic structure and industry performance. Special attention will be paid to the local service concept and to the contrasting problems posed by spectrum allocations for commercial and educational purposes.

THE STANDARD BROADCAST ALLOCATION PLAN

When market support lags, any resultant nonuse of allocated broadcast spectrum may well constitute the price of avoiding costly subsequent dislodgment in a system riddled with de facto squatters' rights. The defensibility of this price is another matter, for it depends on the magnitude of the nonuse, the seriousness of errors in long-range regulatory predictions, and the spectrum manager's willingness to reexamine basic allocation decisions in light of such errors. At issue also are potential arrangements (namely, secondary rights) to reconcile regulatory priorities with fuller spectrum utilization. (See Chapter VII.)

Furthermore, any allocation plan will exclude certain classes of users who are ready, willing, and able to enter, if it sets aside spectrum for others who are not. This is true whether the plan provides a number of specified pre-determined, pre-engineered assignments as in television, or a set of general channel allocations geared to accommodate individual grants on a case-by-case basis, as in standard (AM) broadcasting. By setting aside a number of nationwide channels for long-distance transmissions by a few high-powered "clear channel" stations, the Standard Broadcast Allocation Plan initiated first in 1928, now necessarily excludes those many lower-powered local or regional radio stations which would otherwise be able to enter. On the other hand, the FM and TV Allocation Tables, in imposing a grid of pre-determined and pre-engineered assignments, have excluded not only numerous private non-broadcast users who are clamoring for more spectrum, but also many TV applicants still unable to secure grants in the nation's leading markets. Similarly, the granting of daytime-only radio licenses has long excluded whole classes of licensees from the lucrative nighttime radio audiences, leaving the field to the higher-powered full-time stations. The reservation of special FM and TV channels for noncommercial educational use may (in some cases) have excluded interested commercial broadcasters.

Under the FCC's Standard Broadcast Allocation Plan, full-time and part-time grants are now authorized for AM broadcast stations to operate on four kinds of channels.[4] One special group of nationwide clear

[4] See FCC Rules & Regulations for AM Broadcasting, paras. 73.21–73.29.

channels is reserved exclusively for one or two powerful stations expected to serve very large areas free from objectionable interference, where market support for local stations is inadequate. A second group of clear channels is open to medium-powered licensees, consistent with the right-of-way of so-called dominant stations which operate thereon. "Regional" channels are reserved for medium-powered stations geared to serve metropolitan districts. "Local" channels are designated to accommodate low-powered stations that serve small communities in and out of the larger urban centers.

Like the Television Plan, the Standard Broadcast Allocation Plan has from the outset sought to maximize the number of persons served by one or more signals and to widen program choice in the process. In both cases, one unintended consequence has been to grant to different classes of licensees access to quite different-sized markets with different economic potential. A second consequence has been to limit the number of competing stations in some cases for the sake of other regulatory objectives. The unique value of the clear channel license is suggested by the simple fact that, from a strict technical viewpoint, more than 150 low-powered local stations could satisfactorily operate on a single clear channel, as compared with the very small number and types of stations now enfranchised. Signal quality and service to remote areas are still cited to justify the continued restriction on entry.

One consequence of the power variations that characterize the Standard Broadcast Plan has been surprisingly neglected. This is the limitation on maximum transmission power of the clear channel licensees. For present purposes, we are mainly interested in the implications for efficient spectrum utilization. If these were fully recognized, the power limitations might well be reexamined, although in the context of various regulatory priorities.

There is of course no question about the economic value of clear channel privileges as preferential grants that authorize higher power than other grants, for extensive service in choice market areas. Time sales, profits, profit margins, and returns on tangible property all vary significantly among the several classes of FCC radio licensees (irrespective of community size) and the clear channel licensee appears to be the most favored.[5] The question is how successful are these arbitrary limits on clear channel power—and the consequent underuse of spectrum—in furthering the regulatory goals of maximum area service, multiple services, and local service.

[5] See Ch. XIII below, especially text associated with Tables 41 and 42, and fns. 5–6.

For argument's sake, let us accept as valid some tentative new engineering evidence that permitting the clear channel stations to raise their power tenfold or more may facilitate a far more acceptable service to people in 40 per cent of the nation who now get no service at all at night.[6] Suppose also that this increase in power will, as claimed, bring two to eight services to many listeners who now have fewer options. In that case, the increased power would clearly promote the FCC's all-important area service goal and its multiple service goal too. But suppose finally, as seems likely, that the local service goal might be impaired in the process.

Viewed as a regulatory problem, the question would then become twofold: What price in forgone area coverage would be imposed by limiting the clear channel power in order to preserve local stations? Is this price worth paying in terms of the benefits derived from a local service that might be impaired technically or rendered uneconomic? At this point, the strictly allocational and regulatory dimensions of the problem become virtually indistinguishable.

To justify the forced underuse of clear channels, for example, the FCC would presumably have to demonstrate that unlimited power would (a) hurt existing local stations economically even if they too could raise their power; (b) deter potential local entrants by impairing their chances to survive; (c) that the deprived listeners actually prefer a local service; and (d) that the network rules and nonnetwork system of program suppliers and advertisers alone cannot guarantee viable local outlets in the face of clear channel competition. Contrariwise, greater freedom for licensees to set their own power levels would be justifiable, as would fuller spectrum occupancy, only insofar as:

a. clear channel stations cannot "divert" listeners who presently lack any local service (or nighttime service);

b. listeners who do have local service and may turn to the clear channel stations for superior signal quality and better-financed programming constitute no reason to protect the local station, because the "viewer knows best";

c. local stations delegate many program responsibilities to their networks and advertisers anyhow, and this constitutes still another reason why they merit no special protection from clear channel competition.

Only a factual determination can help resolve these issues.

[6] The writer was briefed on the technical propositions examined in this section in conferences with A. Barghausen and K. Norton, Institute of Telecommunication Sciences, Boulder, Colo., in the summer of 1966, and permitted to review internal memoranda on the subject.

Another illustration of how allocation and regulatory problems intermesh relates to the rise of the national radio networks twenty-five years ago in the face of Commission rules on authorized transmission power and multiple station ownership. These rules may merely have shifted the locus of the industry's economic and political power from "superpower" and "chain ownership" to the network-affiliate relation. At least, some of the same factors that generated the national network system, such as large-scale programming economies, would presumably have led to more extensive multiple ownership and a fuller use of unlimited power by the "clears" (clear channel stations). The big difference would have been the smaller amount of spectrum needed to generate any designated number of signal options in various market groupings by means of a handful of high-powered clears as compared with the spectrum needed for a like number of nationwide network hookups of local stations.

Unless local service is, or can be made, distinguishable from other services in the face of network-affiliate relations, it seems hard to justify rigid power limitations. Even assuming local service to be distinguishable, the question is whether the extra national services which unlimited power might generate for more listeners are "worth" the potential deterrence of new local services. In seeking an answer, it is not enough to ascertain simply the number of people tuning in to the national and local services today. This is at best an imperfect market standard. A handful of viewers deprived of local service might, if permitted, be willing to pay more than a much larger number of viewers would to retain the competing national services. Pay-TV would help clarify this. Moreover, the FCC does not even now weight viewers equally in all cases. If local service were truly distinguishable, it might be appropriate to quantify and compare the potential listeners who would get more service of some sort under FCC priorities #1 and #3 as listed above, against those who would lose potential local community service under priorities #2 and #4. Without prejudging the outcome, the case for continued rigid power limitations might conceivably emerge the strongest here.

These few examples illustrate the interrelations of the technical, economic, and social parameters of allocation and regulation in the standard broadcast field. Comparable interrelations emerge from a more detailed analysis of the Television Allocation Plan of 1952.

THE TELEVISION ALLOCATION PLAN

The Television Allocation Plan assigned 12 VHF channels and 70 UHF channels in their entirety to television. These were located, respectively, in the 54–216 Mc/s and 470–890 Mc/s regions. Although VHF assignments were widely distributed among cities and states (under the equitable geographic dispersion priority), most of them went to cities over 50,000 in population. UHF assignments were then added to the VHF to give the larger cities a number of alternative outlets. The UHF channels made theoretically possible a first local outlet in over 1,000 communities. TV assignments went to all communities with a radio station though the smaller communities normally got a UHF outlet, except in the West where VHF was plentiful.

By and large, the number of TV assignments varied with community size:

1950 population of central cities	No. of assignments (VHF plus UHF)
1 million and more	6–10
250,000–1 million	4–6
50,000–250,000	2–4
Under 50,000	1–2

One interesting question is why even the largest cities still have no more than 10 to 15 assignments, and why most major cities have only 5 to 10, even though 82 channels have been derived from the spectrum now allocated to TV broadcasting nationally. The reason is that intense adjacent and co-channel interference simply precludes the assignment of more than a handful of these channels in any single community. From the outset, minimum co-channel spacing has ranged from 170 miles in the crowded Northeast, to 220 miles in the Gulf region where ionospheric interference was more pervasive, and 190 miles elsewhere. An attempt was made also to equalize the service range of all stations by setting the same minimum and maximum power limitations within the two TV bands, while at the same time permitting UHF grantees, with well-known technical deficiencies in coverage, to utilize much greater power than VHF grantees.

In addition, the plan normally intermixed VHF and UHF assignments in most communities on the assumption that (a) the demand for the older VHF program service would soon spill over into the newer UHF service and induce set conversion and the production of more sets; (b) failure to intermix would leave UHF outlets in markets overshadowed by VHF in nearby metropolitan areas, or in more remote, less economic markets. Finally, the plan initially reserved 242 outlets for noncommercial educational stations, 68 VHF and 174 UHF.

The financial plight of UHF stations during the years following the first UHF authorization in 1952 need not be recounted in detail. Even eight years later, only 75 (14.6 per cent) of the 575 commercial TV stations were UHF. (See Table 38 below.) Yet roughly 70 per cent of the nation's total channel assignments were UHF at that time and only 30 per cent VHF. Hence UHF television, with more than twice as many assignments as VHF nationwide, had less than one-fifth as many stations on the air. Indeed more than four times as many UHF as VHF construction permits had been surrendered unused by June 1958. One decade later, in January 1969, though UHF financial prospects had clearly started to improve, still only 168 (25 per cent) of 674 commercial TV stations were located there.

The interplay of technical and economic factors that explain the "UHF problem" is well known. Lacking adequate resources or affiliations with a major network at the outset, UHF stations could not transmit programs of wide appeal. Viewers would therefore not pay extra to convert their sets or to buy all-channel receivers. Their reluctance to convert was accentuated by UHF's initially limited range. Without adequate set penetration, the UHF stations found it hard to secure choice network and advertising affiliations, their programs deteriorated still more, and the vicious circle was complete. For such reasons there was an early, pronounced inverse relation between the number of VHF signals received by TV homes in any UHF market, and average revenues per UHF station, the percentage of TV homes with UHF reception, and the number of network program hours carried per station.[7]

At the outset, the networks understandably preferred to affiliate with VHF stations insofar as they enjoyed the greatest TV set penetration and were normally owned by the networks' older radio affiliates. In addition, ample NBC–CBS programs and the prosperity of those networks both reflected and helped explain early VHF prosperity. The absence of NBC–CBS programs and the availability of poorer, less popular ABC and Dumont programming reflected and explained much of the UHF troubles. A final factor in the relative profitability of VHF stations was doubtlessly the FCC's decision to stop issuing new TV grants during the period 1948–52 while it ironed out numerous technical problems pursuant to adoption of a new Allocation Plan. This so-called TV freeze operated inadvertently to entrench the first 108 VHF stations with the choicest network and advertising affiliations and has left an impact on industry structure and performance felt almost down to this very day.

Intentions and Results

What was the FCC after, and how has the TV Allocation Plan worked out to date? Three of the Commission's key priorities were maximum area service, local community service, and multiple competing

---

[7] See H. Levin, "Economic Structure and the Regulation of Television," *Quarterly Journal of Economics* (August 1958), especially citations on pp. 431–34.

TABLE 37. ACTUAL AND POTENTIAL NUMBER OF COMMERCIAL TV STATIONS BY NUMBER OF STATIONS IN MARKET, BY MARKET GROUPING, AND ALL MARKETS, 1966

Channel assignments in market	On the air		Potential	
	Number of markets	Number of stations	Number of markets	Number of stations
Top fifty markets				
Less than 5	40	132	1	4
5–9	10	61	41	290
10–14	0	0	5	57
15 and over	0	0	3	46
Total, top fifty markets	50	193	50	397
All markets				
Less than 5	214	487	113	294
5–9	15	90	102	675
10–14	1ᵃ	10	11	126
15 and over	0	0	4	63
Total, all markets	230	587	230	1,158

Source: Derived from Television Factbook No. 36 (for 1966).
ᵃ Hawaii (market rank 111).

services. Because most Americans live within the range of at least one TV signal today, and less than 6 per cent of all households lacked any TV receiver in 1967, maximum area coverage is virtually achieved. However, only some 400 (40 per cent) of 1,000 communities with commercial TV assignments actually had a local station in 1967. And only 117 (41 per cent) of 285 TV markets (as listed by the FCC in that year) had three or more stations.[8] It is clear that the local and multiple service goals are not yet achieved, even though the three national networks do provide some alternatives for most stations, viewers, and advertisers.

A still more dramatic way to contrast the Commission's vision of long-run industry structure with the facts as they now are appears in Table 37, which shows the number of TV markets with varying numbers of commercial stations on the air in 1966 and the potential number of such markets (and of stations) if all assignments (both UHF and VHF) were activated. This is simply another way of showing that the economic plight of UHF stations still constitutes a major factor in the Allocation Plan's failure to have its intended results.

Looking at major markets only, where all but three VHF outlets were spoken for in 1966, the Plan at that time had generated fewer than five stations in 40 of 50 top markets (132 stations in all), and

[8] A higher percentage of viewers were within range of three or more signals, but the multiplicity of stations on a market basis is still important.

five or more stations in only 10 markets. Yet if all UHFs were activated, the plan could theoretically accommodate 10 to 14 stations in each of five markets, 15 or more stations in each of three markets, and 5 to 9 stations in as many as 41 markets. Even in the country at large, most TV stations could potentially be located in markets with five or more stations each—not, as in 1966, in markets with fewer than five stations.

Have UHF financial prospects now taken a significant turn for the better? It is probably still too early to tell with certainty. The number of UHF stations on the air has risen consistently relative to total commercial stations since 1960, most notably in recent years. Until recently, also, the percentage of UHF stations showing a profit has risen fairly steadily, its relative decline in 1966 and 1967 presumably reflecting, in part at least, the larger number of new UHF stations then taking to the air. (See Table 38.) In addition, the number of UHF stations authorized to be built but not yet on the air, is substantial, having risen from 95 in 1966 to 157 in 1969, as compared with 22 and 17 for VHF, respectively.

Nevertheless, such data must be evaluated with care. Over the years, many authorized UHF stations have never been built or operated. Construction permits are frequently retained for long periods before construction starts or ends; so long, in fact, that the Commission has on frequent occasions had to prod UHF grantees to activate their assignments.

Even the growing proportion of TV sets with all-channel capability may be deceptive. The FCC estimates this as over 50 per cent in January 1969, as compared with only 16 per cent in 1962, 22.8 per cent as late as August 1965, and a projected 75 per cent by 1970. But markets with four or more stations tend to have higher UHF set penetration ratios than other markets—and poorer UHF profit records. In these big markets where one or more stations will lack a network tie, the UHF licensees will most certainly do so. This helps explain why so many of them report losses, notwithstanding the relatively high UHF set penetration ratios.[9]

The UHF stations actually fare best in one- and two-station markets where they do have network ties. (See Table 39.) In 1966, only 55

---

[9] In the 24 markets with four or more stations for which data are available, the median UHF set penetration ratio in 1967 was 62 per cent, compared to about 42 per cent nationally. Ratios in these markets ranged from 42 per cent to 97 per cent. *Television Factbook* No. 38 (1968–69). The profit record of VHF and UHF stations for network affiliates and independents is summarized in FCC TV Broadcast Financial Data for 1967, Table 5.

TABLE 38. NUMBER AND TYPE OF TV STATIONS ON THE AIR, 1952–69, AND NUMBER AND PERCENTAGE OF COMMERCIAL STATIONS REPORTING PROFITS

	Stations on the air								Stations making usable financial reports (commercial only)					
	Commercial				Educational									
	Number		Per cent[a]		Number		Per cent[a]		Number		Number with profits		Per cent with profits[b]	
Year	VHF	UHF	VHF	UHF	VHF	UHF	VHF	UHF	VHF	UHF	VHF	UHF	VHF	UHF
1952	108	*							108	(41)	94	(8)	87.0	(19.5)
1954	233	121	65.8	34.2	1	1	50.0	50.0	*	(87)	*	(13)	*	(14.9)
1955	297	114	72.3	27.7	8	3	62.7	37.3	292	85	200	28	68.3	32.9
1956	344	97	78.0	22.0	13	5	72.2	27.8	342	85	248	33	72.5	38.8
1958	411	84	83.0	17.0	22	6	78.6	21.4	402	73	284	27	70.6	37.0
1960	440	75	85.4	14.6	34	10	77.3	22.7	435	72	353	36	81.1	50.0
1962	458	83	84.7	15.3	43	19	69.4	30.6	448	75	362	43	80.8	57.3
1964	476	88	84.4	15.6	53	32	62.4	37.6	458	78	391	53	85.4	67.9
1966	486	99	83.1	16.9	65	49	57.0	43.0	463	94	401	55	86.8	58.5
1967	492	118	80.7	19.3	71	56	55.9	44.1	449	105	374	44	83.3	41.9
1968	499	136	78.6	21.4	75	75	50.0	50.0	452	118	387	53	85.6	44.9
1969	506	168	75.1	24.9	75	97	43.6	56.4	**	**	**	**	**	**

Source: See Appendix A.
* Data for VHF and UHF not comparable.
** Not available.
( ) UHF data not comparable to rest of UHF series.

[a] Per cent of total stations on air that are VHF and UHF.
[b] Per cent of all VHF reports that indicate profits; and per cent of all UHF reports that indicate profits.

TABLE 39. MEDIAN REVENUES OF PROFITABLE STATIONS IN TV MARKETS, BY CHANNEL TYPE, NUMBER OF STATIONS IN MARKET, AND AGGREGATE VOLUME OF MARKET REVENUES, 1966 (STATIONS OPERATING FULL YEAR ONLY)

TV markets ranked by descending volume of revenues in each group	Stations reporting						Median revenues of profitable VHF	Median revenues of profitable UHF
	Total number		Number with profits		Per cent with profits			
	VHF	UHF	VHF	UHF	VHF	UHF		
Total, all markets	463	94	401	55	86.6	58.5	$1,553,043	$ 771,431
Markets with four or more TV stations								
Total, 29 markets	103	30	94	12	91.3	40.0	4,527,588	1,033,259
Markets with three TV stations								
1–25	69	5	67	1	97.1	20.0	4,007,116	*
26–50	59	14	55	10	93.2	71.4	1,481,606	1,250,322
51–80	60	23	50	17	83.3	73.9	1,020,874	614,406
Total, 80 markets	188	42	172	28	91.5	66.7	1,782,991	775,482
Markets with two TV stations								
1–25	45	5	40	4	88.9	80.0	1,212,305	1,125,621
26–50	47	2	35	2	74.5	100.0	652,321	*
51–56	6	2	4	1	66.7	50.0	316,755	*
Total, 56 markets	98	9	79	7	80.6	77.8	837,335	961,583
Markets with one TV station								
1–25	25	—	24	—	96.0	—	848,162	—
26–50	21	4	17	3	81.0	75.0	461,976	536,743
51–75	19	6	12	4	63.2	66.7	264,916	258,465
76–100	9	3	3	1	33.3	33.3	111,360	*
Total, 100 markets	74	13	56	8	75.7	61.5	529,338	286,292

Source: Federal Communications Commission.

* Figures not shown because less than three stations are reported.

— No stations reporting.

(58.1 per cent) of 94 UHF stations in all markets earned profits as compared with 401 (86.6 per cent) of 463 VHF stations. In markets with three or fewer stations, however, the disparity between VHF and UHF was apparently far smaller, irrespective of market rank, especially in one- and two-station markets where the median revenues of profitable UHF stations frequently approached (or even exceeded) those of VHF stations in the same grouping. In markets with four or more stations, on the other hand, only 12 (40 per cent) of 30 UHF stations reported profits compared to 94 (91.3 per cent) of 103 VHF stations.[10]

Even if one were to take at face value the large number of UHF stations authorized but not yet built, the degree of effective UHF spectrum utilization may still be exaggerated. The FCC has estimated the total theoretical capacity of 70 UHF channels as 8,800 assignments (with a triangular grid lattice and minimum geographical separations). Even limiting TV assignments for economic reasons to cities only, at the rate of 55 assignments per nationwide channel, the 70 UHF channels could still accommodate as many as 3,850 assignments compared to 1,098 in the present Allocation Plan. Clearly, the Commission can "pack" its UHF assignments far more tightly (outside the major metropolitan centers). The fact that no such move has yet been seriously considered may give further pause to any sweeping claim about the general prospects for UHF utilization.

There is in any case no question that the wholesale activation of UHF frequencies would result in far more competing media voices, more multimedia markets, more independent stations, and even in a technical basis for another national network or at least additional specialized network groups. In the process, one would clearly expect a reduction in the industry's economic rents—at the station level, at least—although it is far less clear how much program choice would widen.

Strategies to Activate the TV Broadcast Spectrum

The fact that broadcasters have been unable to utilize UHF spectrum more extensively by no means implies that no one else would; land mobile and other nonbroadcast users have increasingly requested permission to do so. How much longer a delay due to incorrect prediction of the time pattern of utilization will be tolerable is difficult to say. The Commission has meanwhile considered a number of strategies to activate the UHF broadcast spectrum.

---

[10] Lack of a network tie still figures largely in UHF's problems. Of 26 UHF independents in 1967, only 2 (7.7 per cent) reported profits compared to 42 (53.2 per cent) of 79 UHF network affiliates, 18 (72 per cent) of 25 VHF independents, and 356 (84 per cent) of 424 VHF network affiliates. (Ibid.)

Among the remedies so far explored (and rejected) are these:

1. Tax relief on all-channel TV receivers to offset higher costs than for VHF-only sets.

2. Limit of VHF signals to the station's retail trading area, so as to prevent the overshadowing of UHF stations in nearby communities. This may help further the success of local stations, though conceivably at the expense of total geographic coverage and the number of multiple service markets. The consistency of all three objectives would actually depend on the use of boosters by UHF stations, higher UHF power and better antennas, the relocation of VHF stations directly into their home communities, and their use of directional antennas.

3. Shift of all TV stations into the UHF band, thereby promoting all regulatory objectives simultaneously, fully activating the UHF frequencies, and releasing 12 scarce VHF channels for other uses. The question originally was how to avoid loss of service in fringe areas to over eight million people and transition costs once estimated as high as $1.5 to $2.5 billion.[11] Suggested means included the use of boosters, satellites, and higher-powered UHF assignments, and a ruling that stations must transmit UHF–VHF signals simultaneously during the conversion period.

4. Waiving of multiple ownership ceilings wherever a network or nonnetwork organization sought to purchase or build additional UHF outlets. With his abundant resources, the multiple owner could supposedly survive the long period of losses before UHF became viable. He would presumably be better able also to secure essential network programming and advertiser support. Yet competitive advantages over single-station owners in contests for network and advertising ties and most favorable rates and compensation might be aggravated.

Another option was to devise means to utilize the VHF band more intensively and thus to further the Commission's several priorities without using the UHF at all. Proposed here was:

5. Reduction of the mileage separations of VHF stations to facilitate sufficient new VHF entry to promote the local station and multiple service goals irrespective of the UHF problem. But oppo-

[11] See Senate Commerce Committee, 84th Cong., 2d sess., *Television Inquiry*, 1956, Vol. I, pp. 291–94; CBS exhibit in House Antitrust Subcommittee, 84th Cong., 2d sess., *Hearings on Monopoly Problems in Television*, 1956 Vol. III, pp. 5036–44; CBS statement in Senate Commerce Committee, 83d Cong., 2d sess., *Hearings on S. 3095* [UHF hearings], 1954, pp. 975–76. See also FCC evaluation of above materials in *Hearings on Monopoly Problems in Television*, Vol. I, pp. 3269–74.

nents cited the potential interference to existing VHF stations and the threat this posed to the objective of maximum area coverage. One modified version sought to promote the multiple service objective, with little or no harm to the other goals, by proposing selected changes in the location of VHF stations, modifications of power and antenna heights, and the use of directional antennas. This would hopefully raise the number of major markets with three or more comparable outlets from 52 to 84. Under still another plan, three or more competing outlets would be allocated to each of the top 100 markets, thus making possible a fourth network. But the main objection was that the UHF band would again lie idle, and the local service goal would not be furthered. Cited also were the impropriety of preempting any of the VHF assignments then reserved for educational use, and the urgent military-governmental needs for VHF spectrum.

In the end, the FCC decided to "de-intermix" as many as possible of the so-called mixed TV markets, i.e., those to which its plan had assigned both VHF and UHF channels. The "de-intermixture" was to be managed through a policy of selective allocational adjustments. Lastly, the Commission also urged passage of an all-channel receiver law requiring all manufacturers to equip television sets to receive both UHF and VHF signals.

Under the first strategy, the Commission has followed an ad hoc case-by-case approach on VHF–UHF power, antenna heights, booster stations, directional antennas, relocations and reduced mileage separations—all geared to facilitate new station entry. Here it responded in part to widespread fears that a really full-scale effort at creating homogeneous markets would deprive too many people of all service and also impose substantial costs on the public for new sets and antennas. As early as 1958, the cost of giving each of 1,240 TV communities either all VHF or all UHF outlets, with no overshadowing near the big city markets, was estimated as a billion dollars for conversion of sets, equipment and antennas plus loss of service to several million viewers.[12] Even short of that, a plan at the time to give four homogeneous outlets to as many as possible of 326 leading markets, and thus to further the multiple service goal, was found to help the local station objective but little (owing to overshadowing), to deprive a million people of service, to cost the public $200 million to convert their sets and antennas, and another $30 million for new equipment.[13]

Through the all-channel receiver law enacted in 1962, the Commis-

---

[12] *Television Inquiry*, Vol. II, pp. 797–808.
[13] Ibid.

sion has hoped gradually to build a more dependable market for UHF advertisers and hence for potential UHF entrants. This is clearly the more fundamental innovation and the one on which Congress and the FCC have placed their greatest hopes. Indeed in rejecting several past demands by nonbroadcast services for unused UHF spectrum and in protecting local UHF against CATV competition, the Commission has frequently requested "ample time" for the all-channel law to work itself out. The recent improvement in UHF financial performance, together with the rising numbers of authorizations, applications, and stations on the air, may in part reflect growing UHF set penetration, as one factor among many.

The Local Service Commitment

The FCC is well aware that far less spectrum would suffice to promote its area coverage, competing signals and network competition goals, if only the local station goal were ignored. A major reason for setting aside so much TV spectrum at the outset was the commitment to local service. In response to the growing pressures of next-best users, however, the Commission has more than once put broadcasters on notice that their idle UHF assignments may not remain idle indefinitely; that local live service, not just routine transmission of network shows, is needed to justify any continued channel reservation.

Yet broadcasters are quick to defend their sizable spectrum shares by reference to the Commission's Sixth Report. The Commission's several regulatory priorities are said virtually to require no less than 82 TV channels for effective implementation.[14] The question, however, is whether the FCC would have allocated this much spectrum could it have predicted: the amount that would have remained unused; the duration of such nonuse; the number and urgent needs of the next-best users; and the technical possibilities of transmitting good pictures with narrower bandwidth and therefore of reduced channel spacing.

Indicative of what some commissioners expect of the broadcast in-

[14] See House Small Business Committee, 90th Cong., 2d sess., *Hearings on the Allocation of Radio Frequency and Its Effects on Small Business*, 1968, pp. 98–101; and House Small Business Committee, 89th Cong., 2d sess., *Hearings on Activities of Regulatory and Enforcement Agencies Relating to Small Business*, 1966, pp. 257–62. See also House Commerce Committee, 87th Cong., 2d sess., *Hearings on All-Channel Television Receivers*, 1962, pp. 223–25, 309–11, 395–400. For detailed synopsis of FCC and Congressional statements in support of full utilization of 70 UHF television channels for broadcast purposes, see FCC Dockets No. 18261 and 18262, Comments of Association of Maximum Service Telecasters, February 3, 1969, Part III, Ex. F.

dustry if it is to retain its many underused frequencies are comments by a former chairman, E. William Henry. He saw the broadcasters, relieved from having to compete against potential nonbroadcast users for the same spectrum, as having assumed special program service responsibilities; namely, fairness in the treatment of controversy and local service, locally originated, supported by local advertisers, and using local talent.[15]

According to Henry, local service was the principal goal, mainly because the Commission could have accommodated the TV industry in only one-third of the spectrum that was in fact allocated, had it not sought to provide local community assignments. A broad blanketing of the nation by a handful of high-powered stations in the major urban centers—with service ranges extended by boosters or translators—could also have given service throughout the country. Hence, the failure to activate local talent and resources, or otherwise to exercise local discretion in program scheduling, would weaken the case for continued retention of the TV spectrum.[16] So too would any protracted failure to activate the UHF band for commercial and educational purposes.

Whether the broadcaster's share of spectrum is adjudged to be excessive will depend in part on whether he can successfully retain it in a competitive market. But an answer depends also on whether the standards, to further which the regulators protect him from such a market contest, are furthered adequately in return. Finally, the better the broadcaster discharges his public service responsibilities, the less he may be able to bid for the spectrum he needs, whereas the less faithful he is to public service standards, the better he may fare in any market contest for spectrum. These and related issues will be discussed further in Chapter XIII.

EDUCATIONAL TELEVISION RESERVATIONS

In the TV Allocation Plan of 1952, the FCC chose between two alternatives. On the one hand, it could encourage speedier development of more commercial stations and more programming checked by pro-

---

[15] See "Address of E. Wm. Henry before the Annual National Broadcast Editorial Conference, Arden House, Harriman, N.Y., July 7, 1964," FCC 53986-G, pp. 8–9. Compare with L. Loevinger, "Broadcasting and the Journalistic Function," address before Association for Education in Journalism, FCC mimeo. 40060, August 26, 1963, and "Role of Law in Broadcasting," *Journal of Broadcasting* (1964), pp. 116–17, 120–21.

[16] FCC Docket No. 14863, "Report of the Presiding Officer in Inquiry into Local TV Programming in Omaha, Nebraska," FCC mimeo. 42231, October 24, 1963, pp. 1–7.

gram controls and the cooperation of commercial and educational broadcasters. On the other hand, it could opt for slower development of the spectrum, temporary nonuse, and perhaps ultimately fewer outlets activated, though with conceivably more or higher-quality cultural-informational-educational service. In choosing the second alternative, the FCC considered and rejected such factors as the past financial failure of the educators, the history of cooperation between the industry and the educators, the availability of free time on commercial stations and their willingness to cooperate, the availability of foundation resources for blue-ribbon commercial programming, and the public service responsibilities of commercial stations.[17]

Risks that the allocated spectrum might never be activated were viewed as less inimical to the public interest than risks that access would be quickly preempted by the burgeoning commercial interests. In the early 1950s, a flood of broadcast applicants actively sought available VHF assignments in many markets. Many of the reserved VHF channels would probably have been snapped up quickly if not set aside for educators. Ironically, the commercial broadcasters' initial arguments against the reservation of channels for educational TV (and FM) are almost identical with those that the manufacturer, trucker, or taxicab service now make against the continued allocation of unused FM and UHF spectrum to broadcasters.[18]

Today the private nonbroadcast user represents the opportunity costs of idle UHF and FM space. He criticizes the FCC's Allocation Plan for conferring privileged, protected market positions on broadcasters with no tangible social return; imposing avoidable costs and inconveniences on the excluded nonbroadcast user; and depriving the nation of net increments to public safety, security, and economic productivity. Fifteen years ago the commercial broadcaster predicted a protracted nonuse of TV channels reserved for educators on very similar grounds. And he saw his own past cooperation with educators, the FCC's program policies, and foundation support as sufficient guarantees

---

[17] FCC Sixth Report & Order in Docket No. 8736 et al., FCC-52-294 74219, April 14, 1952, paras. 33–62.

[18] See, for example, testimony by Justin Miller, President, National Association of Broadcasters, reprinted in *Textbooks & Television* (Washington: NARTB, 1951), especially pp. 12–19. Miller opposed any indefinite extension of the ETV reservation largely on grounds of the "waste" of a precious national asset through long periods of nonuse. On this basis he opposed permanent (or any) reservation of even one-fourth of allocated TV spectrum for noncommercial ETV notwithstanding longer time requirements of the educators and the fact that only 1/20 of all assignments in the TV Plan had been taken up at that time. Miller proposed instead that educators compete for licenses later at renewal time in the event that suitable outlets had become preempted by commercial broadcasters.

for program diversity and blue-ribbon programming without separate ETV outlets.[19]

Then, as now, the question was whether the price we pay in stockpiled spectrum to further the ends in view is inordinately high, and whether there might be some way to have our cake and eat it too—a fuller use of the spectrum consistent with allocational priorities. Some of these issues were anticipated in Chapter VII. Here it will suffice to focus on the unique prediction problems posed by almost any educational TV allocation.

It appears far more difficult for economics to predict the rate of development of future educational needs for spectrum than of effective commercial demand. The latter can at least be extrapolated from past trends in such objective economic determinants as advertising revenues, population, and competitive media available. However difficult it may be to analyze commercial market potential precisely, it is surely more predictable than the budgetary decisions of legislatures and school boards on which the level of support for ETV activity depends. The resulting gap between the allocation and utilization of educational channels appears to be of a different order from the comparable gap in the commercial services.

This fact is borne out clearly by data in Table 40 which indicate that relatively fewer allocated channels are in use today in ETV than commercial TV, irrespective of market size and channel type. The sole exception to this pattern occurs in the top 50 markets where slightly more educational UHF stations are in use, relatively, than commercial UHF stations, and where relative number of activated VHF stations is about the same for both services. However, even there, the percentage of channel allocations "outstanding" (i.e., neither on the air, under construction, nor applied for) is significantly higher for educational VHFs and UHFs than for comparable commercial assignments. This also holds true for all other market groupings. Hence, while the relative number of activated allocations for both services tends to vary directly with market size and is larger for VHFs than for UHFs, educational demand as such has consistently materialized more slowly than the commercial demand for TV spectrum.

[19] The initial industry position on ETV reservations was well stated by Miller, "The Commercial Broadcaster Views Educational Television," address at Georgetown University, October 16, 1952; and H. Fellows, "Televisional Education," address at University of Georgia, January 29, 1953, p. 6. Compare changed attitudes a decade later when Congress considered ways to activate the allocation of ETV spectrum. Some industry spokesmen then took a more sanguine view in support of the ETV Facilities Act. See especially Senate Commerce Committee, 87th Cong., 1st sess., *Hearings on Educational Television*, 1961, pp. 18–22, 77–83, 142–47.

TABLE 40. NUMBER OF TV ALLOCATIONS IN USE AND NUMBER OUTSTANDING, BY MARKET SIZE, CHANNEL TYPE, AND STATION TYPE, JUNE 1966

Market group[b]	Number of allocations — Commercial VHF	Commercial UHF	Educational VHF	Educational UHF	In use (on air) — Commercial VHF Number	Per cent[b]	Commercial UHF Number	Per cent	Educational VHF Number	Per cent	Educational UHF Number	Per cent	Outstanding[a] — Commercial VHF Number	Per cent	Commercial UHF Number	Per cent	Educational VHF Number	Per cent	Educational UHF Number	Per cent
1–50	161	236	27	160	155	96.3	38	16.1	25	92.3	35	21.9	4	2.5	95	40.3	2	7.4	103	64.4
51–100	140	184	36	136	118	84.3	46	25.0	22	61.1	10	7.3	18	12.9	100	54.4	11	30.6	110	80.9
101–150	126	97	27	109	107	84.9	14	14.4	14	51.8	2	1.8	16	12.7	58	59.8	8	29.6	91	83.5
151–200	97	60	18	74	68	70.1	7	11.6	2	11.1	1	1.3	21	21.6	47	78.3	13	72.2	69	93.2
201–250	40	17	6	29	27	67.5	7	41.1	1	16.6	0	0	7	17.5	8	47.1	4	66.7	28	96.6
Total	564	594	114	508	475	84.2	112	18.9	64	56.1	48	9.4	66	11.7	308	51.9	38	33.3	401	78.9

Source: Derived from Television Factbook No. 36 (for 1966).

Note: Percentages refer to total number of allocations within any category of market size, station type, and channel type.

[a] Total allocations minus stations on air, under construction, or where applications have been filed for construction permits.

[b] Ranked in descending order of American Research Bureau data listing markets according to net weekly circulation in March 1965.

This does not deny the critical importance of channel type for success in both ETV and commercial TV. The strikingly higher percentages of educational VHF than of commercial UHF channels activated, in all market groupings but the smallest, indicate otherwise. Nevertheless, when market size and channel type are comparable, as noted above, the educator's handicaps are unquestionable. And some additional implementation of his utilization of spectrum therefore seems very much in order. What the nation presumably needs is: (a) a more rational balancing between the cost and benefit of ETV and other educational inputs; and (b) a more careful coordination of the resulting investment decisions with the needed frequency allocations.

From the educator's viewpoint, when no further change in budgetary expenditure patterns will yield greater net educational benefits, the optimal demand for each input is determined, including the demand for spectrum. Today he may choose between closed-circuit facilities and microwave frequencies to interconnect ground-based broadcast stations; broadcast frequencies for the ground-based stations; microwave frequencies for airborne operations direct to a school system or via terrestrial microwave relays.[20] Frequencies for direct satellite broadcasting may eventually become still another option. But the educator must also trade off added investments in TV broadcast hardware against added investments in such nonspectrum substitutes as instructional film, audio-visual aids, and classroom teachers, or added investments in wire circuitry and video tape for interconnection.

From the spectrum management viewpoint, on the other hand, the allocation of ETV spectrum will ideally depend not only on some such rational appraisal by educators of the relative cost and productivity of alternative educational inputs but also on the known alternative uses for the frequencies in question. Because the latter have been minimized (or ignored), the allocation of ETV spectrum may have been notably larger, and the constraints imposed on educators to consider nonspectrum substitutes less onerous, than would be true in a market-type spectrum system with prices.

The managers' inability to make better long-run predictions of edutional demand, then, partly reflects the failure of school boards, state education departments, and universities to evaluate the relative efficacy

[20] For a handy review of major alternatives with systematic comparative cost estimates see M. Sovereign, "Comparative Costs of Instructional Television Distribution Systems," unpublished Ph.D. thesis, Purdue University, 1965, especially pp. xiii, 117–64. The main technical distinctions between interconnecting microwave, broadcast, and closed-circuit systems are reviewed also in National Association of Educational Broadcasters, *Standards of Television Transmission* (Washington: NAEB, 1964).

of ETV and alternative inputs in maximizing educational opportunity.[21] Basic studies are badly needed of the trade-offs among these several possible inputs in regard to retraining, literacy, rehabilitation, the spread of superior teaching skills, enhancement of teachers' productivity, and lowering of per student instructional costs. Such studies would facilitate not only more rational decisions by educators, but also better long-range predictions by the spectrum managers.[22]

In retrospect, to have made available hundreds of millions of dollars worth of spectrum for educational use with but niggardly sums over time to activate it, seems the height of irrationality. Had a healthier respect existed in 1952 for the economic value of frequencies, this might not have happened. Either we would not have tolerated idle channels so long but turned them over to others ready to put them to productive use in manufacturing, transportation, public safety, and perhaps even commercial broadcasting;[23] or we might have been willing to make additional investments, equal to some percentage of the value of this "hidden" investment, to activate the idle ETV spectrum. These outlays would not only have included more for physical plant but for programming and operating costs as well. Without such efforts at implementation, the efficacy of channel reservations, at best an uncertain tool of spectrum management, seems dubious.

The precise form of long-range financing is less important than recognition of the fact that special efforts are needed to coordinate the nation's decisions on investment in ETV plant and equipment with its decision to stockpile needed spectrum. This does not mean that long-run projections of commercial demand for spectrum are always easy to make. But it does underline the difference between the two broadcast services and the need to extend governmental responsibility from the mere provision of a public resource to educators to the more systematic provision of financial capabilities to utilize it.

[21] Indicative of how subjective the data on educational "needs" may be for purposes of projecting the demand for spectrum is evidence presented in U.S. Department of Health, Education, and Welfare, *The Needs of Education for TV Channel Allocations* (U.S. Government Printing Office, 1962). Yet this study later provided inputs for National Association of Educational Broadcasters, *UHF Television Channel Assignment Plan—Report to Develop a UHF Plan Using Digital Computer Methods* (Washington: NAEB, 1963).

[22] Even the National Association of Educational Broadcasters had little to say about the time period within which its proposed Table of Allocations would be activated and for which it urged extended and enlarged reservations. See citations in fn. 21.

[23] The increased tax revenues generated could have furthered education more effectively through more conventional means, or perhaps by feeding the ETV stations already on the air.

CHAPTER **XIII**

THE EFFECTS OF BROADCAST LICENSING

As a regulatory technique, broadcast licensing has two major drawbacks: those inherent in the distribution of valuable rights by administrative regulation; and those posed by special problems in recovering "sufficient" public service to offset the privileges conferred. Underlying both these difficulties is the inadvertent creation of sizable franchise values.

License distribution has long posed problems such as: improper influence in awarding grants, in the face of elusive selection criteria and inflated franchise values; frequent circumvention of the Commission's screening procedures, when broadcasters or newcomers pay large premiums for old licenses to avoid the risks and delays of winning new ones; and diversion of Commission attention from the substance to the form of regulation.

Moreover, in attempting to recover an adequate public service, the Commission has been faced with frequent criticism on just how much of specifically what kinds of programming at what times of the day would constitute an "adequate" quid pro quo. The dilemma is painful. If government imposes too rigorous a standard, there is danger of political influence and censorship or economic injury. Subterfuge is the danger when the Commission is anemic or is prevailed upon to sanction market power under the guise of public interest.

To help appraise the efficacy of the Commission's current regulatory techniques, inquiry is made here mainly into the relation between licensing-allocation policies, economic structure, and the magnitude of rents capitalized in the prices of broadcast stations at the time of sale. A second critically important relation between the number of available program services, by market size and type of station, and the resulting character of program choice, will be reviewed only in passing here. (Appendix E considers problems in analysis of this area.)

The licensing-allocation function confers sizable franchise value without guaranteeing its effective diversion to a diversified and widened program choice or one with higher quality. The question arises at once, therefore, as to whether a positive program to widen choice may not merit serious consideration. But, since the crucial quantitative studies essential to any such determination really transcend the scope of this book, comments here must be limited to certain analytical aspects and to the basic requirements of an empirical inquiry.

These issues must in any case be resolved irrespective of overall spectrum allocations. However, the rising marginal value of broadcast spectrum to next-best users in other services underscores the urgency of resolution. The rationale of large TV spectrum allocations actually lacks persuasiveness today to the excluded mobile, space satellite, or government users, insofar as the FCC's licensing-allocation function confers private advantages out of all proportion to the regulatory priorities furthered. Nor do the goals of broadcast regulation necessarily rule out wire distribution modes or sources of financial support other than broadcast advertising, hard as the merits of these options may be to compare with those of the current broadcast system.

ECONOMIC EFFECTS

The American broadcaster operates in a market heavily influenced by regulatory policies of the FCC. Managerial ingenuity in program innovation, production, distribution, and financing operates within a range delimited by external conditions imposed largely by the Commission through its licensing-allocation function. Limitations are placed on the broadcaster's permissible signal power, and length of his broadcast day, the location of his spectrum and his base of operations, and the maximum number of rivals against whom he must compete.

As a consequence, broadcast licenses are generally agreed to have an economic value and the FCC's licensing policies to affect this value. But there has been little attempt to quantify these propositions, mainly because the basic data are lacking.

It should be noted that not all segments of broadcasting are equally affected by the Commission's licensing-allocation function. There is, for example, considerable evidence that standard broadcasting has in general behaved as a competitive industry should, both in regard to the secular behavior of its rates of return, aggregate investment, and profit margins, and in the pattern of new station entry over time.

In television, on the other hand, barriers to entry are higher, franchise values and monopoly rents more substantial. However, even in

standard broadcasting, any generalization about the overall competitiveness of industry behavior must be qualified in the light of evidence that
licensing and allocation confer differential advantages on different
classes of AM broadcast licensees.

Secular Behavior of Time Series in Standard Broadcasting

In an industry responding to competition, one would expect high
returns to industrial pioneers to bring forth new investment sufficient to
reduce earnings rates to a competitive level. Where competition is effective, one would also expect these adjustments to occur at least as rapidly
as is consistent with technology of the day. In some cases, one might
further expect sharp cutbacks in profit margins as rates of return commence to fall (in response to new investment), in an attempt to stabilize
industry earnings.

What do the facts on standard broadcasting show? Looking at AM
radio stations only (and excluding the national and regional networks),
the FCC data shown in Figure 5, which are available only for the years

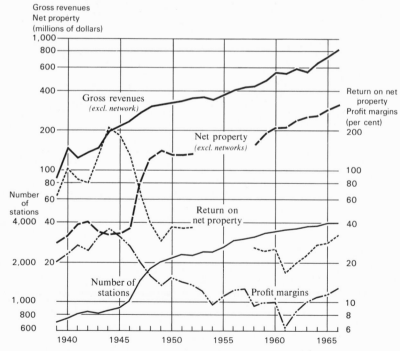

*Figure 5. Net tangible property, gross revenues, profit margins, and rates of re-
turn: standard broadcasting, 1939–66. (For source, see Appendix A.)*

1938–66, do suggest broadly that the abnormal returns of the late depression and war years induced a burst of new investment and new station entry in the postwar period sufficient to reduce returns and profit margins towards more competitive levels. At the same time, Figure 6 makes clear that the industry's national network component declined dramatically after 1945, while its competitive national nonnetwork (spot) and local station components have tended to flourish.

To examine standard broadcasting over a still longer time period (1930–66), and in somewhat greater detail, Figure 7 uses another set of time series, this one derived from Internal Revenue statistics on the

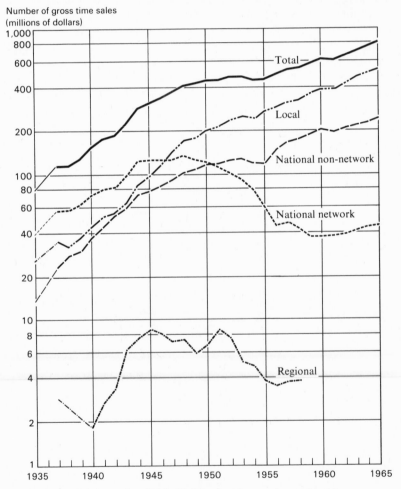

Figure 6. Radio time sales, 1935–65. (For source, see Appendix A.)

broadcast industry as a whole (radio plus television). This helps us examine the depression years more carefully for, even though the data refer to the entire broadcast industry, the FM and television components did not really become a factor until 1946 or 1947. For convenience, comment will be limited to Figure 7 alone.[1]

After losses in the early depression years, the broadcaster's rate of return on total investment rose from 11.1 per cent before tax in 1934 to 22.8 per cent in 1939, 25.7 per cent in 1940, and 37.1 per cent in 1944. The returns actually averaged 20.0 per cent during the late depression years and 30.0 per cent in the war period. On the other hand, the book value of total assets rose roughly from $60 million in 1934 to $80 million in 1939, $100 million in 1940, and almost $179 million in 1944. Likewise, the number of stations on the air rose from 591 to 778, 847 and 985 for those years (including some FM and TV licensees). In other words, at a time when returns on total assets rose some 105 per cent (1934–39), net investment and the number of operating stations rose by only 32 to 33 per cent. The wartime inflation of capital values then produced a rise in total broadcast assets of 79 per cent during the 1940–44 period, when returns rose by 44 per cent, but the number of stations rose by only 16 per cent, owing to wartime materials scarcities.

After the war the trends reversed. Between 1945 and 1959, rapid rates of new station construction and net new investment came in the face of falling returns on investment. The number of broadcast stations (AM, FM, and TV) rose some 380 per cent—from 1,000 to 4,900—while total investment grew even more rapidly, from some $209 million in 1945 to over $1.6 billion in 1959, a rise of about 660 per cent. Returns on investment dropped from 28.8 per cent in 1945 to 13.3 per cent in 1959, averaging only 15.3 per cent before tax during the whole period. Indeed during the next five years, 1960–64, returns before tax averaged only 12.6 per cent, as compared with average returns of 20 per cent in the late depression period and 30 per cent in the war years. Whether the latest rates on the chart were in fact "competitive" is hard to say. But the average rate of return on stockholders' equity for broadcasting of 11.5 per cent after tax (1960–64) approximates the average

[1] Television's profitability in the late 1950s and 1960s obviously operates to raise the average of returns and profit margins for the combined radio-TV broadcast industry in Figure 7. One may therefore question the relevance of this figure here for much of the postwar period. Nonetheless, it does have special value for analyzing the years before 1950. Furthermore, the reader can draw his own conclusions about the more recent period by checking back to Figure 5 and by reference also to the time series data for the number of AM, FM, and TV stations, which are plotted in Figure 7 as well.

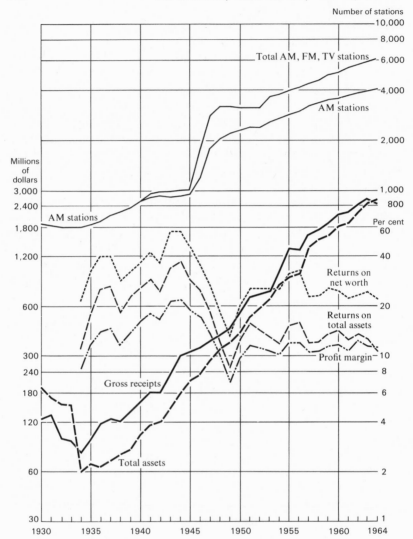

Figure 7. Total assets, gross receipts, profit margins, and rates of return: radio-TV broadcasting, 1930–64. (For source, see Appendix A.)

rate of 11.1 per cent for some 1,800 leading manufacturing corporations listed by the National City Bank Letter, and barely exceeds the average rate of 9.4 per cent for more than 3,400 major corporations which NCBL lists for *all* economic sectors.

Even granting that broadcasting's response to the high earnings rates of the late depression and wartime years is broadly consistent with a competitive standard, did the adjustment in new investment come as rapidly as possible under existing technology? Or did restrictive practices slow up the industry's response?

There is of course no question that new station construction lagged far behind the rise of earnings rates during the late depression and war years. Only when the war ended did the surge in construction and in total assets (including intangibles) assume spectacular proportions. And only then did the surge of new investment result in a decline in the industry's rate of return towards competitive levels. But why was this adjustment not more rapid, and why did it not occur sooner?

Wartime control of scarce materials would clearly prevent any expansion of existing plant, let alone the construction of new plant. This alone would interrupt a competitive response that may have come earlier. But what about the failure to respond more quickly during the late depression years? The launching of two national networks by 1927 and a third in 1934 had created the economic base for a profitable industry. Why was there not more investment in fixed plant and program facilities during the seven years ending 1940?

One factor may simply be the failure of long-run profit expectations to recover after 1929 as rapidly as actual earnings did, in the face of general instability. Yet the industry was well aware of the public's growing investment in radio sets and hardly reticent about claiming inroads into the printed media in those years. Trade restraints implicit in the network-affiliation contract may also have played a role. But the major impediment to new investment was simply the high entry barriers raised in part by the technology of the day and in part by the FCC, both of which eased substantially in the immediate postwar period.

Until the *Sanders Bros. Radio Station* decision in 1940 (see Chapter II), the Commission generally required new applicants to demonstrate the economic as well as social "need" for their service. New applicants had to bear the burden of proof to demonstrate that a particular market could support a new station without imposing economic hardship on an existing one. Aside from the legal and social consequences, the economic effects of this decision are believed to have been substantial. It is quite conceivable therefore that the volume of new construction during the late depression period would have been larger, and the resulting rates of return lower, if the Supreme Court had spoken out five or six years earlier.

The Commission's allocation of 59 clear channels for highly restricted use may also have placed a brake on new entry into some of the choicest urban markets. To be sure, there was a flood of postwar construction despite this restrictive allocation plan. But the surge of new investment was much facilitated by such factors as: sharply improved directional antennas; the Commission's willingness to tolerate debased signal standards; the growth of market support in small communities where there was insufficient advertising potential before 1940 but where the early postwar expansion actually occurred; the end of wartime materials scarcities. Finally there was the perfection of the FM and TV technology and the availability of those bands as new investment outlets. By the same token, the absence of such supporting conditions during the 1930s may well have intensified the restrictive impact of the Standard Broadcast Allocation Plan and the Commission's position on "economic injury."

The development of FM and television after 1945 is crucial in any explanation here. By and large, standard broadcasters entered these new bands, as well as expanding in their own, as logical steps in their development. Following the war, the AM radio interests bought or built additional AM, FM, and TV stations, short of the ceilings on group ownership. Newcomers who had learned the rudiments of broadcasting during the war also tried their hand at small AM and FM operations. Prior to the war, FM and TV had not reached the point of development to warrant this kind of investment.

Another way to look at the competitive adjustments within standard broadcasting since World War II is to examine the relative importance of national network, national (spot) nonnetwork, and local radio time sales. The networks' steadily declining portion of gross time sales charges (before commissions and discounts) contrasts with a continued rise in national spot business and an even more dramatic growth in local time sales. (See Figure 6.) Increased competition is clearly suggested by the steady growth of a national spot alternative to network radio advertising and also by the greater strength of station time sales at the local level.

The Pattern of New Station Entry

Broadly consistent with the above picture is the pattern of new station construction, by class, time, and power of AM radio station and by community size, during selected periods since 1939.[2] For eight classes of AM radio stations, in five community sizes in excess of 50,000 population, the computed relationships are those that would be expected to emerge under competitive conditions. The pattern of new station con-

[2] Sufficiently detailed published data are not available before 1939. Combined with the rise of television after 1950, the data limitations make the period 1939–50 the most pertinent for our analysis.

struction, 1945–48, by class of station and size of community, tends to coincide with the pattern of changes in per station income during 1939–45. The pattern of declines in broadcast income, 1945–48, coincides with the pattern of new construction during those years; profits fell most in communities where construction grew most rapidly for the various classes of stations. The pattern of new construction, 1948–50, tends to reflect the pattern of per station income changes during the years just prior, 1945–48.[3]

The rank order techniques used here permit no sweeping generalizations, but the results do suggest that AM station entry during a current time period (T_0), by class of station and community size, depends on the rate of change of per station income during a preceding time period (T_{-1}), and in turn induces inverse changes in per station income during the current period. Revised profit expectations, based on this profit experience in the current period, then result in a new pattern of station entry in the next period (T_{+1}), along lines which roughly reflect changes in the distribution of profits as between different classes of stations and community sizes.

In television, on the other hand, aggregate broadcast revenues and income in the leading markets have risen steadily since 1950, with marked stability in the number of stations operating there. This is perfectly clear from data on the 11 leading markets reported by the FCC for 1950.[4] The median rise in aggregate revenues, 1950–56, was 453 per cent, notwithstanding virtual stability in the number of stations. Even by 1958, the average number of stations in these communities had only risen from 3 to 3.2.

A similar trend is clear in a more recent analysis of the 43 identical TV communities listed in the Commission's financial reports for 1956 and 1966. In that case, the average number of stations per community rose only from 3.4 to 3.8, while the median percentage increases in

---

[3] The following variables were each ranked in descending order with the greatest percentage change ranked first: (1) average per station income, 1939–45; (2) numbers of broadcast stations on the air, 1939–45; (3) number of stations on air, 1945–48; (4) average per station income, 1945–48; (5) number of stations on air, 1948–50; (6) average per station income, 1948–50. In communities of 50,000 people and over $(N=30)$, the following coefficients of rank correlation were computed: $\rho_{1.2}=.1093$; $\rho_{1.3}=.3885$; $\rho_{3.4}=-.6650$; $\rho_{4.5}=.4936$; $\rho_{5.6}=-.1045$. At the .01 level of significance, $r=.4487$; at the .05 level, $r=.3494$.

[4] In this early year in television's history, the Commission reported only data on aggregate broadcast revenues (not income), and then only for 11 major markets. (See FCC Financial Report for 1950.) The swift rise in TV revenues enjoyed by these stations by 1956 presumably implies at least a comparable rise in aggregate broadcast income too. On the other hand, the average number of stations in the 11 markets rose from 3 in 1950 to 3.1 in 1956.

revenues and income for the same communities were 214 per cent and 246 per cent, respectively.

Technical limitations on the number of comparable TV outlets are the main reason for these high entry barriers to date.

In television, of course, these tight entry restrictions are inevitably reflected in any regression analysis of TV station sale prices, as shown later in this chapter. Sale prices necessarily incorporate the capitalization of income-earning expectations of TV station licensees. However, in AM radio too, notwithstanding the evidence on competition cited above, the Commission's licensing-allocation function has a further demonstrable impact on differential relative profitability of different classes of radio stations.

Economic Benefits Conferred by Broadcast Licenses

Because the initial impact of broadcast licensing policies is on the licensee's potential audience and thus on his maximum time sales revenue, one simple way to ascertain the existence of any economic impact of licensing is to analyze variations in average time sales by station class and community size. The relative abundance of time sales statistics facilitates the use of such techniques.

The thesis tested here is that the licensing policies governing a radio station's power, range, time on the air, location in the spectrum, and freedom from competing signals influence its relative profitability. To check for reliability, all three proxies for profit rates are used. Ideally one would want to estimate the variance in these three sets of data over time for the FCC's eightfold classification of standard broadcast stations, both by community size and by the number of stations in the market. Because serious discontinuities in the data make this impossible, the analysis was limited to selected time periods. Only in the time sales series were statistics broken down by community size for years prior to 1951. Nonetheless, the reliability of the results of several tests is pointed up by their high degree of consistency with one another.

Tests summarized in Table 41 indicate that average time sales per station, the ratio of income to gross revenues, and the ratio of income to net tangible property all vary significantly for the period 1939–60 among the eight classes of stations licensed by the FCC.[5] The tests summarized in Table 42 reveal that time sales and profit margins also vary

[5] This classification includes full-time and part-time stations licensed to operate on four groups of channels: "primary" and "secondary" clear channels; regional channels; and local channels. See Ch. XII.

TABLE 41. RESULTS OF VARIANCE ANALYSIS OF PROFIT MARGINS, RATES OF RETURN ON
NET TANGIBLE PROPERTY, AND AVERAGE GROSS TIME SALES, BY CLASS OF
STANDARD BROADCAST STATION, 1939–60[a]

Data analyzed	Period	Computed value of F	Theoretical value of F at 0.01 level
Ratios of broadcast income to revenues	1939–49	14.0038	2.87
Ratios of broadcast income to net property	1939–49	8.1134	2.87
Average time sales per station	1939–49	132.9640	2.87
Ratios of broadcast income to revenues	1939–52 1958–60	13.0896	2.79
Average time sales per station	1939–52 1958–60	173.0660	2.82

Source: Basic data derived from financial reports of the Federal Communications Commission. Series were incomplete.

[a] The eight station classes analyzed include: 50-kw clear channel unlimited and part-time; 5–25 kw clear channel unlimited and part-time; regional unlimited and part-time; local unlimited and part-time.

significantly among the eight classes of stations irrespective of community size. Likewise, time sales (but not profit margins) vary significantly among nine community sizes irrespective of station class. Finally Table 42 suggests that station class, time, and power may be more important factors than community size in explaining variations in time sales and profit margins.[6] In sum, the data do not rule out the possibility that a radio broadcaster's economic opportunities may be limited by conditions created by the licensing authority and normally beyond his control. The facts are also consistent with the hypothesis that broadcast licensing has differential economic effects.

The differences in earning power conferred by licenses to enter different broadcast bands are as suggestive as the variance in earnings of different classes of station within a single broadcast band. The marked differences between the economic opportunities conferred by FM and AM radio licenses, or by UHF and VHF television licenses, are familiar by now. What may be less familiar is just how valuable the licenses to operate in certain segments of the broadcast industry really are. Some rough idea of this can be obtained from a comparison of earnings rates in broadcasting with those in the major economic sectors and in comparable "creative" industries like newspapers and magazines.

The most profitable TV stations (those in the VHF band that were on the air before 1952) have generally earned profit margins since 1953 far in excess of the margins earned by several thousand nonfinancial

[6] The F-values for community size are not only considerably smaller than those for station sales, but one of them is also statistically insignificant at the .01 level.

TABLE 42. RESULTS OF VARIANCE ANALYSIS OF PROFIT MARGINS AND AVERAGE GROSS
TIME-SALES CHARGES, BY STATION, CLASS, AND COMMUNITY SIZE, FOR
STANDARD BROADCAST STATIONS, 1946–50

	Computed value of F	Theoretical value of F at 0.01 level
Type of variance		
Profit margins:		
By community size[a]	1.2823	2.69
By station class[b]	17.6574	2.82
Average gross time sales:		
By community size[a]	21.6625	2.85
By station class[b]	54.6677	2.98

Source: Basic data derived from financial reports of the Federal Communications Commission.

[a] Nine sizes of communities.
[b] Eight classes of stations as in Table 41.

corporations operating within six major economic sectors.[7] (Broadcasters in the UHF band as a whole actually had outright losses as late as 1968.)[8] Likewise the most profitable standard broadcast stations—those with licenses to operate full time on clear channels with 50,000 watts power—have consistently ranked high on the comparative basis just cited, whereas the low-powered part-time standard broadcast stations generally rank very low. (Independent FM stations as a group have actually shown losses to this very day.)

Profit margin comparisons must be interpreted with care. Low margins and high capital turnover are as likely to result in high rates of return on total assets as will high margins and low capital turnover. The different economic characteristics of industries in the above interindustry comparisons make any generalization tentative at best. Yet the return on net tangible property is in some ways an "unfair" measure of profitability in broadcasting because it excludes all-important intangible assets from the investment base. One can actually defend the profit margin as more appropriate for this industry because fixed plant is a relatively small part of total investment.[9] In the absence of data on the actual rate of return on total investment, probably the best that we can do is

[7] The median ratio of pre-tax broadcast income to revenues of the older VHF stations, 1953–60, was 33.5 per cent. (The distinction between VHF stations on the air before and after 1952 was not made after 1960.) This contrasts with a median ratio of 12.1 per cent for all leading corporations reported annually by the First National City Bank, adjusted for comparability.

[8] This was true even though the median revenues of profitable UHF stations in 1966 equalled or exceeded those of profitable VHF stations in markets with two TV stations, and in some markets with one TV station too. (See Table 39.)

[9] See written testimony of the Columbia Broadcasting System in Senate Commerce Committee, 84th Cong., 2d sess, *Television Inquiry*, 1956, Vol. IV, pp. 2017–30.

to devise ways to use one or both of these measures as a reasonable proxy.

An earlier study for the years 1945–57 compared the profit margins and returns on net tangible property of different segments of the broadcast industry with those of the leading newspaper, magazine, and motion picture companies, as listed in Moody's *Industrials*.[10] The comparability of the mass media for this purpose was suggested by the fact that they had long had operating and capital turnover ratios much closer to each other (and to nonrail transport) than to public utilities and railroads. It was also argued there that broadcasting should rightly be compared with other "creative" industries, much of whose assets are intangible, rather than with utilities and rails, where fixed costs are high and tangible property constitutes the bulk of investment. On both counts such a comparative study was presented as the best available proxy for a comparison of the actual rates of return on total investment of broadcasting and other industries.

Throughout the years studied, it was found that the profitability of certain key broadcast segments generally exceeded by far the profitability of these comparable "creative" industries. Likewise, the reverse was true for other segments. Without exaggerating the implications, suffice it to note the conclusion there: that not only do some classes of broadcast licenses offer far greater economic opportunities than others but the magnitude of the differences in these opportunities appears to be substantial.

Analysis of TV Station Sale Prices

Moving from the relative profitability of different classes of radio and television stations to the analysis of TV station sale prices, we may now try to identify still more explicitly the probable economic impact of the FCC's broadcast licensing function.

Conceptually the value of a license to a station-buyer roughly equals the sum he is willing to (or does) pay for a station, minus the sum that he would have to pay to duplicate the physical plant, business contacts, and good will he acquires. That is, the price of a station reflects the buyer's expectations about future earnings over the life of the property

[10] The original study appears in my article, "Economic Effects of Broadcast Licensing," *Journal of Political Economy* (April 1964), p. 155. Of interest also is the similar pattern that emerges in a comparable analysis of more recent data derived from the *Sourcebook of Income Statistics* for the motion picture production and exhibition industries, newspapers, periodicals, and broadcasting. There I examined returns on net worth and total assets, and profit margins on sales, for selected periods, 1930–65.

he acquires, discounted by the rate of interest. The price of a license, on the other hand, is that portion of the excess of total price above replacement costs which the buyer is willing to pay for temporary, renewable rights to operate in a certain market under certain conditions. The margin between sale price and replacement cost should therefore be smaller, the greater is the number of rival signals received in the market and the smaller the market's retail sales and advertising potential. The margin should also be smaller the cruder the engineering characteristics of a station's frequency, the lower its power, the shorter its permissible broadcast day, the harder it is to get a network affiliation, the easier it is to get permission to build a new station there, the more rigorous the FCC's service standards, and the less certain a broadcaster is of pro forma renewals.

One would of course like to examine the thesis that the excess of the current value of a TV station's expected income over the replacement cost of its physical assets varies, *cet. par.*, with both the size of its market and its competitive position therein. One would like further to establish the effects of the FCC's licensing-allocation policies on both these variables. However, the replacement cost data are at best rough estimates subject to all the vicissitudes of divergent accounting practices, and by no means comparable to standardized public utility data. More important, my earlier work along these lines was obscured by the use of a composite dependent variable (sale price minus replacement cost),[11] the subsequent simplification of which (to sale price-only) led to marked improvement in the results.

Accordingly, I propose here to examine sale prices only and, through multivariate analysis, to determine the relative importance of (a) market size, (b) number of stations, (c) age of station, (d) network affiliation, (e) average daily circulation, (f) original cost of assets, and (g) authorized signal power.[12] The main task is to determine whether the level of sale prices responds relatively more to changes in potential or actual circulation (a,e) or in strategic structural and regulatory factors (b,c,d,g) than to changes in initial station investment (f). To the extent that the impact of initial investment is large, but that of the other factors less so, doubts may be raised as to how much broadcast licensing affects TV station sale prices. However, the effects of licensing would seem greater where initial investment has only a negligible relative impact but

[11] Ibid., pp. 157–62.

[12] For computational details see Appendix C. The variables in this new study contrast with those of the earlier analysis of 1964, where I had examined: sales price minus replacement cost, retail sales, effective buying income, TV homes per TV station, network hourly rate, national spot rate, age of station, network affiliation, and percentage of urbanized population.

factors like market size, or number and age of stations, are important. High coefficients for network tie and daily circulation are more complex to interpret, but even these would be consistent with a conclusion, grounded on the other coefficients, that regulation creates sizable franchise values.

In brief, entrepreneurial discretion is reflected in the licensee's investment and programming decisions, whereas the Commission's licensing-allocation function is reflected more in the size of market to which a license permits access and in the number, age, and signal power of the stations permitted to operate therein. Thus the value-creating effects of licensing appear more likely to exist where regulatory constraints (and not licensee ingenuity) explain the major variability in TV station sale prices.

Regressions run on sale price with the four independent variables, which preliminary work indicated to be the most pertinent for this study did in fact reveal each factor as significant. Listed according to relative impact these variables were: TV homes, average daily circulation, age, and network affiliation. In addition, tests were run for authorized signal power, original cost of assets, and number of stations in the market. Each of these additional variables was included separately in a six-variable regression, but in no case was any of them significant.

Following this exploratory inquiry, and for purposes of further clarification, a separate eight-variable regression was run, the results of which are reported in Table 43. Throughout the analysis, TV homes (X_2) and average daily circulation (X_5), in that order, have the greatest relative impact of any variable on sale price.[13] The dummy variables for network status (X_4) and age (X_3) are both significant, to be sure, and the former appears to have the greater relative impact. But their main function is simply to take account of important qualitative factors at play here and thereby to enhance the reliability of the other regression coefficients.

In Equation 4, holding constant X_3 and X_4, the introduction of circulation (X_5) not only raises the value of $\bar{R}^{-2}$ but its coefficient is significant in its own right at the 1 per cent level. In Equation 5, on the other hand, the coefficient for number of stations (X_6) is statistically insignificant at the 5 per cent level, but its introduction nonetheless raises

[13] Other regressions of circulation on sale price run elsewhere have actually shown it to be a highly significant predictor, holding constant age of station, network affiliation, and type of seller. This suggests that its limited relative impact in Table 43 may be due largely to the high intercorrelation with TV homes $(r = .91)$. See United Research Inc., *The Implications of Limiting Multiple Ownership of Television Stations* (1966), Vol. II, Appendix H, tests 19–24 (incorporated in the record of FCC Docket No. 16068, October 1966). See also selected results in Appendix C below, tests 7–8.

TABLE 43. MULTIPLE REGRESSION ANALYSIS OF TV STATION SALE PRICES, 1956–57

Equation number	Constant term	Regression coefficients and their standard errors							Coefficient of multiple determination adjusted for degrees of freedom (R^2)
		TV homes X_2	Age[a] X_3	Network status[a] X_4	Circulation X_5	Number of stations X_6	Signal power X_7	Cost of assets X_8	
1	3.3518	0.7596[b] (0.0653)							0.6619[b]
2	3.6965	0.7950[b] (0.0627)		−0.2885[b] (0.0959)					0.6985[b]
3	5.0926	0.7258[b] (0.0662)	−0.5598[c] (0.2210)	−0.2906[b] (0.0922)					0.7216[b]
4	5.5315	0.4112[c] (0.1573)	−0.7307[b] (0.2285)	−0.2627[b] (0.0904)	0.3297[b] (0.1505)				0.7372[b]
5	5.5635	0.4180[b] (0.1565)	−0.7647[b] (0.2288)	−0.2330[c] (0.0929)	0.3661[c] (0.1523)	−0.0961 (0.0748)			0.7398[b]
6	5.6365	0.4284[b] (0.1581)	−0.7454[b] (0.2318)	−0.2320[c] (0.0933)	0.3890[c] (0.1570)	−0.0994 (0.0753)	−0.0539 (0.0829)		0.7373[b]
7	5.3643	0.4194[b] (0.1613)	−0.7198[b] (0.2444)	−0.2249[b] (0.0962)	0.3835[c] (0.1589)	−0.1005 (0.0759)	−0.0604 (0.0855)	0.0486 (0.1374)	0.7334[b]

Source: See Appendix C.
Note: N = 68; data are in logarithms for all variables except X_3 and X_4.
[a] Dummy variables.
[b] Significant at 1 per cent level in two-tailed test.
[c] Significant at 5 per cent level in two-tailed test.

$\bar{R}^{-2}$ slightly from .7372 to .7398 which indicates some possible impact and the need for further investigation. Beyond this, finally, the coefficients for signal power (X_7) and cost of assets (X_8) in Equations 6 and 7 are not only insignificant but their introduction actually reduces the value of $\bar{R}^{-2}$.

For the purposes at hand, the following tentative conclusions appear to be in order. In regard to regulatory constraints, the number of TV homes to which the FCC permits access unquestionably has the greatest relative impact on sale price of any variable studied. But age of station, with reference to the TV "freeze" in 1948–52, is also significant. On both counts, the data are consistent with the thesis that broadcast licensing-allocation policies affect the level of sale prices.

On the other hand, the insignificance of signal power presumably reflects the Commission's success in equalizing the service range of TV licensees in contrast with its quite different objectives in standard (AM) radio. Hence the insignificance of this variable is also fully consistent with the above conclusions. But the insignificance of the negative coefficient for "number of stations" raises more serious questions. The effects of broadcast licensing should presumably be revealed through the maximum number of stations permitted to operate in different markets, as well as by market size. The lack of significance may be attributable in part to intercorrelation with TV homes and circulation (for both of which the value of r is roughly .51).[14]

In regard to managerial ingenuity the results are rather more complex. Clearly the impact of network affiliation and daily circulation reflects in part the networks' program innovations and the licensee's programming decisions, respectively. On both these counts the facts would seem consistent with business discretion as a factor in sale price variations. Yet the networks' ingenuity in program innovation not only provides the basis for network power but also relieves the affiliated stations from any need to exercise their own ingenuity.

As noted earlier, the broadcast licensee delegates much of his program selection-innovative function to a network company. The network provides him with a varied, popular program service even before receivers are widely owned in his market and later provides him with a

[14] There is indeed some indication that number of stations may be more significant than appears to be the case here. For example, in the regressions United Research ran on prime time quarter-hour viewing—a more refined measure of audience size than average daily circulation—number of stations was in fact significant at the .01 level. It also had a greater relative impact (beta coeff.=.5623) than network affiliation (.1826), channel number (−.1667), type of ownership (.0685), or type of frequency (−.0285). See ibid., Appendix I. It should be noted however that the value of $\bar{R}^2$ in this test was only .32 (N=490).

steady source of advertising revenue. The network helps him also to fulfill his public service responsibilities by providing a balanced service that includes free sustaining programs that fill in the time slots which may be vacated by sponsors (a requirement whose urgency the industry's peculiar cost function underscores). Accordingly, the statistical significance of network affiliation in this analysis is fully consistent with the existence of economic rents at the station level.[15]

On the other hand, the number of homes any station actually reaches (circulation) will necessarily reflect total TV homes in the market and the maximum number of stations the FCC permits to enter therein, as well as program popularity, format, and scheduling. Hence the importance of daily circulation cannot be viewed as a reflection of managerial ingenuity alone.

On balance, the significance of network ties and circulation is at least broadly consistent with the enjoyment of large economic rents by TV broadcast licensees, a conclusion supported by the remainder of the analysis. Finally, the statistical insignificance of original cost of tangible assets further corroborates this conclusion. Licensee discretion regarding investment in physical plant (including studios and equipment) appears to exercise no significant influence on sale prices and thereby on franchise value.

By way of confirming this exploratory analysis $(N = 68)$, brief reference will now be made to a comparable study of a far larger sample $(N = 198)$ I helped organize and conduct for United Research Inc.[16] From listings of all major TV station sales published in *TV Factbook*, 1949–65, URI eliminated sales which involved more than one television station plus one radio station, as well as transactions for which complete data for selected independent variables were not also available. To ensure further that sales involving radio-TV stations, or sales of less than 100 per cent stock would not distort the analysis, all sales were grouped into three categories. First were all 100 per cent ownership transfers with cash and noncash elements combined to secure a total price. Second were sales of more than 50 per cent but less than 100 per cent interest transferred, with calculated price (including all cash and noncash items) imputed to reflect a 100 per cent ownership transfer price. Third were sales where an AM and/or FM station was

---

[15] Of additional relevance may be the barriers to new station and new network entry imposed by the Commission's TV Allocation Plan. In this special and limited sense, the value of a network affiliation can thereby be related at least in part to the restrictive impact of the Commission's licensing-allocation function.

[16] See United Research Inc., *Implications of Limiting Multiple Ownership*, Ch. VI and Appendix H.

also included and only a combined price for the package was available but the TV portion of the package was presumed to account for the bulk of the combined price.

To isolate the power of major independent variables in a more refined fashion, separate tests were run for all markets, for the top 50, and for the top 100. Separate tests were also run for each of the three types of sales for all markets. However, data limitations required a limitation of the explanatory variables to TV homes, network affiliation, age of station, and for URI purposes, to an index of "groupness" (where station sellers and buyers were scaled according to whether a group or nongroup entity).

Once again, one important finding was the significant relative impact of TV homes, network ties, and age of station on TV station sale prices. Each of these factors when taken separately emerged as significant irrespective of all others and irrespective of "groupness." The URI analysis, conducted for other purposes, corroborates the regressions cited earlier and underscores the conclusions drawn here regarding the economic effects of broadcast licensing. (See Appendix C below.)

EFFECTS ON PROGRAM CHOICE

Having examined the differential effects of licensing and allocation policies on entry, profits, and franchise values in several parts of the broadcast field, we shall now consider what assurances, if any, there are that the franchise values will be used in part at least to support relatively unprofitable public service. Here broadcast regulation follows two approaches: first, a type of Commission-induced internal subsidization of public service by commercial licensees; and second, a policy to promote competition and diversity through new station entry on one hand, and the growth of public television on the other.

The critics of exclusive reliance on the procompetitive approach generally express concern over the excessive program duplication they find in the nation's television markets. According to their theory, the limited number of TV stations in most markets today raises a serious likelihood of such duplication and, through that, the possibility that few listener groups can satisfy their top-level preferences. It has at least been argued that: (1) a second, third, or n^{th} station in any market will prefer to imitate what an initial station produces (rather than to innovate a new program type), so long as its expected audience would thereby exceed that which would result from the innovation; (2) this situation (and hence duplication) is more likely to occur when a new station enters a market, *cet. par.*—(a) the fewer the stations then in the market,

(b) the greater the disparity between the sizes of the different listener groups; and (c) the smaller the disparity between the audience shares of the competing stations.[17] More recently, it has been argued further that duplication will be more likely to occur (a) the greater the tendency for audience preferences to cluster around a "middling" program type—the lowest common denominator—(this being true the more that listener groups disagree on their highest or lowest program preferences); (b) the smaller the absolute size of different preference groups; and (c) the larger the number of conceivable program types.[18] One conclusion is that while there may be an inverse relation between program duplication and the number of competing stations, even the addition of a rather large number of new stations will reduce program duplication but a little.[19]

The proponents of this a priori thesis have not yet subjected it to any really conclusive empirical test. Nevertheless, searching inquiries of a preliminary sort already provide broadly corroborative evidence.[20] And the thesis does provide a suggestive explanation for the alleged difficulty of most viewing groups to satisfy their highest program preferences. It may also explain the Commission's dual efforts to increase the number of competing stations and program suppliers sufficiently to enhance program diversity notwithstanding such factors, *and* to require *each licensee* to diversify his program output irrespective of strict profit considerations.

To assess the potency of broadcast licensing and allocation as instruments to widen viewer choice, however, what we really need are systematic in-depth inquiries into at least three areas: first, the observed relation between multiple station entry and the range of program choice under *current* transmission and interconnection technology, program

---

[17] This thesis has been set forth at length in a landmark paper by P. Steiner, "Program Patterns and Preferences: and the Workability of Competition in Radio-broadcasting," *Quarterly Journal of Economics* (May 1952), pp. 194–223. His conclusions are basically the same whether or not listener preferences are assumed to be independent of the particular programs broadcast.

[18] See J. Rothenberg, "Consumer Sovereignty and the Economics of Television Programming," *Studies in Public Communication* (Autumn 1962).

[19] But compare with the different conclusions drawn from an alternative analysis by J. McGowan, "Competition, Regulation, and Performance in Television Broadcasting," *Washington University Law Quarterly* (Winter 1967), pp. 503–13. A priori analysis alone clearly cannot resolve this question.

[20] See in particular H.W. Land Associates, *Television and the "Wired City"* (Washington National Association of Broadcasters, 1968), Ch. 2. See also J. Dimling, R. McCabe, and W. Schmiedeknecht, "Identification and Analysis of the Alternatives for Achieving Greater Television Program Diversity in the U.S.," Appendix A to Staff Paper No. 6, President's Task Force on Communications Policy (U.S. Department of Commerce, Clearinghouse for Federal Scientific and Technical Information, June 1969).

production costs, and tastes; second, the projected maximum number of stations expected to operate in markets of varying sizes, over time, under varying economic, technical and legal assumptions; and third, the inferences one may draw about the above from new knowledge about program production and delivery costs, per program option, under cable television.

The magnitude of this task suggests that the work can best be broken down and done separately. By the same token, it must be borne in mind that any observable relation between viewer choice and multiple station entry could conceivably change with the advent of public television networks, pay-systems, wire service, satellite- or microwave-interconnected local CATV systems, or even satellite-interconnected local ground-based broadcast systems. For one or more of such modifications may operate to alter the number and the capabilities of independent program suppliers, and the costs of program production and delivery.

Stated otherwise, the critical factual questions for effective use and regulation of the broadcast spectrum are these: Will the sheer numbers of stations and signals act to widen and diversify program choice where (a) interconnection costs, program costs, and the number of national networks and of other program sources *all remain constant*? Or where, irrespective of the above, (b) the mix of advertiser-supported, pay-TV and ETV services *also* remain constant? If not, are rising numbers of stations at best a better way to reduce industry rents and supernormal profits than to diversify choice with reference to minority as well as majority preferences? Finally, and of major importance in its own right: How will viewer choice and diversity respond to changing numbers of stations where the number of national program suppliers (including TV networks) and the mix of conventional, pay-TV, and public television service *also vary*? (See further partial discussion in Appendix E.)

In sum, the principal dilemma that the FCC confronts in diffusing benefits in the broadcast field may well lie, as often alleged, in the asymmetrical relation between the number of stations and economic rents on one hand, and the number of stations and range of program choice on the other. If so, it would take far more new commercial stations in markets of varying sizes to widen effective choice there, than to reduce industry profits, rents, and franchise values. Entry-opening cost-reducing technology that activates the UHF band, or intensifies VHF utilization, would in that case be a better way to bring rents down than to raise standards or widen choice.

By the same token, suppose rising numbers of public TV stations could, as many observers hold, enhance diversity far more effectively than comparable increases in the number of commercial stations. A strengthened national policy in support of institutional diversity would then look more promising than any procompetitive policy in the commercial sector alone. But there are additional considerations. Public television's high rating in widening program choice must be qualified by its low rating in actual audience size. It must be qualified also by its undemonstrated capability of building substantially larger audiences over time (although it can of course be argued that a society "should" have available certain options almost irrespective of who actually uses them).

At this juncture, what spectrum managers most need to do is to measure the spectrum and nonspectrum costs of establishing alternative nationwide public television systems, and to compare them with the same costs of underwriting alternative commercial systems with enough stations, in enough markets, to widen the range of choice *comparably*. The viability of all projected systems would of course depend on the cost and availability of the needed programming, with prorated credit given also for any release of the radio spectrum.

Until such studies are undertaken, it is hard to predict the precise relative impact on effective viewer choice of an additional megacycle of broadcast spectrum allocated to educational or to commercial licensees. Allocation and licensing decisions will doubtlessly have to be made without such factual evidence; but that is all the more reason to underwrite these studies soon.

CONCLUSION

There seems little point to any perfunctory summary here of the factual findings in each chapter. But a word does seem in order on one of the book's principal conclusions; namely, that far more attention is needed in high policy-making circles to determining the proper form for market-type constraints in the present spectrum system and also the distance that such constraints will take us in discharging major government responsibilities.

In recapitulating the basis for this conclusion, let us first consider the principal thrust of the argument in Parts Two, Three, and Four and then examine two related propositions.

THE PROPER FORM FOR PRICE INCENTIVES

In Chapter IV, we cautioned against oversimplifying the case for freely transferable rights, and especially against grounding the case for some market-type system on that approach alone. There are a number of economic obstacles to any full-fledged market, arising mainly from cost and benefit externalities. But the major practical obstacles are, and will presumably continue to be, factors of a political, institutional, and international sort.

As a more judicious way to proceed, therefore, Chapter V proposed an interrelated package of middle-range options; viz., shadow prices, rental charges, and intraband auctions. Throughout Part Two we emphasized the need to limit or constrain administrative discretion, not to eliminate it. By the same token, though market norms can be overridden for cause, the burden of proof in so doing must be made more explicit and heavier. Much of Part Two attempted to indicate how this could be done, and the problem was reexamined again in Part Four, from a related viewpoint.

How Far Will Market-type Constraints Take Us?

Even assuming that market-type constraints can be instituted effectively, the question is how far this will take us in allocation, promotion, and regulation. That is, how much of the spectrum managers' threefold function would really be rendered superfluous by a market-type spectrum system, and how much would still remain?

Because it is important to draw this line carefully, we shall now capsulize the major conclusions of Parts Two through Four, as follows.

In Part Two we found that market incentives would unquestionably help move us towards optimal allocation in economic terms and, on that score, enhance the economic efficiency of spectrum utilization. The manager could still override any market verdict for cause, we concluded, and there are several performance dimensions he might want to further notwithstanding their cost in forgone efficiency. But costs and benefits must be balanced with care. Perhaps the most viable approach is to undertake cost-effectiveness studies of alternative allocational decisions as between users who enjoy comparable social-regulatory priorities. This would enable us to minimize the cost of implementing any given management goal.

In Part Three we showed that a market-type spectrum system would generate a pattern of spectrum-developing incentives different from, but comparable to, those inherent in the present nonprice system. Spectrum scarcity, we saw, is now associated with technological change at the intensive and extensive margins of spectrum, whereas auctions, rental charges, or shadow prices would presumably alter the pattern of innovative activity, possibly making it more consistent with consumer welfare and economic efficiency. Yet even so, the federal government's traditional pragmatic role in generating new telecommunications capabilities would remain. Because spectrum development is costly, risky, and characterized by substantial benefit externalities, far more thorough analysis is needed as to the appropriate investment criteria. This is of course true under the present system. But, we saw it would also be true if a market-type system were instituted. Furthermore, selected public R&D programs would still be needed in such areas as atmospheric noise and TV bandwidth compression.

In Part Four there was again no question that the use of market-type devices to eliminate the subsidy element in free spectrum grants today would alter the character of regulation needed in the broadcast and common carrier services. But it would surely not eliminate that need. Major economic and social problems would remain owing to exceptional technical barriers to entry and benefit externalities in the broadcast field, and unusual scale economies among the carriers. Regulation would therefore be needed even assuming some ideal articulation of spectrum costs. The practical crudities of whatever price incentives we do in fact manage to inject into the spectrum system would further underscore the need to reexamine our regulatory concepts and techniques. In rejecting market-type verdicts for reallocation, the government must regulate the broadcast or common carrier services in ways that justify the extra costs their incumbency imposes on others and the outputs the nation forgoes thereby. The greater rigor with which market-type incentives in spectrum utilization would force the FCC or the DTM to justify any regulatory action would do just that.

TWO MAJOR PROPOSITIONS

Moving beyond the specific conclusions just described, a word is now in order on two related propositions to which much of the whole study can be reduced. First, that regulatory problems, difficult enough in their own right, are rendered even more complex and urgent in the face of spectrum stringencies, scarcities which the institution of market-type arrangements could help reduce. Second, that the de facto burden of proof which newcomers are forced to bear in the present spectrum system would be more equitably shared with incumbents in a system where economic incentives played a larger role.

In regard to the first proposition, the rising marginal value of broadcast or common carrier spectrum to next-best users in other services requires careful reexamination of the interplay between competition and regulation in both those fields. Part Four has initiated a preliminary inquiry into such issues. The need for rethinking is separate and distinct from, though clearly related to, the bearing of new allocational techniques on the level of spectrum development and the government's more general promotional responsibilities.

In regard to the second proposition, one major implication of the opportunity cost concept, as applied to spectrum allocation, would be to sharpen (and conceivably shift) the burden of proof as between newcomers and incumbents. This issue is subtle but extremely important. For administrative regulation has long conferred de facto property rights on the basis of prior access and use of the spectrum, legal fictions to the contrary notwithstanding. Incumbents have what lawyers call "standing" in the evaluation of regulatory change. It is their investments that must be considered in phasing in the new and phasing out the old, over time. Yet there is no question that the excluded newcomer has rights too, neglected though they often appear to be. The better articulation of opportunity costs in spectrum utilization would help rectify this imbalance in regard to who has how much standing to contest what.

Let us conclude with a further look at both propositions.

COMPETITION AND REGULATION REVISITED

As shown in Chapters X and XI, the case for competition between ComSat and the carriers can be judged on the merits. So, too, can the case for competing private domestic satellites. The building of such competitive elements into present telecommunications structure does appear a likely way to limit tendencies toward overinvestment and inefficiency inherent in regulated industries as such. The case for diversifying the number and type of broadcast stations and national program suppliers also stands on the merits. (Chapters XII–XIII.) Indeed one may therefore ask why these matters are examined at such length in Part Four. After all, the bulk of this study deals with the problems of spectrum allocation as narrowly viewed, not with market structure, competition, and regulation in the broadcast and common carrier fields.

The point is, however, that the policies in question clearly illustrate the kind of regulatory task which spectrum scarcities and the demands of deprived next-best users virtually impose on the government today. They illustrate also the regulatory requirements for any deliberate decision to override economic factors in allocating spectrum under a modified market-type system with prices.

Let us assume for example that relative intraband auctions were to favor land mobile over television, or that relative shadow prices were to do likewise, or that outright interband contests did so. The status quo in allocations could still be justified if particular regulatory dimensions were thereby implemented in return. In this regard, diversity is an overriding goal of broadcast regulation. To tie up so large a spectral region as we now do for local ground-based broadcast stations is defensible only if the diversity that results is commensurately greater than it would otherwise be. And here, the analysis in Chapter XIII suggested that the mere multiplication of commercial stations may be less potent than the addition of educational television. For such reasons, indeed, we underscored the special role of ETV in any context of spectrum scarcity and excluded next-best users. (See Appendix E.)

Because spectrum requirements of the present local ground-based system so far exceed those of conceivable systems which generate a small number of national services, the rising marginal value of broadcast spectrum to next-best users further compels the FCC to scrutinize network-affiliate relations from the viewpoint of an adequate local live service, public service prime time clearances, and other important considerations.

The regulatory implications of the rising opportunity costs of microwave and space satellite spectrum also merit consideration. To permit private systems to operate in these spectral regions may impose higher spectrum costs on the nation, but it clearly makes possible lower (nonspectrum) communications costs for the user. (Chapter X.) Having once allocated spectrum towards this end, it seems illogical then to stop the carriers from trying to match these advantages, under a variety of regulatory safeguards. (Chapters X–XI.) On the contrary, the initial goal in allocating spectrum to the private systems notwithstanding higher spectrum costs—viz., lower communications costs and rates—requires otherwise. And even the small general user will stand to gain from the significant cost-reducing innovations that the carriers may make in response to the "threat" of private systems.

If we permit spectrum sharing between terrestrial microwave and space satellite systems, and on that score lower the entry barriers to the latter, the logical corollary once more seems to be to try to build (not block) a framework conducive to more (viable) competition between the two, albeit consistent with other regulatory priorities. (Chapters X–XI.)

"STANDING" TO CONTEST THE STATUS QUO

The basic thrust of Parts Two and Four, finally, can be reduced largely to the question of who shall bear what burden of proof where market-type criteria are deliberately overridden in the allocation of spectrum. Part Two made very clear that many problems which currently plague spectrum management would recede in an organized spectrum market, but that the task of management necessarily involves important noneconomic criteria and standards as well. One major contribution of market-type systems would be to force the manager's hand in spelling out and justifying more explicitly any decision to reject market criteria.

As already noted, Part Four reviews two cases where regulatory policies, defensible on the merits, assume even greater persuasiveness in the context of spectral stringencies and constraints. To reject evidence in support of a market-type reallocation of broadcast spectrum to mobile radio, or space satellite users, the FCC must be doubly sure that the present broadcast allocation is used most expeditiously to widen effective program choice. And here the case for public television assumes new significance.

To reject additional evidence in support of reallocating some microwave spectrum to space satellites (or from the common carriers to private users), the Commission must be comparably certain that the common carriers will pass on the gains of new microwave or satellite technology in the form of lower rates. Competition by the private systems generally is one guarantee that this will happen; competition by ComSat is another. Unless we endorse some such principle of competitive alternatives, the higher spectrum costs of competing private systems may not be adequately offset by rate reductions on the common carrier side.

One final place where a new look at the burden of proof in regulation is crucial relates to incumbents and newcomers. The practical tendency of regulation is to phase in changes gradually in ways least likely to disrupt the current state of affairs. Willy-nilly, regulators act to safeguard the substantial equities which incumbents derive from their past investments and the essentiality of their ongoing service. Special attempts are made to reconcile most significant reforms with financial stability of the existing regulated entities. That this is rationalized as safeguarding the wherewithal for adequate service is nowhere clearer than in the broadcast and common carrier fields.

But a major finding in Parts One, Two, and Three is that the newcomer should also have "standing." True, he has no past investments which his exclusion would impair. But that exclusion, in favor of the incumbents, may still impose serious economic costs on him. (See Chapters II, V.) Nor does the fact that the newcomer is not yet providing an essential service necessarily warrant his exclusion. It is all a matter of degree, and the costs and benefits must be balanced with care.

Exclusion may of course force the newcomer to show considerable ingenuity in innovative change. (Chapter VIII.) But there is a question at least as to whether these are the kinds of innovations that are economically desirable or most consistent with consumer welfare, or whether the spectrum is at best the kind of resource for whose rational and efficient development we can really rely entirely on unaided private innovation anyway. (Chapter IX.)

The effective articulation of opportunity costs (via auctions, rental charges, and shadow prices) could, in any case, prod the manager to explore new ways to reconcile more efficient spectrum utilization with other overriding national policy goals. The principle of temporary interim usage by secondary grantees is one such possibility. So far, the risks appear to have been all on one side. What the government mainly fears is that the incumbent's equity and standing due to past investments and current service will generate political forces that subvert regulatory action, priorities, and change. Normally, these are the risks that the government wants to avoid. But with new market-type constraints, the newcomer may also gain standing; and the risk of inconveniencing or sacrificing his interests may come to be weighed more judiciously in the regulatory process.

APPENDIXES

APPENDIX A—NOTES ON SELECTED TABLES AND CHARTS

TABLE 1 AND FIGURE 1

The typical uses of the major ITU frequency bands are derived from Joint Technical Advisory Committee, *Spectrum Engineering: The Key to Progress* (New York: Institute of Electrical and Electronics Engineers, 1968); a Frequency Spectrum Chart, appended at end of volume, is reprinted as Figure 1 in pocket at end of this book. Reference is also made to another publication of the Joint Technical Advisory Committee, *Radio Spectrum Utilization* (New York: Institute of Electrical and Electronics Engineers, 1965), pp. 214–15.

TABLE 14

Table 14 ranks 25 Land Mobile services according to the percentage of total transmitters in the services located in the Electronic Industries Association's "areas" with 50 per cent, 70 per cent, and 90 per cent of U.S. population, respectively.

The basic EIA table on which Table 14 is based was tabulated as follows. First, all 2,938 of the 30-minute by 30-minute areas into which the EIA Card Study divided the United States (EIA Communities) were ranked in descending order according to population size. The number of transmitters was then calculated for each area, by band of service, for each of 25 services. Finally, the number of areas containing each decile of U.S. population was ascertained next—starting with the most populous area. The EIA computer was also programmed to ascertain the percentage of transmitters in each of 25 Land Mobile services, located in each population decile, by band of service, again in descending order of EIA areas. For further discussion of the EIA Study, see Appendix B below.

TABLES 25 AND 26

Table 25 is adapted directly from Electronic Industries Association, Land Mobile Section, *Report to the Federal Communications Commission Concerning Licenses Issued to Land Mobile Radio Services as of June 1963* (Washington: EIA, 1964), Vol. I, Exhibit C. Table 26 is derived from estimates contained in Exhibit F, and more fully described in Appendix B, pp. 553–54.

FIGURE 2

The transmitter data were taken from FCC Annual Reports. Comparable series are normally available for the year 1935 and for the years 1947–66. GNP in constant prices and U.S. population from *Statistical Abstract of the United States.*

FIGURES 3 AND 4

Value of output of total electronics, consumer products, industrial products, government products, and replacement components, from *Electronic Industries Yearbook* (1967), p. 2. GNP in current prices from *Statistical Abstract.*

TABLES 35 AND 36

The positions summarized here are found in the following FCC proceedings: Authorized Users, Docket No. 16058; Early Bird Circuits, Docket No. 16070, File No. 1-CSS-L-65, et al.; Earth Station Ownership (plus interface issue), Docket No. 15735 RM-644; and Domestic Satellites, Docket No. 16495.

Not all entities tabulated entered each proceeding; nor do all participants always speak to each issue examined herein. Furthermore, where perusal of the several filings which individual participants normally made in each proceeding left their precise positions unclear but there is some general evidence, we have used parentheses to so signify. Parentheses are used also, as is self-evident, where the major position is further qualified by additional views.

TABLE 38

Data for "stations on the air" from Annual Reports of the Federal Communications Commission. Data for commercial stations "making usable financial reports" from FCC Annual Financial Reports for Television Broadcasting.

FIGURE 5

All AM broadcast financial data derived from FCC annual financial reports. Number of AM stations from FCC Annual Reports.

FIGURE 6

Time sales from FCC annual financial reports.

Figure 7

Number of AM, FM, and TV stations from FCC Annual Reports. All other series derived from *Sourcebook of Income Statistics* (Internal Revenue Service).

APPENDIX B—STATISTICAL ANALYSIS OF LAND MOBILE TRANSMITTERS

The main thrust of the regressions run on land mobile transmitters, and the principal conclusions derived therefrom, were set forth briefly in Chapter VIII. By way of further documentation this note will now restate more explicitly the variables under scrutiny and the form of the postulated relationships among them. A word is in order also on the problems and procedures of data compilation.

Multiple regression analysis permits us to estimate the relative importance of variations in two or more independent variables in explaining variations in one or more dependent variables. The main statistical task here has been to measure the degree to which variations in a cross-section of land mobile transmitters in different radio services are explained by variations in population and in the number and type of channels. Preliminary analysis of time series was also undertaken.

The tests performed can be described briefly as follows (exclusive of numerous exploratory runs).

I. Cross-Sectional Analysis, 1963
    A. Land Mobile Transmitters in 25 Major Population Centers

        Number of Regressions Run on Individual Services: 6
        Number of Observations per Regression: 75
        Variables Analyzed:

X_1 = number of transmitters	EIA Land Mobile Study
X_2 = size of population	Statistical Abstract
X_3 = number of mobile radio channels	EIA Land Mobile Study
X_4 = type of channel (scaled as 0, 1, 2)	EIA Land Mobile Study

    B. Land Mobile Transmitters per Channel in 25 Major Population Centers

        Number of Regressions Run on Individual Services: 6
        Number of Observations per Regression: 75
        Variables Analyzed:

X_1 = number of transmitters	EIA
X_2 = median family income*	Statistical Abstract
X_3 = population per square mile	Statistical Abstract
X_4 = channel type (scaled as 0, 1, 2)	EIA

II. Time Series Analysis, 1950–64
Number of Services for which First-Order Correlations
Computed: 16†
Number of Observations per Correlation: 15
Variables Analyzed:

X_1 = number of transmitters	EIA
X_2 = U.S. population	Statistical Abstract
X_3 = channel spacing	EIA

* An alternate set of regressions was also run with "value added by manufacture" as X_2.

† Plus three summary series.

The prime basic statistical source for all regressions here was the Electronic Industries Association, Land Mobile Section, *Report to the Federal Communications Commission Concerning Licenses Issued to the Land Mobile Radio Services as of June 1963* (November 1964) (cited hereafter as EIA *Land Mobile Study*). The EIA Study applied computer programming to 350,000 land mobile frequency cards on file with the FCC to make "a thorough study of the use of the [land mobile] frequency spectrum . . ." Specifically, EIA sought to ascertain the geographic distribution of licensed transmitters per channel, by all mobile radio services, by state and major metropolitan area. A second objective was to project probable future trends in "channel loading" on the basis of past trends.

Notwithstanding EIA's explicit acknowledgment (Vol. I, pp. 9–28) of several basic limitations of "transmitters per channel" as any adequate index of spectrum utilization (or congestion),[1] the study is still an invaluable mine of statistics in a field subject to massive obstacles to data collection. Indeed the industry's whole costly effort sought ostensibly to fill serious gaps in the data base on which emerging Commission policies should rightly be grounded. Early access to the Study enabled me to derive some series of usable data for a number of regressions which throw at least limited light on the issues reviewed in Chapter VIII. In the absence of more directly relevant data the study was a valuable place to start.

[1] See Electronic Industries Association, Land Mobile Section, *Report to the Communications Commission Concerning Licenses Issued to Land Mobile Radio Services as of June 1963* (Washington, D.C., 1964), Vol. I, pp. 9–28. According to EIA, an arithmetic tabulation of actual transmitters per channel "grossly overstates the number of channels available for licensing," especially in the major metropolitan centers. Among the factors which could limit the effective number of transmitters in use on any band, for any service, and in any area, are these: technical standards and hardware design; co-channel occupancy; proximity of broadcast stations, especially TV; sunspot activity; terrain; man-made noise; weather conditions.

CROSS-SECTIONAL ANALYSIS

The cross-sectional data presented a number of problems.

Transmitters

Much of the EIA Land Mobile Study (the bulk of Vol. I) focuses on 72 so-called "channel-loading" maps of the United States. This material includes separate maps for each of some 25 mobile radio services and for each band any service utilizes.[2] Separate symbols are superimposed throughout each map to convey visually the computer-estimated distribution of transmitters-per-channel, by service, band, and area.[3]

Because no summary statewide statistics were published, and none were readily available from EIA (without considerable expense in transforming them from the EIA tapes), I devised a simple procedure to utilize the symbols themselves. But it soon became apparent that the statewide data produced were either erroneous for mechanical reasons, seriously heterogeneous on other counts, or both. Accordingly, I focused instead on the data for 25 leading metropolitan centers.[4]

There, in an awkward form, were the estimated ranges of transmitters per channel licensed to each of 22 services, by band utilized. Using these estimates I calculated the total number of transmitters as mid-point of range times number of channels in the service, by city, by service. Transmitters were than introduced as the dependent variables (X_1) in six cross-sectional tests (see Table 12). In the remaining twelve cross-sectional tests, transmitters per channel data were used without further adjustment (Table 13). Judging from the statistical results (e.g., the substantial values of R^2), compared to those derived from preliminary analysis of the statewide data using the same independent variables, the EIA "population centers"[5] appear to be a more relevant area to analyze than the mere arbitrary administrative boundaries of a state.

[2] Ibid., Vol. I, Exhibit E.

[3] A grid network of ½ degree latitude and longitude lines was superimposed on a map of the U.S. Each of these squares represents an area of roughly 60 miles on each side. Letters are then used to indicate the average number of licensed transmitters per channel therein, and red dots are superimposed to indicate communities with populations of 5,000 or less (the minimum population associated with the need for land mobile radio service). The steps followed to program a computer for purposes of generating such channel-loading maps are set forth in detail in ibid., Vol. I, Exhibit D.

[4] Ibid., Vol. I, Exhibit F, Summary Maps.

[5] The 25 EIA major population centers appear to be larger than city units and most nearly comparable to standard metropolitan areas. However, in calculating the effective coverage areas of the top 25 metropolitan centers in 1960, adjustments were made in line with topographic and other information. For example, a transmitter atop a 6,500-foot mountain might enjoy a range up to 100 miles. (Ibid., Vol. I, pp. 24–25; also see Los Angeles Area Study, ibid., Vol. II, Exhibit H.)

For analytical purposes my final regressions were limited to services which operate within all three mobile radio bands. With three observations for each of the 25 EIA population centers, therefore, $N = 75$ in all regressions reported in Tables 12 and 13. The six services examined most intensively (and recorded there) include a representative sampling of land mobile radio usage: viz., special industrial, business, power, fire, local government, and motor-interurban property.

Channel Type

Channel Type refers to the three land mobile bands, Band A (at 50–74 Mc/s), Band B (at 150–174 Mc/s), and Band C (at 450–474 Mc/s). The task here was to scale the three bands in a dummy variable according to the probable degree to which they would facilitate spectrum utilization on sheer technical grounds.

As noted more fully in Chapter IX, the technical character of the three bands can be summarized as follows:

A. Band A, offering the longest range, is most useful in rural areas, but it is more vulnerable than Band B to i.terference from man-made noise and long-distance skip.

B. Band B provides a more reliable medium-range service and is therefore better suited than Band A for combined rural-urban (or suburban) needs.

C. Band C is best suited to meeting special urban needs, its range being the shortest and its service freest from interference.

D. Highest in the spectrum, however, and the most recently developed, Band C confronts more rigorous natural constraints than Bands A or B, with a technology that has had less time to develop and hardware costs which are higher.

Bearing in mind this general contrast I then sought to scale the three bands separately for each test depending on the special character of the service in question. In every case, Band C was scaled the "lowest" (0), as least propitious for land mobile usage mainly on grounds cited in point *D* above. The scaling of Bands A and B was more difficult but a judgment had to be reached for the purposes at hand.

Knowledge of the character of the services and bands in question provided a start but would not in this case suffice. Therefore the following procedure was devised. Two forms of the X_4 dummy variable were prepared, the first on the assumption that Band A was the most propitious for the service in question; the second, that Band B was the most propitious. Each form of X_4 was then introduced into a separate regression along with two other independent variables. Subsequently selected was the form of X_4 which produced the highest first-order correlation with X_1 (transmitters). In each of the 18 regressions whose results are summarized in Tables 12 and 13, this was the form of X_4 (and the scaling of channel type) that contributed most to the value of adjusted R^2.

In other words, the procedure insured that the dummy variable X_4 would be cast in the form most likely to remove any significant distortions in the principal regressions due to the heterogeneity of transmitter data drawn from three different bands. This would presumably enhance the reliability of the regression coefficients of X_2 on X_1, and X_3 on X_1.

Other Variables

The other variables introduced in different tests, for reasons stated in the text, included median family income, value added by manufacture, population, population per square mile. The data for these were all taken from standard statistical sources for the Standard Metropolitan Areas.

TIME SERIES ANALYSIS

Statistics on total U.S. transmitters, by service, 1950–64, are readily available in the EIA Study (Vol. II, Exhibit I) and the FCC's Annual Reports. EIA's simple regressions of population on transmitters in Exhibit K and the projections in Exhibit M are both suggestive of the basic relationships under scrutiny here. However, the data on channel bandwidth are far less reliable for the task at hand. Improved technical capabilities clearly underlie the FCC's successive actions to "split" the land mobile channels; but there are many obstacles to using reduced bandwidth as a proxy for technological change.

First, there is the difficulty of constructing a single index of channel spacing in a situation where the proportion of transmitters located in the Low, High, and Ultra High mobile radio bands varies considerably among the twenty-five land mobile services. Second, there is the problem of distinguishing between the time of an FCC decision to "split" the channels, and the time the industry actually puts the new standards into effect. The "phasing in—phasing out" process makes raw annual data on channel bandwidth far too crude an indicator for present purposes.

For such reasons I soon decided against undertaking any refined analysis of time series. Utilizing the raw data on channel spacing for the High Band only, the first-order correlation coefficients which follow (see Table B–1) must on all counts be interpreted with the greatest care. They are, however, superficially consistent with my cross-sectional regressions. Licensed transmitters appear to vary with rising population (as the ultimate source of demand for land mobile spectrum), and inversely with the width of channel spacing (reflective of technical knowhow). The analysis does not, of course, indicate the relative importance of either explanatory variable or the precise role of spectrum congestion in triggering the administrative actions to "split" the Land Mobile channels.

TABLE B–1. FIRST-ORDER CORRELATIONS BETWEEN LICENSED TRANSMITTERS, POPULATION AND CHANNEL SPACING, FOR SELECTED LAND MOBILE SERVICES, 1950–64

Type of service	Transmitters— population	Transmitters— channel spacing
Police	.9906	−.9281
Fire	.9940	−.8519
Forestry-conservation	.9730	−.9122
Highway maintenance	.9851	−.8484
Special emergency	.9724	−.8797
Power	.9866	−.9100
Petroleum	.9877	−.8742
Forest products	.9962	−.8864
Relay press	.9967	−.8688
Motion picture	.9844	−.8895
Business	.8660	−.6074
Special industrial	.9885	−.8498
Railroad	.9823	−.8167
Urban transit	.9209	−.8772
Taxicabs	.9243	−.7676
Auto emergency	.9850	−.8291
Total, public safety	.9968	−.8699
Total, land transportation	.9913	−.8484
Total, industrial	.9684	−.7771

Source: See text.
Note: $N = 15$; theoretical value of r ($n = 13$, $P = .01$) = .6411.

APPENDIX C—REGRESSION ANALYSIS OF TV STATION SALE PRICES

The main statistical task here has been to measure the degree to which variations in a sample of TV station sale prices are explained by variations in TV homes, age of station, network affiliation, average daily circulation, number of stations in market, authorized signal power, and original cost of assets. The relative power of each independent variable to explain the dependent variable is estimated, holding constant all other independent variables.

The stepwise regression technique was essential here in view of the large number of variables being tested. By permitting the computer to determine the order in which the independent variables enter, we ensure an ordering reflective of the relative size of each one's contribution to the coefficient of multiple determination, *at each step in the analysis.* This enables us to ascertain the point at which the contributions are no longer significant, as well as the relative explanatory power of each variable at each step.

ANALYSIS IN TABLE 43

The variables analyzed and the form of the analysis will now be described.

Sale Prices

Notwithstanding their potential value for appraising industry behavior, TV station sale prices are among the least accessible economic data. The FCC rarely compiles such statistics at all. On the few occasions when it has done so, the crude form of the data has posed very real problems to any investigator without large sums to spend for basic compilation purposes. For that reason I am indebted to two industry consulting organizations[1] whose research has produced a set of basic statistics compiled for quite different purposes. Without these data my own analysis could never have been conducted.

The analysis of 68 sale prices summarized in Table 43 was based in part on materials prepared by Checchi and Co. in 1959.[2] These sales all took place in the years 1956–59, as recorded in *Television Factbook* at the time. The original listing included all CBS and NBC affiliates sold during the period, together with many ABC affiliates and some independents. I eliminated a few cases rendered useless by gaps in the data needed to fill out the independent variables in the analysis.

The Commission's Transfer and Renewal File was utilized extensively in the original listing to make the prices comparable in all major regards. The procedure followed was threefold. First, in cases where the sale included AM and/or FM stations as well as TV, but where only a combined price was recorded for the package, the TV portion was allocated according to the ratio of the TV station's one-minute spot rate to the sum of the TV and the radio station's spot rate. Second, where a 100 per cent ownership interest was transferred, all cash and noncash

---

[1] Checchi and Co., of Washington, D.C., and United Research, Inc., of Cambridge, Mass.

[2] *Statistical Appendix to Analysis of TV Station Sales, 1956–1959,* prepared for Fly, Shuebruk, Blume, and Gaguine, May 1959, who released it to me.

components in the transaction were combined to secure a total price. Finally, where less than a 100 per cent interest was transferred, the calculated price, inclusive of all cash and noncash items, was projected accordingly to estimate a 100 per cent ownership transfer price.

The Hypothesis

As noted in Chapter XIII, the hypothesis under scrutiny is that the level of TV station sale prices varies, with both the size of the station's market and its competitive position therein. Presumably prices will be higher, the larger the number of TV homes in the market and the fewer the sellers competing to reach them. The Commission's licensing policy would affect both sets of determinants: the former, by permitting or refusing entry by any licensees into markets of varying sizes or viability; the latter, by setting limits on the number of competing sellers.

In analyzing variations in the level of sale prices (X_1), I defined the relevant market to include all counties for which each station reached at least 10 per cent of the families with TV sets once a week. I then estimated total TV homes in the market (X_2) and the station's average daily circulation (X_5) as indexes of total potential and actual audiences, respectively.[3] These variables are of crucial importance to advertisers in their media budgeting.

Age of Station

Two dummy variables, age of station (X_3) and network affiliation (X_4), were introduced next as two other major determinants of sale price. In regard to the former, it is well known that the cessation of the issuance of new TV licenses during the period 1948–52 enabled 108 VHF pioneers to entrench themselves in the largest urban markets and to earn exceptional earnings ever since. To ascertain the influence of this factor all stations were scaled in X_3 according to whether they had commenced operations before 1952 (1) or after 1951 (2). Our further assumption here was that the older stations are more likely to have choice advertising and network affiliations, and to have built up a loyal audience following.

---

[3] All data on TV homes and average daily circulation were derived from A.C. Nielsen's confidential *NCS Complete Circulation and Audience Reports*, No. 2 (Spring 1956) and No. 3 (Spring 1958). These data, and data for all other variables examined, were all placed as close as possible to the actual date of the sale in question.

Network Affiliation

Network affiliation is another well-known determinant of station profitability and hence of sale price. The network affiliation contract has been called a station's most valuable economic asset. It guarantees a steady source of popular programming and advertising revenues even before markets and stations become established economically. However the two major networks—CBS and NBC—have until recently outstripped the third network, ABC. Hence stations have normally sought to affiliate with one of the two major networks. However, where this is not possible (in markets with three or more stations), they have preferred an ABC affiliation to no affiliation at all. In the smaller markets, with one or two stations, each station is pretty sure of a major network tie, although ABC has not been sure of a primary affiliate. Under existing network rules, affiliations would be shared in these cases. Some stations thereby gain ties with two networks or with all three.

To ascertain the power of network affiliation as a factor explaining sale prices, the stations in the sample were scaled according to whether they had ties with a major network (1), a major network plus ABC (2), ABC or no network (3). This would avoid any distortion that might result from a more detailed scaling in a sample this small. It also provides three groups of comparable size.[4]

Other Variables

Two other characteristic FCC-imposed constraints were introduced in the form of authorized signal power (X_7) and number of stations in the market (X_6). Holding other factors constant, one would normally expect audience size, profitability and sale price to vary directly with signal power, and inversely with the number of stations in the market. However the interpretation of the relation between these variables is really more complex, as noted in the text.

Lastly, original cost of assets (X_8) was introduced as a final determinant of sale price. Here the question was whether variations in the cost of physical plant (including studio, transmitter, antenna, etc.)

---

[4] The above-cited scaling of "network affiliation" and "age of station" would lead us to expect a negative regression coefficient if these factors were indeed significant—i.e., if the older stations and those with preferred (major) network ties did sell for higher prices. The reverse scaling in another set of regressions cited below (by URI) would imply a positive coefficient if the same factors were significant. For example, URI scaled the older stations as 2, and the newer ones as 1, whereas I scaled the older ones as 1 and the newer ones as 2.

would help significantly to explain variations in sale prices, when all other factors are taken into account.

In sum, the variables analyzed are these:
X_1 = TV station sale price
X_2 = TV homes in market
X_3 = Age of station as related to TV "freeze" (dummy)
X_4 = Network status (dummy)
X_5 = Average daily circulation of station
X_6 = Number of stations in market
X_7 = Authorized signal power
X_8 = Original cost of assets

The general form of the estimating equation is:
$$\log X_1 = a + b_2 \log X_2 - b_3 X_3 - b_4 X_4 + b_5 \log X_5 - b_6 X_6 - b_7 \log X_7 + b_8 \log X_8.$$

For reasons cited in the text, estimating equation number 5 in Table 43 is the most pertinent for our purposes:
$$\log X_1 = 5.5635 + .4180 \log X_2 - .7647 X_3 - .2330 X_4 + .3661 \log X_5 - .0961 X_6.$$

The most relevant elasticities in this equation, holding constant the dummy variables, are these:

For every 10 per cent rise in	Sale price changes
TV homes	+4.2%
Circulation	+3.7%
Number of stations	−0.1%

URI Multiple Regressions on TV Station Sale Prices[5]

As noted in Chapter XIII, United Research, Inc. prepared a number of regressions on sale price, the results of which are at least broadly consistent with those reviewed in this Appendix, and summarized in text Table 43. For the reader's convenience I shall include some of the most pertinent URI findings, leaving him to seek out more details in FCC Docket No. 16068 where the full study appears.

The URI analysis was based on all major station sales recorded in *Television Factbook* (No. 36) for the years 1949–65. To ensure com-

---

[5] As economic consultant to United Research, Inc. (1965–66) on a study of TV Group Ownership, I worked extensively with URI's Chief Statistician, Mrs. Rose Kneznek, in designing a set of regressions on sale prices. That study drew heavily on my earlier work which was published in the *Journal of Political Economy* (April 1964) and elaborated in Chapter XIII and earlier in this Appendix. A summary of URI procedures and key results appears in the public record in FCC Docket No. 16068, United Research, Inc., *The Implications of Limiting Multiple Ownership of Television Stations* (October 1966), especially Vol. II, Appendix H.

parability, we eliminated all UHF sales, and sales involving more than one TV station plus one radio station. Some other sales were also eliminated where deficiencies were encountered in the published data on TV homes in the station's market, network affiliation, type of ownership of buyer, and seller at time of sale.

To preclude any distortion due to heterogeneity resulting from the inclusion of sales which include a radio station, or of those which involve less than 100 per cent of the stock, we grouped all VHF sales as follows:

Type A: 100 per cent ownership transfer, with all cash and non-cash elements combined to secure a total price.

Type B: transfer of less than 100 per cent but more than 50 per cent interest, with calculated price (including all cash and noncash items) adjusted to project a 100 per cent owner-ship transfer price.

Type C: TV station sales where an AM and/or FM station in-cluded in sale and only a combined price for the package was available, but where TV portion of package is pre-sumed to account for bulk of combined price.

The URI study worked extensively with the following variables:

X_1 = TV station sale prices
X_2 = TV homes in market
X_3 = Age of station
X_4 = Network affiliation
X_5 = Type of owner

Depending on data availability, separate tests were run for all markets and for major market groupings (top 50, top 100); for all sales (A + B + C); and for each of the three classes of sales separately.

Several dummy variables had to be introduced, and these were scaled as follows:

Type of owner: group owner, 2; nongroup owner, 1
Age of station: on air before 1952, 2; on air after 1951, 1
Network affiliation: 4 = primary tie with CBS or NBC
                      3 = primary tie with a major network and ABC or DuMont
                      2 = primary tie with ABC or DuMont
                      1 = independent (nonaffiliated)

In each test the general form of the estimating equation was:

$$X_1 = a + b_2X_2 + b_3X_3 + b_4X_4 + b_5X_5.$$

The results most pertinent to the problems under scrutiny here appear in Table C–1.

TABLE C–1. SELECTED RESULTS OF STEPWISE REGRESSIONS ON TV STATION SALE PRICES (URI)

Variables[a]	Regression coefficient	Standard regression coefficient	Significance	N	R^2 (adjusted for degrees of freedom)[d]
1. All sales (types A + B + C)—All markets (Av. sales price = \$2,710,500)					
TV homes	3.7098	0.5604	.01		
Age of station	12.5956	0.1595	.02		
Network affiliation	442.6682	0.1443	.02		
Type of seller	320.7540	0.0484	below .05	198	0.4062
2. All sales (types A + B + C)—Top 50 markets (Av. sales price = \$4,879,500)					
TV homes	3.0731	0.4913	.01		
Network affiliation	1080.0636	0.2918	.02		
Type of seller	995.5662	0.1146	below .05		
Age of station	4.6273	0.0492	below .05	64	0.2879
3. All sales (types A + B + C)—Top 100 markets (Av. sales price = \$3,833,500)					
TV homes	2.9949	0.4691	.01		
Age of station	16.3104	0.1936	.05		
Network affiliation[b]	521.5431	0.1643	below .05		
Type of seller	303.8216	0.0400	below .05	110	0.3367
4. Type A sales—All markets (Av. sales price = \$2,710,000)					
TV homes	3.3282	0.6571	.01		
Age of station[c]	11.2077	0.1643	below .05		
Type of seller	768.4656	0.1305	below .05		
Network affiliation	155.8537	0.0608	below .05	64	0.5466
5. Type B sales—All markets (Av. sales price = \$2,662,000)					
TV homes	3.0886	0.5017	.01		
Network affiliation	1010.1273	0.2798	.05		
Type of seller	1681.2164	0.2294	below .05		
Age of station	9.6155	0.0912	below .05	46	0.2668
6. Type C sales—All markets (Av. sales price = \$2,736,500)					
TV homes	5.6094	0.5874	.01		
Age of station	16.2302	0.2090	.05		
Type of seller	−476.0788	−0.0706	below .05		
Network affiliation	185.7948	0.0543	below .05	88	0.4613
7. Type A sales (Av. sales price = \$3,316,500)					
Net weekly circulation	5.0483	0.7389	.01		
Age of station	9.4040	0.1256	below .05		
Type of seller	421.3093	0.0645	below .05		
Network affiliation	−32.9666	−0.0120	below .05	35	0.6342
8. Type C sales (Av. sales price = \$3,553,000)					
Net weekly circulation	21.9427	0.9065	.01		
Age of station	10.5541	0.0879	below .05		
Network affiliation	−272.1245	−0.0654	below .05		
Type of seller	431.3476	0.0618	below .05	34	0.7663

[a] All variables listed in each test in order of relative explanatory power.

[b] Significant at Step 3 at .05 level.

[c] Significant at Step 2 at .01 level.

[d] All values of R^2 significant at .01 level.

Any detailed comparison of the URI results with those summarized in Table 43 is unnecessary for our purposes. Suffice it to note that the category of "TV homes" clearly and consistently has the greatest relative impact, except in tests 7 and 8 where net weekly circulation is used instead and produces even better results. The relative impact of age of station and network affiliation varies somewhat from test to test. However at least one of them emerges as significant, too, in all but one of the first six tests and there, too (test 4), one of them is significant at a prior step in the analysis. The consistently higher values for $\bar{R}^2$ in the successive equations 1–5, probably reflect the nonlinear distribution of data for certain variables. In my earlier study, but not URI's, those variables were transformed into logarithmic form.

The reader may want to probe these issues more deeply in the cited source. Suffice it here to note only these few high points of a more extensive study, conducted for other purposes, as broadly corroborative of findings based on my more limited sample, drawn from a shorter time period.

APPENDIX D—INCUMBENTS, NEWCOMERS, SPECTRUM COSTS, AND RENTAL CHARGES

The purpose of this Appendix note is to set forth more systematically than in Chapter V the relations between incumbents, newcomers, spectrum costs, and rental charges. The note bears also on issues raised in Chapter VIII as to the potential effects of rental charges on the pattern of spectrum development.

In the formulation that follows, the note attempts to structure the issues confronting spectrum management-cum-allocation in ways that point out fruitful areas where those with line authority may want to develop rules of thumb.[1] Without attempting to develop any specific formula for a rental charge, the note will analyze instead the probable effects on spectrum allocation (and development) of a charge related to the costs incurred through exclusion from designated spectrum.

It will be convenient first to identify a number of key variables:

S = incumbent
N = newcomer
F = frequency space occupied by incumbent and sought by newcomer
C_1 = incumbent's current costs of operation

---

[1] This formulation emerged in several discussions with John V. Krutilla.

V_1 = present value of F to incumbent

*C_1 = incumbent's operating cost with a next-best alternative (another frequency, a wire mode, the use of transportation, storage space or labor instead of radio, etc.)

*V_1 = value to incumbent of his best alternative input

C_2 = costs imposed on newcomer by exclusion from F

V_2 = present value of F to newcomer

*C_2 = cost of newcomer's best alternative input

*V_2 = value of newcomer's best alternative input

Now, let the options open to incumbent and newcomer under spectrum management practice be as follows:

1. Incumbent may squat.
2. Incumbent may vacate.
3. Incumbent may share.
4. Incumbent may lend.
5. Newcomer may reimburse incumbent to induce him to vacate, share, or lend.
6. Newcomer may turn to a next-best alternative.

Finally, let there be two procedural rules under which the above options must be exercised:

Rule I: Incumbent may, but need not, vacate, share, or lend spectrum for reimbursement of his adjustments costs by newcomer.

Rule II: If incumbent will not adjust for this cost reimbursement, he must then pay "rent" to the spectrum manager equal to the extra costs imposed on newcomer through exclusion.

The regulatory import of the two rules can be contrasted as follows: Under Rule I:

1. Incumbent may squat.

2. But newcomer would be willing to pay him to move, share, or lend the F-space in question, provided these cost reimbursements fell short of the newcomer's extra costs due to exclusion.

3. Incumbent would accept this payment provided that these cost reimbursements (and hence newcomer's costs due to exclusion) just exceeded the value of F to incumbent. Otherwise, incumbent would prefer to squat, and newcomer would be forced elsewhere (bearing his own costs due to exclusion). Only where the latter costs (C_2) exceed the value of F to incumbent (V_1) would incumbent vacate, share, or lend, exacting his full monopoly rent at that point. Only at that point, moreover, would incumbent yield F to the "better" user and thus increase the efficiency of spectrum utilization.

Under Rule II:

1. Here incumbent may squat provided he pays "rent" (to the spectrum manager) equal to newcomer's extra costs (C_2). That is, incumbent may vacate, share, or lend F (and be reimbursed for his trouble); or he may refuse to do so, but must then pay the "rent" instead.

2. Where newcomer's extra costs (C_2) exceed the value of F to incumbent (V_1), then incumbent would move under *either* rule. Likewise, where V_1 exceeds C_2, incumbent would *not* move. But under Rule II, when latter chooses to squat, he will retain only the *difference* between V_1 and C_2. That is, he will be deprived of part of his economic rent when he pays spectrum manager a sum equal to newcomer's extra costs due to exclusion. (Under Rule I, incumbent would retain the full value of F to him, V_1, when choosing to squat, with newcomer forced to pay his own exclusionary costs, C_2.)

3. We have so far assumed that $V_1 = {}^*V_1 = V_2 = {}^*V_2$; but that $C_1 \neq {}^*C_1 \neq C_2 \neq {}^*C_2$. The question is whether the newcomer will be allowed to share, acquire, or borrow F to do the *same* thing that he now does, more cheaply; or be forced to do it elsewhere, at greater cost. And also whether the incumbent will be forced to vacate and go elsewhere at higher cost *to him* to do the same thing, but at a lower *increment* to his costs than to newcomer's costs were *he* excluded. In either case, the use of Rule II should act to (a) improve the utilization of F; and (b) reduce incumbent's monopoly rent.

Let us now consider briefly the bargaining range within which the result is indeterminate under Rule I but determinate under Rule II (and presumably under competitive bidding). Note, that is, the sense in which Rule II provides an administrative equivalent of competitive bidding, no small consideration in that multiple bids may not be forthcoming and bargaining may therefore occur within a fairly wide range.

Basically, the incumbent's range of discretion is greater under Rule I than under Rule II. Under Rule I, only when C_2 exceeds V_1 will he vacate, for only at that point would he exact his full monopoly rent. To be sure, incumbent might feel constrained to settle for something short of that because of pressures in the regulatory arena for him to be "reasonable." However, incumbent's "unreasonableness," and the concomitant pressures on him to adjust, would emerge only where he and newcomer could both use F equally well *and* where incumbent's cost of adjustment was substantially less than the costs he would impose on newcomer by refusing to adjust. Holding out for the full monopoly rent (until C_2 exceeds V_1) would in that case cast incumbent in a highly unfavorable light. Although a full divulgence of these facts might constrain him to settle somewhere short of that point, the precise point is indeterminate under the stated assumptions.

Under Rule II, however, the solution will be determinate: incumbent will move if, but only if, the difference between $*V_1$ and $*C_1$ exceeds the difference between V_1 and C_2; or, under the postulated assumptions, where C_2 exceeds C_1. For clearly, whether or not he adjusts, incumbent's rents will be reduced from what he would have retained under Rule I. So that the question is only what decision will minimize the extent of the reduction.

When C_2 exceeds C_1, incumbent will accept C_2 as reimbursement for his adjustment costs if, but only if, the net value he can expect to retain with his next-best alternative exceeds what he would retain by standing fast (and paying "rent" equal to newcomer's exclusionary cost instead). That is, incumbent will adjust when $*V_1 - *C_1 > V_1 - C_2$. Under the postulated assumptions, this will be true whenever C_2 exceeds C_1.

On the other hand, whenever incumbent's *new* costs ($*C_1$) exceed newcomer's *current* costs due to exclusion (C_2), incumbent will stand fast and pay "rent" equal to C_2, as a less costly alternative than adjusting himself. Once more, the solution is determinate. But once more, too, incumbent retains only V_1 minus C_2, which, while it may exceed $*V_1$ minus $*C_1$, is still less than he would have retained under Rule I. It is presumably closer, too, to what he would have retained in a competitive market for spectrum.

The rudiments of this conception can be related also to the level of spectrum development (as reviewed in Chapter VIII). Under Rule II, at some point a rise in C_2 will just make it worthwhile for incumbent to invest in intensive (or extensive) spectrum development. For at that point he would expect the innovative activity to enable him to adjust at newcomer's expense and also to avoid having to reimburse newcomer for C_2. Under Rule I, incumbent might also invest in this fashion, but only when C_2 exceeds V_1. Therefore, the likelihood is less under Rule II than under Rule I that the level of spectrum development will be retarded until incumbent exacts his full monopoly rent. By the same token, the imposition of Rule II would provide incentives for innovative activity by incumbent comparable to those presently imposed on newcomer by the extra costs due to exclusion. As suggested in Chapter VIII, finally, the result should be a more equitable and economically rational distribution of the burden of spectrum development as between new-comers and incumbents at large.

APPENDIX E—EMPIRICAL PROBLEMS IN THE ANALYSIS OF EFFECTIVE VIEWER CHOICES

Long-standing interest by government and industry officials in the concept and measurement of program diversity derives largely from broadcasting's special economic-regulatory framework. At play here are the technical barriers to new station entry, the absence of relative demand prices for particular program outputs, and the sensitivity of all parties to direct intrusions on programming by industry and government alike. At issue also are cleavages among informed experts on the precise ingredients of a program mix suitable for democratic social-political processes, and the government's reluctance to impose minority preferences on the majority.

Any quantitative study of program diversity and choice must at some point consider the programming itself, and the costs and methodological risks of using it. Reference must of course be made to the necessarily arbitrary character of program classification schema and principles of allocation, as well as the related need to guard against investigatory bias. Hitherto neglected data which economists could more fruitfully cooperate with behavioral scientists in analyzing include the quarter-hours of broadcast time devoted to specific program types and subtypes. Using such data, the relation between viewer choices and the number and types of stations on the air could be analyzed by at least two methods.

One approach would require answers to questions like these: For any set of TV program logs, drawn from all stations in a sample of markets, throughout a representative broadcast week, how does the share of program time devoted to major selected program types vary with changes in cogent independent variables? How, e.g., do program prime time shares vary for any and all such program types, say, with changing numbers of commercial stations in the market? With the addition of a public television station? By market size? By net weekly circulation per station in the market?

The task of compilation would be costly and time-consuming, but once the data are in hand quantitative answers should not be hard to produce. Interpretation is another matter, and one beset with more intractable problems. There we must consider the bearing of the cited regularities on (a) the character and determinants of program duplication and diversity more generally; (b) variations in the level of program standards as such. Does marked stability in program time shares indicate growing program duplication as the number of stations rises? Would systematic changes in the time shares suggest increased diversity and choice? And/or any alteration of program standards relative to minority taste group preferences?

One trouble with such a study is that reporting the full array of time shares information for a substantial breakdown of program types, separately, by number and type of station and market size, would produce a bewildering mass of results from which it would be impossible to draw any but the most general conclusions. Yet to calculate the mean values of the program time shares of selected groups of specific program types, assigned to a few overall program categories, might well mask intertype shifts as the number and type of stations vary.

A more direct analysis of viewer choices, and some simplifying statistical construct are clearly needed. A second approach, therefore, is to construct an operational Index of Diversity that quantifies the program mix available in any and all markets and implies thereby the range of viewer choices. Once again, does the Index vary with changes in the number and type of stations? With market size? With net weekly circulation per station? Of what relative importance in explaining its behavior are changes in the number of commercial stations compared to changes in net weekly circulation per station? Changes in the number of commercial vs. public television stations? Answers to these and similar questions will take us a good step forward in essential fact-gathering for rational spectrum management in the broadcast field. But here too, serious problems will remain.

As noted in Chapter XIII, H. Land Associates constructed such a Diversity Index under commission by the National Association of Broadcasters, for transmittal to the Rostow Communications Task Force in July 1968.[1] However Land Associates did not explicitly estimate effective viewer choices at each and every point in the broadcast week. Nor did their Index demonstrably imply this range, though it did quantify the program mix in the full-time and nighttime TV schedules.

Briefly, Land Associates defined the Diversity Index as a weighted mean rank of program categories in the market using the number of broadcast hours as weights. Specifically, $DI = \frac{\Sigma rh}{\Sigma h}$, wherein "$r$ is the rank

[1] H. Land Associates, *Television and the Wired City* (Washington: National Association of Broadcasters, 1968).

(1–20) in the particular market for any program classification, determined by ordering categories according to total broadcast time devoted to each (during a sample week); and *h* is the number of half-hours of programming time devoted to the category."[2] Because this Diversity Index was based on the distribution of programs within the twenty defined categories, low values indicated concentration toward the most popular types, and high values greater equality of time to the less popular types, of greater interest to minority groups.

Though a useful advance, this approach also has its own problems. Conceivably, low diversity as thus measured would be consistent with significant viewer choices on an hour-by-hour basis. Suppose that each station in a two-station market carries the identical number of 30-minute units of four selected program types. Because the program rankings (and the weights) are the same for both stations, the Land Index would indicate zero diversity. But suppose the stations actually staggered the 30-minute periods during which they broadcast any common program type, such that viewers in each period during the week had a choice of two different types. One could then say that viewers had gotten the *maximum* effective choice; that is, two different program types for each 30-minute period, or 70 "actual" choices out of 70 "potential" choices.

The Land Index is probably not as unrelated to the facts of viewers' choices as this extreme example suggests. Nor would even unusual regulatory constraints normally induce profit-maximizing stations to stagger their programs in this manner. However it does seem essential (a) to cast a Diversity Index into a form more responsive to the measurement of hourly viewer choices; (b) in so doing, to employ other independently compiled program data; and (c) given the hazards of investigatory bias in the classificatory and allocation schema used, preferably to employ a different though related set of program types. It would then be interesting to see how such a Coefficient of Viewer Choice responds to postulated variations in the number and type of stations, market size, net weekly circulation, etc.

As a start, one could define the coefficient as $\frac{\Sigma P_o}{\Sigma P_t}$, where $P_o =$ the total number of program choices that stations in each market generate, and viewers enjoy, during some series of arbitrarily defined time periods; and where $P_t =$ the maximum number of choices viewers *could* have if each period were filled by each station with a program type different from that simultaneously broadcast by all other stations in the market. The coefficient would in that case vary between the reciprocal of the

---

[2] Ibid., pp. 37–38.

number of stations in the market (perfect duplication), and one (perfect diversity).[3]

After a preliminary inquiry into its relation with the above-cited independent variables, alternative versions of the coefficient could be formulated and tested, and the specific form and number of the explanatory variables also recast with an eye on still other regulatory constraints. One promising possibility might be to focus on the *absolute number* of viewer choices and then, holding constant market size, to isolate the relative impact of the programming broadcast by public television and by commercial stations classified as independent and network-affiliated, single and group-owned, newspaper- and nonnewspaper-owned, etc.[4]

---

[3] This formulation is closer to P. Steiner's "Coefficient of Diversification" than to the Land Index. Steiner's Coefficient is $1 - \dfrac{D}{X-1}$, where X, the number of stations, must be at least two; and where D, the amount of duplication, is defined as "the difference between the number of stations and the number of program types being produced." (See P. Steiner, "Program Patterns and Preferences, and the Workability of Competition in Radio Broadcasting," *Quarterly Journal of Economics*, May 1952, pp. 199–201.)

[4] The author's preliminary results from using this approach were presented at the 1970 Meetings of the American Economic Association in a paper entitled, "Program Duplication, Diversity, and Effective Viewer Choices."

GLOSSARY OF SELECTED
TECHNICAL TERMS AND ABBREVIATIONS

Absorption: The irreversible conversion of the energy of a radio wave into other forms of energy as a result of interaction with matter.

Aeronautical fixed service: A fixed service intended for the transmission of information relating to air navigation, preparation for and safety of flight.

Aeronautical mobile (R) frequencies: Frequencies used by air carrier aircraft on established air routes. The designation "(R)" indicates "on route." "(OR)" indicates "off route."

Aeronautical mobile service: A mobile service between aeronautical stations and aircraft stations, or between aircraft stations, in which survival craft stations may also participate.

Aircraft radiotelephone identification: Method of identifying an aircraft by use of radiotelephony, generally, though not necessarily, the call sign.

Amateur service: A service of self-training, intercommunication, and technical investigation carried on by amateurs; that is, by duly authorized persons interested in radio technique solely with a personal aim and without pecuniary interest.

Amplitude modulation (AM): Transmission of information by varying the amplitude (strength) of a radio signal, the earliest form of broadcasting. Broadcast and shortwave stations as well as certain classes of nonbroadcasting stations use AM.

ARPA: Advanced Research Projects Agency.

Assigned frequency band: The frequency band the center of which coincides with the frequency assigned to the station and the width of which equals the necessary bandwidth plus twice the absolute value of the *frequency tolerance* as a means of protecting signal quality.

Attenuation: A general term used to denote a decrease in magnitude in transmission from one point to another. It may be expressed as a ratio.

AUTODIN: An automatic communications network, using private lines, that transmits digital data for the Department of Defense. Abbreviation for "automatic digital data network." See *Private line service.*

409

Band: Used as applying to a group of radio frequencies assigned to a particular type of radio service, a range of frequencies (per second) within two definite limits.

Bandwidth: The band of frequencies comprising 99 per cent of the total radiated power of a transmitter plus any discrete frequency on which the power is at least 0.25 per cent of the total radiated power.

Bit: Single, smallest element of information in computer technology.

Broadcasting: Dissemination of radio communication intended to be received by the public, directly or through relay stations.

Carrier wave (carrier):   The wave whose amplitude, frequency, or phase is to be varied or modulated to transmit a signal. See *Modulation.*

CARS: Community Antenna Relay Service. A microwave service owned by a *CATV* system for the purpose of bringing in television signals for use over the system.

CATV: Community Antenna Television. System by which television signals are collected at a central point and distributed to subscribers by wire, for a flat fee. Differs from *Pay-TV*, which has scrambled signals that must be decoded for reception.

CCIR: International Radio Consultative Committee (Comité Consultative Internationale Radio). An international committee formed to study radiofrequency assignment problems.

CCITT: International Telegraph and Telephone Consultative Committee.

Channel: That segment of the radiofrequency spectrum assigned to an individual station. The width will vary according to the type of transmission, ranging from a few cycles for telegraphy to several million cycles for television and radar. Center of channel is station's assigned frequency.

Channel splitting: Reducing the width of individual channels to permit two or more stations to operate in the space previously used by one.

Class I station: A dominant standard broadcast (AM) station operating on a clear channel and designed to render primary and secondary service over an extended area and at relatively long distances. Its primary service area is free from objectionable interference from other stations on the same and adjacent channels, and its secondary service area free from interference except from stations on adjacent channels and from stations on the same channel in accordance with the channel designation in Section 73.25 or 73.182 of FCC Rules. Operating power shall not be less than 10 kw nor more than 50 kw.

Class II station: A standard broadcast (AM) secondary station which operates on a clear channel and is designed to render service over a primary service area which is limited by and subject to such interference as may be received from Class I stations. Whenever necessary, a Class II station shall use a directional antenna or other means to avoid interference with Class I stations and with other Class II stations.

Class III station: A standard broadcast (AM) station which operates on a regional channel and is designed to render service primarily to a principal center of population and the adjacent rural area.

Clear channel: Nationwide AM broadcast channel set aside for long-distance transmission mainly by a few high-powered stations. One special group of these channels is reserved for one or two powerful stations each, which serve very extensive areas free from objectionable interference.

Coast station: A land station in the maritime mobile service.

Co-channel: Use of the same channel by stations located in different geographical areas. Not to be confused with *"Sharing."*

Communications common carrier: Firm, organization, or individual making wire or electronic communications services available for hire.

ComSat: Communications Satellite Corporation. Entity created by the Communications Satellite Act of 1962 to establish and manage the U.S. segment of a global satellite system.

Contour: A line drawn on a map connecting points of equal signal strength (field strength contours) or points of equal elevation above sea level (elevation contour).

Cross talk: Electrical disturbances in a communication channel as a result of coupling with other communication channels.

DASA: Defense Atomic Support Agency.

DME: Distance-Measuring Equipment. A radio system for measuring distances en route to an aircraft's terminal area.

DTM: Director of Telecommunications Management. The official responsible for overall telecommunications policy within the Executive Branch; also serves as Special Assistant to the President for Telecommunications; heads Office of Telecommunications Management, which is FCC counterpart for federal government communications. On April 22, 1970, his duties were transferred to the Director of a newly created Office of Telecommunications Policy, also located in the Executive Branch.

Daytime-only stations: AM radio stations restricted to operation between local sunrise and sunset.

Double sideband (DSB): Transmission with two sidebands. See *Sideband* and *Single sideband.*

Early Bird: ComSat's Early Capability Satellite System. An initial developmental and operational synchronous satellite relay, orbited over the Atlantic on April 6, 1965, and phased out of regular commercial service 43 months later.

Earth station: A station in the earth-space service located either on the earth's surface or on an object which is limited to flight between points on the earth's surface.

Earth-space service: A radiocommunication service between earth stations and space stations.

Electromagnetic compatibility: The capability of electronic equipments or systems to be operated in the intended operational electromagnetic environment at designed levels of efficiency.

Emission: Production of radiation by a radio transmitting system; radiation produced.

Facsimile: A system of telecommunication for the transmission of fixed images, with or without half-tones, with a view to their reproduction in a permanent form.

FAS: Frequency Assignment Subcommittee of the Interdepartment Radio Advisory Committee (IRAC).

FCC: Federal Communications Commission.

Field strength: The strength of a radio signal at any given location. Usually expressed in microvolts per meter or millivolts per meter.

Fixed service: A service of radiocommunication between specified fixed points. Sometimes called "point-to-point" service.

Frequency: In communication circuits, the number of times per second an alternating current or voltage goes through a complete cycle.

Frequency allocation: The designation of frequencies (or frequency bands) to be used in particular geographical areas without specifying the radio stations which are to be assigned such frequencies.

Frequency assignment: The assignment of a specific radio frequency (or frequency band) for use by a particular radio station.

Frequency modulation (FM):   Transmission of information by varying the frequency of a radio signal. Operating in the VHF spectrum just above TV channel 6, FM broadcasts are characterized by high-quality sound, freedom from manmade and natural static, and absence of long-distance interference. FM also is used for the sound portion of television and most of the nonbroadcast services.

Frequency tolerance: The maximum permissible departure either by the center frequency of the frequency band occupied by an emission from the assigned frequency or by the characteristic frequency of an emission from the reference frequency. A precondition of acceptable signal quality.

Gateway cities: The major coastal cities where the international common carriers have normally had their headquarters and facilities for picking up traffic from domestic carriers for overseas transmission or for delivering overseas traffic to such entities. See *Interface*.

Geneva Radio Regulations: A multilateral international agreement to which the U.S. is a party and signatory country. The regulations prescribe the use and allocation of radio frequencies.

Gigacycles per second (Gc/s):   Unit of frequency equal to one billion cycles per second. Also known as GigaHertz (one billion Hertz).

Grandfather rights: From time to time FCC changes its rules and makes certain new conditions applicable to stations thereafter licensed but permits stations already authorized to continue under the old conditions. The latter stations are said to have grandfather rights. See *Squatters' Rights*.

Groundwave: Radio signal traveling along and over the surface of the earth. The higher frequencies tend less to follow the earth's curvature and weaken rapidly beyond line of sight. See *Skywave.*

Harmful interference: Any emission, radiation, or induction which endangers the functioning of a radionavigation service or of other safety services or seriously degrades, obstructs, or repeatedly interrupts a radiocommunication service operating in accordance with FCC regulations or Geneva Radio regulations.

Harmonic interference: Interference caused by a spurious wave which occurs on a frequency two, three, or four times the proper (fundamental) frequency of the signal.

ICAO: International Civil Aviation Organization.

ICAS: Interdepartmental Committee for Atmospheric Sciences. A governmental committee promoting research into the atmospheric sciences.

ICSC: Interim Communications Satellite Committee.

IEEE: Institute of Electrical and Electronic Engineers. A professional organization of engineers working in the field of electromagnetics, including communications, computers, electrical power, and the like.

IFRB: International Frequency Registration Board.

Instrument landing system (ILS): A radionavigation system which provides aircraft with horizontal and vertical guidance just before and during landing.

INTELSAT: International Telecommunications Satellite Consortium, sometimes referred to as ITSC.

Interface: A device or surface forming a common boundary between two bodies, spaces, or phases. Often relates to the common boundary or hardware that interconnects domestic and overseas communications traffic, or the terrestrial and space satellite services. See *Gateway cities.*

Intermodulation: A phenomenon with no close parallel in resources other than the radio spectrum, wherein radio signals transmitted on two different frequencies cause interference to a transmitter which operates at the same time and in the same area, but on a third distinct frequency. Intermodulation relates to the production of frequencies that are the sums or differences of frequencies of different inputs or of their harmonics.

Ionospheric scatter: The propagation of radio waves by scattering as a result of irregularities or discontinuities in the ionization of the ionosphere.

IRAC: Interdepartment Radio Advisory Committee. As an advisor to the Director of Telecommunications Management, IRAC includes representatives of all federal government users of radio and also of the FCC.

ITFS: Instructional TV Fixed Service.

ITU: International Telecommunications Union.

JTAC: Joint Technical Advisory Committee. An organization formed by the Electronic Industries Association and the Institute of Electrical and Electronic Engineers. Its objective is to obtain and evaluate technical and engineering information concerning radio and to advise governmental bureaus, industry, and professional groups as required.

Kilocycle per second (Kc/s): Unit of frequency equal to 1,000 cycles per second. Identical with kiloHertz (KHz).

Kilowatt (Kw): Unit of power equal to 1,000 watts or 1.34 horsepower.

Land mobile service: A mobile service between a base station and a mobile station, or between mobile stations, all on land (e.g., service used in dispatching taxicabs, etc.).

Line-of-sight: 1. Distance to the horizon from an elevated point including the effects of atmospheric refraction. 2. Straight line between an observer or radar antenna and a target. 3. Unobstructed or optical patch between two points. 4. TV and FM radio transmissions are also line-of-sight, but not those of AM broadcasting. See *Skywave.*

Marker beacon: An aeronautical radionavigational aid that provides in-flight information to aircraft as to their location.

Megacycle per second (Mc/s): Unit of frequency equal to one million cycles per second or one megaHertz (MHz).

Meteorological aids service: A radiocommunication service used for meteorological (including hydrological) observations and exploration. See *Radiosonde.*

Microwave: Term applied to that portion of the radio spectrum above approximately 1,000 Mc/s. The wavelength is less than one foot and decreases as frequency increases.

Microwave relay station: A radio station at a fixed location that transmits to another fixed location on frequencies above 952 Mc/s.

Mobile service: A service of radiocommunication between mobile and land stations or between mobile stations.

Modulation: Process which causes the amplitude, frequency, phase, or intensity of a carrier wave to vary in accordance with a sound wave or other signal, the frequency of the signal wave usually being very much lower than that of the transmitter. Frequently applied to the application of sound-wave signals to a microphone to change the characteristic of a transmitted radio wave. See *Carrier wave.*

Multiplex operation: Simultaneous transmission of two or more signals on a single frequency.

NARBA: North American Regional Broadcasting Agreement. Agreement to minimize interference between AM stations in the United States, Canada, Cuba, Dominican Republic, and the Bahama Islands.

Natural noise. Noise having its source in natural phenomena and not generated in machines or other technical devices.

Necessary bandwidth: For a given class of emission, the minimum value of the occupied bandwidth sufficient to ensure the transmission of information at the rate and with the quality required for the system employed, under specified conditions. Emissions useful for the good functioning of the receiving equipment.

OTM: Office of Telecommunications Management. See *DTM*.

Pay-television (Pay-TV): A subscription service broadcast over the air, or delivered by wire, where programs are scrambled and will be decoded for intelligible reception only upon payment of prorated charges per program viewed. May or may not be associated with *CATV* systems.

Point-to-point service: See *Fixed service*.

Polarization: Direction of the electric field as radiated from the transmitting antenna. A vertical antenna radiates a vertically polarized signal; a horizontal antenna radiates a horizontally polarized signal.

Pollution: See *Spectrum pollution*.

Port operations service: A maritime mobile service in or near a port, between coast stations and ship stations, or between ship stations, in which messages are restricted to those relating to the movement and the safety of ships and, in emergency, to the safety of persons.

Prime time: Broadcasting term referring to peak nighttime audience periods for which top prices are charged to advertisers for time.

Private-line service: A service in which facilities for communications between two or more designated points are set aside for the exclusive use of a particular customer during stated periods of time.

Private mobile radio facilities: Radio facilities licensed for use by private users (nonbroadcast and noncommon carrier) for business and operational communications.

Propagation path: Course taken by a radio signal from transmitter to receiver.

RACES: Radio Amateur Civil Emergency Service.

Radar: A radio determination system based on the comparison of reference signals with radio signals reflected or retransmitted from the position to be determined.

Radio: A general term applied to the use of radio waves.

Radio altimeter: Radionavigation equipment, on board an aircraft, which can determine the height of the aircraft above the ground.

Radio astronomy: Astronomy based on the reception of radio waves of cosmic origin.

Radio communication: Telecommunication by means of radio waves.

Radio determination: The determination of position, or the obtaining of information relating to position, by means of the propagation properties of radio waves.

Radio direction-finding: Radio determination using the reception of radio waves for the purpose of determining the direction of a station or object.

Radio location: Radio determination used for purposes other than those of radio navigation.

Radio navigation: Radio determination used for the purposes of navigation, including obstruction warning.

Radio propagation: The manner in which radio waves travel from one location to another.

Radiosonde: An automatic radio transmitter usually carried on an aircraft, free balloon, kite, or parachute, which transmits meteorological data. See *Meteorological aids service.*

Radio spectrum: The full range of radio frequencies from the lowest to the highest usable for radio communications.

Radio waves (or Hertzian Waves): Electromagnetic waves of frequencies lower than 3,000 Gc/s, propagated in space without artificial guide.

Relay: To retransmit a signal received at a given point.

RF: Radio frequency.

Safety Service: A radio communication service used permanently or temporarily for the safeguarding of human life and property.

Satellite communications: Service either between earth stations by using active or passive satellites for the exchange of communications of the fixed or mobile service or between an earth station and stations on active satellites for the exchange of communications of the mobile service for retransmission to or from stations in the mobile service.

Satellite relay: A fixed station on a satellite used for the reception and retransmission of signals from other stations.

Scatter: The diffusion or dispersion of a radio wave, caused by collision with precipitation, buildings, or other obstacles in its path.

Sharing: Use of the same channel by stations in the same geographical area. Interference is avoided by strictly observed hours of operation, or by narrow directional beaming of the signals. Not to be confused with co-channel operation.

Ship station: A mobile station in the maritime mobile service located on board a vessel, other than a survival craft, which is not permanently moored.

SHORAN: Short-range radio navigation. System used for offshore petroleum exploration and calculation of ranges and distances.

Sideband: A band of frequencies produced by modulating a carrier wave. Such emissions may be above or below the signal being modulated.

Signal wave: A wave whose shape conveys some intelligence, message, or effect.

Single sideband (SSB): Transmission with one sideband. With SSB transmissions, only half the spectrum space is needed as in the case of double sideband. Introduction of SSB normally reflects technical improvements which reduce the spectrum requirements of acceptable radio-communication.

Skywave: That portion of the broadcast signal that travels upward and is reflected to earth by the ionosphere, permitting long-distance over-the-horizon reception of frequencies below approximately 30 Mc/s. Higher frequencies usually penetrate the ionosphere and are lost in space. Used in AM and HF broadcasting. See *Groundwave* and *Line-of-sight*.

Space service: A radio communication service between space stations.

Space station: A station in the earth-space service or the space service located on an object which is beyond, or intended to go beyond, the major portion of the earth's atmosphere and which is not intended for flight between points on the earth's surface.

Spectrum: A complete range of frequencies or wavelengths of electromagnetic waves.

Spectrum pollution: Decreasing utility of any spectral region or band for communications purposes due mainly to noncommunication usage for medical, scientific, industrial, or locational purposes.

Spurious emission: Transmission of unwanted and unnecessary signals outside the authorized channel. This may include harmonics, parasitic emissions, and intermodulation products. Emissions in the immediate vicinity of the band, resulting from the necessary modulation, are not considered as spurious.

Spurious response: Sensitivity of a receiver to signals whose frequencies are other than those frequencies in the channel to which the receiver is tuned.

Squatters' rights: Claims to radio frequencies that may be granted to spectrum users who occupy these frequencies under temporary initial grants, or without prior legal authorization. In the international field, the term is most frequently associated with usage of the High Frequency radio band where claim staking by entities in different nations once posed the problem most explicitly. Domestic licensees in the U.S., on the other hand, normally hold temporary renewable rights only. However, the business equities derived from good behavior and large investments (as in TV) may produce de facto property rights however meritorious the subsequent applications from latecomers may be. Equally pertinent are the temporary experimental grantees, often hard to dislodge when their licenses expire—prior promises to the contrary notwithstanding.

Standard frequency service: A radio communication service for scientific, technical, and other purposes, providing the transmission of specified frequencies of stated high precision, intended for general reception.

Switched network: Normally refers to common carrier facilities which provide voice or message service to large numbers of general users of communications who cannot afford, or have no need for, leased circuits of their own, or their own systems outright. "Switching" refers to the connection, disconnection, or redirection of communications circuits. See *Private line service.*

TASI: Time Assignment Speech Interpolation is a device that operates by taking advantage of pauses in conversation to use the temporarily idle channels for other calls. TASI was first used in 1960. It is not economical to use with overland systems and is therefore associated with submarine cable systems alone.

Telecommunications: Any transmission, emission, or reception of signs, signals, writing, images, and sounds, or intelligence of any nature by wire, radio, optical, or other electromagnetic systems.

Telegraphy: A system of telecommunication which is concerned in any process providing transmission and reproduction at a distance of documentary matter, such as written or printed matter or fixed images, or the reproduction at a distance of any kind of information in such a form.

Telemetering: The use of telecommunication for automatically indicating or recording measurements at a distance from the measuring instrument.

Telephony: A system of telecommunication set for the transmission of speech or, in some cases, other sounds.

TELEX: Automatic dial teleprinter exchange of Western Union.

TELPAK: Private line service offered by AT&T and Western Union with bulk rates to heavy service users.

Translators: Low-power devices receiving a signal on one frequency and transmitting it on another without significantly altering its original characteristics. Used to bring FM and TV programs to areas where direct reception is unsatisfactory.

Tropospheric scatter: Propagation of radio waves by scattering as a result of irregularities or discontinuities in the physical properties of the troposphere. Can transmit signals over-the-horizon.

TWX: Teletypewriter exchange service.

Ultra high frequency (UHF): Band of frequencies extending from 300 to 3,000 Mc/s (MHz). Television stations assigned to TV channels 14 through 83 operate on frequencies between 470 and 890 Mc/s and are known as UHF TV stations.

Very high frequency (VHF): Band of frequencies extending from 30 to 300 Mc/s (MHz). Television stations assigned TV channels 2 through 6 (54 to 88 Mc/s) and channels 7 through 13 (174 to 216 Mc/s) are known as VHF TV stations.

WADS: Wide Area Data Service. System for data users comparable to Wide Area Telephone Service for telephone users (*WATS*).

WATS: Wide Area Telephone Service. System by which telephone user is allowed unrestricted number of calls in specified areas for one overall rate. *Inbound WATS*—System under which incoming calls to a specific number are charged at one overall rate.

WARC: World Administrative Radio Conference of International Telecommunication Union.

Waveguide: Broadly, a system of material boundaries capable of guiding electromagnetic waves. Specifically, a transmission line comprising a hollow conducting tube within which electromagnetic waves may be propagated.

INDEX